THE SHAPING
OF AMERICAN
CONGREGATIONALISM
1620–1957

JOHN VON ROHR

THE PILGRIM PRESS
CLEVELAND, OHIO

The Pilgrim Press, Cleveland, Ohio 44115
© 1992 by The Pilgrim Press

Biblical quotations are from the New Revised Standard Version
of the Bible, © 1989 by the Division of Christian Education of the National
Council of the Churches of Christ in the U.S.A., and are used by permission

Printed in the United States of America
The paper used in this publication is acid free and meets the minimum
requirements of American National Standard for Information Sciences-Permanence
of Paper for Printed Library Materials, ANSI Z39.48–1984

97 96 95 94 93 92   5 4 3 2 1

Library of Congress Cataloging-in-Publication Data
Von Rohr, John.
The shaping of American congregationalism : 1620-1957 / John von Rohr.
        p.   cm.
Includes bibliographical references and index
ISBN 0-8298-0921-X
1. Congregational churches—United States—History.   2. General Council of the
Congregational and Christian Churches of the United States—History.
3. United States—Church history.   4. United Church of Christ—History.
I. Title.
BX7135.V6   1992
285.8'73—dc20   92-29485
CIP

THE SHAPING
OF AMERICAN
CONGREGATIONALISM
1620–1957

To the memory of

Louis H. Gunnemann,

co-worker in historical and theological studies

for the United Church of Christ

CONTENTS

Introduction

The rebirth of interest in Puritan studies and the intensification of research in general American religious history have provided in recent decades added insights into the nature and development of American Congregationalism. Despite this new knowledge, scant effort has been made to draw it into a comprehensive retelling of the Congregational story. This volume undertakes that task, seeking to provide for the late twentieth century a fresh account of Congregationalism's pilgrimage throughout the course of its American journey.

In this account the story of Congregationalism is explored as the story of a religious community, the story of a church. Although there is focus on individuals who comprise it, the larger intent is to portray the life of the institution as it has played its role in American history. For that purpose this analysis of Congregationalism has been channeled through several components of the denomination's nature and life. In the book's plan all chapters, as they deal with given time periods in the story, present their material through five identical topics: history, theology, polity, worship, and mission. The first provides broad narrative; the others probe those particular elements that constitute the nature and activity of the church. *Theology, polity,* and *worship* all refer to the inner essence of the church as a religious community. The outreach of the church in evangelism and social responsibility is caught up in its *mission,* a more contemporary term for such activity when employed in this broader sense. The arrangement also makes possible a consecutive reading in any or all of these topics, tracing over the course of Congregationalism's history the church's development in these areas.

Congregationalism was shaped and reshaped during the course of its history. Lines of continuity persist, constituting a central pattern in this evolution, but in all areas of its being Congregationalism also adapted to new circumstances and needs. The story is therefore one of growth and change, as those who made up the living organism of Congregationalism found new ways to live out the faith that impelled them.

In 1957 the major portion of twentieth-century American Congregationalism, by then having become Congregational Christian by virtue of a 1931 merger, entered into further union with the Evangelical and Reformed Church to create the United Church of Christ. It is primarily for that total church that this volume is written, portraying this particular portion of UCC heritage. There is little new scholarship for the academic world here, for the writing draws largely on that which has already been discovered by others. The intent, however, was to organize and analyze that material in such a way that a clearer sense of what Congregationalism has been may appear. It is the hope that seminary students, clergy, and laypersons now in the United Church of Christ will find this helpful in understanding one of the major denominational sources of their church. Additionally it is the hope that Congregationalists who have continued their denominations separate from the United Church of Christ will find this account useful as a story of their past. Suggestions for further reading are appended to assist additional study.

Readers will note that quotations from historical sources sometimes contain noninclusive language, despite current practice rejecting such usage. This form has been followed, however, for historical accuracy. Readers will also note the occasional use of lowercase *c* in the word *congregational*. In such instances the reference is to a form of church government, rather than to the denomination.

This research and writing were pursued with assistance from the Emeritus Faculty Research and Publication Fellowship awarded by Pacific School of Religion, Berkeley, California, and I am grateful for its help. I wish to express appreciation also to the Graduate Theological Union Library, Berkeley, and the Congregational Library, Boston, for help in research. Assistance in the former institution was rendered by Mr. Oscar Burdick and in the latter by Dr. Harold Worthley. I am likewise grateful to friends and former colleagues who read and commented on the manuscript in progress. Portions were read by Louis Gunnemann, Elizabeth Nordbeck, and Richard Norberg, and the full manuscript was read by Barbara Brown Zikmund and Charles Hambrick-Stowe. Suggestions from these readers were immensely helpful, and any remaining faults are my own. Finally, I want to thank my wife, Helen, who has been for a long time a patient in-house listener to her husband's reading of the manuscript, bit by bit, during the late afternoon hours. Her responses have been a good and final check on whether the writing makes any sense.

CHAPTER ONE

OLD WORLD ANTECEDENTS
1558–1660

American Congregationalism was initially shaped through the influence not of the New World, but of the Old, for it was born from the womb of sixteenth- and seventeenth-century English Puritanism. Although the umbilical cord was in due course cut and ensuing centuries witnessed a development marked by an intricate interrelationship with the ongoing evolution of American life, that early English gestation was central to the character of both the childhood and maturation of the American Congregationalism that followed. This dependence on Old World antecedents is, of course, not unusual among major American religious denominations, for the larger number of such Christian and Jewish groups in America had their origins in Europe. Yet it is of particular importance to note this explicitly with respect to Congregationalism, for too often American historians have neglected old English roots in their recounting of the New England story. Neither New England nor the ongoing American Congregationalism that it initiated can be truly understood, however, apart from their English Puritan heritage.

HISTORY

The Elizabethan Church

Puritanism in Elizabethan England arose as an effort to reform further a church that the sixteenth-century English Reformation had already restructured and renewed. It was under the rule of Henry VIII (1509–47) that separation from Roman Catholicism began, especially in the repudiation of papal authority. The brief reign of Edward VI (1547–53) accelerated greatly that movement, giving it certain Protestant characteristics long thereafter to endure. In these years the Book of Common Prayer was developed to constitute the church's prescribed form of worship, the Articles of Religion were written to summarize the

1

church's faith, the sacraments were reinterpreted to express emerging Protestant understanding, and altogether a remarkably changed church began to appear. The reign of Mary (1553–58) brought this transformation to a momentary halt, with the restoration of Roman Catholicism as the official religion of the nation, but the tide again turned when in 1558 Elizabeth I ascended the throne. The daughter of Anne Boleyn and Henry VIII, a union deemed illicit by the pope, Elizabeth was in a sense fated to return to Protestant reform. Yet as a politician, she knew well the dangers inherent in pursuing too intensely that goal. Thus her "Elizabethan settlement" looked in two directions in its establishment of the national religion, and features of both the Catholic and the Protestant traditions thereafter characterized the Anglican church.

Elizabeth pressed Parliament to legislate both the Act of Supremacy and the Act of Uniformity as instruments for control of the religious establishment. The first was patterned after an earlier enactment in her father's reign in which Henry was declared "the only supreme head in earth of the Church of England," though in Elizabeth's case "supreme head" was altered to "supreme governor" as a verbal concession to the Catholics. The second act also had precedent, in this instance in Edward's reign, mandating the use of the Book of Common Prayer as the sole form of worship to be practiced throughout the land. Penalties were prescribed for any deviation by clergy and also for any failure by laity to attend the church's required worship. And the law was to be enforced not simply by ecclesiastical courts, but by civil judges as well. Strictures such as these were not unduly harsh, however, if seen against the practices of the times. One of the "givens" of sixteenth-century Protestant nations was some form of this relationship between church and state. Whether in Lutheran or Reformed lands, the civil ruler was understood to rule by divine authority, having among royal responsibilities at least a protecting, if not an ordering, of the life of the church. So it was with Elizabeth and her obligation to the nation, and added to her titles was "defender of the faith."

The Puritan Protest

There were questions in the minds of some, however, concerning the kind of faith Elizabeth should defend. As those questions emerged, not only in their theological but also in their practical implications, the

Puritan movement came into being. The term *Puritan* was coined in the mid-sixteenth century as a term of contempt to vilify those who presumed to be engaged in a "purifying" of the church. Oddly, it was first employed in this manner by English Catholic writers critical of the reforming efforts involved in changing Mary's Catholicism into the Anglicanism of the Elizabethan establishment. But soon the term was adopted by the Anglican bishops themselves and applied to those in their now-reformed communion who remained dissatisfied by a renewal that seemed to have stopped halfway. Puritanism first arose, therefore, as a protest movement within the national Anglican church.

The precise nature of the movement defies easy description, for it was multifaceted and often in flux. Much of it reflected the influence of religious thought and practice in Calvin's Geneva, where some of its early leaders spent years of exile during Mary's reign. But English Puritanism was more than a direct transplant from Genevan soil, drawing upon other Continental traditions and building upon native impulses within English life itself. Despite the varieties within it, however, certain predominant characteristics gave Puritanism recognizable form. For one thing, it focused upon the Bible as supreme authority much more rigidly than did the church of the English establishment. In addition to the Bible, the English church acknowledged the authority of church tradition and the natural powers of human reason, whereas for the Puritans ultimate authority in all matters of theology, ethics, worship, and church government rested in the Bible alone.

Further, Puritanism developed a theology of sin and salvation both more pessimistic and more enthusiastic than that generally expressed in Anglicanism. It knew more of the depths in its Calvinist portrayal of the magnitude of sin, and it knew more of the heights in its dwelling upon the joys of a new life through grace. Focusing its positive message upon the divine transforming power proclaimed in the gospel, Puritanism became what some now call an "evangelical Calvinism." Although Bible centered, it was also experience centered to a degree not found in the established church.

In addition, Puritanism was distinguished by its many efforts to purify the visible forms and practices of the church. Using the New Testament as its guide, it sought simplicity in worship, criticizing with vigor the elaborate ceremonial of Anglican liturgy. It also sought simplicity in church organization, stressing the role of the laity in church government and rejecting the hierarchical structure by which the Elizabethan church was both served and ruled. Issues concerning the quality of clergy leadership were of special concern, as parish posts increasingly were being given to less-than-competent persons through political appointment and family favor. One Puritan, when asked if the wine of the sacrament could be served in a wooden chalice, is reported to have replied that whereas once the church had wooden chalices and golden priests, now it has golden chalices and wooden priests! The Puritans wanted to put qualified clergy into the parishes and their pulpits to proclaim the converting and empowering word of grace.

There were disagreements within the Puritan movement, however, concerning the degree of resistance to the established church. A distinction can be made between *conforming Puritans*, engaged in passive resistance within the establishment, and *nonconforming Puritans*, who actively rejected the Anglican way. And to some extent the distinction can be connected to views held on church polity, those favoring presbyterial and congregational government being identified with the more aggressive attack, and those supporting episcopal government seeking change within the system.

But Nonconformism itself had both passive and active dimensions. The early stages of presbyterial protest relied upon the possibility of persuading the crown, either directly or through Parliament, to abandon episcopacy for representative church government, and it was not until such hopes were completely dashed in the 1630s and 1640s that resistance took the form of outright revolution. Similarly, those holding to congregational polity combined active and passive approaches. Early expressions of Separatism led to withdrawal from the English church and flight to Holland. Later, however, an important non-Separatism arose that sought to pursue its congregational agenda while remaining to some degree within the English church's fold. Finally, in the 1640s and 1650s, as the political revolution reached its climax in the execution of the king, the abandonment of episcopacy, and Parliament's mandating of a national presbyterianism, these radical dissenters rejected even the latter establishment and worked in Cromwell's Commonwealth for such freedom of religion as would give state coercive power to no single church. Thus in its organizational and political dimensions Puritanism showed much variety as it sought to achieve its underlying goals.

The first Puritan protest against Elizabethan church rule appeared in the 1560s and was directed solely at imposed practices in worship and clerical dress deemed objectionable when examined in the light of the biblical norm. Where was scriptural authority for kneeling to receive Communion, for the use of the ring in marriage, or for the making of the sign of the cross in the administration of baptism? These "noxious ceremonies" were seen as remnants of a priestly order and a papal church rather than as biblically authorized elements in the true worship of God.

Moreover, it was held, there were many more such evils in the complex liturgy of the Book of Common Prayer, especially when one compared it with the simple worship of the church of the New Testament, which was made up largely of preaching, prayer, and psalms of praise. One Puritan of this period scornfully characterized the antiphonal elements in the Anglican service as a "tossing to and fro of psalms and sentences like a tennis play whereto God is called [to be] judge."[1] The requirements for clerical dress also drew Puritan fire, for here in cope and surplice were further remnants of a priestly order, even "the badges of Anti-Christ." Actually, this protest had its roots back in Edward's time when John Hooper, sometimes designated the first English Nonconformist, refused to wear episcopal vestments following his appointment as Bishop of Gloucester. Finally a compromise was reached, and he agreed to wear them on a selective basis, for preaching in his own cathedral and for preaching before the king, but on no other occasions. Many Puritans of Elizabeth's day were even less inclined to compromise.

The church's disciplinary rejoinder was the Archbishop of Canterbury's publication of the Advertisements of 1566, a set of instructions for liturgical conduct and clerical dress. The Advertisements explicitly mandated many of the practices to which Puritan objection had been voiced. There were precise directions for the administration of baptism and the celebration of Communion, with the child signed by the cross and the communicants kneeling. Specified vestments had to be worn for the administration of the sacraments, surplices in all parishes and copes in collegiate churches. And there were many other details prescribed by this ecclesiastical law for clerical vocation and life. Protests followed, and dissenting clergy were first suspended and then deprived. As the struggle was joined, a movement of increasingly focused Puritan protest began.

The next stage in the conflict shifted from concern over ceremonies and vestments to matters of church organization and government, a succession of disputes promoted by those committed to presbyterial and congregational patterns. Leading divines of presbyterial persuasion opened the new protest by presenting two "admonitions" to Parliament arguing against episcopacy and asking for the development of representative government within the church. The first admonition appeared in 1572 under the authorship of John Field and Thomas Wilcox, and the second shortly thereafter, penned by Thomas Cartwright, leading English advocate for presbyterial polity in the sixteenth century. John Whitgift, ultimately to become Archbishop of Canterbury but at the time vice-chancellor of Cambridge University where Cartwright was Professor of Divinity, prepared the response. When intense pamphlet debate followed, Cartwright was dismissed from his faculty post and subsequently fled to the Continent to minister to English congregations there. All manner of ecclesiastical issues were drawn into the discussion, but in its essence it centered on two matters: the relationship of church authority to New Testament authority in determining the church's polity and the precise nature of what the New Testament itself prescribed.

True to his fundamental Puritan convictions, Cartwright argued that the New Testament contains a thorough model for church order. And in it, he insisted, there is no place for episcopacy with its variety of hierarchical offices, for all pastors in the New Testament church were of equal rank. Moreover, the laity deserved a more elevated role in church government, for their rights and responsibilities in the earliest Christian community included participating in the election of their ministers, sharing in the administration of discipline, and joining with the clergy in the work of the church's representative governing bodies. Although there may be some minor things for the church to decide anew in each age, the basic pattern for church structure and government, Cartwright held, is extensively prescribed in the New Testament.

Whitgift disagreed. He denied the existence of such exact form of church polity in the Scriptures and argued that in the absence of biblical prescription, the church itself had authority to shape polity in the manner that seemed most wise. For him church order was more a matter of expediency than of faith. Beyond this basic impasse Cartwright and Whitgift had another significant disagreement. For Whitgift the authority of the church to determine and enforce church government gave, by virtue of the Acts of Supremacy and Uniformity, essentially arbitrary power to the crown to control spiritual affairs. Cartwright did not disavow royal supremacy in civil matters, nor the royal responsibility to defend the true church, but the New Testament, he held, did not give the "power of the keys" to the holder of the power of the sword. Church order and ceremonies must be in accord with the Word of God, and ecclesiastical discipline and government must be administered by the clergy and laity of the church. This position was soon to be affirmed even more emphatically by Puritans of congregational persuasion.

The Early Separatist Churches

Cartwright and those who joined with him in the "admonition controversy" did not seek separation from the Church of England. Their policy was to protest and to influence those in power, but also to wait for further reformation to occur. Others, however, believed such waiting would itself be a denial of faith and chose the more radical route of establishing independent self-governing congregations completely separated from the national church. Theirs were small churches of deeply dedicated persons who gathered in secrecy for worship and who began to develop a congregational form of church life. In this sense these Nonconformists pioneered, though only in a limited manner, American Congregationalism. They bequeathed to the New World many of the basic principles ultimately found in the polity of later Congregational churches. Their wholesale repudiation of the Church of England through radical Separatism, however, led to their persecution, exile to Holland, and, often, the early demise of their congregations. Only one of their congregations, with modified views, reached New England shores.

Actually, the major source of American Congregationalism was a later English and Dutch non-Separatist movement in which congregational polity was practiced but continued communion with the Church of England was sustained. This movement supplied most of the clergy and laity who subsequently migrated to New England and founded its early Congregational churches. Because the somewhat fleeting Separatist churches did initiate the basic congregational conception prior to their disappearance from history, it is sometimes affirmed that they belong to the "prehistory," rather than the ongoing ecclesiastical history, of Congregationalism. They were a source of certain basic aspects of the "congregational idea," although not of the subsequent living family of churches called Congregationalism.

Although their early records are meager, these "privy churches" separated from the national church go back to the days of Mary's reign. Such early defections, however, were in all likelihood protests against presumably idolatrous worship and other nonbiblical practices, not expressions of a positive principle of congregational church order. Yet as early as 1568, the tenth year of Elizabeth's reign, the first intimations of a more constructive Separatism did appear in a congregation meeting secretly in London under the ministerial leadership of Richard Fitz. Drawn in part from an earlier and less clearly defined Plumbers' Hall congregation that had been dispersed by English authorities and had several of its members sent to prison, this new gathered body of believers combined protest with the beginnings of a new form of church life.

The church's protest was evident in its self description as "a poor congregation whom God hath separated from the Church of England and from the mingled and false worship therein." But a new style of church organization and government also was evident, including covenant commitment by each member and the congregation's assumption of responsibility for election of its minister and discipline of its membership. Yet this novelty in church form only made it more threatening to Anglican uniformity, and the new congregation was likewise suppressed, its ministers and several members being put to death. The last record of the church was a petition presented to the queen in 1571 by its few survivors, justifying on scriptural grounds its withdrawal and asserting that unless further national reform takes place "the Lord's wrath will surely break out upon this whole realm."[2]

Some clandestine Separatism may have continued in the years following, but it was another decade before these principles were again practiced in public view. Not until the 1580s and 1590s, when given guidance by a new group of radical church leaders, did a renewed Separatism appear. The first of the new leaders was Robert Browne, who revived the Separatist movement and enlarged considerably the understanding of congregational church order. Born into a family of prosperous English gentry in probably the year 1550, Browne became a student at Cambridge University when Cartwright was lecturing there on Puritan divinity and carrying on his dispute with Whitgift over the polity and practices of the established church. Thus as a young man Browne came to imbibe fully of the Puritan protest and quickly identified himself with the cause of church reform. At the outset he shared Cartwright's presbyterial viewpoint on church government, but his impatience with episcopal ways led him soon into more active protest than others were at that time inclined to make. When asked to preach at Cambridge some time after the completion of his studies, he vowed not to seek the authorization from the bishop required under ecclesiastical law. When his brother, anxious about the possible consequences of such action, secured for him a license granting preaching privilege from the Archbishop of Canterbury himself, he first destroyed it and then began to preach! As a result Browne was forbidden by authorities to preach further, and his commitment to active reform increased.

It was at this point, 1579, that Browne abandoned his conforming presbyterial views and became a Separatist. He became convinced, so he later wrote, that "the kingdom of God was not to be begun by whole parishes, but rather of the worthiest, were they never so few."[3] If the church is to be reformed, he believed, it must be done through the gathering of congregations of genuine believers from out of the larger multitude of nominal Christians, for according to Scripture they, and no others, constitute the true church. The church cannot be reformed from above, through the mandating of new practices that are then applied to the people; its renewal must come from below, from those who are of sound faith and who unite to practice that faith in local congregations separated from the corrupt life of the larger church and the world.

With this new conviction Browne joined another Puritan friend, Robert Harrison, in the city of Norwich. There the two worked out many of the implications of this emerging congregational conception of church polity, including the use of a covenant for church membership and a system of church government in which the congregation as a whole played a major part. Finally, in 1581, the time was ripe to put theory into practice. Browne and Harrison gathered their followers and, according to later report, they all "gave their consent to join themselves to the Lord, in one covenant and fellowship together, and to keep and seek agreement under his laws and government, and therefore did utterly flee disorders and wickedness."[4]

Opposition was immediately encountered, the Bishop of Norwich complaining to an official of the queen that Browne was encouraging worshipers to come together in private houses and conventicles, a violation of the proper ways of church assembly. Browne was arrested and detained briefly in prison before he, Harrison, and the congregation found it expedient to flee to Holland. In Middelburg they renewed practice of their church order, but this state of affairs did not last long. When a quarrel broke out between the two leaders, Browne was charged with excessive severity, the congregation divided, and Browne and his supporters returned to Britain to settle in Scotland. No peace was found, however, within the domain of the established Church of Scotland, for persecution there was as severe as it had been in England under its established church, and in 1584 the whole enterprise was abandoned. Within a short time Browne was back in England where, after recanting his Separatism and submitting himself anew to the ecclesiastical authority of the queen, he was assigned to a small parish in which he served as Anglican priest until his death in 1633.

Although the two years Browne spent in Middelburg contributed little to the practice of congregational order in actual church life, those years were of immense significance in the development and clarification of congregational ideas for subsequent generations. In that brief span Browne wrote and published extensively, two of his treatises being of major importance for congregational understanding. His chief work was a manual of theology, ethics, and ecclesiastical principles titled *A Book which sheweth the life and manner of all true Christians.* In this he set forth his congregational view of the nature of the church, its membership, its ministry, and its sacraments. Although Browne was ultimately repudiated by early New England Congregationalists because of his Separatist stance and later return to Anglican priesthood, his treatment of congregational church structure and government anticipated in remarkable manner much New England Congregational thinking of the following century.

Browne's other important work was titled *A treatise of reformation without tarrying for anie.* There he sounded his clarion call to separation. Browne deplored the hesitancy of those who held back from separation by waiting for the ruler to enact the reform. When they say they must "tarry for the magistrate," Browne argued, they make the will of the ruler, rather than the will of Christ, the supreme authority in the church. Browne believed that in England it was the duty of the ministers and people of Christ, not only the duty of the queen, to take the venturesome step. To them God had given gifts of preaching and revelation of truth, and these must be used to confront corruption and to restore the true church. Moreover, true Christian faith and its expression in faithful church practice, insisted Browne, should be a voluntary matter, never one brought about by compulsion. "The Lord's people is of the willing sort," he said. Thus genuine reform can never come by royal decree or legislative enactment, for neither of these can really sway the heart. The triumphant rule of God, he affirmed, never comes "by battle, by horses and horsemen, that is, by civil power and pomp of magistrates, by their proclamations and parliaments," for "inward obedience, with newness of life, is the Lord's kingdom." The burden for reform falls on believers, and believers should begin it "without tarrying for anie."[5]

It was not long before others in England, although apparently not directly influenced by Browne, took up again the Separatist cause. The next instance was initiated in the mid-1580s by two ardent advocates of this radical reform, John Greenwood and Henry Barrow, and came to public view when their secret London congregation, meeting in a member's home, was discovered by authorities in 1587. Greenwood, the leader of this conventicle, was a former Anglican priest who had been deprived of his benefice in Norfolk because of his Puritan sympathies and who, after serving briefly as a domestic chaplain for a member of the Puritan gentry, came to London to form this private church. Leadership of the congregation was shared with Barrow, a London lawyer who abandoned his profession when converted by a Puritan sermon that he chanced simply out of curiosity to hear. Little is known about the congregation prior to its detection, although its reasons for separating from the Church of England are set forth in one of Barrow's later writings. Four monumental abuses, he said, prevail in the life of the English ecclesiastical establishment. There one finds a false membership ("mixed" congregations of believers and nonbelievers), a false ministry (ordination and appointment by a bishop), a false worship (the Book of Common Prayer), and a false government (denial of the rights of the congregation in both the election of officers and the disciplining of members). On all these grounds, he argued, separation is not only justified, but called for, and more scripturally sound congregations must be gathered.

The discovery of this London group in its private worship led quickly to the imprisonment of its leaders and some of its members. Greenwood and Barrow particularly felt the heavy hand of persecution, with the former knowing only occasional freedom and the latter none at all during the remaining six years of their lives. Both were subjected to severe interrogation by Whitgift, Archbishop of Canterbury, and by other representatives of the episcopacy, as well as by civil officials. Barrow's sharp tongue did not help his cause, leading him on one occasion to identify the archbishop as "a monster" and "the second beast" spoken of in Revelation. Fiery indignation was Barrow's style. But his legal skills, along with the literary abilities of Greenwood, were brought into constructive and ingenious use during their imprisonment. Under the mantle of secrecy the prisoners were able to draft significant writings on Separatist reform, which were smuggled by friends sheet by sheet to the outside world. Here, as earlier in Browne's treatises, the congregational idea was expounded, though in a highly polemical manner. Yet the vituperative condemnation of the English church and its oppressiveness, especially in Barrow's writings, did not lead to a countenancing of such public aggressiveness as would infringe upon the "magistrate's authority" or intrude upon the "royal dignity." In Barrow's understanding, different here from Browne's, the power for reforming the "public enormities" of the "false church" rested with the ruler to whom God has given this authority. In the meantime the task of true Christians was to separate from such evil, and their lot was to suffer the consequences this would bring.

To some degree a "theology of martyrdom" was present here, as had been the case for certain of the sixteenth-century Continental Anabaptists who suffered greatly for their faith but welcomed the opportunity for heroic witness. Certainly Barrow's witness was brash and bold, despite the inevitability of severe recrimination. His charge of cowardice was equally emphatic against the "tolerating preachers" who compromised their faith by inaction. Wrote Barrow to them, "Christ crucified you all abhor, you cannot abide his cross, you will not suffer."[6] And the final suffering for Barrow and Greenwood was indeed martyrdom. In 1593 they were brought to public trial on the charge of publishing and dispensing seditious books seeking to overthrow the royal authority by attacking the ecclesiastical order. Found guilty, they were put to death by hanging.

Shortly thereafter a third member of the London congregation suffered the same fate. John Penry, a Puritan preacher from Wales more interested in evangelism than in church formality, joined the remnants of the little conventicle while Barrow and Greenwood were in prison. Eventually Penry also came under suspicion for his writing. He was believed to be the author of the Martin Marprelate tracts, a scurrilous set of documents that ridiculed the bishops and their church, although such authorship was never proven. But discovered among Penry's private papers was an accusation critical of the queen's rule of the church, for her reign, it said, had "turned rather against Jesus Christ and his Gospel than to the maintenance of the same."[7] With the precedent of Barrow and Greenwood freshly in mind, Penry also was tried, found guilty, and consigned to death on the scaffold.

Despite the imprisonment of their leaders and the harassment of their meetings in the early 1590s, the London Separatists continued to gather, as occasion permitted, to engage in worship and to practice a congregational form of church order. Joining them, probably in 1591, was Francis Johnson, soon elected their new pastor. Johnson's pilgrimage to this Separatist leadership was unusual. Ordained initially to the Anglican priesthood, he gradually developed sufficient Puritan sympathies to lead to emigration to Holland. There he took over the ministry to a congregation of English merchants previously served by Thomas Cartwright. Having no Separatist sympathies at the time, he presided on one occasion over the burning of copies of a book by Barrow confiscated from a printer preparing them for secret shipment to England. He saved a copy to study the nature of its errors, and upon reading it, found himself persuaded. The result was a return to London, a visit with Barrow in prison, and a uniting with the Separatist group. Harassment of the congregation continued, however, Johnson himself being thrown into prison and most members fleeing into exile. After some years Johnson was released and rejoined his people in Amsterdam. At the same time Henry Ainsworth was added to the membership and elected to the office of teacher in the congregation. Ainsworth had fled England in 1593 and now, as a renowned scholar, gave further intellectual leadership to the Amsterdam church. It was largely through his work that a remarkable document of congregational faith and polity was published, the Confession of 1596.

The subsequent history of this conventicle, however, contained more trouble, this time internally inflicted. For some years disputes plagued the congregation concerning the degree of severity to be employed in dealing with violations of morals. The breaking point came in 1610, though over a related polity issue, namely, the locus of authority for administering this discipline. Francis Johnson felt that such power was in the hands of the officers, whereas Henry Ainsworth placed it in the hands of the congregation. The result was a secession of a group led by Ainsworth and a fatal division of the church. After Johnson's death his group sought relocation in Virginia, but was almost totally decimated in a disastrous voyage. With Ainsworth's passing, his followers continued for several years without a pastor or teacher, finally being absorbed into Holland's Reformed Church.

Separatism in the Reign of James I

In the midst of this turmoil in England for Puritanism in general, and in exile for Separatism in particular, a political change occurred, momentarily giving new hope. In 1603 Elizabeth died and was succeeded on the English throne by James I, at that time also James VI of Scotland. Although all religious parties had reasons, often political, for expecting favorable support from the new king, Puritan hopes rested especially on the fact that he was coming to them from a Puritan land. For some decades Scotland's national church had been shaped by influences from Calvin's Geneva, and this, they believed, could augur well for greater leniency for Puritan practices than Elizabeth had shown, even though the king's personal sentiments had not yet been disclosed. Efforts were undertaken immediately to garner his support for the English Puritan cause.

The Millenary Petition was submitted to James upon his arrival in England, containing nearly eight hundred signatures of ministers of Puritan sympathies within the established English church. This was a moderate proposal asking simply for relaxation of the laws enforcing church ceremonies, improvement of the quality of persons granted ordination to ministry, some reform of the ecclesiastical courts, and the prohibiting of the preaching of "popish" doctrines from the church's pulpits. No request was included for the abolition of episcopacy nor for the establishment of a presbyterial polity. But the king was alarmed, clearly fearing that an urging of that change in church government was next to come. The result was a conference with Puritan representatives in 1604 at Hampton Court at which James so politicized the potential peril of presbyterianism as to equate survival of the monarchy with retention of episcopacy. A presbytery, he told Puritan delegates, agreed as little with monarchy "as God with the devil." And turning to his supporting bishops, he said, "If once you were out and they in place, I know what would become of my supremacy. No bishop, no king!"[8] With this response Puritan hopes were dashed, and no changes were made to reform more fully the English church.

It is little wonder, then, that Separatist attempts to gain concession from the new king were likewise without success. Eager to obtain relief from its long persecution, the Amsterdam congregation sought a word of favor from the crown, sending successively three petitions, all either ignored or rejected. The second petition is of special interest because it was accompanied by a concise statement of congregational polity, undoubtedly drawn up by Johnson and Ainsworth, framed in terms of fourteen "points of difference" with the English church. The overall intent, however, was not the seeking of a transformation of the ecclesiastical establishment but simply the obtaining of permission to return to England and to practice their church way in peace. But such toleration was not the king's policy. Upon the death of Whitgift, shortly after the Hampton Court conference, Richard Bancroft was appointed Archbishop of Canterbury. For many years Bancroft had served the former archbishop as one of Puritanism's fiercest and most vigilant enemies, and his appointment made James's hostile response complete.

During the next seven years, while Bancroft served in this high office, Puritanism in all its forms was repressed with utter severity. A new set of Constitutions and Canons was developed by the church and approved by the king, extending the punishment of excommunication to all manner of acts of nonconformity and adding large loss of civil liberties. When Puritans objected that such laws could be created only with Parliament's approval, James obtained from his legal counselors an opinion that he had this legislative authority as part of the king's "supreme ecclesiastical power." Moreover, under Bancroft a new anti-Puritan conception of church polity appeared. Whitgift had argued against Cartwright that the New Testament contained no precise model of church government, and that the early church had simply chosen episcopacy wisely as its governing form. Bancroft, however, saw it differently, affirming that episcopacy was the New Testament model and that bishops were therefore a separate and ruling order of clergy by divine right. The door to reform was now fast being closed for the Puritan movement.

One additional strong effort at developing a viable Separatism in England was attempted during these years of political transition, although in the end it too was driven into exile. In the longer range of history, however, its labors had a lasting consequence denied its predecessors, for it led to the first carrying of the congregational form of church order to American soil. For years there had been religious ferment in northern England, several of the parishes in Lincolnshire and Nottinghamshire being served by Puritan-minded pastors, and in the early 1600s there emerged from this unrest a new Separatist group. Meeting originally in the village of Gainsborough under the leadership of its elected pastor, John Smyth, it grew quickly to the point of branching off a second congregation that gathered in the home of one of its elders, William Brewster, postmaster in the neighboring village of Scrooby. Within a short time, the Scrooby congregation drew to its membership another Puritan preacher, John Robinson, ultimately to become the most prominent and influential leader of English Separatism.

While engaged in his university studies at Cambridge, Robinson was introduced to Puritan concerns and appears to have been among those at the university seeking purification for the church. He was ordained, however, into the ministry of the Church of England, probably in 1599. His more radical views did not fully appear until after he had been suspended in 1605 from his position as curate in St. Andrew's Church, Norwich, for failure in some respect to conform to the new Constitutions and Canons promulgated the previous year by church and king. Then, however, he turned to Separatism, and after joining the Scrooby congregation in 1606, he led its members in an act of covenant-taking. Each promised the Lord "to walk in all his ways made known, or to be made known unto them, according to their best endeavours, whatsoever it should cost them,"9 an act that bound them together in a new and independent "church estate." For about a year thereafter the congregation met secretly each Sabbath for worship, increasingly enlarged by persons attracted through Robinson's continued unauthorized preaching in neighboring parish churches. In time the congregation, like its Separatist predecessors, was subjected to severe harassment, directed in this case by the Archbishop of York. By 1608 both the Gainsborough and the Scrooby groups had fled to Holland. Robinson remained behind for a period "to help the weakest." Twelve years later he did the same when some of his people left Holland to journey to the New World.

Under Smyth the Gainsborough congregation settled in Amsterdam and quickly became engulfed in controversy with the Separatist group led by Francis Johnson and Henry Ainsworth already located there. Growing increasingly radical in this new setting, Smyth became extreme in his Separatist convictions and practices. For example, he stressed more and more the need for reliance on the presence of the Spirit in the act of worship, concluding that all of its aspects—prayer, preaching, singing—must be carried on without visible aids. Not only prayer books, as other Separatists believed, but also hymn books and even the Scriptures were impediments to voicing praise. The Spirit must freely express itself, through sanctified memory and inspiration, in the church's worship of God. This also meant a blurring of the traditional distinction between clergy and laity, for the Spirit's presence was available to all. But still further, Smyth became convinced that baptism of infants was not scriptural and that the sacrament should be administered exclusively to adult believers. Then, in an ultimate Separatist act, he rebaptized himself and a number of his followers in order to, in his judgment, reconstitute more properly the true apostolic church. The congregation split when Smyth and some others attempted to join with Dutch Mennonites, a goal accomplished only by his followers after Smyth's death. The remaining members turned to Thomas Helwys for leadership and later, on return to England, became the initiators of the English Baptist churches.

Meanwhile the Scrooby congregation, with John Robinson as pastor, chose to avoid the controversy in Amsterdam, locating in the city of Leyden. There a change in the nature of Separatism also occurred, but in a manner quite different from that of Smyth's design. Rather than intensifying the sense of alienation and separateness from England's national church, Robinson moved over the course of the years to a more moderate position, accepting certain ways by which a measure of relationship with the Church of England could be restored.

The main thrust of Robinson's early years in Leyden, however, was a sharply defined rejection of the Anglican establishment. Responding in 1608 to a bishop's urging that he recognize the Anglican church as his "mother," he wrote, "So may she be, and yet not the Lord's wife," adding that even a mother can have children by fornication![10] Two years later he systematized his protest in a lengthy treatise titled *A Justification of Separation from the Church of England,* detailing the abuses in membership, ministry, worship, and discipline that made necessary the judgment that this church, "till it be separated and free from the world, and the prince of the world that reigneth in it, cannot possibly be the true church of God, or wife of Christ." In contrast, he added, "a company, consisting though of but two or three, separated from the world, and gathered into the name of Christ by a covenant, is a church, and so hath the whole power of Christ."[11] Under these principles the Leyden congregation flourished, a major and vital expression of English Separatism.

The Non-Separatist Churches

At this time, however, a second type of congregationally minded exiles appeared in Holland, pursuing a more moderate stance in relationship to the Church of England. Their chief leaders were William Ames and Henry Jacob. Unwavering in their commitment to the basic principles of congregational church order, these exiles hoped nevertheless to achieve reform in such manner as not to break communion with the church of their birth. Separatism had sought purification in church life by the strategy of a "root and branch" severing from the impure body. But to this group there seemed to be a less drastic method that could be pursued. They sought to create small churches within the large church, *ecclesiolae in ecclesia,* participating in the larger to the extent that conscience permitted, while always in the smaller adhering to the principles of the congregational way. The hope was that by being faithful to the congregational idea, but not disloyal to the establishment to the point of separation, the seeds of reform could be planted within and changes in the national church gradually attained.

This non-Separatism, however, was not merely a strategy for reform. It also represented an earnest desire to preserve the unity of the English church even in the face of many deficiencies. For these reformers the Church of England was indeed "mother," from whom they had been born and by whom they had been nourished in faith. For them it still housed the true church, even though burdened with faults, and must not be abandoned. Theological justification for this stance was needed, however, in view of its leaders' underlying conviction that the only true church, scripturally prescribed, was one of congregational order. Christ's church, they were convinced, must be a gathered church of genuine believers, united by common covenant and in which the clergy are elected and ordained by common consent.

But the ingenuity of these non-Separatists was equal to the task. Despite all the errors in Church of England government, they declared, there was still sufficient free consent in its parish congregations to create therein true churches before God. Although in each parish persons were gathered by law, there were some at worship for whom this was also a matter of free choice, and these worshipers were bound together by an implicit covenant of mutual faith and purpose. Similarly, the element of a people's free consent was operative in each congregation's willing acceptance of its clergy. Here was implicit authorization of clergy power, even though formal ordination and assignment had been by bishop's act. So, they argued, the congregations of England are true churches and the ministers are true ministers—in effect, churches congregationally gathered and ministers congregationally ordained! Yet that which is implicit should be made explicit, and other abuses must be resisted. So a cautious movement gradually emerged to gather congregational churches that could exist to some degree within the frame of the larger Anglican church.

The major theologian of this effort was William Ames, author of *The Marrow of Sacred Divinity*, which became throughout the seventeenth century the primary textbook for the training of Congregational clergy in England and America. Ames's professional life was spent largely in Holland, to which he fled in 1610. There he served initially as minister to a British congregation in The Hague. Later he was for many years professor of theology at the University of Franeker in north Holland. Then shortly before his death in 1633 he returned to parish ministry, serving as co-pastor of a Congregational church in Rotterdam.

More extensive early pastoral leadership was given to this movement, however, by Henry Jacob, who spent a decade in Dutch exile before returning to his native England to establish its first non-Separatist Congregational church. Educated at Oxford, Jacob received

Anglican orders and probably served a parish in Kent prior to his development of congregational nonconformity. The latter became clearly evident, however, by 1604 when he published a volume titled *Reasons . . . Proving a Necessity of Reforming our Churches in England*. The work was directed in its prefatory letter to the newly enthroned king, James I, and not only detailed a severe criticism of Anglican church government but also affirmed the congregational pattern as the only polity scripturally prescribed. Wrote Jacob: "Only a particular ordinary constant congregation of Christians in Christ's testament is appointed and reckoned to be a visible church."[12] As a consequence Jacob was imprisoned in London. After his release, he fled to Holland, where he ministered to a congregation in Middelburg for many years. Throughout this period he emphasized the non-Separatist form of congregational understanding, a view that appeared in his writings as early as 1606. Later this was shared not only with William Ames but also with others such as Robert Parker and William Bradshaw, who were also early leaders among the exiled English in Holland.

Finally, in 1616, Jacob returned to England and established a small non-Separatist Congregational church at Southwark, in south London. This was the first such church gathered on English soil and was the actual beginning therefore of Congregationalism, or Independency as it was later called, as a continuous part of British church life. The congregation was formalized into a church when, according to the record, its members "stood in a ringwise" and "covenanted together to walk in all God's ways as he had revealed or should make known to them."[13] Following this they elected and ordained Henry Jacob to be pastor and began their new independent existence. Yet their independence in meeting apart from the parish churches of England, probably with some secrecy, did not mean severance of all communion with the Anglican establishment. Where such relationship could be maintained without giving approval thereby to "any mere human tradition," Jacob fully voiced encouragement. From this beginning there developed in England that perception of the congregational way that produced the early generation of leaders who carried Congregationalism to the New World.

The influence of these non-Separatist exiles also was felt in Leyden by John Robinson and his Separatist congregation. From 1610 onward Ames and Jacob were in contact with Robinson and succeeded in leading him to modify some of his Separatist views. Although Robinson has not been seen in this light, and has normally been labeled a strict Separatist whose congregation carried that outlook in 1620 into Plymouth colony in New England, recent research has corrected the story. In the end Robinson did not fully change his earlier views, but after 1616 he recognized the validity of Jacob's non-Separatist congregation, and near the end of his life he published *A Treatise on the Lawfulness of Hearing Ministers in the Church of England*. Years later John Cotton, one of New England's leading ministers, wrote that Robinson "came back indeed one half of the way, acknowledging the lawfulness of communicating with the Church of England in Word and prayer, but not in the sacraments and discipline." Cotton termed this "a fair bridge, at least a fair arch of a bridge for union."[14] By means of this "bridge" the followers of Robinson were able to join hands with the flood of non-Separatists who soon followed them to New England to create a harmonious beginning for American Congregationalism.

The Renewed Struggle under Charles I

In England, however, the conflict continued. In 1625 Charles I succeeded James I in England and Scotland, and his reign brought to a climax the royal conflict with the Puritan movement. Charles's policies were like those of his father. In civil matters he maintained the divine right of kings and attempted to rule by personal authority, allowing as little interference as possible by the democratic forces represented in Parliament. In religious matters he continued the anti-Puritan program of his predecessor, leading the Church of England to further rejection of the reform movement. He encouraged its "high church" element, permitting the development of a growing Anglo-Catholic tradition. Communion tables were changed back into altars, and uniformity in vestments and liturgical practices was enforced with increasing severity. In addition he supported a growing modification in theology that pitted a more liberal Arminian perspective against the Calvinism characteristic of Puritan thought.

Charles I relied upon the counsel and heavy-handed action of William Laud, a cleric whom he appointed Bishop of London in 1628 and then Archbishop of Canterbury in 1633. Laud's high church views were vigorously anti-Puritan. Puritan preachers were kept from their pulpits. Puritan lectureships, a form of midweek instruction within the

English parishes, were broken up. Even the Puritan attempts at a greater honoring of the Sabbath were mocked through the reissue of the *Book of Sports*, which mandated recreation on that holy day. As Laud placed Arminian clerics in high ecclesiastical positions, Puritan leaders found themselves increasingly exposed to hostility to their faith and their desire for ecclesiastical reform.

Although one effect of this oppression was the encouragement of flight to the New World, another was resistance and, finally, revolution within England itself in which Puritanism and Parliament joined forces against the Church of England and the king. The struggle was partly constitutional, a defense of political liberties against a despotic ruler. It was also partly religious, an effort to resist the tyranny of the archbishop and even to replace episcopacy and its liturgy with a presbyterian pattern of polity and worship. In 1641 Parliament impeached Laud for treason and imprisoned him in the Tower of London, later decreeing his execution. In 1642, when Charles attempted to arrest leading Puritans within the House of Commons, civil war began. Scotland joined the fray, having suffered under the king's effort to impose upon it the Book of Common Prayer, and signed with Parliament a Solemn League and Covenant, committing the parties to resistance to the crown and to reformation of the church.

Early in 1643, to fulfill its religious commitments, Parliament passed an act abolishing episcopacy from the English church and also called an assembly of clergy and laity to advise in additional reform work. The overwhelming majority of delegates in this Westminster Assembly were Puritans of presbyterian sympathy, with minorities holding episcopal and congregational convictions. The assembly met for almost five and a half years and produced results of major significance. In 1644 it completed a Directory of Worship, which Parliament adopted after abolishing the Book of Common Prayer. Shortly thereafter it presented to Parliament a system of presbyterian government for the national church, which also was adopted in its major parts. Two years later it produced the Westminster Confession of Faith, subsequently acknowledged as one of the major theological statements within the Reformed tradition. Approved by Parliament for England, it became the confession for the Church of Scotland as well, and later it was affirmed by Congregationalists in both England and America. In addition to these documents the Westminster Assembly prepared two catechisms, a Larger Catechism for use in the pulpit and a Shorter Catechism primarily for the instruction of children, each approved by Parliament in 1648. Puritan reforms and Calvinist theology then prevailed in the established English church, presbyterian forms of faith, government, and worship being mandated for the national religion.

Among the delegates to the Westminster Assembly, however, were a few who kept alive the voice of Congregationalism. Five especially were active in its deliberations, and late in 1643 they presented their views in a unique document that they titled *An Apologeticall Narration*. Led by Thomas Goodwin and Philip Nye and known to history as the "five dissenting brethren," these men sought to stem the tide of a developing ecclesiastical dogmatism that would reform church government simply by replacing episcopacy with a required presbyterian system. They had all known persecution under the former, each having been an exile in Holland during the time of Laud's ascendancy. And now they were seeing on the horizon the possibility of more of the same, only administered by Puritan colleagues with whom they had otherwise shared so much in religious conviction. While defending in their document the way of Congregationalism against the presbyterian charge of its leading to heresy and even schism in church affairs through lack of centralized and controlling power, these men also opened up a significant new approach to the establishment of a nation's church polity by pleading for toleration of minority views.

Although these Congregationalists believed that Scripture contained "a complete sufficiency to make the Churches of God perfect," they resisted absolutization of any group's current understanding of that plan. One of their principles, they said, was "not to make our present judgment and practice a binding law unto ourselves for the future." They added that they wished this principle "were enacted as the most sacred law in the midst of all other Laws and Canons Ecclesiastical in Christian states and churches throughout the world." This was a plea for open-mindedness. The five dissenting brethren attempted to halt the rush toward a new ecclesiastical tyranny. Then applying this to their own situation in the face of what could be further exile, they asked permission for themselves to enjoy in their own country the ordinances of Christ, "with the allowance of a latitude to some lesser differences, with peaceableness," for they did not know "where else with safety, health, and livelihood," they could "set their feet on earth."[15] Quite unexpectedly, however, the toleration that soon came was broadly extended to almost all religious groups and was administered by a Congregationalist who was one of their own.

Cromwell and Congregationalism

While the Westminster Assembly debated theological and ecclesiastical matters, the civil war ran its course. In 1644 the army of the king was defeated in the critical battle at Marston Moor, and in the following year Charles himself was taken captive. The hero of these military exploits was a member of Parliament, Oliver Cromwell, who had created a "new model" army made up of men of religious enthusiasm, many of them members of new religious sects then beginning to appear. Some were Congregationalists; others were Baptists, Levellers, Diggers, or Fifth Monarchy men. More and more they found themselves fighting not only for political freedom but also for the religious toleration that, in the face of a coercive nationalized presbyterianism, would enable them to live freely according to their convictions. While winning on the battlefield, the army likewise began to take control of Parliament. In late 1648 Parliament expelled its presbyterian members and in the following year tried, condemned, and executed the captive king. Meanwhile Cromwell extended his military victories, first subjugating the Irish and then defeating the Scots, who had risen briefly in revolt.

By 1651 all opposition had been overcome, and in 1653 Cromwell dismissed the remainder of the previous Parliament, calling a new body to establish the Commonwealth of England, Scotland, and Ireland. Then, refusing the title of king, he was chosen to rule as lord protector. A deeply religious person of Puritan sympathies, Cromwell inclined more toward Congregationalism than toward any other church form, but he created a religious settlement that provided a large degree of toleration for almost all groups in the nation. Only Anglicans using the Book of Common Prayer and Roman Catholics celebrating the Mass were barred from their worship under the Commonwealth's laws. But this was largely because of fear that these practices would revive old political loyalties adverse to the new peace. Cromwell himself was lenient in administering the legislation, and both groups were largely left alone if they did not disturb the public order.

Toleration, however, did not mean religious indifference on the part of the lord protector. His religious settlement, crafted especially in consultation with the five dissenting brethren and other clergy among the Congregationalists, created a national program for Protestant evangelization along Puritan lines, though without the establishment of a national church. The key was to improve the quality of preaching in the local parish congregations, and to that end both a national commission and local commissions were set up to evaluate clergy competence and to foster changes where needed.

In this system Congregationalists, Baptists, Presbyterians, and Anglicans participated alike. Although Calvinist theology in general was the norm, there were no prescribed creeds, nor forms of worship. The intent was an intensification of Puritan Protestant faith in a context permitting free expression of other religious views. In this setting Congregationalism thrived. Congregational clergy were Cromwell's chaplains, and Congregational churches were gathered to practice their polity without obstruction. In 1658 a conference of Congregational ministers and lay delegates was held at the Savoy Palace in London to state more explicitly the principles of their churches' faith and practice. It produced the Savoy Declaration, subsequently endorsed in part also in American Congregationalism. Although the Savoy Declaration's confession of faith was based largely upon that of Westminster, the section entitled "The Institution of the Churches" became an important late seventeenth-century document depicting the congregational form of church order. The Commonwealth had enabled English Congregationalism to come out of the shadows and to prosper.

Neither Oliver Cromwell nor the Commonwealth, however, were to survive long. The lord protector died in 1658, and he was succeeded by his son, Richard, a person of lesser competence for the inherited undertaking. This and other factors conspired to bring the new politics to an end. In 1660 Charles II restored the Stuart kingship to the throne and the Anglican church to ecclesiastical power. With episcopacy re-established and the Book of Common Prayer again mandated, the liberty of the Commonwealth years disappeared. Uniformity of religious practice was once more required, nonconforming clergy were deprived, and legal restrictions were placed against all forms of conventicle gathering and worship. Congregationalists, Baptists, and Presbyterians, along with member of the smaller sects, were consigned to live again under the cloud of persecution. It was not until the Act of Toleration of 1689, when in a new revolution William and Mary came from Holland to occupy the English throne, that religious liberty was restored.

THEOLOGY

The theology of early American Congregationalism came in a very broad sense from the totality of English Puritanism. The Congregational émigrés leading the exodus to the New World counted as their theological mentors such men as William Perkins, Paul Baynes, William Ames, Richard Sibbes, Robert Jenison, and John Preston, leaders of the "spiritual brotherhood" of theologian-preachers who, without regard to polity differences, developed English Puritan thought throughout the late sixteenth and early seventeenth centuries. Some of these men held academic professorships, some were private pastors in Puritan households, some served as lecturers or special preachers to congregations, some were even chaplains in the court. In their variety of locations and callings they comprised a leaven within the church, contributing by written and spoken word to spiritual and theological renewal. Dedicated to intensive biblical study, they sought to recapture and reinvigorate major themes in the Reformed tradition's interpretation of Christian faith. Through their work a broad Puritan theological consensus arose, which was transported to the New World.

Authority

Puritan theology began with a reliance upon the Bible as ultimate source and authority for Christian truth. In this it reaffirmed a central theme of the early sixteenth-century Protestant Reformation itself, whether in its Lutheran or Reformed expression. Fundamental to all else in that revolt against Catholicism was the assertion of the supremacy of the scriptural Word. Roman errors had come, it was felt, from the subordinating of Scripture to ecclesiastical tradition and to interpretation given by a supposedly infallible church. Protestants argued that infallibility can be ascribed only to God's voice, rather than to that which is human, and that the locus of the divine voice is the biblical Word. John Calvin wrote that the Bible obtains "full authority among believers" only when they regard it "as having sprung from heaven, as if there the living words of God are heard."[16] With this biblical literalism Puritans agreed.

Yet the Bible needed always to be interpreted, and Puritans, although heirs of the Reformation, were also heirs of the Renaissance, placing great confidence in the power of human reason to carry out that task. Their confidence, however, was not in the power of natural reason, for sin had corrupted that. But God's restoration of human persons in Christ brought the gift of an enlightened and renewed reason. One Puritan divine even said, "Our Saviour Christ hath taught us how to argue."[17] So logic was deemed a trustworthy tool to be applied to divine revelation. Furthermore, there were different types of logic—and Puritans did not follow the medieval logic of Thomas Aquinas as used by the Roman Catholic Church. They turned to a newer logic used by Petrus Ramus, a French humanist and Protestant of the late sixteenth century. It differed from the former not only in context but also in style and intent. Medieval thinking was designed for complex analysis and proof; the logic of Ramus upheld the task of simple assertion. It was a system to be used as a means of exposition or declaration. It was not a means of inquiry, employing the syllogisms of Aristotle for reaching conclusions of truth, but rather it served as an instrument setting forth in logical order a truth already received. Puritans found it ideal for explaining and expounding the biblical Word.

Covenant of Grace

The theology Puritans found in the Bible was covenant theology. Scripture told them that God's chief means of dealing with humanity was by way of covenant, and for Puritan theologians, therefore, the whole understanding of Christian faith related to this central theme. A covenant was a relationship of mutual commitment, binding two parties in sworn promises. In a certain sense it could be seen as a compact, with a quid pro quo not dissimilar to contractual arrangements in various areas of human association. However, when a covenant was visualized in the realm of divine-human relationship, it took on added dimensions. There the calculus of contractualism receded before the more compelling power of religious consciousness. Terms suggesting commercial barter gave way to those emphasizing friendship, loyalty, and love. The covenant between God and God's people stressed the element of divine promise rather than of human payment—and although human obligation was present, its impulse was less a grasp for recompense than gratitude for a gift. Indeed, the biblical covenant between God and humanity was called a *covenant of grace*, for it was God's grace that provided the enveloping context for divine-human relationships. So Puritan theological reflection was conditioned by this religious awareness as it sought to explore the covenant's meaning.

In Puritan exegesis of the biblical story the covenant of grace was preceded by a covenant of creation, commonly termed a *covenant of works*. In the creation of the human race the divine expectation was one of receiving perfect human obedience, and the divine commitment was to grant to such behavior the blessings of happiness and eternal life. This was a covenant of mutual obligation in which obedience brought reward. But Adam in the garden, representing the entirety of humanity, did not obey, and the covenant of works was broken. With the breaking of the covenant, moreover, came that fall in the human condition called *original sin*. Its consequence for Adam and Adam's posterity was both guilt and corruption, that is, liability to eternal punishment and the presence in this life of spiritual death. Although originally created in the image of God, humanity now bore the marks of confusion and inability to conform to God's expectations. In all of the human faculties this taint appeared, with the mind, the conscience, the will, and the affections sharing in the plague of rebellion and pride that turns one away from a loving obedience to God. So there was no way, as one divine put it, for humanity "to patch up a broken covenant."[18] It was only by a new God-given covenant that help could come. That covenant was the covenant of grace.

In expounding its understanding of the biblical message of redemption under the language of the covenant of grace, Puritanism expressed a warm pietism and a theology marked by distinct evangelicalism. This Puritan characteristic has been minimized or lost in many descriptions of the movement, the Puritans often being pictured as dour and their theology as too bound up with the necessity of detailed obedience to God's law. It is true that for the Puritans life was a serious business, and no little part of that business was religious commitment and faithfulness in the duties it entailed. But the overriding spirit of Puritan covenant theology was evangelical, not legal. English Puritanism was in fact a forerunner of the larger Pietist movement that blossomed on the Continent during the succeeding century.

God's new covenant extended to the heirs of Adam the promises of forgiveness of sin and power of more obedient life. This was the good news of the gospel and, for the Puritan divines, needed to be constantly conveyed through sermon and theological treatise to draw those alienated from God and neighbor into newness of loyalty and love. Consequently in Puritan practice theology itself was never an abstract exercise. Reformed scholasticism on the Continent in the latter part of the seventeenth century was more abstract, and in its speculations it became an arid intellectual pursuit less and less related to the realities of human experience. For Puritan thinkers the existential note was always present in the theological enterprise. William Ames even defined theology in his textbook, *The Marrow of Sacred Divinity*, by declaring, "Theology is the doctrine of living to God."[19]

Puritan covenant theology spoke, therefore, of God's covenant promises to relieve the pangs of guilt and to restore the power of righteousness, promises vastly different from those of God's first covenant given at creation and quickly broken by human act. The covenant of grace, unlike its predecessor said the Puritans, is a free covenant, a sure covenant, and one that is everlasting. It is a free covenant offered by God without recompense required. There is no quid pro quo as in the covenant of works. If the covenant of works said, "Do this for life," in the covenant of grace it is said, "Do this from life." The gift is prior to the deed, not the deed prerequisite for the gift. William Perkins, leading systematic theologian of the movement, wrote that God's promises "are not made to any work or virtue in man, but to the worker; not for any merit of his own person or work, but for the person and merit of Christ."[20]

Furthermore, whereas the covenant of works was uncertain as to its fulfillment, the covenant of grace is sure. The freely given promises of God are covenant promises, that is, the committed mercies of God. Unlike the offering of blessings contingent upon obedience, these are divine promises for which God commits certain fulfillment. Puritans often marvelled that God should thus "become a debtor" to humankind.

Finally, a covenant that is free and sure is also everlasting. Here is the fullest expression of confidence in the certainty of the divine promises. Whereas the covenant of works was ephemeral and readily broken by human sin, this new covenant is subject to no such termination. The covenant conveys the forgiveness of sin and the restoration of the sinner. In this it is not contingent upon merit, but rests solely upon grace, a grace that reaches out without ceasing to embrace and to renew. Thomas

Sutton's word of assurance to those in covenant was, "Be glad and rejoice, for God has given you the keys of the kingdom. Though you fall, yet you shall rise again. Therefore you are not to be cast away."[21]

The Covenant as Conditional

The covenant of grace is a gift of God's free promises, not to be earned. And yet God's promises must be received. This, too, was the word of the gospel and an important reason for God's use of a covenant in dealing with humanity. In Puritan thought God's act of covenanting was above all an appropriate way of inviting the response of rational and voluntary creatures. A person, said these theologians, is not a "block or stock," a wooden entity simply to be moved, but a living being to be appealed to in both mind and will. Human decision very much enters the picture in this covenant relationship. Richard Sibbes wrote, "God honors us by having our consent. Indeed he will not accomplish the work of eternal salvation without it."[22] There is mutuality in the covenant, and God's action by covenant is not only a committed promising, but a calling upon human persons to be freely participating covenant partners. The covenant of grace is therefore a "conditional covenant." The receiving of God's covenanted gifts depends upon a fulfillment of covenant conditions, the human commitments necessary for being in covenant relationship with God.

Yet this is no covenant of law calling for merit, as had been that first covenant at creation. The conditions leading to covenant completion are never matters of merit. The gifts are not given to the worthy, but to the needy. What is required is the trusting relationship in which the covenanting partner personally receives that which the Giver gives. Far from being a legal covenant, the covenant of grace is an evangelical covenant whose primary condition is faith.

It was important, however, that the nature of saving faith not be misunderstood. Faith could be seen by some as simply an intellectual act, the assent of the mind to the doctrines of Christian revelation. Medieval theology, so Puritans felt, often yielded to this fault, and Protestantism was being similarly tempted. Such faith, however, was not life changing. Did not "even the devils believe?" Puritans knew that saving faith must touch the deeper loyalties of life. It had to do with one's fundamental being.

Or again, faith could be construed as simply a comforting addendum to divine work already accomplished, a view that appeared on the more "enthusiastic" fringe of the Puritan movement. This antinomian emphasis stressed the overwhelming presence of God's inflowing Spirit, in the light of which faith was no more than assurance that God alone had made things well. But authentic Puritan thought viewed faith as a decisive act of human participation in that saving relationship. Faith, as trust in God's mercy, constituted a necessary, though nonmeritorious, fulfillment of the primary condition for entrance into the covenant of grace.

Gifts of the Covenant

In the traditional language of Protestant theology the main gifts of God received in the covenant were those of *justification* and *sanctification*, that is, the forgiveness of sins and the cleansing of inward being that leads to new holiness of life. In the covenant relationship God both pardons and purges, dealing with human sin in terms of not only its guilt but also its grasp. Although these divine actions may be concurrent in human experience, they represent distinct and separate ways in which life under God can be portrayed. Justification is a relational matter and signifies God's acceptance in forgiveness of the unworthy. By God's pardon alienation is overcome and relationship is restored. Sin leads to separation and judgment, whereas forgiveness means restoration and peace. As a legal term, justification implies the passing of a sentence, and the sentence upon the sinner is one of acquittal. Thus the classic Protestant principle of "justification by faith" emerged in Puritan covenantal terms. For those who enter the covenant of grace, through the faith that is trust in God's mercy, forgiveness of sins is a covenantal gift.

Similarly, sanctification was affirmed as a gift of the covenant, for God's love brings a cleansing. Puritan concern for a life of godliness was expressed here. If justification, said Puritan theology, represents acceptance by God for God's kingdom, sanctification represents the moral renewing that more and more fits one for God's kingdom. A favorite biblical metaphor for this was the "new heart," and Puritan theologians spoke of God as not only the "heart maker," but also the "heart mender" who would bring to pass this inner healing. By God's act life at its center is transformed, the direction of its loyalty and love is changed, and one becomes a "new creature." Indeed, in its most profound sense this is "union with Christ," and Puritan writing expressed unhesitatingly the joy of this divine presence and power. The gift of sanctification, therefore, ennobles the very core of one's being. Ames said that it is "a new principle of life communicated by God unto us" that "resembles the highest perfection which is found in God."[23]

Lest this ecstasy lead to self-deception, however, Puritan thought quickly entered its qualifiers. For one thing, sanctification is gradual, lifelong in development, and in earthly experience never complete. Despite the divine power at work within, there still remain the "stubs and reliques" of human corruption—so much that, as Paul Baynes noted, sin "doth fight against the work of grace, more than water fighteth with the heat of fire."[24] Puritanism never allowed itself to lapse into the dream of historical perfectionism. Furthermore, sanctification as God's gift must also be preserved by sustained human obedience. Again, this was not deemed meritorious, for no human obedience is fully worthy. Sanctity and sin are too intermixed. But in the conditions of the covenant, faith needs to express itself in faithfulness, and the Christian's life embraces a constant spiritual struggle for greater and greater fidelity. In his interpretation of Puritanism, historian William Haller portrayed that life as "a wayfaring and a warfaring."[25] It is both a pilgrimage and a battle in the effort to fulfill the conditions of the covenant and to continue in covenant relationship with God.

The Covenant as Absolute

Yet all this consideration of mutuality was not a fully sufficient way, in Puritan understanding, to view the covenant of grace. For all its value and biblical warrant, it was only a partial picture and contained inadequacies in at least two respects. On the one hand, if the covenant with God is merely conditional, dependent for fulfillment on human response, there is really no likelihood that it will ever be fulfilled. Conscious of the weakness of the fallen will and the magnitude of human corruption, Puritan thought refused to believe that one could rise by one's own strength and turn oneself from sin to faith. If this were the necessity, said Robert Jenison, it would leave the blessings of the new covenant through Christ as uncertain as those once available in the first covenant to Adam, which he lost "when it was left to his own keeping."[26] And Thomas Blake noted that if we are in covenant simply by our own frail responses, then Christ "might have been a Savior, and not one person in the world would have been saved."[27] The doctrine of human depravity left a heavy impact on the Puritan view of covenant. Human persons need God's decisive and compelling act, which gives even the gift of faith, so that the covenant may be truly initiated and its primary condition fulfilled. Considering, moreover, the persistent tenacity of sin even in those to whom faith has been given, the same need recurs for the Christian's perseverance in faithfulness. For conditions to be met, the covenant must be more than conditional. It must also be an absolute covenant conveying, along with divine promises, a decisive completion through the power of God's own act.

There was also a second inadequacy in the idea of a merely conditional covenant. It violated God's sovereignty with its erroneous belief that, as Robert Jenison again wrote, differences between "the children of God and of this world, as suppose between Peter and Judas, should be wholly made from nature, not from grace."[28] Here an additional major element in Puritan theology was exposed, the conviction that in the last analysis historical events and human destinies are under God's ultimate rule and determination. In all things it is God's unconditioned decree that must prevail. So, drawing upon its reading of the biblical message and its Protestant heritage, Puritanism affirmed a doctrine of predestination, an aspect of its belief in the unqualified sovereignty of God. The difference between the destinies of Peter and Judas was by God's free determination. Faith itself is a fruit of divine election, and the chosen therefore are God's chosen, not simply those who choose themselves.

Covenant theology thus emphasized God's final and decisive efficiency in covenant action. The covenant of grace gives to those to whom it is bestowed not only forgiveness and new life, but also the very receiving of those gifts in covenant partnership. Although in the covenant one brings faith to God, it is the covenant that gives the faith that brings one to God. The covenant is not merely conditional. It is also absolute.

Puritan theology of the late sixteenth and early seventeenth centuries, therefore, looked simultaneously in two directions, toward the poles of piety and predestination. On the one hand, it enthusiastically proclaimed the biblical evangel, presenting the good news of God's promises and urging the responses of faith and faithfulness. On the other hand, it affirmed with equal conviction the biblical message of divine election, the sovereign choosing by God of those who are to be God's people. Yet the two convictions, though different, were conjoined through the idea of the covenant of grace. The covenant was conditional and called for response. But the covenant was likewise absolute in that the very response itself, in fulfillment of the conditions, was empowered by God's freely chosen giving. In this covenant theology human decision and divine decree were held together in close interrelationship, although subject always to the possibility of the tension being broken through greater stress given to one or to the other. This theology was what the leaders of the Congregational exodus brought in the seventeenth century to the New World.

POLITY

For English Puritans committed to a congregational form of church order, theology flowed naturally into polity. The structured organization of church life and the practical procedures by which it should be carried out were based upon an understanding of the nature of God's working, not on some independent type of human consideration detached from the realm of faith. In part this was due to the literalistic manner in which the Bible was approached in Puritan thought. As the infallible and comprehensive Word of God, it contained, in Puritan conviction, a model for the government of the church, and for these particular Puritans that form was congregational. But faith and order were related in more than this purely legalistic way. For Separatists and non-Separatists alike the church was seen as a locus of divine activity, to be understood even in its manifold practical dimensions in a theological manner.

It is sometimes said that congregational polity and practice represent a "low church" view of church order. To a certain degree this is undoubtedly true, for its more simplified approach to matters of ministry and worship are less complex when contrasted with hierarchical structure and ornate liturgy. Yet in another sense this congregational understanding of radical English Puritans was a "high" conception of the church. The gathered congregation itself was seen to be a holy vehicle, a sanctified instrument in God's hands for divine purposes. As a covenant community the church was called into being by God and endowed with God's own authority and power that it might carry out a saving ministry to God's people. Therefore it is within this context of high vocation and mission that congregational church order must be viewed. Polity had theological grounding.

The Church Invisible and Visible

When William Ames turned to the subject of the church in his *Marrow of Sacred Divinity*, he wrote first about "the church mystically considered." Whatever else the church is in its visible and structured manifestation, it is even more fundamentally an invisible, universal reality that "embraces believers of all nations, of all places, of all times" and that may be spoken of as "mystically one." Indeed, it is the mystical "body of Christ," Ames noting that the relationship between Christ and the church is "so intimate" that in apostolic understanding "not only is Christ the church's and the church Christ's, but Christ is in the church and the church in him." Other scriptural metaphors, in Ames's judgment, stressed the fact that Christ is "the beginning of all honor, life, power, and perfection in the church"—the church is a city and Christ the king; the church the branches and Christ the vine; the church a body and Christ the head. So behind all visible manifestations is this catholic character of the church, a mystical unity permeated by divine presence and rule.[29]

The mystical church becomes concrete and visible, however, in local congregations of Christian believers—and this provided the sphere of distinctive affirmation in congregational polity. In the political and ecclesiastical context of sixteenth- and seventeenth-century England this meant, in a negative sense, the denial of authority to such visible hierarchical bodies as Roman Catholicism, Anglicanism, and even Presbyterianism in their claim to be universal or national churches. Papal decree, diocesan rule, and imposed decision by presbytery or synod had no power over locally gathered communities of faith. Positively stated, the power and authority granted by Christ resided directly and separately in each congregation.

A Church of Believers

The most fundamental aspect of this congregational conception was the conviction that the locally gathered church is a church of believers. If the church expresses the life of Christ, it must be composed of those whose personal lives embody that reality. One of the major failings of comprehensive state churches that by law compel membership from all in the nation is the "mixed" character of the resultant congregations, with believers and unbelievers, the faithful and the nominal, even the good and the wicked, intermingled. Separatist and non-Separatist protestors within the English establishment inveighed unremittingly against such a travesty. Limitation to a committed membership was, in their understanding, the manner of the church's composition in its New Testament manifestation. Such commitment was the very "rock" upon which Jesus said his church was to be built. Congregational exegesis of the famous ecclesiastical passage in Matthew 16:18 denied that the rock was, as Roman Catholic interpretation had long declared, the person of Peter who had made confession of faith in Christ. It affirmed instead that the rock was the confession itself. So the church was to be built upon the foundation of this confession, made up of those who willingly professed their faith and took their stand with others of like dedication in gathered Christian community.

Moreover, profession of faith, in this perception, could never be separated from expression in holiness, the believer's manifestation of the power of new life. So, in New Testament terminology, the church was seen as a "society of saints." This could be more problematic, however, for the ethic of saintliness was subject to varied interpretations, and deviations from a life of godliness were both more tempting and more easily discernible than those from a profession of faith. Despite continued imperfection, however, the emphasis upon purity remained strong and became a constant, sometimes obsessive, element in this early congregational understanding. There were strong disciplinary procedures promoting its realization, so that each local congregation would be made up of persons of faith and faithfulness. Called by God out of a wicked world and an impure national church, these persons alone must comprise the local churches if those churches are truly to reflect the life of Christ.

Church Covenant

The bond by which a gathered congregation was united in its common profession and allegiance was the church covenant. Robert Browne's simple statement in 1582 provided the first clear indication of this policy and practice. "Christians," he said, "are a company or number of believers, which by a willing covenant made with their God, are under the government of God and Christ, and keep his laws in one holy communion."[30] This meant that the covenant relationship with God known by individual believers in the covenant of grace was extended in church covenant to corporate religious life. The church was a community participating in the mutuality of divine-human commitment. As God's covenanted promises were given to a gathered people to be their God in governing and protective care, so the community's promises were made to live faithfully under that government. Furthermore, this corporate commitment to God involved a common commitment to one another, the pledge of a gathered people to "walk together" in promised obedience. Through this bonding by covenant a gathering of Christian people was transformed into a church. Ames declared that believers, simply as an assembly, do not constitute a church even though they may regularly meet together. Only unification through covenant, with its shared commitment to perform requisite duties toward God and toward one another, creates church estate.

Church Government

For a congregation to be constituted into church estate meant that it possessed within itself, as God's gift, the power and responsibility of church government. Placed into each congregation's hands was the awesome task of perpetuating faithfully the life Christ intended for his people. One bold way of conceiving this responsibility affirmed that the "offices" of Christ had now been assumed by each participating believer in the life of the congregations. In Calvin's theology Christ was spoken of as prophet, priest, and king. These were the roles Christ took on, the functions Christ performed in his earthly ministry. As prophet, he conveyed by his words the truth of divine revelation. As priest, he offered to God prayers and ultimately the supreme sacrifice of his life. And as king, he led persons from an earthly to a spiritual kingdom and exercised power of judgment over evil. But as Christ now lives in each local congregation, these sacred roles are shared with the humblest of members. Each can be prophet, participating in teaching and exhorting. Each can be priest, offering spiritual sacrifices of prayer and praise. Each can be king, participating in the community's government and helping to cleanse the church from all evil. Because not only the mystical church is the "body of Christ," but each visible congregation also carries that label, the power of acting for Christ falls heavily into local hands. So two things characterize the covenanting local church: the authority to administer its life and the obligation to use that privilege in obedience to its Lord.

One major responsibility of the local church in its self-government was the election and ordination of officers. Although the church, by virtue of its covenant, could exist as a church without officers, the authorization of and guidance by officers were important for its more complete functioning. This was especially true with respect to the administration of the sacraments, for celebration by a member of the ordained clergy was necessary for their use.

Both Separatists and non-Separatists consistently found five offices of "ordinary ministry" represented in the churches of the New Testament, and each was to be filled through the congregation's election. This power of election, however, was for males only, for early Congregationalism limited the franchise by denying women the right to vote. In the exercise of this free consent each voting member was urged to attempt to "divine the mind of Christ," that is, to determine those among one's companion believers whom God had particularly qualified to assume these leadership tasks. It was not appropriate to use this privilege to advance one's own will in the church. The overarching concern was always the accomplishment of Christ's will—and thus the selection of the "fittest" to bring this about. The business of the church and its government was a divine business, and participation in it a sacred trust. Elections were therefore to be preceded, in the words of Browne, "by prayers and humbling of all, with fasting and exhortation, that God may be chief in the choice."[31]

The five offices of ministry for each congregation were pastor, teacher, ruling elder, deacon, and widow. The functions of the pastor and teacher were primarily a proclaiming of the Word, the former by exhortation and the latter by instruction, and an administering of the two sacraments, baptism and the Lord's Supper. The ruling elder helped in the administration of church affairs, particularly as related to the admission of new members and the exercise of discipline, and also presided at meetings of the congregation for election and ordination of officers. Deacons were given the responsibilities related to financial matters, collecting the voluntary contributions of members at worship and dispersing these funds as relief for the poor and maintenance of the officers—in Browne's words they were "to gather and bestow the church liberality."[32] The office of widow was for older women who prayed for the church and attended the sick and afflicted.

Acts of ordination formalized the entrance of church officers into their places of responsibility. In all cases these were acts of the congregation, rather than of some ecclesiastically superior body, a people's setting apart of those whom they had chosen for leadership tasks. It was to the believing congregation that the "power of the keys" had been given, that is, the spiritual power of government within the life of the church. Yet important as the ceremony and prayers of ordination might be, the actual authorization of a pastor or teacher to perform a ministry of Word and sacrament occurred in the election itself, not in the formalizing liturgy. Because the latter had been subject to long historical abuse, Browne even proposed that within the congregation's ordination service the traditional imposition of hands should not be included if "it is turned into pomp or superstition."[33] The simple voice of the congregation in election was respected as the confirming and authorizing voice of Christ.

Despite this strong emphasis on the role of the congregation in church government, however, these early advocates of congregational polity resisted the allegation that their Separatist and non-Separatist churches were ruled simply by "popular democracy." In an age when civil rule was still largely monarchical and church rule was largely hierarchical, democratic tendencies were seen as leading to "mob rule." Congregational leaders tried to avoid that judgment by interpreting their church order as a mixed form of government in which monarchic, aristocratic, and democratic strains were joined. Congregational government, they said, is first a monarchy because it recognizes in the church the headship of Christ. In all aspects of church organization and practice the congregation seeks obedience not to its own will, but to that of its risen and ever-present Lord. But this government is also an aristocracy, for elected officers have been granted certain powers of rule. Particularly in the "eldership," that is, the offices of pastor, teacher, and ruling elder, major authority in ministerial function has been established. Although some divergences appeared in early congregational practice concerning the degree of this authority, the tendency was to affirm the elders' decisive leadership in guiding the congregation. The eldership was chosen by the congregation for these duties, and members should follow their "guides." Yet beyond all this, the government of the congregation is a democracy, for it rests on a people's free consent. Officers chosen by election could be removed, in cases of dereliction of duty, by the congregation's act, and the addition of members through admission or their removal through discipline, though recommended by the eldership, could occur only by the congregation's assent. Yet all such action, again, had to be in accord with the rule of Christ. So this "mixed government" was declared by early Separatists and non-Separatists as proper for each local church—and as something quite different from a democracy embodying no more than the people's will.

Church Discipline

One of the distinctive aspects of local congregational church practice in this earlier period was its emphasis upon the use of disciplinary measures to keep the church pure, including as last resort the sentence of excommunication. The employment of discipline was not a novel matter on the English church scene. Roman Catholic and Anglican officials had used it to preserve conformity to their ways, and leaders of Scottish and English presbyterian Puritanism enforced it at the point of selective admission to the Lord's Supper. But these congregational procedures now gave disciplining authority to the local congregation to keep pure the congregation's life. Each local church had responsibility to detect and deal with those faults in members' behavior that could seriously compromise the church's standing before God. And so crucial was this matter that the administration of discipline became in early Separatist and non-Separatist literature one of the designated "marks" by which the true church could be known.

Ample directive for practical procedures was found in the "tell it to the church" passage of Matthew 18:17, seen generally throughout the Reformed tradition as the basis for the exercise of discipline. In the congregational interpretation of this text, ruling elders were charged, in matters that could not be settled privately, to bring to the church for public disciplinary action those persons judged in violation of the church's covenant commitment to walk together in God's ways. If change of heart was not forthcoming, the disciplinary penalty was applied by the church's consent. Interestingly, at this point John Robinson allowed women members of the church to join in the voting process, making it a fully congregational act. Whatever the degree of penalty, however, including the most severe step of excommunication, the declared intention of the congregational groups was encouragement to repentance and restoration. The motivation was the return of both the church member and the church to greater spiritual health in the sight of God. This was seen to be in accord with the frequently declared Pauline affirmation that the goal for congregational life was "edification," a process leading to growth in godliness. Discipline was one of the divinely given means for movement toward this ideal.

Indeed the whole of congregational church order for these radical Puritans constituted a divinely given means, not only for earthly edification but also for eternal salvation. Ecclesiastical exclusivism had long been a common characteristic of Christian churches, frequently employing the classic dictum "Outside the church there is no salvation," although with varying meanings. In Roman Catholicism this pointed to the necessity for recognizing papal authority and receiving the sacraments, whereas Protestant Reformers maintained the assertion by affirming the church as essential proclaimer of the Word and home of saving faith. But a form of church order was now urged by radical Separatists and non-Separatists as God's prescribed and necessary way for leading persons to their eternal destiny. The ancient slogan was revived, with the proviso that outside of a congregationally organized and governed church there was no salvation. One slight qualification was the admission that God could save in other ways if God so chose— but this was God's "ordinary" means and thus the safest route for churches to follow. Henry Jacob spoke a representative word when he said that congregational form of church government "is plainly the way to heaven and the outward means which must bring us thither, or else ordinarily we cannot come there."[34] Despite the plaintive hope expressed in 1643 at Westminster by the five dissenting brethren that no form of polity would be fixed into a binding law for the future among either themselves or other churches, the time for such open-mindedness on polity matters had not yet come.

WORSHIP

In 1605 William Bradshaw, a non-Separatist exile in Holland, wrote that "the word of God is given by Christ, the Head of the Church, to be the sole rule in all matters of religion and the worship and service of God. And whatsoever done in worship cannot be justified by the said word, is unlawful."[35] As authorization by the Bible was deemed the basis for theology and polity among early congregational Puritans, so too the Bible was the ground for determining the content of divine worship. All Puritans followed Calvin in this conviction, differing from Luther, whose criterion for inclusion in worship was somewhat broader. Luther was willing to incorporate into the service certain elements, both traditional and novel, if the Bible did not prohibit them. For Calvin and the Puritans, however, worship should include only what the Bible specifically prescribed.

From this scriptural absolutism came a strong Puritan critique of Anglican liturgy. When Browne characterized the Book of Common Prayer as containing "written rotten stuff," he spoke the harsh judgment of Puritan divines concerning the way in which it required purely human traditions to be forms for the worship of God. There were the various ecclesiastical vestments mandated for conducting the services of the church. There were the "noxious ceremonies" of kneeling for communion, the sign of the cross in baptism, and the ring in marriage. There were the formal prayers crafted for repeated use. There were the elaborate services for the sacraments, different from the simple administration practiced in the New Testament church. There were the prescriptions for the reading of officially approved homilies by clergy who did not preach. There were the ceremonies for wedding and funeral, occasions Puritans considered to be of a civil, not religious, nature. There was the calendar of the church year, with its saints' days and holy seasons, unnecessary addenda to the biblically prescribed Lord's Day, on which could be celebrated each week the total drama of salvation. Worship in the biblical manner meant a vast simplification of that which was practiced in the national church.

Preaching

Puritans believed that biblically sanctioned worship for each Lord's Day should be centered on the proclamation of the Word. Although there were other important elements of prayer and praise, the heart of honoring God was found in preaching and hearing the biblical message. Both Luther and Calvin identified this as one of the marks of the true church, and Puritans agreed. If the church is an agent of saving faith and continuing faithfulness, providing stimulus and nourishment for Christian believers, it must speak the Word of the Lord with persuasive power. Through its voice must come encounter with the rigors of God's law and the promises of God's gospel, and this is found through the publicly read and preached Word. By no other means does God speak so clearly, for the voice of God is in the Bible, and the Bible must be the content of preaching. In fact, the reading of the Bible in the course of worship ought itself be an interpreted reading. Puritan practice opposed the "dumb reading" found in the Anglican service, favoring inclusion of the pastor's explanatory comments to promote a meaningful hearing. But the fuller explication of Scripture comes through the sermon that follows. This was the centerpiece of all Puritan worship.

In accord with the evangelical concern of Puritanism the sermon was constructed and delivered so that it might penetrate the hearts of its hearers, leading to conversion and then to further deepening of faith and strengthening of obedience. Mere communication of knowledge, even biblical knowledge, was insufficient purpose. Although the sermon should inform, its more significant goal was to transform, that is, to serve as an instrument in the hands of the Spirit for radical change and renewal in human life. Puritans deplored the innocuousness of preaching in the national church. Richard Greenham complained that such preaching had "no more taste in it than the white of an egg," and urged instead that the sermon be "powdered with salt, that it may give grace to the hearers and make their souls thirst after the waters of life."[36] Puritans criticized what was called the "witty" preaching of the day. They felt that sermons preached especially in the larger parishes were often more displays of erudition than channels of communication. The style of such sermons was ornate, employing elaborate rhetoric, literary allusions, and quotations in the classic tongues, and their subject matter often seemed more superficial than significant in relation to the central themes of Christian faith.

In contrast Puritanism developed what came to be called "spiritual" preaching delivered in the "plain style." It was spiritual preaching in that it dealt with the journey of the human spirit under the design of God. Using the Bible as its source, it focused on the reality of sin and the drama of salvation. It aimed at enabling its hearers to travel the difficult pilgrim route, portrayed later by John Bunyan as leading from City of Destruction to Celestial City. It dealt with the tragedy of the fall and the continuation of temptation and struggle, but even more it proclaimed the grace of God in Jesus Christ and the strength this gives for triumph. Far from displaying the "wisdom of words," Puritan preaching portrayed the "word of wisdom," the eternal Word and its salvation.

Puritan preaching was "plain" not because it was unimaginative, but because it was directed toward plain people and was intended to make fully intelligible to them the saving message of the Word of God. Puritans used enhancing illustration and suggestive metaphor to achieve this end, but had no place for learned allusions that distract nor for Greek and Latin phrases that obscure. Clarity and persuasiveness were the goals, and the structure of the sermon itself was influenced by this intent. Customarily the Puritan preacher developed his sermon along a threefold pattern. First, he would "open" his text by reading it from the Scripture and explaining it briefly in relation to its biblical setting. Next, he would "divide" his text by extracting from it the relevant points of doctrine, to which more "proofs" would be added. Finally, he would "apply" the text by expounding on the "uses" to which it could be put in relation to the hearer's spiritual pilgrimage. All this was to make it plain—and also to convey the conviction that through the words of the preacher the very Word of God was being heard. William Perkins felt the minister must so frame his sermon "that all, even ignorant persons and unbelievers, may judge that it is not so much he that speaketh, as the Spirit of God in him and by him."[37] That was the sermon's high goal.

In addition to the formal preaching of the Word, characteristic of all Puritan worship, the worship of the congregationally gathered groups included further exposition by less formal "prophesyings." This was a practice of extemporaneous interpreting of Scripture and had its origin during the Elizabethan period in extraecclesiastical weekday conferences sponsored by Puritan-minded clergy to encourage biblical preaching. Gatherings included clergy and laity, several of the clergy speaking on a given text for the specific instructing of one another, as well as for the general edification of all others assembled. Although prophesying was suppressed by Elizabeth, who saw great danger in its dissemination of Puritan doctrine and encouragement of Puritan preaching, the practice, in altered form and with lay participation, found its way into the regular worship of both Separatist and non-Separatist groups.

In its more extreme form it was part of the Smyth congregation's worship in Amsterdam, where a text was read and several members of the church then successively engaged in interpretation. In Browne's congregation in Middelburg the minister first took his full hour, and then, says an account, another stood up to make the text more plain! The practice in Robinson's church in Leyden was still more regulated, with prophesying limited to those who had previously been recognized as having this special qualification and calling from God. Further, lay exhortation was combined in Leyden with the putting of questions by church members to the minister for clarification after the sermon. Although women were not permitted to participate in the questioning, they were allowed to share in the prophesying if they were "immediately, and extraordinarily, and miraculously inspired."[38] In varying ways, therefore, the interpretive work of the Spirit was believed present in worship's act of proclamation of the Word.

Praying

Even more expressively the presence of the Spirit was expected in the act of the minister's spontaneous public prayer, and one of the distinctive contributions of early congregational-style worship to the nonliturgical tradition was that of free prayer subject to the Spirit's inspiration. Anglican worship utilized set prayers from the Book of Common Prayer, and Reformed churches in the Calvinist tradition similarly employed set liturgies for public worship. English Puritans of presbyterian allegiance had John Knox's Genevan Service Book, along with other prayer books developed in exile on the Continent. But for Separatist and non-Separatist congregations the use of "stinted" prayers was an unscriptural act and a stifling experience. Set prayers in a liturgy, they said, cannot present to God the changing and special needs of a gathered people in worship. They suffocate the very Spirit that should be present to enable significant voicing of the congregation's petitions and praise. Their words are mere lip service before God; genuine prayer comes from deep within. John Robinson noted that "if our prayers be not conceived first in our hearts before they be brought forth in our lips, they are an unnatural, bastardly, and profane birth."[39] For this reason even the Lord's Prayer was rejected as a prayer to be used in Lord's Day worship. Through thoughtless repetition it can lose its meaning. The Lord's Prayer was not a prayer to be recited, but a model for shaping one's own petitions to God. In practice, public prayer in the worship of these dissenting congregations was labored, intense, and entered into with strong feeling. The "long prayer" was a major element in their Lord's Day service, often consuming more than a half hour, the people standing throughout. And when the prayer ended, the congregation responded with "Amen."

Singing

In addition to preaching, prophecy, and prayer, worship in a biblical manner included singing psalms of praise. This appears to have been less true for the early radical Separatist groups, whose worship was more didactic and expressed largely through the spoken word. Nevertheless, Robinson's Pilgrims in Plymouth were good psalm singers, and both earlier and later non-Separatist congregations shared in this broadly approved use of music in Puritan worship. Music, however, was limited in worship to this one form. Although records indicate that Puritans enjoyed instrumental music and other forms of vocal music in private, they believed that Scripture prohibited the employment of such pleasures in worship. Church organs were silent and sometimes even removed when it became possible in the mid-seventeenth century to worship in former Anglican sanctuaries. The use of choirs in worship was similarly abandoned. Nor was there hymn singing in the style of the Lutheran chorale. Following, rather, the precedent established by Calvin in Geneva, the Puritans limited their texts to psalms that they then put to simple musical settings. No harmonies were introduced, for the basic concept was that of a single melodic line, with one note to each syllable, to be sung in unison without accompaniment. Because of the metrical rhythm this was easy for the congregation to master, and where illiteracy made psalm books of little use, the preceptor would sing out the psalm for repetition line by line. Eventually the "lining out" of the psalms became the standard practice. In this mode of worship, through the text of the psalms, Puritans engaged in further exposure to and use of the Word of God.

Sacraments

A final major element in early Separatist and non-Separatist worship was the celebration of the sacraments. Both baptism and the Lord's Supper were incorporated into the Lord's Day service and were administered only by the pastor or teacher of the congregation. The meaning of the sacraments in these congregations was drawn from Calvin's theology and was in accord with the mainstream of Puritanism. Sacraments, it was held, are seals of the covenant of grace. They are visible signs that God has given to confirm to the individual person God's covenant promises made through God's Word. They cannot be separated from the Word and have no independent significance apart from it. Rather, they are adjuncts of the Word, servants of the Word, and render more explicit the divine commitments of forgiveness and renewal. They also signify the response of the believer in trust and renewed dedication, a matter essential to receiving that which is promised.

Baptism signifies the washing away of sin and the rising to new life in Christ. It is given to believers, if previously unbaptized, and to the children of believers. Infant baptism was justified by the general Reformed conviction that baptism was the Christian successor to Jewish circumcision as the covenant's seal. Moreover, administration to infants indicates that grace is by divine, not human, initiative, so that, as Robinson urged, the main end is not on our behalf toward God, but on God's behalf toward us. Baptism of children does not in itself guarantee their salvation, for that is limited to the elect and in one's maturity is contingent upon saving faith. But baptism gives children a presumption of election as they are granted a "federal holiness" that places them in the church under God's care. Then the promises of cleansing particularized in this act can have further and even lifelong significance as they are returned to time and again in faith. Separatists also faced the question of the validity of earlier baptism in a false church. Most of them upheld a sense of sacramental objectivity, and none but Smyth opted for rebaptism. Robinson maintained that the seal could come through the false church, but that repentance would later be required for the baptism of the Spirit accompanying regeneration. The actual act of baptism was administered in the name of the Trinity by means of sprinkling or pouring. The practice of having godparents was seen as lacking biblical warrant.

In agreement with Puritanism as a whole the Lord's Supper was also deemed a seal of the covenant, a "visible gospel" in which the elements in its celebration are themselves "preachers" of the Word. Representing the broken body and shed blood of Christ, they become a sign of the redemption promised in covenant by God to persons of faith, even as the receiving of the sacrament in faith is a responding act of covenant renewal. But the sacrament is more than a "bare sign" of God's promises. Following again the general Puritan understanding, the Lord's Supper was viewed as an occasion for nourishment of the soul through a "feeding on Christ," who was spiritually, though not physically, present.

The impulses of congregational polity also led to appreciation of the sacraments in terms of their significance for the life of the church itself. Far from being limited to the individual's experience, they had corporate value and meaning. Baptism, administered always within the congregation's worship, signified preliminary entrance into the covenant community. By this act infants were brought into the closer circle of God's love and care. And in the Lord's Supper, said Browne "we grow into one body, the church, in one communion of graces, whereof Christ is the head."[40] This latter affirmation brought to the fore again the significance of the administration of discipline within the local church. Barrow, in his bitter attack on the English establishment, asserted that celebrating the Lord's Supper in an impure church is "casting the precious body and blood of Christ to hogs and dogs."[41] Sharing this conviction, both Separatists and non-Separatists were committed to honoring the sanctity of the table by an attesting to the purity of the congregation to which the sacrament is offered. Because identification of worthiness rested upon the local congregation and its elders, unknown outsiders were not admitted to a church's communion and the pastor did not administer it elsewhere than in his own church.

The administration of the Lord's Supper was simple, the elements being offered in silence after a recitation of Christ's words instituting the sacrament. The celebration, however, was always preceded by preaching, lest it be as meaningless as "the seal on a blank document." The elements were received in a seated position, because kneeling was viewed as implying a "worshipping of the bread." Following Calvin's proposed, though never realized, practice, Separatists favored weekly

Lord's Day observance of the sacrament, and Congregationalists in Cromwell's Commonwealth also followed this plan.

MISSION

In recent times some have spoken of the local church in terms of two aspects or modes: "the church gathered" and "the church dispersed." The former involves the internal life of the church, with emphasis upon matters such as its membership, organization, worship, and inner spiritual health; the latter relates to the church's "mission" in society. Differing times and circumstances help shape varying understandings of that mission, from evangelization of the unchurched, to programs of material aid in places of need, to labors for social justice and peace, to efforts at improved ecumenical relations among the several churches, along with other significant causes leading the local church into broader areas of service. Such tasks may be seen as tasks for individual members who leave the gathering for their dispersal into daily labors and as responsibilities for the church as corporate body. In both instances, however, the movement is outward, as the church encourages and assumes obligations that its faith impels for the living out of its life in the larger, and secular, world.

Perfecting the Church

The history of American Congregationalism has shown a remarkable evolution on the part of its churches in conceptualizing and engaging in that mission. At the beginning, however, particularly in the early English Separatist congregations, the understanding of the nature of the church and the energies applied to the realization of its destiny were directed almost exclusively inward. An image of the church used in Separatist writing was that of the "walled garden." The garden contains the lush growth representing the beauty of Christian faith and faithfulness, the congregation that has grown up into the stature and likeness of Christ, where dedicated leaders have planted and watered and God has given the increase. But the garden is walled, closed off from the impurities of surrounding false churches and corrupted society. In the garden, free from external contact and contamination, the rule of Christ is found, and energies must be directed toward its preservation.

Obviously, the political situation contributed to the dissenters' focus on isolation and self-protection. Where the only alternative to withdrawal was persecution by state and by established church, the choice ran readily to seclusion. The best that could be found was toleration, but until the mid-seventeenth century that was persistently denied.

Separatism also turned inward, however, because of its understanding of the nature of the church itself. Its passion, even obsession, became the congregation's purity, and in seeking this goal fear of contamination led to withdrawal and preoccupation with each local church's inner state. Moreover, the criteria for purity were self-serving and limited to life within the select community, with discipline employed for enforcing their realization. Separatists devoted their efforts to fleeing from the hostility of the surrounding world and creating a reclusive world acceptable to God. By an inversion of meaning, isolation became their mission in the midst of perceived peril and evil.

To a considerable extent this tendency toward isolation was also true of non-Separatist Congregationalism as it gradually developed on English soil. However, non-Separatism's more relaxed attitude in interchurch relations from 1616 onward and its less perilous political situation in the 1640s and 1650s tempered its degree of self-preoccupation. In addition to maintaining from the outset some measure of communion with the Church of England, it extended at least a limited openness to other churches in its Savoy Declaration of 1658. There it noted that those churches, "though less pure," can still be judged true churches and that there can be communion with "such members of those churches as are credibly testified to be godly."[42] Moreover, in the political arena, Cromwell's support and broad toleration gave non-Separatist Congregationalism a brief opportunity to establish itself as an accepted part of the larger society. In practical terms this resulted in participation in Cromwell's attempts, through evaluation committees, to improve the quality of ministry and preaching in all the churches of England. It also led in the Savoy Declaration to specific instructions to Congregational ministers that their work of teaching and exhorting should go beyond the membership of their congregations "so far as their strength and time will admit," to include others living in their parochial bounds. Yet the more restrictive principles of earlier Separatism were also there, as major emphasis was placed upon right church order and the disciplining of members to keep the local churches unblemished in the sight of God. Even among non-Separatists the mission of the church was perceived as being directed mainly toward itself. The time for the church's assumption of a larger role of servanthood within the social order was yet to come.

SUMMARY

American Congregationalism initially was shaped by its antecedents in English Puritanism. Holding, on the one hand, to the fundamental Puritan conviction that the Bible alone is the authority for all matters of faith and practice, Congregationalism's early leaders shared much common ground with the mainstream of the Puritan movement in affirming that conviction's consequences. General Puritan developments throughout the late sixteenth and early seventeenth centuries included a focus on the biblical motif of covenant as a central theme in theology, a pruning of Anglican worship back to what was understood to be the more simple biblical norm, and a calling upon the church's preaching ministry to guide persons along the perilous spiritual journey from sin to salvation. Those who carried Congregationalism to America shared in these emphases and transported them to the new land. All early Congregationalists were fully engaged participants in the larger ethos of Puritanism.

On the other hand, the form of church organization and government transported by the founders of American Congregationalism was representative of only a minority in the total English Puritan movement. Most Puritans favored a presbyterial church structure, and some even retained episcopacy. Congregational polity was limited to the radical few. Appearing first among the Separatists, the congregational idea took the shape of a total repudiation of the established English church. The Separatist congregations were persecuted, however, resulting in flight, exile, and, for the most part, a disappearance from history. But practice of a congregational way was preserved by others who developed it without withdrawing from communion with the church of their birth and who then carried it in a non-Separatist form to the New World. In America Congregationalism came from this more limited segment within the Puritan movement, and on matters of church polity its advocates were in disagreement with others who equally bore the Puritan name. Thus in this twofold sense the Congregational heirs of English Puritanism drew on their past to initiate what they called their "errand into the wilderness."

CHAPTER TWO

NEW WORLD BEGINNINGS
1620–1660

A contemporary chronicler of the early seventeenth-century migration from England to the New World was Edward Johnson, lay member of Boston's First Church and later founder of the town of Woburn where he served in public office. In 1650 he began writing his *Wonder-Working Providence of Sion's Savior*. This was a tale of England's "decline in religion, like lukewarm Laodicea," and then of the heroic acts of those summoned by Christ to a "voluntary banishment" by which they carried the seeds of the true church into a new land. Johnson wrote that Christ's heralds had issued the call: "Oh yes! oh yes! oh yes! All you, the people of Christ that are here oppressed, imprisoned and scurrilously derided, gather yourselves together, your wives and little ones, and answer to your several names as you shall be shipped for his service in the western world." And after the call came the promise of what would transpire under God's "wonder-working providence" in that new land: "Know this is the place where the Lord will create a new heaven and a new earth in new churches, and a new commonwealth together."[1] Johnson's words caught up the faith and the vision underlying much of the migration— and those new churches, by the Lord's design, were to be Congregational.

HISTORY

Pilgrim Beginnings

Although all early immigrants fleeing to the New World for religious reasons embarked upon a pilgrimage, the privilege of precedence bestowed the name *Pilgrim* upon the little group from Robinson's Leyden congregation that arrived in 1620 to found the colony of Plymouth. They were called Pilgrims by one of their number, William Bradford, soon to be governor and later historian of their venture, and the designation has remained. In time Plymouth Colony was incorpo-

rated into the larger colony of Massachusetts Bay, but the initial planting of American Congregationalism was accomplished by Plymouth's
Pilgrims.

Life in Holland for these people had been relatively peaceful, but
after a decade they longed to move. Bradford noted in his recollections
their fear of loss of English identity, increasingly felt during their years
of exile, as well as their struggle for economic survival in a strange land.
Although return to England under the rule of James held no promise for
freedom of worship, they believed that religious liberty probably could
be found in the proposed English colony across the Atlantic. In 1617
they began negotiations toward the realization of that goal.

First they needed to obtain the crown's permission to be included
in the colonizing venture, and this was sought through submitting to
the king's council seven articles of belief. Signed by John Robinson and
William Brewster for the Leyden congregation, this conciliatory document acknowledged the king's far-reaching authority as "Supreme Governor in his Dominion in all causes and over all persons," including even
some measure of civil control in the religious realm.[2] When the royal
adviser responded favorably, informing the king that these petitioners,
though troublesome when in England, could be of value in America,
the way was opened for their approved migration as English citizens to
the New World. Soon arrangements were made with a group of seventy
London merchants who had obtained a patent to settle lands in Virginia
with the goal of developing a fishing industry. The merchants would
contribute the financing, the Leyden Pilgrims would contribute the
labor, and on that basis a joint-stock company was formed. The agreement was for seven years, after which the merchants would consider
themselves repaid. The bargain laid a heavy burden on the colonists.
But now, both approved and financed, the journey could begin.

In July 1620 the Pilgrims set forth, sailing first on the Speedwell
to England and then on the Mayflower to the New World. Not all of the
Leyden congregation could go, or even desired to go, for the hazards
were great. The congregation agreed that Robinson, their pastor, would
accompany them if the majority went. If not, their leader would be
Brewster, the ruling elder. Because only a minority chose to make the
first trip, Robinson stayed, but he sent the Pilgrims off with a farewell
address containing words now firmly fixed in the historical memory of
Congregationalism. One of the immigrants, Edward Winslow, pro-

vided the report. Robinson spoke first of his past leadership of the congregation, but then told those departing that they were now to follow him no further than he had followed Christ, adding, wrote Winslow, that "if God should reveal anything to us by any other instrument of his, [we should] be as ready to receive it, as ever we were to receive any truth by his ministry. For he was confident that the Lord had more truth and light to break forth out of his holy word."[3] The journey of the Mayflower was lengthy—and off course. When the travelers sighted land in November, it was not Virginia, as intended, but the coast of New England, and the ship found its way into the shelter of Cape Cod. Months of difficult travel had brought the Pilgrims to Plymouth.

Not all of the 101 passengers on the Mayflower were members of the Leyden congregation. Some had joined the group in England as colonists seeking adventure and fortune. The group from Leyden, however, provided the leadership and initiated the colony's first official act, the establishment of a government by covenant, patterned after the covenanting in Scrooby that had created their church. Signed by forty-one adults in the cabin of the ship, the Mayflower Compact affirmed that "we whose names are underwritten . . . solemnly and mutually in the presence of God and one of another, covenant, and combine ourselves into a civil body politic . . . unto which we promise all due submission and obedience." Although they also described themselves in this compact as "loyal subjects of our dread sovereign Lord King James," their plans for self-government were clear.[4]

The physical hardships suffered by the Plymouth Colony in its early stages are legendary, but difficulties also developed with respect to pastoral leadership within the church. In Robinson's absence responsibility for conduct of worship fell to Brewster, who preached twice each Sabbath for several years. Yet there could be no administration of the sacraments without an ordained pastor or teacher. Attempts were made to convince the merchant partners to finance the journey of the remainder of the congregation to bring Robinson to Plymouth. The London merchants were not interested, however, for they felt Robinson's radical reputation could be harmful to the colony's image in British eyes. One abortive attempt to provide pastoral leadership was made in 1624 when the merchants sent John Lyford to be the community's minister, but Lyford's presumed Puritan sympathies proved to be hypocritical. In collusion with a small group of disaffected colonists, he attempted to set up worship according to the practice of the Church of England and also was discovered seeking to overthrow the Leyden Pilgrim's political control of the colony. He was brought to trial and expelled. Another attempt to send for Robinson and the remainder of the Leyden congregation was made after the colony gained independence from the merchants through early payment of the balance of their debt. But before the trip began Robinson died, and even in reunion the congregation was left without a pastor. Finally in 1629 Ralph Smith was secured as a satisfactory minister, and he was joined in 1631 by Roger Williams as assistant, whose own brand of radicalism, however, was to bring the colony further unrest.

For almost nine years Congregationalism in America was limited to the Pilgrim church in Plymouth. Although the church prospered despite many difficulties, it was a meager beginning. Historical myth making has given it a prominence beyond its actual influence by arguing that Plymouth introduced the congregational form of church government to the later Puritan colonists flooding into other parts of New England. It was long said that Plymouth's physician and deacon, Dr. Samuel Fuller, while ministering in 1629 to the sick in newly founded Salem, also taught them the principles of the Congregational way. More recent historical research, however, shows that those who settled Salem and the other early communities of Massachusetts Bay were already Congregationalists upon their arrival. As the non-Separatist heirs of Ames and Jacob, they were unwilling to sever themselves completely from the English church, but they sought liberty for congregationally organized churches in the new land. So Plymouth was not a mentor, but became a partner, in this larger venture. Its Separatist heritage gave it a somewhat more spirit-filled worship and democratized church life than found in other Puritan communities during the early years, but it shared with them cooperatively in shaping an emerging New England Congregational way.

As the 1630s began, new settlements were developed and new churches were formed in the outlying districts of Plymouth Colony. Among these were the village of Scituate and its congregation, notable for the presence of members of the former Henry Jacob non-Separatist Congregational church in England founded in 1616. By 1634 a group of approximately thirty members of that London congregation, now under the pastoral leadership of John Lathrop, chose to flee from the increasing oppression experienced at the hands of Archbishop Laud and, after arriving in Scituate, were soon joined in church covenant by additional persons moving from the Plymouth congregation. Five years later a major portion of this group withdrew from the church at Scituate, moving out for better farmland to Barnstable on Cape Cod where further covenanting created another church. Similarly, settlements and their non-Separatist churches began to appear in Duxbury, Taunton, Sandwich, and other locales. So within the colony of Plymouth itself non- Separatism joined with the early "semi-Separatism" of the Pilgrims in developing the growing body of Congregational churches. The yet larger migration of non-Separatist Congregationalists was already beginning to take place, however, into the colony of Massachusetts Bay.

The Great Migration

Although the 1620s witnessed frequent sailings from England to parts of New England, these were largely forages for fish and furs rather than efforts at colonization. The church was not significantly represented in these expeditions, despite the occasional presence of a venturesome Anglican parson. But toward the end of the decade, as pressure against Nonconformists mounted in England and as published reports, such as Winslow's *Good News from New England*, told of the progress of the Plymouth Pilgrims, Puritan interest began to focus on seeking refuge in the New World. English Puritan merchants organized themselves as the New England Company, a group combining commerce and Congregationalism, and this led to the planting of the Salem colony in 1628 and the gathering of its church in 1629. John Endecott, a military captain, was chosen at the outset to be governor, and after a church was organized, Samuel Skelton and Francis Higginson, two clergy among the colonists, were selected to serve as pastor and teacher.

The non-Separatist character of the venture was clear from the beginning. As the colonists' ship left the British shore, Higginson exclaimed, "We will not say, as the Separatists were wont to say at their leaving of England, 'Farewell, Babylon! Farewell Rome!' But we will say, 'Farewell dear England! Farewell, the Church of God in England!'"

. . . We do not go to New England as Separatists from the Church of England, though we cannot but separate from the corruptions of it."[5] Church ties with the past were not to be severed. At the same time the congregational character of the venture was apparent. The gathering was not by law, but by covenant. Those who voluntarily assembled voiced the commitment binding them into church estate: "We covenant with the Lord and one with another; and do bind ourselves in the presence of God, to walk together in all his ways, according as he is pleased to reveal himself unto us in his blessed word of truth."[6] In due course came the electing and authorizing of the church's ministry. On the given day, reads the record, "every fit [that is, male] member wrote, in a note, his name whom the Lord moved him to think was fit for pastor, and so likewise, whom they would have for teacher," Skelton being chosen for the former office and Higginson for the latter. Despite the fact that in England both had bishops' ordaining hands laid upon them, they were then ordained anew by "several of the gravest members of the church."[7] In this manner Salem began the practices of a church life that were repeated often in the years to follow throughout the colonies of New England.

As the Salem enterprise progressed, others became interested in finding religious freedom in the New World. To facilitate further colonization the New England Company added substantially to its membership from among Puritans of influence in economic and political circles, transformed itself into a newly organized Massachusetts Bay Company to cope more adequately with its task, and obtained directly from the king a royal charter giving it specific privileges for the administration of the territory in its domain. Here an unexpected turn of events took place. For reason unknown, whether of carelessness or indifference on the part of those preparing the document in the king's court, the charter did not designate a place from which its governing body would carry out its supervisory responsibilities. Presumably it would have been in London, but it was not so prescribed. So the door was opened to a colonial venture that could have greater independence of self-government than any had ever envisioned, for if the whole governing body moved to New England it could function beyond the range of control of an unsympathetic king. Rather than being simply a hiding place of refuge from persecution, the new land could become a positive center of reformation where state and church might unite in creating a new society for God's people. Gradually, cautious steps were taken to bring this development about.

A leading figure in the plan was John Winthrop, lawyer and statesman of strong Puritan sympathies and immense political talents. Winthrop had for some time been considering the possibility of a move to New England, but had struggled with the question as to whether such action would be an avoidance of the responsibility to use his life in constructive public service. His Puritan conscience relentlessly reminded him that his talents and vocation must be employed not simply for self-advancement, but in labors of love for the glory of God. Would it not therefore be an escape from duty to leave in this time of peril for dissenters and take up distant residence for personal safety? However, Winthrop was approached by members of the Massachusetts Bay Company with an invitation not only to join their venture but also to lead— and with the argument that God could indeed be better served in the building of a new society than in the preserving of the old. In New England, they said, leaders of dedication and godly character were needed to govern and to attract others of faith to make their commitments as well. As Winthrop weighed these arguments, he came to see the invitation as God's call, convinced that were he not to accept, his talents "were like to be buried" rather than used. He joined the company, endorsed the plan, and was elected while still in England to be the first governor of the colony of Massachusetts Bay.

Under Winthrop's leadership plans for more extensive colonization moved quickly. Eleven ships were outfitted within a few months in 1630, and soon the Great Migration was under way. Altogether in that first year seventeen vessels sailed from England to New England, carrying more than one thousand new inhabitants for the Massachusetts Bay Colony. This was more than three times the number found in Plymouth at the end of its first ten years. In the succeeding decade religious refugees were joined by many others emigrating in search of economic advantage, and by the early 1640s more than twenty thousand had made their way to New England shores. The 1630s in Massachusetts, therefore, were a time of rapid growth, witnessing the founding of more than twenty towns and churches. Under the central guidance of the colony's government, located in Boston, towns were laid out in a systematic manner, each with a meetinghouse at its center for both civic and religious purposes. Town governments were developed, selectmen were elected to be in charge of local affairs, militia companies were organized, and churches were voluntarily gathered, in Congregational fashion, for corporate worship.

Among the colonists were many clergy. University educated and frequently having served parishes in the Church of England, these men, mostly of Congregational Puritan conviction, now found freedom from the persecution and release from the struggles of conscience earlier known. Coming to the new land, often accompanied by groups of zealous former parishoners, they were called to new ministries through which leadership could be given. Much of the life of New England in its first century was, in fact, significantly shaped by them. Respected in the churches for their knowledge and their piety, they also increasingly exercised political power through their influence upon the government. Their convictions were strong, and their commitments to the new order were great. Their roster contains names of genuine eminence in New England history.

John Cotton stands out as one of the most prominent among them. Cotton's university training had been at Emmanuel College, Cambridge, where he was deeply influenced by its Puritan teachings. In his twenty years as vicar of St. Botolph's Church, Boston, in Lincolnshire, he struggled with the problem of conformity to Anglican practice. Early in his ministry at this prestigious post he was obedient to the church's ecclesiastical requirements, but with the passage of time he gradually gave them up, and his parish supported him in his new ways. In his last years at St. Botolph's he drew together a small group from the larger parish to serve as a covenanted body to call him to its ministry. In 1632, however, Cotton was summoned before the Court of High Commission to answer to charges of Nonconformity. Rather than appear, he fled to London, hiding there while consulting other Puritan clergy about his response. Some urged him to compromise and resume his position, but his conviction grew that conformity was a form of idolatry, a sin against the second commandment. He then persuaded others, who soon became Congregational leaders in exile, of the validity of this view. Naturally his eyes turned to New England, and, further urged by some former parishoners who were themselves undertaking the journey, he set sail in 1633 for another Boston in the new land. Almost immediately upon his arrival he was called to be teacher in Boston's First Church, to serve in joint ministry with its pastor, John Wilson. In that post he labored for nineteen years until his death in 1652. Despite some temporary theological differences with other colonial clergy, John Cotton played a major role throughout this period as shaper and defender of the New England Congregational way.

A fellow passenger on that same journey to the New World was another beleaguered member of the English clergy, Thomas Hooker, who also became a prominent New England leader. Hooker's university work had been at Emmanuel College, Cambridge, alongside Cotton. The first years of his ministry were spent in relative quiet, serving as a private chaplain in the household of a well-to-do Puritan family, but in 1625 he accepted the offer of a public lectureship at St. Mary's Church, Chelmsford, located in the see of London. There his persuasive preaching and Nonconformist ways in worship and clerical attire not only drew large Puritan audiences but also brought him to the attention of church authorities. By 1629 his preaching had been silenced, and soon thereafter, when it was discovered that his home was being used as a meeting place for young Puritan clergy, he was summoned to appear before the Court of High Commission. Like Cotton he first went into hiding, but in 1631 he fled to Holland where he became co-minister with John Paget of the English Reformed Church in Amsterdam. By this time, however, his Nonconformity had evolved from matters of ceremony to issues of polity, and his congregational views were unacceptable in his new position. He next served a brief ministry in Delft, but as a preacher of strong evangelical inclination, he was disturbed by the lack of "heart religion" in the Dutch churches. Returning to England, he joined Cotton in the pilgrimage to Massachusetts Bay where, with a group of settlers who had supported his ministry in England, he founded the church in Newtown, soon to be renamed Cambridge. After three years, however, Hooker led his congregation to found a new settlement on the Connecticut River, which they named Hartford and which contributed to the beginning of Connecticut Colony. Nevertheless, throughout the remaining eleven years of his life Hooker preserved close contact with the churches and clergy of the Bay Colony, continuing as a major leader in the common labors of New England.

The year 1635 brought two important additions to the Congregational clergy of New England. The first was Thomas Shepard, who followed Thomas Hooker as pastor at Cambridge, where he also served as unofficial chaplain of Harvard College after its founding in 1636.

Like others before him, he had struggled in England with Anglican authority. His education, too, had been at Emmanuel College, Cambridge, though some two decades later than Cotton and Hooker, and upon entering ministry he found his Puritanism leading him similarly into conflict with the established church. After three years he was barred by his bishop from preaching, and for the next five, he later wrote, he was "tossed from the south to the north of England"[8] and back again, preaching publicly when possible, otherwise privately in the homes of Puritan patrons. In 1634 he set off for America, but was forced to return because of stormy seas. He hid once more until the next year when the journey could be safely made. More a pastor to souls than a political figure, Thomas Shepard's perceptive insights into Christian experience gave him power as preacher and writer and became the means for his valued contributions to the developing theology and polity of Congregationalism. It was New England's loss when Shepard died in 1649 at the early age of forty-three.

Also joining the migration in 1635 was Richard Mather, ultimately to become pastor at Dorchester and progenitor of a family that contributed in exceptional fashion over the next two generations to New England ministry. A village school teacher in his youth, Mather's conversion under Puritan preaching at the age of eighteen led him, after brief study at Oxford, to the receiving of holy orders and a fifteen-year ministry in the established church. Over time, however, his Puritan inclinations became increasingly evident, precipitating his suspension in 1633. Influential parishoners managed to get him restored, but by then his convictions were clearly congregational and his suspension was soon renewed. Viewing the state of religious affairs in England as inviting God's judgment upon the nation and seeing the opening of the New World as an act of God's providence, Mather then followed what he termed "the clearness of my calling" to a ministry in New England. In America his talents were employed not only in preaching but also in writing, and he was often called upon by his ministerial colleagues to interpret for those both at home and abroad the nature of the Congregational way. Living to the age of seventy-three, Richard Mather, more than any other of the pioneer clergy, transmitted the hopes of New England's founders to the succeeding generation. A man of robust health, he is reported never to have missed preaching a Sabbath sermon throughout the entirety of his active ministry—a period of fifty years!

Equally important among the early New England clergy was John Davenport, one of the founders of New Haven Colony. Davenport had been vicar of St. Stephen's Church, Coleman Street, London, but had become troubled in conscience by the compromises of his Puritan convictions that his ministry required. Discussing this dilemma with John Cotton, who was then in hiding in London, Davenport came to the conclusion that he needed to leave England to practice without inhibition the Congregational way. Accordingly, in 1633 he went to Holland where he served an English congregation for four years, following which both he and members of his congregation made the journey to America. In 1637, when they landed in Boston, they were warmly welcomed by Massachusetts authorities for residence in the colony, but the immigrants desired more independence and within the next year made their way southward to establish the colony of New Haven. Davenport, as their pastor, was a man of strong opinions who became an ardent conservative, resistant to change in his defense of Congregationalism. He remained a close friend of John Cotton and in his last years was called to a ministry in the Boston church that Cotton had served earlier.

These are but some of the many members of the clergy who joined in the Great Migration and shared in the early shaping of American Congregationalism. Altogether some sixty ministers arrived in Massachusetts between the years 1630 and 1641, the vast majority of whom were of non-Separatist Congregational persuasion. Their unwillingness to divorce themselves entirely from the Church of England was, however, more a theoretical than a practical matter. Once removed from England geographically and separated from control by the Anglican bishops in ecclesiastical practice, they were free to pursue in uninhibited fashion the forms of polity and worship they understood the Bible to prescribe. They were also free, along with Winthrop and others in the political realm, to develop self-rule under a new form of government—and thus to work in both church and state for the creation of a holy commonwealth.

Civil Government in Massachusetts Bay

When Winthrop sailed to Boston on the *Arbella* in 1630, probably the most valued piece of cargo on shipboard was the charter for the colony of Massachusetts Bay. Once transported to New England, beyond the reach of king and court for alteration, and with its prescribed governing body also about to be located in the new land, providential opportunity could be translated into significant reality. Winthrop began by setting a theological context while still in the course of the Atlantic journey, delivering a lay sermon in which he spoke to the colonists concerning his vision of the work they were undertaking. They were entering, he said, into a new covenant with God in this enterprise, and their obligation was to develop a community living in accordance with the gospel law of love. They were summoned to be knit together as a single body in which private interests would be subordinated to public concern. All must make the needs of others their own, so that they might "rejoice together, mourn together, labor and suffer together," keeping "the unity of the spirit in the bond of peace." This was their covenant commission as a people whom God had called. If they should fail in this purpose, Winthrop warned, "the Lord [would] surely break out in wrath" against them, for that is "the price of the breach of such a covenant." But if they "avoid this shipwreck" through faithful obedience, they will be blessed in ways far beyond any they have heretofore known. Moreover, such divine favor will be the hope of "succeeding plantations," for New England, he said, is to be "as a city upon a hill" with the eyes of all people upon it.[9]

Winthrop titled his sermon "A Model of Christian Charity," and its vision saw a revolution in social relationships through shared love. But the sermon also contained another emphasis. By the wise providence of God, Winthrop affirmed, the condition of humanity is such that "in all times some must be rich, some poor; some high and eminent in power and dignity, others mean and in subjection."[10] Winthrop here set forth a classical justification for the hierarchical structuring of the social order, based on the divine creation of human differences leading to roles of authority and submission. Government must be for the common good, with the Christian society of shared concern and compassion as its ultimate goal. But government must be guided by those whom God has peculiarly qualified for the task, the godly rulers. To such persons divine authority to govern has been given, whereas those governed are called to obedience. In another address some years later, after a period of struggle with colonists who desired more political power of their own, Winthrop reiterated this theme by interpreting the meaning of *liberty*. On the one hand, he said, there is a natural liberty, essentially a freedom to do as one wants. This, however, is incompatible with authority and leads all too readily to evil. On the other hand, there is a moral liberty, essentially the "liberty wherewith Christ hath made us free," a liberty for the doing of "that only which is good, just, and honest." This liberty is "maintained and exercised in the way of subjection to authority."[11] Freedom can create the godly society, but it must be expressed through voluntary submission to godly rule.

When Winthrop translated this philosophy into the actual machinery of government, it led to "popular aristocracy," where despite a role for the people's voice, primary emphasis fell upon the chosen leaders, who were to be respected and obeyed. From the beginning Winthrop favored to a certain degree the democratic principle. The charter originally established the General Court as the colony's governing body, whose stockholder members were "freemen" charged with the responsibility of coming together four times a year to make laws and, on one of those occasions, to elect the colony's officers for the coming year. One of Winthrop's first acts, however, encouraged the broadening of the base of government by designating all adult male members of the colony's churches "freemen." Although not all of the original freemen's privileges were transferred in the process, a more popular foundation was established for the colony's political life. Winthrop believed that this represented a political form of the entire community's basic covenant with God.

Yet the aristocratic strain also remained in the restructured process, for concurrent with the broadening of the electoral base was a severe concentration of actual power in a few hands. Although the lawmakers, now known as magistrates, were elected by the franchised voters, they alone had the responsibility for choosing the colony's governor. Moreover, with no courts yet established nor colony laws written, these few officials were granted vast executive, legislative, and judicial authority in all colony affairs. Yet this was in accord with Winthrop's philosophy. Ultimately rulers were not agents of the people. On the contrary, whatever their method of selection, they received their commission from God, and their privileged task was to serve the nation as authoritative guides toward the fulfillment of its covenant. Sometimes the wrong person might be elected to the magistrate's office, but limiting the franchise to church members presumably provided some guarantee against such occurrence, inasmuch as membership in the church was restricted to persons of faith and covenant commitment. The godly electorate would choose godly rulers, who would exercise godly rule.

Winthrop's governorship, however, was marked by conflict over these matters. Godly rule often appeared as arbitrary action, and the early decades of Massachusetts Bay witnessed periodic efforts toward further democratization. Over time democratic practices increased, including representation of the towns by deputies in the General Court and a governor elected directly by popular vote. These changes came, however, only after struggle. During the conflict Winthrop often received support and encouragement from members of the clergy. Their understanding of authority was similar to his, and they saw parallels between the role of the magistrates in government and their own role in the ministry of the church. They too depended upon the people's choice, and yet they were more than agents of the people, for their ultimate commissioning and authority came from God.

At one point the clergy resisted the governor and joined the effort to curb his and the magistrates' power. They worked for the development of a body of laws to serve as basis for judicial decisions, whereas Winthrop's view of godly rule had pitted him against such legislative restraint. The terms for the nation's covenant, as found in the Bible, could be interpreted by the magistrates, Winthrop argued, on a case-by-case basis as the need arose. This would build up a body of biblically based common law that could be used for future judicial actions. For most of the clergy, as well as the populace, such an approach left too much power in the rulers' hands. So steps were taken, especially during a period when Winthrop was temporarily out of the governorship, to draw up and enact legislation to limit judicial powers.

The author of the final draft was Nathaniel Ward, minister at Ipswich. In 1641 he finished the Body of Liberties, which was adopted as the fundamental law for Massachusetts Bay. Ward had ten years of legal training and practice in London prior to his entrance into ministry, and brought to this legislation many elements of English law that protected against arbitrary governmental authority. The Body of Liberties included guarantees of matters such as trial by jury, due process of law, and simplified judicial procedures. However, the code was not simply a bill of rights to guard individual liberties; it was also concerned with the Puritan experiment in its larger social dimensions. In the new society seeking to live out its covenant relationship with God, both church and state assumed responsibility. So their roles needed to be defined and the range of their liberties identified. By reference to these matters, the document provided an early constitutional basis for the holy commonwealth.

Church and State

New England Puritan understanding of the holy commonwealth, and the relationship of church and state within it, looked back upon Calvin's achievement in Geneva. Central to Calvin's plan was the conviction that the church and the state should be separate, yet cooperating, entities in guiding the life of a people. Neither should dominate the other and both must be administered in obedience to the authority of the Word of God. In the partnership each has its own responsibility and its own methods to carry that responsibility out. The responsibility of the church is the spiritual realm, the sphere of grace and salvation. It must condemn sin, proclaim the gospel, provide the sacraments, and administer church discipline—all for the life of the soul and its redemption. The responsibility of the state is the temporal realm, the sphere of outward relationships and political order. Its methods are those appropriate to the maintenance of stability in society and, if need be, can include physical coercion. In discharging their responsibilities church and state should never trespass upon each other. Working together, they can join their strengths to aid each other in fulfilling their mission. God has called them both to duty, commissioning ministers and civil magistrates for the common end of a divine ordering of society. Calvin sought this for Geneva, and it became the Puritan goal for New England.

Embedded in this vision, however, were two further principles of great significance for the relationship of church and state. The first was the principle of uniformity, the conviction that within the state only one religion, that is, only one form of the church, could be allowed. This was by no means a new idea, for it had characterized Christian thought throughout most of the church's history. Theologically this idea rested upon the belief that one "true church" had been divinely prescribed and upon a confidence that the correct form of that church could be known. The second principle of importance to Puritans was the political conviction that the state ought to assist the church by law and protect it from corruption. New England Congregationalists believed in both principles as strongly as did English Anglicans or Gene-van Calvinists. Richard Mather noted that because the polity "appointed by Jesus Christ for his churches" is the same for all, and because that "which we here practice be the same which Christ hath appointed," then "we see not how another can be lawful."[12] Thomas Hooker declared himself "not persuaded that the chief magistrate should stand a Neuter, and tolerate all religions."[13] The civil government needed to protect the people from false churches by aiding the true church and permitting only its existence. Legislation and coercion could be employed for that purpose.

At the same time there were restraints on the state to prevent governmental intrusion into strictly religious matters. Doctrine, sacraments, polity, and discipline in the church were controlled by the church through its reading and interpretation, largely by the clergy, of the biblical Word. Moreover, because that Word was interpreted in a Congregational manner, this more precise ecclesiastical restraint was also imposed. This meant an adjustment, unknown in Europe, on the part of the magistrates to church polity. Whereas in European countries the state could compel all persons into membership in the church, this could not be done in New England. Church membership rested on personal religious faith and experience, outside the control of the state. Yet New England's civil government did not view these restraints as an undesirable limitation of power. Magistrates were chosen only from good church members and were in full harmony with the ecclesiastical scheme as it evolved in the new setting. Advised even in governmental affairs by their clergy, magistrates shared in the perspectives, both theological and political, contributed by the church.

The chief characteristic, therefore, of this church-state relationship was one of cooperation, and its chief consequence was assistance to the church through legislative support. This was especially true in Massachusetts Bay, where the General Court set the pattern for the New England way. Beginning in 1630 with a limiting of the franchise to church members in colony elections, the legislative body over the next three decades provided the church with various forms of favor and assistance. There were laws mandating honoring the Sabbath, compelling church attendance by all residents, requiring community financial support of the clergy, permitting only church members to hold political office, allowing the founding of new churches only with the consent of those already established, ordering religious instruction for children, and prohibiting schismatical preaching. The General Court also called the churches together in synods to develop united ecclesiastical responses in the face of common needs. The commonwealth prospers, so it was believed, if the churches receive government aid.

Part of that aid, furthermore, was the employment of the coercive power of government to deal decisively when necessary with instances of false religion. Although the state did not intrude upon matters of purely private belief, any public evidencing of blasphemous or heretical ideas was subject to punishment by civil authority. This was particularly true on those occasions when the magnitude of the offense threatened the very stability of the commonwealth. The preservation of the religious uniformity of society was a major concern, and the "temporal sword" was freely employed for the attainment of that goal.

Uniformity Enforced

Early in the history of Massachusetts Bay Colony two major instances occurred in which this civil power was used, and both reflect the harshness of the colony's dealing with dissent. The first was the case of Roger Williams, Puritan preacher of unorthodox religious and political views, and troubler of both the clergy and the magistrates. When Cotton Mather introduced Roger Williams a century later into his history of America, he presented him through the analogy of a windmill that had been reported in Holland to have so whirled out of control in a windstorm that it became overheated and ultimately set a whole town on fire. Mather said of Williams, "There was a whole country in America like to be set on fire by the rapid motion of a windmill, in the head of one particular man."[14] In the 1630s Williams's contemporaries felt the same.

Massachusetts' problem with Williams began with his Separatism. When Williams arrived in Boston in 1631, he was invited to join its church and to assist in its ministry. He refused, however, because he could not participate, so he said, in the life of an unseparated people. Winthrop was surprised, for in England Williams had shared in the planning of the Massachusetts Bay Company and was looked upon as a "godly minister" for the colony and its Congregational churches. But over time his views became more radical, and now he repudiated the non-Separatist assumptions underlying the colony's founding. The church in Boston could be made up of Christian believers of sound faith and godly life, he felt, but its purity was compromised by its relationship, both past and present, with the impure congregations of the English church. In order to set things aright, church members should first repent "for having communion with the churches of England, while they lived there."[15] And then the church should go on in a full-fledged separated way. Winthrop argued with Williams that the English congregations are not as impure as Williams alleged. Their members may be weak Christians, yet "whores and drunkards they are not"—and what is more, it is possible to achieve reformation "without complete separation."[16] But the argument was of no avail. Although Williams served briefly in two New England ministries, he never softened his radical Separatist view. Yet in the total course of events, that was probably the least dangerous element to the commonwealth in his deviation from orthodoxy.

Williams began his colonial ministry at Plymouth, where for two years he assisted Ralph Smith, the newly called pastor. But even there, in a congregation that had itself only recently come out of a Separatist history, he found a lack of concern for Separatist purity. Members of the Plymouth congregation were known freely to attend services of the Church of England on visits to their native land and upon return were not disciplined for having done so. Other matters, soon to be made more public, began to trouble Williams as well. Later Governor Bradford remembered him as "a man godly and zealous, but very unsettled in judgment," who "began to fall into some strange opinions," and who then quite abruptly left the church.[17]

It was at Salem, where in 1633 Williams was called first to assist Samuel Skelton and then to succeed him in ministry, that the "strange opinions" began to become more generally known. For example, Williams raised questions about the legitimacy of the colony's ownership of and control over the land of Massachusetts Bay as granted by patent in the royal charter tendered by the king. The land in fact, he said, was not the king's to grant, for it belonged to and should be purchased from its original inhabitants, the American Indians. The king, therefore, he declared, was a liar; the charter was worthless; and the colonists should engage in an act of repentance for having accepted illegitimate title to a land they did not truly possess. They should also send the charter back to the king with the request that all references to the granting of land be removed. To raise these questions at any time was troubling enough, but this was a period when reexamination of patents was taking place within England. A commission led by Archbishop Laud had been appointed by Charles I to conduct an inquiry into the Massachusetts Bay patent. This produced much anxiety in the colony, even leading to fortification of Boston harbor. Fortunately, troubles at home distracted the archbishop and king, enabling the colony to escape what could have been a disastrous investigation into the interpretation and use of its charter.

Soon other disturbing opinions were heard from the pastor at Salem. In the midst of the crisis concerning the charter, the magistrates in Boston asked all residents in the colony to take an oath of allegiance in which they promised to support the government against its enemies. Williams objected that this had religious implications violating his basic Separatist convictions. Taking an oath, he felt, was an act of worship, and a magistrate, who is one of the regenerate in the church, engages improperly in acts of worship with the unregenerate when he calls them to swear allegiance before him. In addition, as Williams considered further implications of this radical view, he became convinced that great care must be taken not to engage in any religious act at all with the impure. He went so far as to announce that one must not pray in the company of one's wife and one's children if they are among the unregenerate. Furthermore, he began to advocate a separation between church and state, holding that magistrates have no authority in religious matters. They cannot, for example, enforce the honoring of the Sabbath. Their authority to punish offenses against the "first table" of the Ten Commandments, those dealing with religious concerns, is limited only to violations that disturb the peace.

By 1635 there was grave concern that Williams was undermining the commonwealth. Williams and the Salem church that employed him were addressed by the ministers concerning the problem. In response Williams cited the principle of the local congregation's independence against intrusion by other churches or clergy into its religious affairs. Congregational polity appeared to be in his and his congregation's favor. So the ministers turned to the magistrates for help. The General Court warned both the pastor and the church of the seriousness of the situation. Williams's opinions, it said, were dangerous to the commonwealth, and the church's employing him as pastor was a contempt of authority. Williams responded by intensifying his Separatist stand. Because the other churches, he declared, abandoned the principle of congregational independence by calling upon civil authorities to condemn Salem, they were no longer true churches. He therefore renounced communion with them and urged the Salem church to do the same. But this was too much for his congregation, and the majority refused to go along. With that development, it was left for the General Court to act. Williams was called before the court and charged with erroneous opinions, chiefly his denial of magistrates' authority in religious affairs. He was also accused of attempting to destroy the unity of the churches in the colony. Found guilty, he was ordered to leave the colony's jurisdiction.

Within scarcely more than a year Massachusetts Bay became embroiled in a second controversy in which erroneous opinions threatened the peace and unity of the land. Anne Hutchinson was the center of that storm, and the issue leading to her banishment was largely theological. Anne Hutchinson and her husband arrived in Boston in 1634. They had been members of the parish served by John Cotton during his ministry in England, and Mrs. Hutchinson in particular was deeply influenced by his preaching. Under her urging the couple followed Cotton to New England and became members of the Boston church. A person of many capabilities, Anne Hutchinson became a leader in the community, especially among the church's women. Initially she used her nursing skills to help women in childbirth, and then because of her religious interests, women gathered in her home for religious discussion. On such occasions Hutchinson reviewed and commented upon the sermons of the previous Sabbath, not limiting herself to those of Cotton, but comparing him with ministers in neighboring churches. The meetings were popular, leading Hutchinson to establish another group including men. Altogether more than sixty persons gathered in the Hutchinson home each week to hear her observations on the colony's preaching and current theological issues.

These meetings began simply as neighborhood devotional sessions, a practice encouraged by the clergy. But Hutchinson's aggressive style seemed to usurp the teaching role of the clergy on theological matters. Even more serious in the eyes of the colony's ministers were the theological opinions she expressed. In those weekly gatherings Hutchinson advanced ideas that reflected the antinomian heresy long condemned by Puritan divines. This view so magnified the role of God's overwhelming power in the process of salvation as to negate all human participation. All is done by the might of the Holy Spirit, drawing one into the covenant of grace. Similarly, one's knowledge of being in this covenant with God is dependent upon an inner awareness of the Spirit's presence, and any effort to gain assurance from attempting to see God's favor in outward aspects of one's life is to regress into a covenant of works. Hutchinson argued that she found her views in John Cotton's preaching, and in large measure she did. Cotton was not an antinomian, but in these years he inclined in that direction. His message focused extensively and emphatically upon the power and presence of God's grace. Hutchinson praised Cotton highly in her analysis of the colony's preaching, but then went further and criticized other ministers as simply proclaiming a covenant of works. These opinions and this judgment soon led to trouble.

The tension created by Anne Hutchinson's antinomianism was intensified in 1636 by the arrival of her brother-in-law, John Wheelwright, a Puritan minister who shared her outlook and was proposed by Hutchinson and a number of her followers for a position in the ministry of the Boston church. John Winthrop, deeply distressed over Hutchinson's theology and its potential for divisiveness, prevented the election of Wheelwright by appealing to the church's members to reject him. Shortly thereafter, however, Wheelwright was invited by Cotton to preach, and from the colony's point of view the sermon was a disaster. Winthrop's account of the occasion reported that the preacher, in criticizing the many who walk by the covenant of works, "called them antichrists, and stirred up the people against them with much bitterness and vehemency."[18] That was enough for the magistrates, and at its next meeting the General Court judged Wheelwright guilty of contempt and sedition for having purposely set about to create dissension among the colony's residents. His sentencing, however, was deferred until the next court session.

Meanwhile the clergy determined to seek greater clarification of the theological issues. Much popular talk and emotion had been attached to the conflict, Winthrop reporting that it was becoming as common to categorize a person's affiliation by distinguishing between the covenant of grace and the covenant of works "as in other counties between Protestants and Papists."[19] So in August 1637, with the approval of the magistrates, ministers and delegates from the various churches gathered in Cambridge for the first Congregational synod to be assembled in New England. The magistrates were also present, though with voice and not vote. The meeting lasted twenty-four days and ended with the identification of eighty-two antinomian errors. Of added importance was the fact that John Cotton, after much consultation with the other ministers, joined them in condemning the antinomian views.

The General Court was now prepared to complete its work in this matter. Assembling shortly after the adjournment of the synod, it sentenced Wheelwright to banishment and then took up the examination of Hutchinson. The latter proved to be more difficult than anticipated. Anne Hutchinson was a well-informed woman, learned in Scripture and competent in theological dispute. The ministers were present and testified against her, but had no part in the questioning, which was done by court officials. For more than a day Hutchinson managed, through astute parrying of arguments, to blunt the court's charges. Finally, however, perhaps due to the strain of the occasion, she faltered, admitting something horrendous to orthodox ears. Going beyond simple reliance upon Scripture, she acknowledged that to attain truth she also relied upon an immediate revelation from God. The interrogator exclaimed, "How! an immediate revelation?" And Hutchinson replied, "By the voice of his own spirit to my soul."[20] Here was sufficient evidence, now from her own mouth, of her heresy—the claim of being so possessed by the presence of the Holy Spirit as to be the very mouthpiece for God. Quickly she was judged guilty and sentenced to banishment.

One of the consequences of this early Congregational understanding of the relationship between church and state was the intolerance, even persecution, that it produced. Religious uniformity permitted no compromise, even in instances of the liberty needed by persons fleeing from persecution elsewhere. Nathaniel Ward, author of the Body of Liberties, simply turned that freedom around by proclaiming "to the world, in the name of our colony, that all Familists, Antinomians, Anabaptists and other Enthusiasts shall have free liberty to keep away from us, and such as will come to be gone as fast as they can."[21] Throughout the early decades these Congregationalists, who aspired to keep their churches pure, also sought to keep the commonwealth itself free from the impurities of Nonconformity. In the 1640s and 1650s the question of religious liberty was debated through the long-distance exchange of pamphlets by John Cotton and Roger Williams, now a resident of Rhode Island Colony. Williams argued that civil power should have control only over temporal affairs and not over matters of religious opinion. Too often, he declared, persecutors have insisted that their opinions constitute the only truth and therefore have punished conscientious beliefs on the part of those whom they opposed. Cotton responded with a different view of conscience. His argument was based on the assertion that the essentials of sound doctrine are so clear that any reasonable person, having heard them explained, would accept them. Therefore a person persisting in error "is not persecuted for cause of conscience, but for sinning against his own conscience."[22] A religious liberty based on respect for the integrity of the individuals's conscience, simply as conscience, was not a part of this seventeenth-century American Congregational understanding.

Connecticut Colony

As the 1630s progressed, Puritan New England spread westward and southward into the fertile valley of the Connecticut River. Interest in this land developed initially in England, when in 1635 a group led by John Winthrop, Jr., was sent to take possession under the patent of Lord Brook and Lord Say and Seal. A fort was established in a locale named Saybrook at the mouth of the river, and Winthrop was designated governor of an extensive surrounding territory. The earliest town settlements, however, came not from England but from Massachusetts Bay, when the appeal of the rich meadowlands on the banks of the river motivated migration. In 1635 pioneering groups from Watertown and Dorchester founded the communities of Wethersfield and Windsor, and others soon followed. Of particular importance among these migrations was that of the congregation at Newtown (Cambridge), under the leadership of its two ministers, Thomas Hooker and Samuel Stone. Desiring more land for their settlement and more opportunity for independence, these would-be migrants first sought permission in 1634 to leave Massachusetts Bay. Unwillingness of the General Court to grant the request created delay, and it was not until two years later that the departure took place. With the completion of their journey, the settlement at Hartford was created, from which then came major leadership for both Connecticut Colony and its Congregational churches.

Largely established and initially populated by Massachusetts people, Connecticut developed a political and religious life parallel in many respects to that of the Massachusetts colony. Its form of government, created in 1639 by representatives of the new settlements in their uniting constitution, the Fundamental Orders, followed closely the precedent of its northern neighbor. A general court, composed of a governor, six magistrates, and four representatives of each town, met regularly as the legislative body, and the magistrates and the governor comprised the court to administer justice. Similarly, the idea of a holy commonwealth prevailed, the constitutional agreement being to preserve the "purity of the gospel" and the "discipline of the churches" as "now practiced amongst us." Subsequent legislation required that all residents attend worship each Lord's Day, as well as upon all days of public fasting and thanksgiving appointed by civil authority, the penalty being a fine of five shillings for every instance of neglect. Moreover, all persons were obligated by law to contribute to the maintenance of the ministry of the local churches, and only such churches could be gathered as were approved by the General Court and neighboring congregations. The Connecticut pattern of church-state relationship followed the Massachusetts model.

The two colonies, however, differed in important respects. Unlike Massachusetts, the colony of Connecticut existed in its early decades without a royal charter, the early settlers colonizing illegally on land contested by numerous English proprietors and sought by Dutch adventurers. It was not until 1662 when, following the restoration of Charles II to the British throne, fear of royal action against the colonists' Puritanism led to their obtaining from the English king the charter legitimizing their land claims and their government. Meanwhile the government had grown out of a compact among inhabitants of the towns rather than out of a king's authorization to stockholders and, in the course of it, had taken a less-restrictive shape through the extension of the franchise to others than church members. All inhabitants who took an oath of loyalty could vote in town elections, and participation in colonywide politics was granted to any judged worthy of this by the General Court without regard to church status. Similarly, differences from Massachusetts appeared in the life of the churches. Although the fundamentals of Congregational order continued to prevail, some of the congregations began to modify their admission requirements, leading to a growing variety among the colony's churches and to instances where further movement toward a more presbyterian-type parish system could occur. Even in the early years Connecticut's Congregationalism developed an openness to experimentation and an adaptability to new circumstances that differentiated it, in at least subtle ways, from that of the Bay Colony.

New Haven Colony

The story was different, however, in neighboring New Haven, where, during the colony's brief history, New England Congregationalism was practiced in its most rigid form. Founded in 1638, New Haven Colony was the creation of John Davenport and members of his former English congregation. Their flight a year earlier had taken them first to Boston, where they received warm welcome and generous inducements to remain within the jurisdiction of the Massachusetts Bay Colony. But desiring independence through which an even more perfect holy commonwealth could be established, they finally settled farther south in the as yet unpopulated area of Quinnipiack, soon renamed New Haven. There, joined by others from Massachusetts attracted to their plan, they initiated their venture by a covenanting act reminiscent of that of the Pilgrims on the Mayflower. The instrument was the Plantation Covenant, in which they bound themselves to be governed by "the rules which the Scriptures held forth" in all matters that concern the church or the affairs of civil order. This was to be intensively a Bible commonwealth, and the implementation of that commitment led to the most theocratic of the early New England colonies.

By 1639 the colonists were prepared to establish formally their church and their political government, and this was done in accord with Davenport's understanding of the biblical prescription. Both church and state, he believed, must be built upon "seven pillars," these being leading men in the community, to whom other members could later be added. So the seven were chosen, Davenport among them, and they proceeded by covenant to organize the church. Once established in this fashion, they gathered to elect church officers, including Davenport for pastor, and to admit others deemed qualified into church membership. Not long thereafter the same seven, known in this instance as "the Court," took steps to organize the civil government of the colony. After seeking divine aid, they proceeded to form themselves into a "Body of Freemen" to which they added the others who had previously been admitted as members of the church. Following a solemn charge in which Davenport spoke to them on biblical instructions concerning the character and duties of civil magistrates, this electoral body acted to choose its governor and other civil officers for the administering of the colony's affairs. Church and state were organized, and the intent throughout was to conform both to the scriptural Word.

Davenport developed some of his ideas in conjunction with John Cotton, whose friendship he valued highly. He had known Cotton in England, had been persuaded by Cotton to come to New England, and had stayed with Cotton in Boston during the months prior to the move to New Haven. His views of church and state paralleled closely those Cotton had urged upon Massachusetts; in particular, that in the state the franchise must be limited to church members, and in the church admission must be rigorously restricted to the pure. But Davenport's own personal character, with its uncompromising rigidity, placed a still further stamp upon the New Haven scene, leading finally to alienation of many in the community from the church and rejection of his pastoral leadership.

Symptomatic of this narrowness and the conflict it generated were the church's numerous acts of censure and excommunication under Davenport's guidance. One case in particular became a centerpiece in this struggle, the disciplining of Anne Eaton, wife of Theophilus Eaton, the colony's governor. Mrs. Eaton's offense was her sympathy with Baptist views, leading to a rejection of infant baptism, compounded by her unwillingness to remain submissively docile in holding to this outlook. When Davenport administered infant baptism, she left the church lest she be party to a ceremony not lawful, and whenever he preached defending infant baptism, she could be heard muttering in the pew, "It is not so!"[23] Although Davenport sought to deal gently at first with the governor's wife, her resistance to reform led ultimately to her excommunication. Shortly thereafter, other women rising to Eaton's defense, although not church members, felt the harshness as well. For mocking the proceedings and even attacking the authority of the pastor, the Mrs. Brewster, Leach, and Moore were brought to public trial and convicted by the court. Similarly, many within the church joined the protest, and by the 1650s the community was severely divided over the issue of Davenport's authoritarianism.

Davenport's conservative form of Congregationalism had its followers in New Haven, however, as evidenced by their migration from the colony during a time of liberalization in the mid-1660s. Although by this time other communities, such as Milford, Branford, and Guilford, had been settled and their churches gathered, New Haven Colony as a whole lost its independence by being absorbed into Connecticut Colony in the charter negotiations then taking place. This was a severe blow dealt to New Haven by the British crown and probably was in part a result of the colony's early unwillingness to accept the restoration of the Stuarts' rule, it being the last of the New England colonies to recognize Charles II as king. Among the consequences of this union of the two colonies was the departure of many from New Haven because of Connecticut's more lenient practices in both church and state. Some moved to Long Island, but the larger migration was to New Jersey, thereby initiating the presence of Congregationalism in the Middle Atlantic states. In 1668 John Davenport also departed, accepting an invitation to the ministry of First Church, Boston. Many remained, however, adding their differing perspectives to an already somewhat eclectic Connecticut Congregationalism.

Congregationalism Defined

Although Congregationalism had been carried to these early New England colonies and made the exclusive church form within them, conflicts soon developed in which New England leaders were pressed for greater clarification and defense of the Congregational system. A part of the pressure came through inquiry and criticism from Puritans remaining in England. Some had received reports implying that New England, under the false pretense of non-Separatism, was actually taking the radical Separatist route once initiated by Robert Browne. Others, not misled in this manner, were nevertheless critical of New England's congregational polity. As presbyterian Puritanism gained political strength in England throughout the late 1630s and early 1640s, there was increasing desire for the colonies to be brought into conformity. By

1643 the Westminster Assembly had begun its work leading to the development of a presbyterian system for the British nation and Parliament had established a Commission for Plantations, which could become the instrument for imposing it upon all colonial possessions. New England Congregationalists were therefore quickly drawn into transatlantic debate on these matters.

A major result for the colonial churches was the writing and publication of several treatises by New England divines in which the Congregational system of church government was interpreted and defended. Among the earliest of these was Richard Mather's *Church-Covenant and Church-Government Discussed*, written in 1639 as response to thirty-two questions sent across the ocean by Puritans in England. In 1642 John Cotton, Thomas Hooker, and John Davenport were invited to represent New England at the Westminster Assembly, but chose not to attend in view of the overwhelming preponderance of presbyterian opinion there, opting instead to continue the debate by written word. Thus in 1644 Cotton published his *Keys of the Kingdom of Heaven*, an extended explanation and biblical defense of the Congregational way. He attached to this an introduction by Thomas Goodwin and Philip Nye, two of the "five dissenting brethren" at the assembly, commending this "middle way between that which is called Brownism, and the presbyterial government."[24]

When this treatise generated responses by two Scottish theologians, Samuel Rutherford and Robert Baillie, Richard Mather produced in 1647 his *Reply to Mr. Rutherford* and John Cotton in 1648 his *Way of Congregational Churches Cleared*, a historical account of the emergence of New England Congregationalism as well as a theological defense. Two other major treatises also appeared at this time, rounding out the New England role in the great debate. The first was prepared by John Norton at the request of his clergy colleagues in Massachusetts Bay and, under the title *The Answer*, was a response to questions that had been submitted by a Reformed Church pastor in Holland. The second, likewise prepared with the consent of the New England clergy, was Thomas Hooker's monumental *Survey of the Summe of Church-Discipline*, the most systematic and influential of all the writings brought to the aid of the Congregational cause. Hooker actually prepared the treatise earlier in the controversy, but the ship carrying the manuscript to England for publication was lost on the journey. There then remained for Hooker the tedious task of reconstructing the writing at a time when his health was beginning to fail. He died before the work was completed, but his editors found in his study sufficient notes to enable them to finish the final section on the role of synods in the Congregational system. Published in 1648, a volume of four hundred octavo pages, this became Congregationalism's most comprehensive statement in its dispute with the presbyterian polity of Puritan England.

The more precise defining of Congregationalism was also stimulated by matters within New England. As time went on, some of the colonists, clergy as well as laity, had growing sympathy for presbyterian views. At Newbury in Massachusetts Bay, both pastor and teacher, Thomas Parker and James Noyes, shared this outlook, as did Peter Hobart, pastor at Hingham. So in 1643 the clergy gathered in a conference, with Cotton and Hooker as moderators, to discuss with the dissidents their differences in polity. This was not a formal synod of the churches as had been the gathering half a dozen years earlier to deal with the errors of antinomianism. Rather, it was an assembling of the clergy for a probing of polity concerns. But out of it came the affirmation that "consultative synods" of the churches ought from time to time be assembled, for they "are very comfortable, and necessary for the peace and good of the churches."[25] Expressed here was the growing longing for an instrument that could bring together the independent churches and speak for them with a collective voice. Moreover, in the light of the inclinations even within the colonies for defection from Congregationalism, there was the tacit hope that the churches could develop a stated "platform of church discipline" to give a specific and solid basis for the uniformity in church practice that New England leaders desired.

Movement toward that goal was stimulated by another crisis, initiated in 1645 by a group of Massachusetts residents distressed over the restrictiveness of the Congregational system in both church and state. Under the leadership of Robert Child, a medical doctor in Boston, these protestors complained against the ideas of a selective church membership, the withholding of the sacraments from nonmembers, and the religious restriction applied to the political franchise. They felt that in all these instances the colony was in violation of the laws of England. Thus they presented a petition to the General Court in

Massachusetts asking for a change in practice and further indicating that, if this were not granted, appeal would be made directly to Parliament in London. Here was a precise challenge to key elements in the colony's church order as well as a threat to its political future. Discussion of these issues in a Parliament sympathetic to a nationalized presbyterianism would open up frightening possibilities of English intervention into the central religious basis for the commonwealth. But Child's efforts to obtain Parliament's help came too late in England's own political struggle. Held in Massachusetts for a time on the charge of sedition, after incriminating documents had been discovered in his baggage, Child finally arrived in London to find presbyterianism on the decline and Cromwell and his congregationalism in the ascendancy. The threat had now lost any possible English support.

The questions pressed by Child and his followers, however, added further incentive to the calling of a synod for clearer and more authoritative defining of the Congregational way. So in 1646, at the request of a group of Massachusetts ministers, the General Court issued a summons to the churches to send representatives to such a gathering. But further questions of protocol and polity arose. Some objected to the mandatory nature of the summons as implying state control over the churches. Although not agreeing with the complaint, the magistrates, for purpose of conciliation, changed the summons to an invitation. Problems still existed, however, for two of the major churches, Boston and Salem, refused to send representatives on the ground that the civil authorities were planning to enforce upon the churches such decisions as would be reached by the synod and then approved by the General Court. When finally these fears were allayed, the synod met in Cambridge in 1647 to begin its work. Twenty-eight churches from Massachusetts were represented by clergy and lay delegates, as well as several of the churches in the other Congregational colonies. The first item of business was to declare the importance of the cooperation of church and state in the use of synods for the health of the commonwealth. This done, the synod began the task of developing a "model of church government" by instructing each of three ministers, including John Cotton and Richard Mather, to prepare a draft for consideration at the next session.

The Cambridge Synod met again in 1648 to complete its work. Preferring the draft submitted by Richard Mather as the basis for its statement, the synod developed and approved the comprehensive Platform of Church Discipline, to which was attached a preface prepared by John Cotton. The platform was a document dealing in detailed fashion with most of the major issues in the Congregational understanding of the nature of the church, its organization, its government, and its ministry, as this had evolved by the middle of the seventeenth century. This was a major accomplishment, for it systematically brought together, through the collective voice of the churches, various elements of the polity that, after only furtive English beginnings, had now become the recognized church order in a settled society. Not all matters, it was found, could be settled, and particularly a troubling issue concerning eligibility for infant baptism was set aside for another time. But here was a clear standard in accordance with which the churches could regulate most of their practices and against which serious deviations could be judged. With the completion of this work, one further matter remained for synod action, a responding to the request that had come in the meantime from the General Court to prepare for the churches a confession of faith. This was quickly accomplished, however, by accepting "for the substance thereof" the Westminster Confession, recently developed by the Westminster Assembly and approved by Parliament for the English church. Although the assembly's presbyterian polity was totally unacceptable in New England, there was ready agreement with its Reformed theology as expressed in this statement of faith.

Following the synod's adoption of the platform, the General Court commended it to the Massachusetts churches for their study and response. Some objections were raised to specific details, and Richard Mather was chosen by the ministers to draw up replies that, with their concurrence, were then submitted to the court. Finally in 1651, after more than three years of deliberations, the court gave its approval to the platform, saying that it represented that which the Massachusetts Bay Colony had practiced and continued to believe. This was not unanimous approval, for even then some of the deputies disagreed, but by this action the Platform of Church Discipline became the legally recognized ecclesiastical standard for the colony and remained so until 1780. Recognized also by other New England colonies and then carried westward in the years of expansion, its broader influence in the shaping of American Congregationalism became very great. Although Congregational polity continued to evolve over the course of the years as new situations were encountered, much that the platform contained remained basic for the organization and government of American Congregational churches.

THEOLOGY

The first generation of American Congregational divines received theological training and nurture within the broad mainstream of English Puritanism and brought to America the Reformed faith as seen through those Puritan eyes. With little modification, this theology dominated the thought of the next several decades in New England. One major dispute, dealing with antinomian extremism, did convulse the early theological scene momentarily and, in pitting John Cotton against the other clergy, disclosed some disagreements among the divines. But these were simply matters of differing emphasis within the larger unity of the Puritan pattern. They can, however, be noted in two specific areas to which particular attention was given as the New England leaders began interpreting and applying their theology in the new land.

The Conversion Experience

In this "evangelical Calvinism" preaching was directed toward conversion, the turning from sin to faith. It also was directed toward encouraging a life of continued trust and obedience on the part of those who in faith had "pitched" on Christ, but the first responsibility was to present the gospel message so as to lead to the beginning of Christian experience and commitment. In bondage to sin, the person must first be freed and brought to a new allegiance. In the terms of covenant theology this moment of conversion was an entering into partnership with God in the covenant of grace. Puritan theology, however, also faced the question of the means by which such radical change could take place. It was a long journey from sin to faith, and movement from one to the other was neither a simple nor easy matter. Old ways had to be destroyed before new commitments could be undertaken. So it was important to come to an understanding concerning the process by which this could come about.

From the beginning of the Puritan movement its theologians in England had dealt extensively with this issue. Most generally they held that the process must be a painful one. One cannot truly turn to God except by being willing first to turn attention inward and, in self accusation as well as in awareness of divine condemnation, confront the reality of one's sin. The first words of Jesus' ministry were, "Repent ye," as he announced the coming of God's rule. The grace of forgiveness and the transformation to new being can come, therefore, only as one faces one's moral and spiritual rebelliousness and allows this to be exposed to the purging judgment of God. William Perkins advised his hearers, "You are as God's corn; you must therefore go under the flail, the fan, the millstone, and the oven, before you can be God's bread."[26] That exposure and the remorse it can bring must, moreover, come through the preaching of the law. Simply to proclaim the good news of the gospel is insufficient. Although that is the message of God's bountiful promises, it can fall on deaf ears. Rather, the law must first be heard as a "hammer" to awaken one to one's true condition, to lead one to repentance and, what is more, to bring one to despair concerning one's own power to effect a change. The law is "a John the Baptist to make way for Christ." It serves an instrumental purpose, opening the way to that trusting in God essential for the receiving of grace.

In New England the divines affirmed this role of the law in preparation for faith and dwelled strongly upon it. Thomas Shepard had found it to be the way toward conversion in his own personal experience. In his *Autobiography* he recalled how in his youth he struggled through a long period of agony after being made aware of his "vileness" in the sight of God. Seeing that he could not fulfill the law, "the terrors of God" began to break in upon him "like floods of fire," and he found himself shaken by the thought of eternal torment. But then, on hearing the preaching of the gospel, he felt that God "gave [him] a heart to receive Christ," and in this was a sense of peace.[27] With this way of "painful" pilgrimage so important in his own experience, Shepard became deliberate in his prescription of it for others who would make the same journey from sin to salvation. The goal was the peace that came through yielding in faith to God's proffered love, but the route must first lead through one's seeking a "conviction of sin." One must "labor for" a "sense of misery" in order to attain "marriage union" with Christ.[28]

Among New England's pastors Thomas Hooker spelled this out in fullest detail, examining the psychological, as well as the theological, aspects of the journey toward conversion. The beginning of that journey, he noted, was like the readying of a plant for grafting into another. First the plant must be cut off from the old stock and then "pared" so it will fit into the new. In the process of conversion the sinful person is cut off from sin and fitted "for the ingrafting into Christ." But the paring is painful, and as Hooker analyzed it, he found within it two successive stages. One was the state of "contrition," which, he said, loosens one from one's sin and makes one see the necessity for becoming another kind of person. Here the minister's presentation of the law can be like "darts and arrows," piercing the heart and leading to great sorrow. In contrition one detests sin and wants to be removed from it. Then, however, comes the second state, that of "humiliation," which loosens one from one's self as one sees one's own total inability "to procure the least spiritual relief" for one's soul. This is a paring away of one's sense of self-sufficiency, one's confidence in one's good performances as a shelter from God's judgment. And only then, said Hooker, only in this realization that one cannot save oneself, is one ready for conversion. Now "the coast is clear," and that faith can come by which one is enabled to turn to the saving love of God.[29] Like Shepard, Hooker urged his hearers not only to labor for a saving faith, but also to labor for that sense of sin and judgment that can prepare the way.

John Cotton, however, was critical of his ministerial colleagues on this issue. For one thing, he did not envision conversion involving such a prolonged and strenuous process. Although it includes a sense of sin and inadequacy, the "spirit of bondage" and the "spirit of burning," the saving union with Christ bursts in suddenly on one's waiting, rather than being gradually approached through actions designed to make way. For one's "first union," said Cotton, "there are no steps to the altar."[30] And implied in this was the further complaint that his colleagues were turning the process into a matter of human effort and therefore, in language made strident by Anne Hutchinson's accusations, were fostering a covenant of works. Cotton's concern was to emphasize the primacy of the sovereign action of God, that is, the powerful and captivating work of the Spirit, which comes simply by God's own giving. One cannot rely on the frailty of one's own efforts, even the efforts to seek contrition and humiliation. Yet this is the temptation if a pathway of preparation is prescribed. Moreover, said Cotton, this turning to human doing is also present when faith itself is interpreted as the action of one who comes to Christ. But faith is not an action humanly performed; rather, it is a state into which one is brought by the action of God. Faith is passive; it is not the cause of union with Christ, but is that union itself, bestowed by God. So neither the preparatory process nor the culminating act of faith are "mediators" of salvation. That is the role of Christ alone.

Cotton's colleagues, however, did not divorce divine and human action in the manner of Cotton's thinking. They stood, rather, in the tradition of their English Puritan predecessors who affirmed the simultaneity of divine and human doing in these works of salvation. Their basic presupposition was that divine sovereignty and human activity must be held together. God, who is sovereign, works through secondary causes, both natural and human, and in that divine working respects the integrity of the instruments employed. So when God works through persons, the efficient cause is divine, but the work is also a human act. God, they said, works repentance in the soul, and yet it is the human person who repents. Or conversely, although in the conversion process the human faculties of intellect and will are engaged in remorse and repudiation of self, their acts of contrition and humiliation are "a divine plucking of the soul from sin" through a "holy kind of violence" used by God.[31] So God does not, as Cotton implied, work upon persons as though they were inanimate objects, but God works in and through persons, "moving upon, co-working with, and assisting" in their work.[32] Furthermore, they said, the faith of conversion itself is both the human fulfillment of the condition requisite for covenant partnership with God and a gift of sovereign grace.

Assurance of Salvation

Cotton's near-antinomianism similarly generated conflict with the other divines when dealing with the subject of assurance. Earlier Puritan thought in England again had set the stage. From the time of Perkins onward, considerable attention had been given to the question of evidences confirming one's partnership in the covenant of grace. This was a matter of grave concern for every believer. The Scriptures urged that one seek "to make one's calling and election sure," and personal anxiety also added to the urgency of the task. It was no small or indifferent matter to know whether or not one was included among those whom God had from eternity predestined for salvation. Calvin warned against undue speculation on this subject, seeing peril in intensive self-scrutiny searching for signs. He dealt with the issue largely in terms of one's identification with the church, feeling one could be confident of God's favor if one were a participating member of the Christian community, sharing in its faith and receiving its sacraments.

But the mood of Puritanism was much more introspective, encouraging exploration of the individual's inner spiritual life and the seeking of evidences there. If one were truly a covenant partner with God, receiving by God's grace a healing of the soul, surely there would be some sign deep within that could be recognized and affirmed. One must seek therefore that "experimental knowledge" that can reveal the presence and power of God's working. This Puritan probing searched for a variety of clues. One could look for simply the yearning for salvation, a sign that God is beginning the work of renewal. Or one could search for the presence of faith, a gift that God would have given. Or one could hope to sense an inner transformation of loyalty and love, the presence of a "new heart" created by God's healing act. Or once again, one could take courage in the outward expressions of that new being, the "good works" of one's life in external behavior. Each and all of these could be indications of God's favor and signs of one's election. Perkins saw it to be "the power and pith of true religion" when one, by observation of inward experience, knows the love of God in Christ to be a determining presence in one's life.[33]

In American Puritanism these certifying graces of God were generally clustered under the rubric *sanctification*. In sanctification one knows the healing and cleansing powers of God. Even the good works of one's outward behavior are dependent on the Spirit's inward presence. Good works must come from good motives, but good motives depend upon God's recreating and ennobling the natural impulses of the heart. These changes, it was agreed, could not always be detected with full clarity. God does not heal all hearts alike, and for some these graces might be less discernible than for others. Moreover, it is possible for hypocrisy to enter, especially if the evidence is sought in outward good works. One can even deceive oneself by acts of righteousness and piety, let alone deceive others. Yet despite these difficulties, Puritans turned confidently to the evidence of God's favor that sanctification could provide. God's favor, they also knew, is expressed in justification, the forgiveness of sin. But justification, they felt, is even less discernible. Justification is a relational matter, in which the change is not in the human person but in the divine attitude. The person once condemned is now accepted as forgiven, and in terms of personal experience, that change is more truly hidden. But the God who forgives also heals. Therefore evidence of one's sanctification can likewise be seen as evidence of one's justification, as one searches one's soul for signs of God's love.

Once again John Cotton objected, essentially reversing the argument of the other divines. He not only denied the validating character of sanctification in showing forth justification, but affirmed that "while I cannot believe that my person is accepted, I cannot believe that my works are accepted of God."[34] It is necessary first to know that one is forgiven in order to know that one's works are judged good. Cotton did go on to say that subsequent awareness of sanctification can be helpful in providing assurance, but justification must first be evident. Once again this objection was related to his near-antinomianism, with its emphasis upon the powerful and captivating work of the Holy Spirit. So, he said, it is only from "an immediate light of the Spirit of God" that the desired assurance can truly come.[35] This is entirely a divine work in which the Spirit witnesses to the soul the forgiveness and peace that God gives. This view also reflected the diminution of the human role in the religious relationship that characterized the thought of Cotton. In his understanding human activity has little to do with the regenerating and revealing work of the Spirit, even though such activities may themselves be occasions of God's gracious doing. To rely, therefore, on the evidence of sanctification for assurance is once more to be thrown back into a covenant of works.

Cotton's position on the matter of assurance was as threatening to the thought of the other divines as had been his dealing with the subject of the conversion process. It suggested that in regeneration the Spirit of Christ takes over so completely as virtually to negate the significance of the human person. Thomas Shepard protested that under Cotton's interpretation "there is seeing in a Christian without an eye, and hearing without an ear, and knowing Christ without an understanding, and loving without love."[36] But regeneration, he asserted, is of the person; in it the person is changed and made into a "new creature." This is the gracious healing of human faculties that God performs, the granting of gracious habits that then flow through human acts. In 1637 the synod meeting in Cambridge confirmed this criticism by distinguishing between "Christ manifesting himself in works of holiness" and "Christ nakedly revealing himself to faith."[37] It is in the former sense, but not in the latter, that Christ brings evidence of one's salvation. So New England theology found assurance in sanctification.

The Westminster Confession

Until 1647 there was no official doctrinal standard for Puritanism in either England or America. Puritan divines shared broadly in the convictions of the Reformed theological tradition, as it had developed especially under the influence of Continental Calvinism, finding useful systemizations of Reformed thought in its many confessions of faith, ranging from the First Helvetic Confession of 1536 to the Canons of the Synod of Dort of 1619, a synod attended by John Robinson and other Puritan theologians. In England the doctrinal statement had been the Thirty-nine Articles of Religion, put into final form in 1562, and Puritans coming to faith within the Church of England had accepted its major theological propositions, even while dissenting from its views on matters of church and ministry. In 1647, however, the Westminster Confession of Faith reflecting English Puritan thought was published, and in the following year it was affirmed "for the substance thereof" by the Cambridge Synod for American Congregationalism. Slight changes were made in some of its phrasing by English Congregationalists in the Savoy Declaration of 1658, and these were subsequently adopted in Massachusetts in 1680 and in Connecticut in 1708. But the major themes of Westminster remained and continued to be influential in American Congregationalism for many succeeding generations.

Setting forth the Reformed faith through the consideration of thirty-three separate theological topics, the Westminster Confession presented a strict Calvinist portrayal of classic Protestant beliefs, emphasizing such ideas as the infallible authority of Scripture, God's eternal decrees predestining some to everlasting life and others to everlasting death, and the total corruption of the whole of humanity by Adam's "original sin." But within the classic theological frame it also revealed itself to be a distinctively Puritan document. One major characteristic of the Westminster Confession is its focus on the pathway in Christian experience from sin to salvation. In its evangelical interpretation of the biblical message Puritanism portrayed the Christian life as a pilgrimage of the soul. It is a journey moving through the various stages of experience provided by the plan of God. It begins in calling, which is conversion, God's drawing of the soul out of sin to a willing acceptance of Christ. Then it moves on to justification, in which faith resting on Christ is the instrument for the receiving of God's pardon. Next comes the stage of adoption, in which the forgiven are now more fully granted the privileges of being children of God. Then, in this "order of salvation," there is sanctification, that transformation of inner attitudes leading in outward practice to the Christian's good works. Finally comes glorification, the translation of the soul to the holiness of heaven. And throughout there is the perseverance in faith and faithfulness, which God makes possible, as well as the sense of assurance that the totality of this experience can bring. Presentation of this pilgrimage constitutes, then, one of the major portions of the Westminster Confession, reflecting the Puritan and evangelical version of Calvinism.

The distinctively Puritan cast is also seen in the confession's incorporation of the covenant theme into its interpretation of the manner of God's leading the elect through the pilgrimage to their final destiny. No previous Reformed creed had introduced this idea, but here God is portrayed as covenant-making and covenant-keeping, two affirmations central to Puritan thought. The confession affirms that God is a covenant maker because this is the chosen means to span the great distance between God and God's creatures. The first covenant was the covenant of works, but that was broken by human disobedience. This was then replaced by the covenant of grace in which God "freely offered unto sinners life and salvation by Jesus Christ, requiring of them faith . . . and promising to give unto all those that are ordained unto life his Holy Spirit, to make them able and willing to believe."[38] Moreover, God is a covenant keeper in that God's faithfulness will continue to preserve to the end those within the covenant who may for a time fall away in the midst of the pilgrimage's temptations. Thus embodied here in confession form is the fundamental Puritan paradox of God's covenant as both conditional and absolute. It calls upon the believer for the faith that fulfills the condition, and yet it also affirms that the very believing, as well as its perseverance, is a gift of God's unconditioned grace. The Westminster Confession at this point retained the delicate balance between human and divine action in the saving process that first-generation American Congregational divines held essential in the expression of Christian faith.

POLITY

Among the English Separatists and non-Separatists of the late sixteenth and early seventeenth centuries, the congregational form of church polity was practiced either secretly within the Church of England or in limited fashion within the small congregations in Dutch exile. The migration to New England, however, brought a new freedom. Now congregational polity could be pursued without hindrance— even more, with the state's aid and blessing. Moreover, theologians could freshly interpret it, and experience in practice could modify it as need might require. Basically the main lineaments remained the same, but New England became the first laboratory for the deeper probing and gradual refinement of the congregational perspective.

Church Covenant

In the 1640s New England theological literature interpreting church covenant dealt frequently, in the face of English presbyterian opposition, with justifying this instrument for the gathering of a local church. In the Bible the Old Testament use of visible covenant for founding the Jewish church was seen as model for the New Testament gathering of local congregations of Christian believers after the national church of Israel had been abandoned. But additionally, the church covenant was valued as providing the needed cohesion for the gathered congregation. In the New Testament the local church is called a "house" and a "city," and the church covenant therefore is like the cement that holds the materials of the house together or the compact that binds together a body politic. Further, in the political sense, the covenant becomes the basis within the congregation for the members' exercise of "mutual power over each other."[39] Where responsibility is granted for performance of ministerial and congregational acts, it is by mutual covenant agreement that all partake in the acceptance of the authority employed in that relationship. Although the covenant of grace, therefore, sets the boundaries for the invisible church at large, the local church covenant, made with God and with one another, is necessary both to bound and to bind the local congregation. And further, said the Cambridge Platform of Church Discipline, there is another practical effect of the church covenant, for "the more express and plain it is, the more fully it puts us in mind of our mutual duty and stirs us up" to its fulfillment.[40]

In the founding of the New England churches each congregation created its own church covenant. Some covenants were simple in form, like the one-sentence statement introduced at Salem in 1629. A somewhat similar covenant was used by the Boston church in 1630, which, while noting that those subscribing were by "wise and good Providence brought together into this part of America," called upon them simply to bind themselves to walk according to the rule of the gospel, in conformity to the holy ordinances, and to do so in mutual love and respect for one another, as God shall give them grace.[41] Most early covenants shared this simplicity. Some, however, were more elaborate. The covenant at Watertown in 1630 not only recalled the providentially guided past but also charged the unborn of the future to join with those present in accepting the responsibility of faithfulness, a duty that included a renouncing of "all idolatry, superstition, will-worship, and all human traditions and inventions whatsoever," and a pledging to keep God's "statutes, commands, and ordinances" in all matters concerning "worship, administration, ministry, and government" in the church.[42] The covenant at Windsor in 1647 took the further step of adding a creed to its covenant promises, so that those who subscribed made affirmation of a series of beliefs before promising to bind themselves to God and to one another. The tendency in early New England was for church covenants to become more detailed as time went on.

Covenants also were changed as circumstances made desirable. An early example is the action of Salem church members in 1636, after the church's unfortunate experience with Roger Williams. Remorseful over their part in this episode and the dissension it created within their own ranks, they supplemented their original commitment so that it would more explicitly define their duties. Reflective of the mood of the several additions was the promise to "walk with our brethren and sisters in this congregation with all watchfulness and tenderness, avoiding all jealousies, suspicions, backbitings, censurings, provokings, and secret risings of spirit against them." Also related to the Williams episode was the further promise not to slight their "sister churches, but [to use] their counsel as need shall be."[43] So the churches also bound themselves to specific commitments in the light of changing needs.

Church Membership

From the very outset the English Separatist and non-Separatist proponents of congregational polity, in opposition to the inclusive admission policies of a national church, insisted that church membership be limited to those who were personally qualified. Each local church must be a church of believers. Ideally this meant that the covenant of grace and the church covenant coalesced and that congregations were composed solely of true "saints." Realism prevented a succumbing to the illusion that such perfection was ever attained, but applicants for membership were nevertheless put to the test. The conviction concerning qualified membership remained central to the policy and practice of New England Congregationalists, by whom it was further developed and applied. "A little church with great godliness," said one pastor, "is far to be preferred to a great church (I mean for number) and small purity."[44]

In earlier practice in England and Holland the qualification was expressed in terms of profession of faith and godliness of life, the former involving a knowledge of the main points of doctrine and a personal faith confession, and the latter interpreted as a life free from scandal. No doubt there were difficulties at times in the application of these criteria to specific individual situations, but these general guidelines were initiated in the Old World and then transported to the new. By the mid-1630s, however, especially in the Massachusetts Bay Colony, this manner of testing did not suffice. There the concern became one of determining more precisely whether the candidate for admission had experienced conversion and was thereby incorporated into the covenant of grace. Saints were not true saints unless their hearts had been wounded for their sin and they had been forgiven and healed by God's grace. But this internal condition could not be adequately revealed by outwardly oriented acts such as formal profession and scandal-free living. Intentional hypocrisy, to say nothing of innocent self-deception, could hide the truth of a still-unconverted life. So the test of the description of one's conversion experience was added. This was to come out of one's introspection and was to be a "personal relation" of one's inner awareness of being judged for sin and restored through grace.

The first indication of this new practice appeared in the founding of a church in Newtown (Cambridge) in 1636 under the leadership of Thomas Shepard following the departure for Connecticut of Thomas Hooker and his congregation. Winthrop reported that the newcomers were told by both magistrates and neighboring ministers that "such as were to join should make confession of their faith, and declare what work of grace the Lord had wrought in them,"[45] and this personal relation was then satisfactorily made by each candidate. In the same year the founding of a new church at Dorchester under the leadership of Richard Mather was delayed because of the lack of candidates meeting this qualification. Mather had misjudged the state of religious experience of his would-be church members, and although the candidates were able adequately to confess their faith, they were not able, again in Winthrop's reporting, to "manifest the work of God's grace in themselves."[46] It was not until some months later that a group satisfactorily testifying to regeneration was gathered and the church established. The practice of requiring a relation of one's conversion soon became common throughout Massachusetts Bay Colony and later in New Haven Colony. It was not adopted as requirement in Plymouth, however, which retained Robinson's older policies, and it found only limited reception in Connecticut where several churches followed a less demanding way.

In all colonies, whatever the nature of the criteria, the testing for church membership was generally tempered by the commitment to do the judging in "rational charity." This meant a willingness to accept as adequate the "least measure" of indication of the presence of grace and faith. English Puritan theologians had long emphasized that God receives into covenant partnership the weak of faith as well as the strong, and New England Congregationalists now applied this standard to church membership. Thomas Hooker urged it at Hartford. Even John Cotton, who favored the more strenuous requirement of a personal relation of conversion, said that "we do not exact eminent measures, but do willingly stretch out our hands to the weak . . . for we had rather 99 hypocrites should perish through presumption, than one humble soul belonging to Christ should sink under discouragement or despair." He noted also that it was hard to discriminate between the two kinds of candidates, for "the tares are like to wheat." The practice in admission was not as severe as its image seems to suggest.[47]

Despite the leniency, however, as the years went on fewer inhabitants sought membership in the church. In 1643 Winthrop observed for Massachusetts Bay that "no small company" was left out of church membership, and by the end of the decade it was reported that less than half of Boston's adult male population belonged. Moreover, an increasing number of the children of Massachusetts' faithful were unable to join their parents in church membership by passing, even to charitable evaluation, the test of a relation of conversion. As a consequence a return to the less-exacting standard began, and by 1648 this was affirmed in the Cambridge Platform of Church Discipline commended by the General Court to the Massachusetts churches. Although the practice of personal relation was retained, this act now became a "profession of faith and repentance."[48] Contrition and commitment were its requirements, which, along with doctrinal knowledge and scandal-free living, constituted the necessary qualification for membership in a church.

In the larger variety found in Connecticut Congregationalism, some churches retained an early restrictiveness, but others adopted even more open admission requirements. Hartford provides an example of the change. There Hooker's views initially prevailed, emphasizing the personal and the experiential. For Hooker a true "knowledge" of God involved personal awareness of grace, and one must be able out of experience to "give a reason" for the hope that is within one. Hooker's successor, Samuel Stone, interpreted this knowledge, however, as being doctrinal in character, an acquaintance with "the principal articles of the creed," to which he also added the admission requirement of blameless living. Those who followed his Congregationalism, therefore, opened the church more broadly to membership for the community at large and the application of solely external criteria.

Over the years change also occurred in the procedures for testing and admitting new members, reflecting in this case, however, the larger role played by the elders. In the 1630s the examination of a candidate was conducted by all of the church's male members. In the 1640s that crucial function was taken over by the elders in private interview, the Cambridge Platform specifying that "the officers are in a special manner to make trial" of those who seek membership.[49] Then if the interview satisfied the elders, the candidate was to be commended to the church and required to present there a public confession of sin and profession of faith. For women the statement was generally submitted to an elder in writing, who then read it to the congregation, and this was also done for some men who shied from public scrutiny. Admission was by the church's assent.

Another change in these years occurred in the manner of receiving into membership persons transferring from another New England church. The early practice was to require a new examination and statement before the congregation. Although this procedure was noted in the Cambridge Platform to be valid for churches that desire to employ it, "letters testimonial" from one's former church were by the late 1640s coming to be recognized as providing adequate recommendation for membership in another congregation.

Ministry

The Congregationalists of early New England gave strong endorsement to the major practices concerning ordained ministry inherited from their progenitors in the English and Dutch Nonconformist congregations. Clergy were chosen by the local church, its male membership voting. Ordination was performed by the local congregation, although it was the election, rather than the formalizing ceremony of ordination, that bestowed ministerial status. The clergy, designated as pastors and teachers, were called to a ministry of Word and sacrament. Their authority was given to them by Christ through their election, and yet because of their participation in church covenant, the range of that authority was limited to the congregation they served. Furthermore, the ministerial status granted by ordination was restricted to the tenure of service to that congregation, election to a new ministry requiring a new ordination. Each church was to have not only a pastor and teacher but also a ruling elder who assisted in nonsacramental aspects of ministerial leadership, these three offices comprising the "eldership" of the congregation. In sum, the local congregation was to have a "mixed" government, a monarchy through rule by Christ, an aristocracy through guidance by the elders, and a democracy through consent by the people.

Modification of this general scheme began quickly. For example, many of the small New England congregations were unable to maintain an eldership in the manner ideally envisaged. The Cambridge Platform of 1648 continued to specify the three positions as biblically prescribed, but by that time the ruling elder had largely disappeared from the scene and as many as two-thirds of the churches had not been able to support the ministry of a teacher. Other changes were also beginning to take place, particularly in the interpretation of the role of the clergy in relationship to the laity within the congregation's life.

In earlier English and Dutch precedents two views of the relation of the eldership and the membership in church government had been advanced. Robert Browne gave strong emphasis to the participatory role of the laity in conducting the congregation's affairs, whereas Henry Barrow turned more to the elders to direct the congregation. Consequently there was lack of uniformity in practice, although the tendency was to view the elders more in Barrow's terms. In New England, however, a resolution of this matter was reached, with both theory and practice minimizing the democracy in favor of the aristocracy. Church government, said the Cambridge Platform, is given by Christ to the elders, who are responsible for "church-rule," whereas "the work and duty of the people" consist in "obeying their elders and submitting themselves unto them in the Lord." When this relationship prevails, added the Platform, the church properly takes on the character of a "body politic, consisting of some that are governors and some that are governed."[50] In this understanding the church conforms to the hierarchical view of human relations, which had been introduced by Winthrop into political governance. Democracy functions through the election of rulers who, in office, receive commissioning from God and exercise divine authority in the guidance of the people. In discussing this aspect of the ministry, John Norton said that those in ministerial office "are not the mouth and hands of the church. They are the mouth of God and the hands of Christ."[51] The church designates the person, but God grants the authority and power. However, the church can withdraw the designation if it believes the power has been misused, and the clergy can be dismissed. But the role of the clergy in office is to exercise the responsibilities of rule.

With the translating of this theory into practice in New England churches, the laity suffered over time an increasing erosion of their participatory role in many aspects of the church's life. Lay participation in worship through prophesying was more and more controlled. In the synod of 1637, the practice of asking questions after the sermon was condemned, and in 1648 the Cambridge Platform prohibited lay speaking in church except by prior permission of an elder. In admission of new members and discipline of offenders the role of engaging in prior examination of individuals to be judged was claimed to be a private function for the elders. And in the instance of discipline the elders maintained the right arbitrarily to dismiss certain cases and to fix penalties in others. Concerning this Thomas Hooker wrote, "The fraternity have no more power to oppose the sentence of the censure, thus prepared and propounded by the elders, than they have to oppose their doctrine which they shall publish."[52] It is not surprising that one lay member of the church in New Haven protested that the members "have nothing to do now but to say Amen, we are all clerks now."[53]

Other modifications tipping the balance between clergy and laity were related to a growing practice among local congregations of seeking help from elders in neighboring churches when critical needs arose. This appears, for example, in the decline in lay participation in the act of ordination, as elders from neighboring churches were increasingly called upon to assume the responsibility for the laying on of hands. It is also evident in churches turning to neighboring elders for counsel in matters of a congregation's responsibility such as the election and dismissal of its pastor. The mixed government still prevailed, and the congregation continued to have its right of assent and dissent. Furthermore, in the view of the Cambridge Platform, the "power of government in the elders" and the "power of privilege" in the congregation are not negated by each other but "may sweetly agree together."[54] Yet in point of actual fact, the system was becoming what Samuel Stone, at Hartford, soon declared it to be—"A speaking aristocracy in the face of a silent democracy."[55]

Synods

After the Cambridge Platform had dealt exhaustively with the government and ministry of the local church, it turned to the subject of the "communion of churches," and in a succinct statement affirmed two of the most basic principles of Congregationalism: "Although churches be distinct, and therefore may not be confounded with one another; and equal, and therefore have not dominion over one another; yet all the churches ought to preserve church-communion one with another, because they are all united unto Christ, not only as a mystical, but as a political head."[56] The independence of the local congregation was declared, its life free from external domination. But the independent churches, by virtue of their common union with Christ, were also united with one another. Moreover, the union was not simply the spiritual bond of Christ's common presence; it was a communion in which Christ was the political head. The Christ whose headship gave to each local congregation the "power of the keys" to govern its own life was also the Christ whose headship gave to the churches in united relationship the responsibility for common concern and mutual caring. Under Christ a quality of shared life for the churches was mandated as much as was a quality of independent life for each local church.

Such church communion, said the platform, can take many forms. There was consultation with neighboring churches when a local congregation faced problems or issues on which it needed more wisdom. There was the recommendation of members who moved to new locations. There was the sharing of the Lord's Supper with visitors from other congregations. There was the granting of help in case of lack, experienced by other churches, "either of able members to furnish them with officers; or of outward support to the necessities of poorer churches." But the most "political" of these forms of church communion was the use of synods. With New Testament precedent found in the Jerusalem Council reported in the Book of Acts, synods were declared to be an "ordinance of Christ," not absolutely necessary to the being of the church, yet often through human iniquity and the evil condition of the times "necessary to the well being of churches, for the establishment of truth and peace therein."[57]

In this early New England understanding synods could be summoned by the magistrates, but they also could be assembled by the churches if the civil government proved hostile. Their membership should include both clergy and lay delegates from the churches, and their responsibilities were to deal with disputed issues of faith and morals, to determine the proper ways of worship and church government, to witness against "corruption in doctrine and manners in any particular church, and to give direction for the reformation thereof." In none of this were they qualified to impose their judgments upon a local church by way of discipline, nor through other acts of authority to violate the congregation's independence. Rather, it was said, the conclusions of the synod should be received by each church "with reverence and submission," for they come from a body divinely sanctioned and empowered to interpret God's Word.[58] If, however, such submission was not forthcoming, some decisive action must be taken, and at this point New England Congregationalism walked a narrow line between congregational autonomy and coerced uniformity. Final recourse was the declaration of a sentence of "noncommunion" upon the erring and uncooperative congregation, a withdrawing from it of all relations with other churches. This resolution, however, should come only in the case of an irreparable breakdown. Voluntary compliance with corporate judgment was the overruling expectation for the churches' response to synod decisions, a testimony to their unity in Christ.

WORSHIP

For the New England Puritans there was nothing more important than the worship of God. In divine worship God is honored by ascriptions and songs of praise, God's Word is proclaimed to declare God's judgment and mercy and to lead hearers to faith and obedience, prayers are offered to lay before God the needs of a struggling people, and the sacraments are celebrated as visible testimony of God's covenanted grace. Both Sabbath and other forms of worship occupied a central place in the thought and practice of early New England churches. In their worship New England Congregationalists drew heavily upon the heritage they brought with them to the New World. Preaching, prayer, and psalms of praise were the major elements in the Lord's Day or Sabbath services, and these were practiced largely in the manner of their English and Dutch predecessors. Yet in this new setting, free from the restrictions of past experience, new emphases and concerns appeared.

Sabbath Observance

Life in the holy commonwealth made possible a protected and even legislated observance of the Sabbath heretofore difficult in Puritan practice. The Fourth Commandment, prescribing remembering the Sabbath and keeping it holy, could now be more precisely obeyed, and the day could be kept as a time of solemn rejoicing. For example, it was a day of rest from otherwise incessant toil. Not only the physical necessities of primitive living but also the Puritan doctrine of "calling" kept a people at long labor throughout six days of every week. In Puritan understanding God "calls" persons to places or "vocations" in family and society where one directs one's work not only to personal sustenance but also to common good. Idleness was a sin, and New Englanders were not hesitant to legislate restrictions against it. "No idle drone," said a Massachusetts Bay law of 1629, could continue to live in the colony. So the Sabbath was a welcome day of rest, and this was supported by legislation banning essentially all forms of labor on that day. Malicious later reporting, critical of Puritanism, exaggerated the harshness of these "blue laws" of the colonies. But labor unnecessary for the immediate needs of living was prohibited, supported by penalties imposed through the judicial system. Similarly, all sports and recreation, as well as unnecessary travel, were banned as out of keeping with the purpose of the day.

More positively, the Sabbath should be devoted to spiritual edification. Symbolically, the Sabbath was a memorial to Christ's resurrection, and its hours should be used for public worship and private devotion. Observing the Hebrew practice of defining the day from sunset to sunset, New England Congregationalists began their Sabbath on Saturday evening, its hours to be spent in family worship and private meditation in preparation for the public worship of the day ahead. Then by nine the next morning, as custom had it, the residents of each community gathered in their meetinghouse for the morning service and again at two for a service in the afternoon. For many years attendance by all, whether church member or not, was required by law, this being seen as a desirable legislative prescription for the health and good order of society. The meetinghouse, necessarily primitive in construction, was also simple and bare by intent. It had whitewashed walls and clear glass windows. The only decorations were texts from the Scriptures. Furnishings were sparse, limited to benches for the people, a high central pulpit for the minister, and the communion table between them for the celebration of the Lord's Supper. There was no cross on the table, for this would visibly recall the liturgical setting from which they had fled. The minister, likewise, wore no garments reflecting "popery," being dressed in a simple, black, academic gown representing his place in a learned profession and supplemented solely by the white collar tabs commonly used by clergy in the Calvinist tradition.

John Cotton has provided a record of the content of the Sabbath

services of his Boston congregation, with indication of the order customarily followed. He also noted, however, that orderliness in the
conduct of the different parts of worship was of greater importance than
any particular order for the service itself. For Cotton the services opened
with an extemporaneous prayer of thanksgiving and intercession, taking
into account not only the necessities of the community but also "the
estate of the times" and the needs of those in authority that all "may
lead a quiet and peaceable life in all godliness and honesty."[59] There
followed the singing of a psalm, which after 1640 would have come
from the Bay Psalm Book, the first book printed in the colony. The
practice was to sing the psalms in order throughout the year, not
attempting to relate the selection to the preacher's subject matter. Next
came the interpolated reading of the Word. Generally at least a full
chapter of Scripture was read, lest lifting shorter portions out of context
lead to abuse. Then came the sermon, followed in the earlier years by
the prophesyings contributed by other clergy and "if time permit" by
lay members called upon for this by the elders, and also by lay questioning of the preacher concerning the contents of his sermon. At this point
in the service the "seals of the covenant" were administered, the Lord's
Supper once a month in the morning and baptism as needed in the
afternoon. Also, as needed, the afternoon service at this point included
the admission of new members and the disciplining of offenders. Then
another psalm was sometimes sung, the collection was received as members rose and moved forward to put their offerings in the deacons' box,
and the congregation was dismissed with a blessing.

This was a long day in church for these pioneers in Congregational
worship. Prayer was lengthy, for it was filled with much fervent emotion and earnest pleading. The psalms were lengthy, many containing a
great number of verses, and were doubled in length by virtue of being
first lined out and then repeated by the congregation. The story is
recorded of one preacher who forgot to bring to the meetinghouse the
text of his sermon. Realizing it as he was about to ascend to the pulpit,
he assigned another psalm, walked a quarter mile back to his house,
obtained his sermon, and was back in the pulpit before the psalm was
finished! The sermon in this early worship also was lengthy, never less
than an hour. Perhaps this contributed to Thomas Shepard's complaint
that audiences were becoming "quite sermon-proof!" Various forms of
lay participation—prophesying, questioning, admitting new members,

and disciplining—added to the length of the services. Altogether, three hours for each service would not have been unusual. But this was the Sabbath, to be well observed and fully preserved. Thomas Hooker exclaimed, "Take away a Sabbath, who can defend us from atheism, barbarism, and all manner of profaneness?"[60] The Sabbath was a bulwark for Christian life.

Sacraments

Although the sacraments were honored by New England Congregationalists as significant elements in the worship of the church, there was an ambivalence in that honoring. For one thing, the evangelical character of their religious outlook, with its predominant emphasis upon conversion and the experience of grace, was not easily conducive to a sacramental form of piety. Focus upon the interior aspects of religious awareness, the presence of the Spirit in the life of the soul, led these Puritans to minimize reliance upon material symbols as helps in the spiritual pilgrimage. John Cotton told his congregation to "sit loose from the Ordinances"[61] and not trust in externals. Further, the conception of the church as the pure congregation separated from the world added to this distancing from a sacramental tradition that, in the past, had recognized sacraments as the cementing bond within a national church made up of both believers and nonbelievers. The doctrine of predestination further complicated the picture, for God's sovereign selection could occur quite apart from the ministrations of the church. And yet the sacraments were important gifts of God and means for grace. They were instituted by Christ and offered as material signs for the spiritual welfare of believers and their congregations. The ambivalence created by these conflicting perceptions, although not unknown to earlier Puritanism, was brought out more fully in the New England experience.

The practice of infant baptism created one set of circumstances in which this tension of interpretations was faced. Because baptism was a seal of the covenant of grace, it became a sign of God's saving act. It was not in itself God's saving act, but confirmed in visible manner the grace God invisibly bestows. But this created difficulties in understanding and administering baptism, especially as given to infants. If only the elect among infants are to be saved, then on what basis should those be selected to whom baptism will be administered? Moreover, if salvation, as partnership with God in the covenant of grace, is ultimately conditioned upon a believer's faith, is infant baptism instrumental in leading toward that later mature faith experience? Or again, is there for baptized infants a membership in the church despite the requirement for Christian experience and faith?

Struggling with these issues, the first New England generation found some answers and left others for the future. In the main they found their way by means of the conclusion that God's covenant is both external and internal. The internal covenant is with the elect, chosen from all eternity to be members of the invisible true church, and it is their salvation which is sealed by baptism. For them baptism does not "seal a blank." The external covenant, however, also includes the non-elect, who, though baptized in infancy and brought into the external care of the church, ultimately are destined to fall away. But as effort must be made to limit the external covenant to those who are presumably within the internal, infant baptism should be administered only to the children of those who are church members through faith and the experience of grace. And in this practice there can be consolation, for the biblical promises are to believers and their seed, the sacrament is a sign and, said the Cambridge Platform, this very act of baptism of infants places them "in a more hopeful way of attaining regenerating grace."[62] So despite ambiguity and unanswered questions, baptism was well honored. It does not convey saving grace, but it can facilitate the process of salvation. And although it belongs to the external covenant, the ministry of that covenant can be a means to internal grace.

The problem of qualification for reception of the sacrament also was faced in New England's administration of the Lord's Supper. This sacrament, too, was a seal of the covenant of grace and therefore presupposed reception only by the faithful. Moreover, the restriction in empowerment of ministry imposed by church covenant limited administration in each local church to the members of that particular congregation. So New Englanders struggled here with further aspects of the qualification problem. Discipline, with the use of excommunication, presumably could limit reception in the local congregation to the truly eligible. But what about visitors who were communicants in other New England churches? Some churches would admit them to communion if they carried letters of recommendation, but Salem refused, on the ground that such letters could be counterfeited, and required oral testimony from one of its own members concerning the candidate's fitness. Finally, both of these restrictions were dropped in the Cambridge Platform, where sharing the Lord's Supper with visiting members of neighboring churches was portrayed as a desirable form of interchurch communion. Not so generously treated, however, were visitors from the Church of England, despite the non-Separatist character of New England's Congregationalism. To share in the Lord's Supper required membership in a Congregational church.

The severe restrictions on qualification were made more essential by the theological understanding of the nature of the sacrament. It was "a meal for the holy rather than a meal to produce holiness."[63] Maintaining the Calvinist characterization of the Lord's Supper, held also by their Separatist and non-Separatist predecessors, the New England divines spoke of a "feeding on Christ," who was spiritually present within the elements in the celebration. Various terms were used to depict this presence: the body and blood of Christ were "exhibited" under the bread and wine; or the union of elements and Christ was a "virtual" union, that is, a union presenting Christ's power though not fleshly reality. But beyond the language was the conviction that in the holy meal Christ was at hand to be nourishment for faithful communicants.

Other Spirituality

The piety of Puritanism not only required attendance at public worship but also encouraged participation in other forms of religious devotion. The honoring of God and the nurturing of the soul could not be limited simply to the confines of the meetinghouse. These should likewise be cultivated through less formal and more private spiritual exercises leading to awareness of God's presence and guidance. New England Congregationalism contributed from the outset to the development of group and private practices designed to assist in the progress of the pilgrim's spiritual journey.

Anne Hutchinson's gathering of friends in her home for religious discussion was not a unique phenomenon in early New England. She overstepped the conventional bounds in two respects, by leading a group that included men and by using the occasions for criticism of the preaching of the clergy, but there were women's prayer groups led by women, as well as other groups, mixed and male, led by men. Moreover, these were often strictly lay gatherings, seeking under their own lay leaders to find in meditation and prayer a nurturing of the spirit. Similarly, the clergy initiated gatherings of ministers. To some degree these dealt with professional concerns, but their primary focus was on a more intimate sharing of worship and the devotional life.

Even more the family circle was encouraged to be a center for spiritual nourishment. The family was a "little church" under the guidance of the husband and father who served as spiritual leader. Manuals were prepared to assist in the conduct of the forms and times of family devotion. Apart from grace before meals, there were morning and evening devotions that included the reading of Scripture, the singing of psalms, and prayer. A pattern was also present in the cycle of the day's prayers. Evening was a time for contrition and for dying to sin in preparation for a sleeping under God's care. Morning was a time of thanksgiving for fresh spiritual awakening with the new day. This was a death-and-resurrection theme integrated into the cycle of family devotion. Family religious life was further enhanced by the practice of catechizing children and servants. Sometimes this was led by the father and on other occasions by a pastor who visited the home for this purpose. In Massachusetts the General Court urged ministers to prepare a catechism for use by families, and by the early 1660s at least fourteen had been printed.

New England Puritanism also encouraged private activity in the pursuit of spiritual enrichment. This might take the form of consultation with one's pastor, for persons were regularly advised to seek such conference, especially in time of particular need. But more consistently it could lead to one's private program of Bible reading, self-examination, meditation, and prayer. This more intimate style of devotional practice was for many the center of all significant religious awareness and became a major feature of Puritan spirituality. Manuals were prepared by clergy for these devotional exercises, instructing in subjects and methods for private meditation. In self-scrutiny one was urged to reflect upon one's "particular temptations" and the nature of one's "present estate towards God." In the process one could recall the stages of one's first conversion and, being led through penitence to faith and renewed commitment, one could arrive at the personal sense of a "sanctified mind" and an "elevation of the heart" in assurance of salvation.[64] Records of these experiences were often kept in personal diaries, many of which became remarkable accounts of both the anxieties and the joys of the pilgrim's progress toward not only an earthly, but also a heavenly, destiny.

The art of poetry was sometimes used to record these intimate reflections, as may be seen especially in the work of Anne Bradstreet. An early immigrant to Massachusetts in the company of her husband and later the colony's governor, Simon Bradstreet, she employed her impressive talents to express both the tribulations and the expectations of the pilgrim journey. Particularly in her meditation titled "As Weary Pilgrim, Now At Rest," she voiced the ultimate hope of the believer who longed for death's release from struggle and entrance into eternal bliss:

> *A pilgrim I, on earth, perplext*
> *with sinns and cares and sorrows vext*
> *By age and paines brought to decay*
> *and my Clay house mouldring away*
> *Oh how I long to be at rest*
> *and soare on high among the blest. . . .*
> *Such lasting joyes shall there behold*
> *as eare ne'r heard nor tongue e'er told*
> *Lord make me ready for that day*
> *then Come deare bridgrome Come away.*[65]

MISSION

Migration to America opened up a new sense of mission for transplanted Congregationalism. If the problems of its minority status and persecuted origin in the Old World had driven it largely to self-defense and protectiveness, the new freedom allowed it to think more broadly about responsibilities in the larger society. Beyond its role in guiding the development of the holy commonwealth, it now saw itself as charged with reaching out to more extensive tasks. One was to evangelize the "heathen" in whose land it had settled. But another was to serve, under God's providence, as a model for the ultimate salvation of all of the world.

American Indian Missions

The seal of the colony of Massachusetts Bay had as its design the figure of an American Indian seeming to call out, "Come over and help us." Although this Macedonian cry was inferred as having been initiated by the land's first occupants, in its reverse way it represented one of the original and continuing aims of the migration. The Massachusetts charter of 1629 charged the governor and his company to "win and incite the natives of the country to the knowledge and obedience of the only true God and Savior," further declaring this to be "the principal end of the plantation."[66] No doubt there were some among the settlers of the first several decades who preferred extermination to conversion as the means for dealing with the American Indian presence, but by and large both humanitarian and evangelistic attitudes prevailed. Contrasted with the cruelty and exploitation of much of the nineteenth-century American treatment of the retreating native population on the western frontier, the Puritan practice of the seventeenth century was both restrained and responsible. Land was purchased, justice was enforced, treaties were negotiated, and for some fifty years, with but a brief interlude, relations were peaceful—and in that half-century persistent efforts were made to meet the charter's evangelistic goal.

Although the Massachusetts General Court tried briefly in the early 1640s to organize missionary activity among the American Indian groups, the effort became mainly voluntary through the work of dedicated individuals. First to undertake it was Thomas Mayhew, Jr., who, with his father, led a group of settlers to the island of Martha's Vineyard in 1642. A church was gathered and Mayhew, who had studied theology, was elected minister. Almost immediately he began working with the American Indians on this and neighboring islands, and for the next fifteen years he visited their villages, leading them by his preaching and teaching to acceptance of Christian faith. In this he was greatly assisted by his first American Indian convert, Hiacoomes, who by 1649 was ordained and was preaching regularly to his people. Mayhew's approach was focused on individuals, not relying on change in social structure, and through it he achieved much success. Even when his converts drew up a plan for a covenant and a church in 1652, Mayhew resisted, for he wanted to make certain about the quality of their commitments before this step was taken. In 1657 Mayhew was lost at sea when on a trip to

England, and his work was immediately assumed by his father. Like his son, the senior Mayhew did not attempt to reshape the American Indian social structure, although a Congregational church was organized within it in 1659 and another a few years later. By 1674 it was reported that most of the natives on the islands were at least nominally Christian, many of them being full communicants. In addition to the two churches, there were several congregations, and all were served by ten American Indian preachers. The Mayhew family continued in following years to encourage this work, giving support for five generations.

A somewhat different and more extensive mission program was concurrently developed on the mainland by John Eliot, whose more prominent activity led to him being called the Apostle to the Indians. Eliot was pastor at Roxbury in the Massachusetts Bay Colony when in the early 1640s he also began preaching with the help of an interpreter in neighboring American Indian villages. Meanwhile he studied the native language and by 1646 was able to employ it in the conduct of worship, his first such service including a seventy-five minute sermon in Algonquian! Soon, like Mayhew, he gathered converts but, unlike the former, felt they should be isolated in their own communities and thus protected from contact with unconverted natives and unsympathetic settlers. So he established towns of what came to be called the "Praying Indians." Helped by a grant of land from the General Court, the first town of Natick was founded in 1651 and others soon followed. Eliot believed that social conversion of the American Indians to English ways should accompany religious conversion, and the towns therefore contained schools aimed at providing knowledge and skills necessary for entering the settlers' style of life. Elementary instruction in the English language was given, and agricultural and domestic crafts were taught in order that the inhabitants could be self-supporting and adapted to their new circumstances. For Eliot this was as essential as the preaching. "I find it absolutely necessary," he said, "to carry on civility with religion."[67]

To facilitate the religious development of the Praying Indians, Eliot employed his linguistic skills in the creation of an "Indian library." In 1661 he published the New Testament in Algonquian, and two years later the Old Testament followed. With the aid of additional translators other books were put into the native tongue, including Puritan tracts on personal piety and the Cambridge Platform for administering church life. In accord with Congregational tradition Eliot, like Mayhew, urged caution against the bringing of converts together too hastily into a covenanted church body. Attempts to formulate a church at Natick were made in 1651, 1652, and 1654 before reaching successful completion in 1660. In all earlier instances examination of the candidates indicated that qualifications were still lacking for full communion. So within the American Indian villages strict Congregational procedures were applied, even as the social and economic life of the villages was made to conform to the settlers' pattern.

The next few years witnessed continued growth for this mission. Altogether fourteen villages of Praying Indians were established. Schooling was also provided for American Indian youth in other colony towns with the hope that those qualified could be prepared for college. In the mid-1650s a building was constructed at Harvard to accommodate American Indian students, President Henry Dunster expressing the wish "to make Harvard the American Indian Oxford as well as the New-English Cambridge."[68] Only a very small number were ever enrolled, but the plan was continued for decades even to the point of the authorization of an improved building in 1695 that any American Indians coming to the college should engage in their studies rent free. During these years help for work with these groups was received from England through two societies for the "Propagation of the Gospel in New England," established by Parliament in 1649 and in 1662. Whether under Puritan or Anglican auspices, these agencies provided financial support for the type of American Indian mission activities in which the New Englanders were engaged.

New England's Mission to the World

When Winthrop spoke on the *Arbella* about the colonists entering into a covenant with God concerning their future society and about the colony becoming a "city upon a hill" with the eyes of all people upon it, he spoke about something larger than simply the church covenant and the congregation of the elect. His vision was upon the holy commonwealth in its total political breadth and upon the national covenant in which it was engaged with God. The concept of a national covenant was not new. Puritanism in England had developed this idea by finding a model for national existence in the Old Testament record of the Hebrew people. There God was in covenant with the nation as it moved through the successive stages of its history. Chosen to be God's people, the Israelites were given the covenant promises of divine favor, the blessings of protection, prosperity, and peace. But that favor was conditioned on obedience. The covenant was a two-way relationship, and the nation's obligation was to honor God and fulfill God's law. If national obedience were forthcoming, God would be their God and they would be God's people. If it were not, there would be curses rather than blessings, and God's wrath would come upon them. Unlike the personal covenant of grace, the national covenant rested on the principle of justice, and disobedience would bring destruction. This, Puritans knew, had been the experience of the Hebrew people when their forsaking of God in indifference and idolatry had led to defeat in war and to decades of exile.

For the Congregational Puritans of the early seventeenth century, the application of this analogy seemed plain and focused particularly on the church's reformation. God had chosen England, they said, to be a covenant nation in which the church's long emergence out of medieval corruption could come to final fruition. The idolatry of Roman Catholicism had been partially overcome by Continental reformers such as Luther and Calvin, but their work had not completed the reforming task. God therefore had selected England as the scene for the church's further purification, and this was begun in the Puritan protest, especially in the attempt to put into practice the principles of Congregationalism. England as a nation, however, was rejecting its opportunity, impeding the continuation of reformation through hostility and persecution. So God was now rejecting England, even as God had rejected Israel. While yet in England, Richard Mather wrote of the many signs of "fearful desolation" in the nation, where a still-corrupt church and a stiff-necked people were resisting the divine leading. Thomas Hooker's last sermon in his native land was titled "The Danger of Desertion," a warning that England was fast being abandoned by God. Intensified by a commonly held apocalypticism, the Congregational preachers saw signs of the "last days" in the turmoil of the times, with their awful portent of England's total destruction.

Yet God's plan had not been halted, for by providence a new opportunity had been made available in the discovery of America and in the founding of New England. God might abandon a faithless nation, but not a faithful people who as a remnant continued the work of reformation. In the new place they could build a new nation and even demonstrate to England and to all the world the purity of life in church and society to which they were called. So God's covenant was now with New England, a land summoned to be the instrument of God for this larger purpose. Like Israel, called by God not only to its own purity but also to be a "light to the nations," New England was given the covenant obligation to demonstrate to all humanity the obedience to God's law that could bring divine blessing. Predominantly this obedience was to be in the restored purity of the churches through a restriction of membership to qualified believers and a faithful adherence to other aspects of the Congregational way in ministry, sacraments, and discipline. But church and society were closely related, and political government shared as well in the obligations of the covenant. Above all, that government was to protect the churches in the practice of their Congregationalism and to keep dissidents from despoiling the peace and order of the land. Purified church and committed state were to work together in the creating of the new society. When John Cotton urged John Davenport to come to New England, he saw that ideal already coming into being, saying that "the order of the churches and the commonwealth was so settled" that it brought to his mind "the New Heaven and New Earth, wherein dwells righteousness."[69] So New England was to be a "city upon a hill" in order that, while time yet remained, it might be a beacon to lead England and all the world to the completion of that reformation that would bring divine favor.

The new political situation for Congregationalism in America enabled it, therefore, to enlarge its sense of mission beyond the scope of the local church. That mission remained conditioned by the continued conviction that the Congregational way was the only way biblically prescribed. But it now placed that conviction within the framework of covenant responsibility in the universal plan of God.

SUMMARY

Leaders of the first generation of American Congregationalists were committed to the establishment of a holy commonwealth. Calvinists in their view of the social order, they saw this goal as realizable through the cooperative efforts of church and state. Both institutions were designed by God for the ultimate purification and rule of human society.

First, therefore, these early New Englanders aimed at the development of the pure church. Their Congregationalism led them to locate such purity primarily within the local congregations. Each individual church should be a community of persons who testify to the experience of conversion through the power of God's grace. These are the elect in the scheme of God, chosen from all eternity to be God's partners in a covenant of grace. Gathered under the headship of Christ, they covenant to walk together as a church in obedience to God's ways. They worship faithfully through prayer, the singing of psalms, and preaching. They select and ordain their clergy and, under the guidance of the clergy, administer discipline to maintain purity in the life of the church. They accept the two sacraments from clergy hands to seal further the covenant relationships they and their children have with God.

But their citizenship is on earth, as well as in heaven. Therefore, they organize and administer the state as an additional means of carrying out God's will. To that end the franchise in New England was first limited to church members, and elected officials were chosen with the confidence that their qualifications were given to them specially by God. Among the functions of the state were the protection of the church and the preservation of the faith. Therefore the state's coercion was used against threats to religious conformity, and in extreme cases involving social disruption the punishment was banishment. The religious liberty sought by the early Congregationalists in New England was for themselves alone and not for those whose religious faith and practice were different.

Believing in the special providence of God, these Congregational settlers were convinced that their New England was chosen by God to replace old England in God's ultimate plan. God, they affirmed, was covenanting with this new paradise to make up for the deficiencies of those that had gone before. Their hope was that New England would be faithful, a pure church protected by a God-governed state. This was New England's covenant responsibility, not only for itself, but for the world.

CHAPTER THREE

CONTINUITY AND CHANGE
1660–1730

The late 1640s and early 1650s witnessed the death of many of the founders of the Congregational experiment in colonial New England, and by 1660 a new generation of leaders was largely in place. John Winthrop had passed from the political scene, and younger men were taking hold of the reins of government. Among the leading clergy only Richard Mather and John Davenport remained to serve as transitional figures, leadership of the churches being increasingly assumed by ministers both native born and locally trained.

The colonies, too, were changing in their basic nature. Although life was still primitive in its physical aspects, it had taken on a more settled form. Towns were established, their governments tied in closely to colonial administrations, and a Confederation of New England had been created to unite the colonies for defense. Similarly, economic progress had been made. Along with growth in agriculture, there were the beginnings of industrial development and the emergence of a merchant class. Boston soon became a trading center, its port used for seagoing commerce and its life taking on the characteristics of a growing city. Puritan zeal for diligent labor was making possible the creation of an increasingly stable society.

In like manner the boundaries of that society were being extended. Expansion of settled populations sent pioneering sons and daughters farther from inhabited areas to cultivate new land and to establish new communities. The growing economic opportunities in the colonies attracted continuing immigration from the mother country, and after 1660 a new group of Puritan dissenters made the journey to escape the renewed religious oppression under Charles II. By 1675 the population of New England had reached an estimated 120,000, a fivefold increase over that produced by the Great Migration. Expansion slowed somewhat in the next decades as a result of the perils of frontier warfare, brought on in part by perceived American Indian hostility, but also in part by the colonies being drawn into the struggles of European powers for dominance of the seas and of the New World. With the Peace of Utrecht in 1713, however, rapid growth resumed, not again seriously interrupted until the renewed conflict of the late 1750s in the final French and Indian War.

HISTORY

Congregationalism in New Hampshire and Maine

Throughout the 1600s and early 1700s, New England's expansion included a gradual settling of the northern areas of New Hampshire and Maine. There, as in the earlier colonies, Congregationalism became the church establishment. In the north, however, it took a form different from the two somewhat varied patterns already worked out in Massachusetts and Connecticut. Although doctrine and polity were broadly similar to those of these southern neighbors, the circumstances and manner of Congregationalism becoming dominant in the north have led historian Elizabeth Nordbeck to speak of the region as a "third New England."[1]

The initial settlements in the north came more from economic than from religious motives. Cotton Mather described this in his later writing by recounting the story of a visiting minister urging the residents there to maintain the purpose of their planting by being a religious people, whereupon one of his hearers cried out, "Sir, you are mistaken, you think you are preaching to the people at the Bay; our main end was to catch fish."[2] As early as 1621 and 1622 two English adventurers, Sir Fernando Gorges and Captain John Mason, obtained patents for extensive land holdings along the northern coast and shortly thereafter sent out persons skilled not only in fishing but also in the lumber and fur trades. For several years these forays lacked stability and continuity, but they became more permanent after 1634 when the land was divided into the tracts of New Hampshire and Maine and put under more purposeful administration. Consequently small communities developed, such as Dover, Hampton, and Exeter in New Hampshire and York, Wells, and Saco in Maine, some through migration from England and others through movement northward from Massachusetts Bay.

The early religious life of these communities was marked by considerable variety. Throughout the 1630s two of the six settlements in the area were Anglican; two were made up of antinomians who moved northward from Massachusetts; one had a succession of Puritan, Anglican, and Baptist pastors; and only one was an orthodox Congregational community. Some years later the variety was further compounded by the migration of a large group of Quakers. Changes began to occur, however, when the northern territories were brought under the jurisdiction of Massachusetts and subjected to Bay influence and legislation, a status accorded to New Hampshire in 1641 and to Maine in 1653. Ministers of Congregational training and persuasion then visited northern communities, in some places establishing temporary preaching points and in others accepting calls to settled ministries. Puritan doctrine was proclaimed and Congregational ways of church life were developed. Furthermore, in application of Massachusetts religious laws, towns were required to make provision for public worship, Sabbath breakers were punished, and citizens were obligated by taxation to support the church's ministry. Consequently, by the early 1700s Congregationalism had become the established church in these new areas and remained so in New Hampshire until 1819 and in Maine until 1820.

Yet the likeness of this establishment to those of Massachusetts and Connecticut was a similarity with a difference. A major point of distinction was in the looser relationship that developed between church and state, leading to a greater measure of civic and religious freedom. Lacking a founding Puritan passion for holy commonwealth, these northerners, for instance, created no church membership qualification for the political franchise or the holding of public office, even receiving the approbation of the Massachusetts General Court for this practice when the territories came under the jurisdiction of the Bay colony. This less-rigid tendency likewise prevailed within the life of the churches themselves as they came to understand the nature of their own identity and their role within society. At this point major emphasis fell upon the importance of moral behavior, leading many of the churches to reject the requirement of a "personal relation" of conversion as necessary for admission to church membership. The value of the church to society also was viewed in these terms, for the church's emphasis on morality could be a means for encouraging order and stability in the local community. As the northern areas expanded in the 1700s, it became the practice of developers of new towns to require that those seeking residence first build a meetinghouse and call a minister before taking final possession of their property, thus assuring community stability.

New Hampshire became a separate province in 1679, and its religious life was freed from Massachusetts control. Nevertheless, its Congregationalism was by then well established and, despite the greater flexibility, its churches and ministers continued a close relationship with those of the Bay colony, often relying on them for counsel and support. Maine remained under Massachusetts jurisdiction until it achieved statehood in the early nineteenth century and shared fully in this continuing ecclesiastical kinship.

Half-Way Covenant

Despite the expansion and establishment of Congregationalism, the churches of New England experienced throughout ensuing years some lessening of interest in the concerns of religion. The secular began taking its toll on the sacred, for, as one pastor put it, there were too many in the pews who saw "religion as twelve and the world as thirteen." These persons were "practical atheists," he said, for "farm and merchandise have their hearts."[3] Priorities were changing as colonies founded more for religion than for trade were now developing erosion of original purpose. Moreover, the churches were beginning to rethink their relationship to society, and members of the clergy faced new tasks. In part these involved a preserving of the past, for the way of the founders was still the foundational way. Yet in light of the realities of the present, accommodations needed to be made for translating that past into a viable future. The second and third generations of clergy took as their responsibility both the forwarding and the reshaping of their Congregational heritage.

An initial problem faced by the new generation had actually been bequeathed by the founders, for they had confronted it but left it unresolved. At issue was the nature of church membership and its privileges, particularly as related to the sacrament of baptism, and the problem was generated by the pressure exerted on tradition by the changing character of the times.

The tradition upheld by New England Congregationalism spoke of church membership in a twofold manner. Primarily membership rested upon adult conversion, for admission to the church covenant was limited to those who could profess the personal experience of regeneration. Membership was for those who had been drawn by God into the partnership of the covenant of grace and who had then acted upon this by covenanting with one another. The biblical message, however, added further that God's covenant was not only for the adult faithful but also for "their seed." As God in ancient times had promised to be in covenant with Abraham and his descendants, so in all later days that covenant could pass from parents to their children. Entrance into the covenant and membership in the church embodying it was by birth as well as by rebirth. It was by both conversion and lineal descent. The expectation was that those born into the covenant would progress in adulthood to its full fruition through the experience of conversion. Yet while awaiting that life-changing experience, they were already within the church's membership and subject to its care. Baptism administered to these children was a seal of that covenant, a signification of their inclusion in the church's family and presumably in the grace of God. Correspondingly, bringing these infant children to baptism was one of the privileges exercised by their parents as regenerate members of the church.

This dual understanding of church membership would have created no difficulty if the baptized children making up the second generation were all to have grown up replicating the professions of conversion of the first, for then, as regenerate parents, they would be exercising their church privilege in bringing their own children to baptism. Moreover, like their parents, they could also participate in the second sacrament, the Lord's Supper, a meal restricted to those qualified by such profession. But the times were changing, and the earlier fervor had begun to abate. Though some followed the path of their parents, others could not. Yet many of the latter did not want to desert the church or deny their children the baptism they themselves had received. Their stumbling block was neither lack of belief nor absence of intent, but failure to find conscientiously within themselves that which was most required, the personal life-changing religious experience. How, then, could they be dealt with in their yearning to continue their families in church estate? If they themselves were members, though by descent rather than by conversion, could they not still pass their membership on to their descendants and represent it through their own children's baptism? Or must that privilege, despite its desirability, await their own conversion? The changes in church and society were creating a theological, as well as practical, dilemma.

The problem actually arose as early as 1634 when a grandfather, who was a full communicant in the Dorchester church, sought baptism for his grandchild despite the fact that the parents could make no claim of regeneration. Added requests from parents, as well as grandparents, followed in other localities, and by the late 1640s became sufficiently numerous for the General Court of Massachusetts to ask consideration of the issue by the Cambridge Synod summoned to begin its meetings soon. Pursuant to that request, one of the draft documents for the synod presented an interpretation of baptismal privilege, supported by many clergy, that under specified conditions could meet the new needs. It would have permitted the parents in question to bring their children to baptism if, despite lack of conversion, they "cast not off the covenant of God by some scandalous and obstinate going on in sin."[4] Only by removing themselves from the covenant by grievous behavior could they disrupt the covenant's birthright perpetuation and despoil for their children the right of receiving the baptismal seal. But in the understanding of other clergy this compromised the importance of personal conversion, and the proposed "enlargement of baptism" was opposed. As a result the matter was left unsettled, the founders bequeathing the problem to the following generation.

Failure to deal with the matter, however, could not be indefinitely prolonged. By the late 1650s the need became increasingly great, as a diminishing number of residents were able to bring to the church a personal testimony of their conversion, and individual local congregations began to deal each in its own way with the consequent reduction in presentations of children for baptism. Added therefore to the growing tensions created by the problem itself was the specter of the erosion of uniformity within the religious establishment. Consequently in 1657 the Massachusetts General Court, encouraged also by the General Court of Connecticut, called a select group of clergy to a ministerial assembly to explore the issue further and in 1662 determined to get a definitive judgment from a synod of all the Massachusetts churches. So in that year more than seventy lay and clergy delegates from those congregations gathered in the meetinghouse of First Church, Boston, primarily to answer a question put to them by the General Court, "Who are the subjects of baptism?" In their response they developed the theological position and ecclesiastical practice subsequently nicknamed the "Half-Way Covenant."

The nickname was coined and applied because of the compromise nature of the conclusion. The baptized but still unconverted parents who wanted baptism for their children were seen as both lacking and possessing privileges of church membership. On the one hand, they lacked the privileges of "full communion," chief of which were a partaking of the Lord's Supper and, for males, the right of voting in church matters. On the other hand, these parents were within the covenant by virtue of their birth, and in passing that covenant on to their children they had the privilege of presenting them for the covenant's baptismal seal. Only if they by their own actions had discovenanted themselves was that privilege withdrawn. Yet at this point a further practical consideration was added. As expression of their continuation in covenant, more than simply a scandal-free life was required. For their children to be received for baptism these parents also must profess their assent to the doctrines of the faith and solemnly "own" the covenant, an act in which "they give up themselves and their children to the Lord and subject themselves to the government of Christ in the church."[5] When this is done, their children, by virtue of being born to these parents, are proper "subjects of baptism."

For many in the New England churches in the latter part of the seventeenth century this was, at least temporarily, an adequate solution to a difficult problem. It held within the ministrations and discipline of the church a group of adults otherwise inclined to be marginal to the church's life, and it brought their children into the circle of the church's watchfulness and care. Yet at the same time, by limiting further privileges to the converted, it preserved the concept of the purity of the church so important in early Congregational understanding and in that manner helped maintain the sharp distinction between the church and the world. Particularly prominent among the leaders of those supporting this solution was Richard Mather, whose advocacy of the enlargement of baptism actually dated back to the time when the issue was briefly discussed at the Cambridge Synod of 1648. Not all, however, agreed with the half-way decision. Following the 1662 synod, a minority of the clergy continued to voice opposition, led by John Davenport, also a venerated figure from the earlier era, and supported by the young Increase Mather, son of Richard, soon to be the leading member of the clergy of the new generation. Within the next decade Increase was to change his mind on this issue, but his early years saw him struggling, along with Davenport, against his father.

The main argument of the opponents was that the half-way arrangement did not in fact preserve the purity of the church as its supporters claimed. Although it limited the Lord's Supper to the regenerated, it gave the baptismal privilege to unworthy persons whose inherited covenant membership actually had been lost, so it was alleged, by their failure to come to conversion. Moreover, assumption that the situation could be remedied by their act of "owning the covenant" was deemed by the opponents an exercise in fantasy, for the required pledges that such an act entailed could be kept only by those who acted through the power of God's saving grace. Still further, warned the opponents, the extension of church privileges in this manner would in time lead to additional erosion of standards in the church's practices, not only to a still more permissive extension of baptism, but even to the defilement of the Lord's Supper. And when those developments occur, said Increase Mather, it will be "farewell to New England's peculiar glory of undefiled administration of holy things."[6] The majority party countered such dire prediction by urging that the half-way covenant would provide new protection for the purity of the Lord's Supper, for now parents would not seek full communion by pretense in order to qualify for having their children baptized. Nor would churches be tempted to lower the requirements for admission to full membership in order that the new generation might be kept within the care and discipline of the church. So the dispute continued even after the synod's decision had been reached and had been commended to the local congregations.

The result was at first only a gradual adoption of the half-way practice by the individual churches. In Massachusetts, where the General Court's response to the synod was somewhat indecisive, no more than two-fifths of the congregations had accepted the practice by 1672, ten years after the synod. In First Church, Boston, a division occurred when a majority followed its new pastor, John Davenport, and rejected the

half-way plan, leading to the withdrawal of others from the congregation to form Boston's Third Church, or "Old South." In other instances
whole congregations, loath to give up old ways, resisted their more
venturesome clergy on this matter, while remaining under their leadership. In Dorchester, for example, where Richard Mather was pastor, the
church delayed adoption of half-way measures until 1677, seven years
following his death. Only when a series of severe disasters struck,
beginning in 1675, did the change occur there, and more rapidly in
Massachusetts as a whole, as renewed efforts were made to enlarge and
strengthen the church in the face of new perils. A similar pattern of
gradual adoption prevailed in Connecticut, where the colony government formally voted to permit either the older or the newer baptismal
practice. Yet in time the more rigid way of the past was set aside in
Connecticut as well, and by the early eighteenth century almost all New
England Congregational churches had accepted the half-way view.

For some churches, however, this alteration of requirements for
baptism seemed not fully sufficient to meet the needs of the changing
times. So further modification in baptismal practice was made, even as
the purists had warned, to draw the community more fully into the
orbit of the church. Mainly this involved an extension of baptism to
those who could make no birthright claim to covenant membership, but
would be willing to make the commitment of "owning the covenant" as
a condition for receiving the sacrament for themselves and for bringing
their children to baptism. Here was a further extension of the half-way
system and, in fact, an additional category of church membership. Some
churches maintained triple-entry books to keep this more complicated
record straight: one column for those qualified for full communion by
conversion; a second column for those who received baptism by birthright qualification; and a third column for those parents formerly outside the church who were granted half-way membership. In time this
latter group was expanded more when, in the early eighteenth century,
some congregations offered half-way covenant membership as a recruitment device to attract groups of young people into the church. Although this was membership without the privilege of full communion,
Congregational churches were opening their doors more widely in their
concern for a broader ministry in their communities. Some, by endorsing a more rigorous revivalism, were soon to resist the compromise of

purity that the new practices entailed. Yet in the early 1700s others favored the evangelizing strategy of making a larger place for the unregenerate in the life of the church.

The Reforming Synod

When the synod of 1662 published its recommendation to the churches concerning the enlargement of baptism, it added what it termed "a word of caution and exhortation to the youth of the country, the children of our churches, whose interest we have here asserted." The "rising generation" could now come more easily into the church and must be advised concerning the obligations this entailed. New members were urged to humility and obedience that they might "lie under the word and will of Christ" and "learn subjection to Christ's holy government." All relations with God, it was noted, "come loaden with duty," and so the task of dedicated faithfulness rested heavily on the shoulders of those to whom new church privilege was now being given. With the admonition came a corresponding warning: failure to fulfill religious duties would bring rejection by God as a "generation of God's wrath." Therefore, the instruction concluded, "Let it not be said, that when the first and best generation in New England were gathered to their fathers, there arose another generation after them that knew not the Lord."[7] The struggle for the hearts and loyalties of the successors to the founders was truly under way.

From many of the published sermons of the ensuing decades it would appear that the struggle was constantly in danger of being a losing cause. The preachers of those years catalogued time and again the failure of the new generation to live up to the standards of the past, inveighing against its defection and threatening the divine judgment this would bring. The term _jeremiad_ has been used to identify this type of sermon, reminiscent as it was of the description of Israel's sin and punishment set forth in the Old Testament's Lamentations of Jeremiah. Particularly emphasized in this preaching was religious decline as a national phenomenon, interpreted to be a breaking of the national covenant that God had made with New England. In these sermons the first generation founders were portrayed, in their coming to the New World, as latter-day counterparts of Israel's heroes. They were the "Abrahams" on pilgrimage under the call of God. They were the

"Davids" who by God's guidance brought reformation and order into church and state. But now the glory of their land was fading away. "How is the gold become dim!" exclaimed Samuel Danforth in 1670, "how is the most fine gold changed!" In the churches, he charged, there is "a careless, remiss, flat, dry, cold, dead frame of spirit," where Scripture and sermon and prayer and sacrament are simply formal "matters of custom and ceremony," lest they hinder "eager prosecution of other things which hearts are set upon." Likewise throughout the land there are "inordinate worldly cares, predominant lusts, and malignant distempers" that "stifle and cloak our affections to the kingdom of God."[8]

This indictment was not simply of individual persons, but of an entire people. The condition of New England was being described and its future was at stake. Increase Mather, who contributed abundantly to this condemnatory preaching, spoke in despair about the apostasy that had overtaken the whole land. There was a decay in the "power of godliness" in all places. Whereas the first generation had developed life under an ecclesiastical and civil constitution "like unto new Jerusalem," now "another and more sinful generation [has] risen up in their stead."[9] So, in the manner of the jeremiad, he added the prediction of divine judgment. In 1674 Mather spoke of "the day of trouble coming . . . and such trouble too as the like hath not been."[10] A short while later he declared that in this judgment "instead of peace, there shall be wars, instead of plenty poverty, instead of health terrible sickness, instead of planting, plucking up and destroying."[11] The wrath of God will be painfully known, and the fate of Israel will be experienced again in New England. This was the anguished message of the jeremiad preachers.

Serious question has been raised in recent study as to whether the religious situation was as grave in the late seventeenth and early eighteenth centuries as the jeremiad preachers alleged it to be. Revivals throughout this period continued to stimulate religious commitment, and records of church membership do not reflect the major "decline" in religious interest that historians have traditionally attributed to the times. It may well be that overstatement of sin and peril was a strategy used in the jeremiads to encourage repentance and reform. Yet in the late 1670s it appeared as though these prophecies of judgment were being fulfilled, for a series of catastrophes struck the land. First and most devastating was the outbreak of armed conflict with neighboring

American Indian groups, the King Philip's War. Except for a brief skirmish some forty years earlier, relations with the American Indian people had been friendly. The settlements had expanded through land purchase, laws preventing aggressive behavior against the native population were in place, some Christian missions among the American Indians had developed, and the tribal and colonial governments had formal treaties of peace. But in the summer of 1675 this came to an end through a sudden and unexpected attack, led by a Wampanoag chief known as King Philip in connection with his effort to consolidate several separate groups and increase their power. The violence was severe and the destruction widespread, bringing extensive loss of property and life and terrorizing the colonists for more than a year until the conflict was brought to an end.

Shortly thereafter further calamities were experienced, especially in Massachusetts Bay. In 1676 and 1679 two wide-ranging fires swept through Boston, each destroying large portions of the city. Meanwhile an epidemic of smallpox took its toll and a series of shipwrecks brought unusually heavy losses. Also at this time the colony's political liberties were increasingly threatened through oppression by the restored Stuart monarchy in England, and its religious establishment was jeopardized by corresponding efforts of English officials to introduce into the colony the practice of Anglican worship. The opening of the last quarter of the seventeenth century was a period of both actual and impending catastrophe, and jeremiad preachers easily found within it instances of the wrathful judgment of God. Michael Wigglesworth said the times reflected "God's controversy with New England."

In the thought of the clergy, led by Increase Mather, this situation called for special response. The causes for such intensity of divine punishment must be more clearly understood and the colony as a whole summoned to appropriate acts in seeking God's mercy. The General Court agreed and ordered a synod of the Massachusetts churches to meet in late 1679. Two questions were to be discussed: What are the evils that have provoked the Lord to bring his judgments on New England? and What is to be done that those evils may be reformed?[12] The synod's final report, titled The Necessity of Reformation, responded to each of these queries. First, the condition of the colony's life was examined, and thirteen separate "evils" were identified as constituting its sin in God's sight. These included general decay in spiritual fervor, increase in pride, neglect of worship, Sabbath breaking, decline in family religious exercises, uncharitable attitudes, intemperance, lack of truthfulness, inordinate love of worldly things, and obstinacy that rebels at repentance and reform.

But the synod's task was to encourage reform, and it answered the second question with recommendation of remedies for combatting the evils provoking to God. Some remedies urged a strengthening of the churches, through a vigorous exercise of church discipline, a watchfulness in preserving the purity of the Lord's Supper, an endeavor to provide a pastor, teacher, and ruling elder for each congregation, and encouragement of proper financial maintenance for these officers of the church. Other recommendations focused on more public matters, such as urging greater use of legislation contributing to the moral health of society, encouragement of learning through the founding and support of schools and colleges, and exemplary behavior on the part of those in authority, whether ecclesiastical or civil, that they might serve as beneficial models for all.

Beyond these somewhat conventional remedies, however, the synod encouraged a further action ultimately to play an important role in New England Congregationalism. Seizing upon a practice initiated by some congregations at the time of the King Philip's War, it called upon all the churches to enter periodically into solemn acts of covenant renewal. The problem in the land, the synod held, could be summarized in the last analysis in terms of flagrant covenant breaking. Particularly was this explicit within the churches, for the commitments undertaken in church membership, whether that of full communion or half-way status, were simply not being fulfilled. Covenant commitment must therefore be taken more seriously, if decay in morals and decline in spiritual fervor were to be reversed. And one way to encourage that greater intensity of dedication could be the corporate act of a congregation in which the gathered people offer in common voice a renewal of their pledge of fidelity to God. This covenant renewal, noted the synod's report, was practiced in moments of great crisis in biblical times and now must be performed again in these latter days of peril. Such acts, it said, have special persuasive power, for they put "an awe of God upon the consciences" of persons obliging themselves in this solemn way and therefore can lead to a "more close and holy walking before the Lord."[13] The synod's recommendation struck a responsive chord among the churches, and the setting of special occasions for corporate covenant renewal quickly became an important part of their life.

Stoddardeanism

Soon, however, another and different voice was heard speaking to the need for change in the churches' evangelizing efforts. In 1669 Solomon Stoddard became pastor of the church in Northampton on the Massachusetts western frontier, and in his fifty-nine years of ministry in that position he became an advocate for still more drastic approaches. Some of his views on church and sacraments seemed even to undercut the foundations of traditional Congregationalism.

Stoddard began his ministry by endorsing the practice of half-way church membership, his congregation having adopted it only months before his arrival. For eight years he faithfully baptized according to its requirements and kept membership rolls distinguishing between those who could and could not claim for themselves the experience of conversion. By 1677, however, he became disillusioned with respect to this procedure and began to replace it with a more open system. For one thing, there were good people in the community still being denied baptism who ought to be incorporated into the church's life. So he offered baptism to all "morally sincere" adults making profession of Christian faith and also to those persons' children. Even more, it was shocking to him that among the adult baptized in the Northampton congregation only one in eight was deemed qualified to receive the Lord's Supper, and in the 1690s he began to advocate the further step of enlarging access to the communion. He would make the Lord's Supper available to all baptized adults within the church, the only added qualification being that they live without scandal. The sacrament should no longer be limited to the regenerate few, but should be shared with persons who were still on pilgrimage toward conversion.

Contributing to Stoddard's new view of communion was his conviction that conversion was not as easily identifiable as his predecessors in the Congregational tradition had supposed. There is no certainty from outward appearances, for regenerate and unregenerate often behave alike, and making judgments with respect to the individual's inner life is beyond the capacity of the church. Even in self-examination persons are uncertain concerning the presence or absence of saving grace, for in the last analysis it is only God's prerogative to know the human heart. For Stoddard conversion continued to be the ultimate goal of the church's preaching and discipline, his own efforts in revivalism being emphatic toward that end, but its identification was too uncertain to serve as criterion for admission to the Lord's Supper.

Additionally, the Lord's Supper itself was reinterpreted by Stoddard. He reaffirmed the traditional view of the sacrament as a meal of spiritual nourishment for the regenerate, but he added the conviction that it could equally be a means of conversion for the unregenerate. For those who had begun the spiritual journey through baptism and affirmation of the doctrines of the faith, the experience of partaking of the Lord's Supper could be remarkable assistance along the way. It was a converting ordinance and, he said, should be administered to the unconverted within the church for their "saving good." Most clergy, led by Increase Mather, vigorously protested this practice as further compromising the purity of the church, but Stoddard's view was now entered into the changing theological and ecclesiastical pattern generated by the early eighteenth-century churches of New England.

The Massachusetts Charter

In addition to confronting problems located within the church, the second and third generations faced a drastically changing political scene. The political independence of the colonies was being progressively reduced, and along with it the protection provided for religious uniformity and for the maintenance of a holy commonwealth. This too called for adjustment of the church's outlook and practice in the light of new times.

The troubles began in Massachusetts as early as 1675 when the British government, determining to pay closer attention to the affairs of the American colonies, assigned their supervision to a committee known as Lords of Trade and sent Edward Randolph to Boston as agent to carry out its work. Randolph, it turned out, had little love for New England, and his fourteen years in Massachusetts were marked by unrelenting efforts to curtail the colony's distinctive practices in religious and political matters and to bring it more fully under the home government's control. In this he was supported by a group of Boston citizens, led by Joseph Dudley, who were interested in the commercial advantages that could come from closer alliance with the British crown. As Anglicans, Baptists, and Presbyterians, these leaders were also unsympathetic with the denial of freedom of worship enforced by the Congregationalists of the holy commonwealth.

Randolph's efforts led first to letters from the king to the colony demanding obedience to specific royal decrees. In 1679 the demands included taking an oath of allegiance, repealing laws restricting the political franchise to church members, and granting freedom for Anglican worship. When the Massachusetts General Court's reply contained only vague promises, Randolph continued his efforts, obtaining in 1682 another royal letter threatening legal proceedings against the charter should there be failure to comply and, in the following year, a legal action summoning the colony to show cause before the English courts why the charter should not be revoked. The colony, however, continued to resist. A large town meeting was held in Boston at which Increase Mather compared the British king to ancient Israel's Ahab in his attempt to seize Naboth's vineyard, and when the vote was taken, not a hand was raised in support of complying with the royal demand. Then the blow fell, and in 1684 the charter of Massachusetts was annulled.

The annulment of the charter meant that every legal act upon which the colony had been built in the fifty-five years of its existence was swept away. Institutions of both civil government and ecclesiastical establishment based upon the provisions of the original grant were null and void. Even titles of individuals to their land had no value. The land now reverted to the crown and could be reassigned only through payment of new fees and taxes. Moreover, a new governmental system was proposed, to be inclusive of all the New England colonies and administered by representatives of the crown. Instead of self-government, there would be rule by a royal governor and his council, the laws for the colonies would be England's laws, and Anglican worship would be permitted. With this development the holy commonwealth was doomed and all New England would become a royal colony entirely subject to outside rule.

The plan for this new colonial administration was drawn up during the reign of Charles II, but his death postponed its actualization until his successor, James II, sent Sir Edmund Andros to Boston in 1686 to be the new governor. Andros's short rule bore out many of the colonists' most dreadful fears. The Massachusetts General Court was abolished.

The power of taxation was taken from the town meetings, and arbitrary taxes were imposed by the governor. All private titles to lands were rescinded and heavy fees were assessed for their recovery, and common lands in and around Boston were expropriated for the governor's private use. The press, heretofore an ally of Congregational leadership, was placed under heavy censorship. Anglican worship was introduced. At first the Old South meetinghouse in Boston was commandeered for this purpose when not in use for Congregational services, and then in 1689 King's Chapel, the first Episcopal church in New England, was built. The protective writ of habeas corpus was suspended, and civil liberties were suppressed through vice-admiralty courts appointed by the crown. One observer declared that the people now had no privilege left to them other than that of not being sold as slaves.

Andros also drew other colonies into this administrative system. Quickly Plymouth and Rhode Island were added, and then New York and New Jersey. A dramatic effort to save Connecticut from a similar fate occurred when Andros went to Hartford in 1687 intent on seizing its charter. At an evening meeting the colony's governor was resisting Andros's demands, with the document on a table before him, when suddenly the candles were blown out. Upon their being relighted, the charter had disappeared, carried away by an aide and hidden in the trunk of a great oak tree, where it was secretly preserved. Even without confiscation of the charter, however, the colony was forced to submit.

For three years the people of New England suffered under this new tyranny. Massachusetts especially felt the brunt of its force, but efforts at resistance were also made there. Boston merchants developed the art of smuggling to circumvent new navigation acts. Neighboring towns sustained self-government by continuing their town meetings. Most courageous was the town of Ipswich, which, under the leadership of its minister John Wise, refused to pay any of the new taxes. Wise, who has been called "the first great American democrat," developed a political philosophy early in his public life that stressed the natural rights of the individual and the formation of government by social contract. Rejecting all forms of monarchy and aristocracy, he affirmed that political power rests solely with the people and that political decisions must be made by popular vote. In the struggle with Andros this meant "no taxation without representation," a position in which Wise anticipated the later protests of the American Revolution by more than seventy-five years. For his resistance to colonial authority, however, Wise was imprisoned, fined, and temporarily suspended from his ministry. Although other clergy were sympathetic to the cause, none followed Wise to this political extreme. Preaching during this time of crisis largely stressed the continuing importance of conversion and moral reform as needed conditions for God's covenant care. Yet the most influential political help toward restoring some self-rule soon came from the Bay colony's leading member of the clergy, Increase Mather.

Early in 1689 word arrived in Boston of the overthrow of James II and the calling of William and Mary to the British throne. Rejoicing in this development, the people of Massachusetts, with some clergy among the leadership, acted quickly to restore their old government. Andros, Randolph, and Dudley were imprisoned, eighty-seven-year-old Simon Bradstreet was called back into the governorship, and the old charter was returned to use, changed only to eliminate the church membership qualification that had originally been required for the franchise. Such precipitous action, however, was premature. Although the new British sovereign had no intention of continuing the repressive policies of his predecessor, he also refused to relinquish control of the American colonies and even considered restoring Andros to his lost post. Fortunately, Increase Mather was in England on a self-appointed political mission to negotiate as much independence as could be obtained. With Mather's urging, an order of restraint against Andros was issued. It took two more years of discussion, however, to achieve the final results.

In 1692 Mather returned with a new charter for Massachusetts, incorporating some of the colony's wishes but also indicating that colonial New England was entering a different day. Self-government for the colony was restored through an elected legislature, to which the power of taxation was given. The authority of local governments was recognized in the life of the towns. And the land claims of individuals and communities previously established through the General Court were reaffirmed. However, other provisions of the new charter changed the old order in drastic ways. Massachusetts, enlarged now by the inclusion of Plymouth and Maine, was made a royal province under the administration of a governor and other officials all appointed by the king. English authorities had the right to overrule laws of the colony's legislature if they were unacceptable to the crown. The requirement of church membership for voting privilege was formally abolished, a property qualification being substituted in its stead. And in accord with England's 1689 Act of Toleration, freedom of worship was granted in the colonies for all churches of Protestant faith. The Congregational churches remained the major religious force in the colony, but their monopoly, and the holy commonwealth supporting it, had come to an end.

Brattle Street Church

Within the next decade a further challenge confronted traditional Congregationalism, as the new freedom was employed for introducing liberalizing tendencies into Boston's church life. The main occurrence in this development was the founding in 1699 of the Brattle Street Church, Boston's fourth congregation but different from the others by virtue of its innovations. Initiated by a group of young men serving as tutors at Harvard College while active in Boston area churches, the new congregation committed itself at the outset to a departure from several of the long-standing New England customs in church polity and worship. The ultimate effect was to disrupt still more the religious uniformity that had long prevailed.

In matters of polity the Brattle Street congregation altered the qualification for church membership and the privileges which such membership entailed, easing the strictness previously observed. Admission to the church and eligibility for full communion no longer required the personal relation of religious experience and an examination by the congregation, as had been Boston's custom. It was sufficient that the pastor be satisfied with respect to the individual's "visible sanctity" and that the pastor recommend the person to the church. Members of the congregation could, if they desired, inquire further into the life and behavior of those who are so recommended. But if no objection was raised, this was considered concurrence with the pastor's judgment granting approval for communion. Baptism was also made more generally available, exceeding the latitude previously commended for Massachusetts churches in the Half-Way Covenant decision. Baptism, said the Brattle Street Church founders, should be allowed for three groups of people: (1) those who profess their faith in Christ and obedience to him, (2) the children of such persons, and (3) any child presented by any professed Christian as sponsor committed to the child's education in

Christian faith. This latter provision was a return, in a sense, to the heretofore rejected practice of recognizing "godparent" responsibility.

One further polity innovation expanded the franchise within the church for the election of its ministry. Previous practice limited the vote to male members in full communion. The new arrangement sanctioned voting by all baptized adults, women as well as men, within the congregation. Although women's voting in other churches was long delayed, the extension of the franchise beyond full communicants soon found a more ready reception. The Brattle Street Church founders also instituted two changes, troubling to traditionalists, in the conduct of worship. One was a return to reading Scripture without the pastor's interpretation, a reintroduction of the "dumb reading" practiced in the Church of England and vigorously criticized by earlier Puritan preachers. The second was the restoration of the Lord's Prayer in the public worship of the church.

Disturbing as these innovations were to the clergy of the Boston area, it was even more distressing that the organizers of the new church did not seek approval of neighboring churches for its founding, as both custom and law had long required. Their independence was even more flagrant when they set about the task of obtaining a minister for their venture. Their selection was Benjamin Colman, a young man of considerable gifts who had studied with them at Harvard and who shared their innovating concerns. Knowing, however, that he would not gain approval for ordination from Boston pastors and also aware that he was currently in England, they advised him to obtain ordination there. Colman agreed, and in late 1699 he was ordained in presbyterian fashion to Christian ministry by the London presbytery. Added, therefore, to the Brattle Street Church's other violations of tradition was the fact that its pastor, according to Congregational standards, lacked proper authorization for his office.

Opposition was strong. Letters of protest were sent by members of the Massachusetts Bay clergy to leaders of the new congregation. The irregularities in this venture, said one of the letters, showed the church's founders to be "unstudied" in matters of church order, and this could lead to a "schism that will dishonor God, grieve the good people, and be a matter of triumph to the bad." Further, on the specific point of voting rights in the church for women, the fearful observation was made that "the females are certainly more than the males and consequently

the choice of ministers is put into their hands."[14] Not all were as
hostile, however, and by early 1700 the Brattle Street Church was
granted formal recognition, members of the Boston clergy sharing with
Benjamin Colman in the appropriate exercises. Still the controversy
continued, promoted chiefly by Increase Mather, whose cooperation in
the recognition must have been with great reluctance. Soon he published a tract, under the title *Order of the Gospel*, in which he defended
the traditional New England way as being that which God had prescribed as "the form of his house" and declared that deviation therefrom
in New England would be "a greater sin and provocation to Christ than
in any place in the whole world." Refusing to be intimidated, the
opponents replied with their *Gospel Order Revived*, not only defending
the innovations but also noting the irony of the fact that those who had
fled from the Act of Uniformity should "impose it on their neighbors
and entail the mischief on their posterity."[15] The clergy responded with
a vote protesting the "unadvised proceedings of people to gather
churches,"[16] but religious liberty had now found new allies within
Congregationalism itself.

Efforts Toward Control

Conscious of the threats taking place to the uniformity heretofore
prevailing within Congregationalism, many clergy in Massachusetts
sought to achieve greater effectiveness against the inroads of innovation.
No longer, under the new charter, could they rely on help from the civil
government, and so efforts were advanced to organize agencies of control among the clergy and the churches themselves. In the process these
clergy were actually joined by Benjamin Colman and members of his
congregation who after recognition allied themselves with the more
conservative movement. This may be because that effort tended paradoxically toward a modified presbyterian position in church government.

Meeting regularly throughout the early 1700s in district gatherings, the Massachusetts clergy recommended through their representatives in 1705 a group of proposals to organize the ministers into associations and the churches into consociations, with the expectation that this
structure could function with sufficient authority to protect against
deviations from the generally accepted patterns of church life. The plan

itself, however, embodied sufficient deviation from traditional congregational autonomy to prevent it from being accepted in its entirety in the Bay colony. Critics of the plan, an observer recalled, "thought the liberty of particular churches to be in danger of being too much limited and infringed" by the proposals to warrant their full adoption. [17] In Massachusetts, therefore, historic Congregationalism's self-defense was not to be carried out by a means compromising its own nature.

Connecticut, however, provided a different story. The Connecticut clergy shared the desire of many in Massachusetts for more centralized control in protecting the uniformity of doctrine and discipline within the churches, and their political situation gave them added advantage over their northern neighbor. Thanks to the efforts of the Connecticut General Court the colony did not suffer the serious charter disruption experienced by Massachusetts and found itself in a particularly favorable situation for legislating on ecclesiastical governance when in 1707 one of its own clergy, Gurdon Saltonstall, was elected to the governorship. Consequently in 1708 the Saybrook Synod, made up of clergy and lay representatives of the churches, gathered under court order to deal with the matter, drafting the Saybrook Platform, a plan for organization and government of the churches based on the Massachusetts Proposals of 1705. Once approved by the legislature, this became the legally recognized standard for Connecticut Congregationalism, and its associations of ministers and consociations of churches were gradually created. Opponents protested its presbyterianizing tendencies, however, and the next decades witnessed variety in the extent to which the plan was effectively put into practice. Yet it remained as Connecticut's official arrangement for its churches until 1784 when all reference to it was omitted in the revision of statutes following the American Revolution.

Toleration and Ecumenism

More than anywhere else, throughout the decades of the late seventeenth and early eighteenth centuries, the changes occurring in American Congregationalism were evident in its relationship to increasingly numerous non-Congregational churches. Beginning with its inherited commitment to a strict religious uniformity, developed by the clergy and enforced by the magistrate, it moved under the pressure of the times to recognition of both the necessity and the value of a cooperative

Protestant pluralism. Limitations remained with respect to the degree of validity accorded other churches, but the development of new attitudes led to increased toleration and an emerging ecumenical consciousness.

The most severe mid-seventeenth-century actions to protect New England Congregational uniformity were taken against certain Quakers who sought a place in Massachusetts. Founded in England by George Fox in the 1640s, the Quaker movement, through its emphasis on the unmediated experience of divine revelation, represented to Puritans a perspective akin to antinomianism. Frightened by the uninhibited extremes of ecstacy to which this could lead, New England Congregationalism quickly attempted to close the doors to a Quaker presence. Extremely harsh efforts were used in the process. The first Quaker missionaries appeared in Massachusetts in 1656. On recommendation of the Commissioners of the United Colonies, the Massachusetts General Court passed a severe law against these intruders, with penalties of fines, whipping, imprisonment, and banishment. Quaker determination, however, ignored these restrictions and intensified efforts to bring the Quaker message to Boston. Missionaries continued to arrive, including some who had been banished, and in 1658 the General Court voted to impose the death penalty upon those who returned to the colony for a third time after expulsion. Some among the group, however, were not intimidated, determining "to look the law in the face," and by 1661 four Quakers were executed on the Boston Common. At the same time Quakers began to appear in other communities, and voices, both Quaker and non-Quaker, called for a halt to this severe recrimination. Help soon came from the British crown when Charles II ordered the suspension of the death penalty in these cases. However, the antagonism against the Quakers was by no means set aside.

Treatment of Baptists in the colonies was not as severe as actions against Quakers, but there was also hostility toward this deviation from Congregational uniformity. Although Baptists generally accepted the Calvinist theology and shared with Congregationalists a common Puritan origin, their repudiation of infant baptism led to a fundamental difference in the understanding of the nature of the church and its relation to the surrounding community. The earliest Baptist church in New England was founded in 1639 when Roger Williams, then in banishment in Rhode Island, came to Baptist conviction and led in this venture. Soon thereafter Baptist sympathizers began to appear in the other colonies, Massachusetts legislating as early as 1644 against dissemination of their views. In 1651 a major confrontation occurred in the Bay colony when a group of Rhode Island Baptists conducted services in the home of a Baptist convert in Lynn and rebaptized several adults persuaded by their message. Discovered and arrested, they were fined and one was whipped before being released to return to their home colony. Less severe in penalty, but more disastrous in public perception, was the case of Henry Dunster, president of Harvard College, who because of growing Baptist conviction refused to present his newly born child to the Cambridge church for baptism. The case ultimately went to the General Court, which instructed a committee of clergy and lay elders to confer with Dunster on his responsibility. Unyielding in his Baptist views, Dunster resigned his presidency and went into retirement. Further tension occurred in the mid-1660s when an attempt was made to found a Baptist church in Charlestown. Members were tried, convicted, disenfranchised, and warned of imprisonment by the court if they persisted in their errors. Refusing to recant, the congregation moved to an island in Boston Harbor, where it remained for some years in semiexile as legal controversy continued.

A defense of religious uniformity, with its refusal of toleration for dissenters, was strongly maintained by the Congregational clergy throughout these years and on into the 1680s. The second generation was not inclined to abandon the view of the founders that Congregationalism constituted the only true way and that its monopoly should be enforced by civil authority. In 1672 Thomas Shepard Jr. condemned talk of toleration that might lead magistrates to sheath their swords, noting that the commonwealth is protected by the "uniting conduct of those two great ordinances of God, the magistracy and the ministry."[18] The following year Urian Oakes, in insisting that the magistrate should only "tolerate what is tolerable," refused to allow conscientiousness in false belief as justification for exclusion from restraint. Were that to be granted, he declared, it could lead to the abhorrent possibility of toleration for "a conscientious Papist or Socinian or Quaker (the most notorious heretic in the world)." Political fears likewise underlay these passions. In 1680 William Hubbard charged that Quakers were not only blasphemers but also "open enemies of the government itself." And in 1681 Thomas Cobbett feared toleration of Baptists in New England would cause so many to "flock over hither" that they "would sink our small vessel" and, by "making infant baptism a nullity," destroy both churches and civil order.[19]

It was in the late 1660s and early 1670s that actual changes began to take place. No longer under the threat of capital punishment, thanks to the king's order, Quakers gradually entered the colonies, and by 1674 a Quaker meeting was established in Boston. Resistance by civil authorities continued, the General Court legislating against such gatherings in 1675 and two years later ordering the constables to search out and disperse all Quaker assemblies, with punishment meted out through the Cart and Whip Act. Yet the movement was irreversible, William Coddington observing in a letter to Governor Bellingham that he "may as well withhold the flowing of the tide into Massachusetts Bay" as attempt to prevent "the workings of the God of truth in the hearts" of the Quaker people.[20] Soon Quakers received more moderate treatment under Governors Leverett in Massachusetts and John Winthrop, Jr., in Connecticut.

Similarly, the restrictions against the Baptists were gradually lifted. In 1669 a group of English Congregationalists wrote to Massachusetts magistrates to urge toleration of the Baptists struggling to maintain their small island community in Boston Harbor, and a few years later under Leverett's governorship permission was granted for their move into Boston. In 1679 these Baptists erected their own church building in the city and finally received the General Court's permission for its use for worship in 1681. After 1682 there were no formal indictments brought against the Baptists in the colonies, although it was not until the 1730s that a second Boston area Baptist church was founded.

Change in outward circumstance was accompanied by change in clergy attitude, a development particularly evident in the thought of Increase Mather. Throughout the early years of his ministry in Boston Mather favored exclusion of Baptist and Quaker dissenters from the colony. The Congregational churches, he said, are "tender vines," and dissenters are "little foxes despoiling them." In his biography of his father, Cotton Mather noted that in those early years Increase approved the "civil magistrate exerting his power as a matter of restraint" upon deviation from the Congregational way. By the end of his ministry, however, he favored toleration, participating in 1718 in the ordination of a new minister for the Baptist church in Boston and declaring that, despite his continued disagreement with their view of baptism, the members of that church were "in the judgment of rational charity godly persons."[21] One intervening factor of great importance was the imposition in 1692 of the new Massachusetts charter, which mandated toleration of dissenters. Yet it is clear that Mather's later support for this broad freedom was as much from principle as from political pragmatism. For one thing, Mather came to see the superiority of obedience to conscience over enforced compliance in the making of religious commitment, for to act against conscience is "to deny the God that is above." And further, he came to realize the danger of allowing the magistrate the power of the sword over religion, for the one with the power will decide what is right and "always assume the power of persecuting."[22]

Also significant for these developments in early eighteenth-century Congregationalism were the additional contributions of Cotton Mather, who advanced the passive permissiveness of toleration to a more active concern for genuine ecumenism. Like his father, Cotton Mather accommodated himself to the political necessities created by the new charter. No longer, he knew, could a religious monopoly be maintained by magistrate's might, nor should such effort to throttle liberty be approved. Preaching the sermon at the Baptist ordination in 1718, he identified himself with the new order, declaring liberty of conscience to be a natural human right and designating freedom of private judgment in the affairs on one's salvation as necessary protection against "church tyranny."[23] But for Cotton Mather, now leading a third generation in the new land, there was an additional ideal to be pursued. This was the goal of Christian unity. He had observed at a distance an experiment in church unity in the early 1690s when Congregational and Presbyterian clergy in England declared themselves to be "United Ministers" and accepted, as a joint proclamation, the Heads of Agreement, a detailed identification of areas of common polity and practice. Although the union lasted only half a dozen years and never involved the laity of the churches, it gave Cotton Mather inspiration for a bold, new emphasis in his ministry. More than simply accept one another, he came to affirm, churches must join together in Christian union, sharing in common endeavor "to advance the Kingdom of God."[24]

For Cotton Mather, however, no technical ministerial agreement nor other institutional structure could suffice for this purpose. Rather, the union of churches must be the unity of Christian persons joined in common Christian experience and committed to its expression in socially significant acts. Mather's vocabulary contained two basic terms summarizing this emphasis: *piety* and *do good*. Drawing upon new impulses coming from European Pietism, with whose leaders he corresponded, Mather believed that personal experience of redemption was superior to all else in determining Christian identity. Although orthodox doctrine must be urged as God's truth and Congregational polity commended as God's way, these in the last analysis were of lesser importance than the saving experience of God's mercy. So this "piety" of heart religion was Christianity's most distinguishing mark, realized in a personal faith receptive to and empowered by divine grace. Furthermore, the saving private experience also must have completion in outward moral action, and Cotton Mather therefore equally stressed the commitment to "do good" as the public form of a Christian presence. Developed as early as 1710 in his influential *Essays to do Good*, this theme called upon Christian persons for active engagement in a variety of good works for social improvement. "Sirs," he wrote, "you must get up and be doing,"[25] and to aid in this he encouraged the founding of numerous societies devoted to programs of human welfare. Theologically understood, this was the supreme work of the Holy Spirit, touching the heart and empowering the will with divine love.

Within this work of the Holy Spirit also resided the hope for Christian union. If doctrine and church organization sometimes divide, the experience of the Spirit can unite. Piety and good works are not confined by the narrow borders of theological definition or polity prescription, nor are they limited by the denominational divisions such restrictions often create. Sectarianism, Cotton Mather believed, can be overcome by attention to this more basic level of Christian experience, where Christian persons of differing creeds and forms of church life can have access to Christ's redemption and join in commitment to its moral manifestation. "Godliness" of life is the key. And then, Mather mused, there could even be intercommunion among the churches: "To see a godly Presbyterian, a godly Independent, a godly Antipaedobaptist, a godly Episcopalian, and a godly Lutheran, all sitting down together in communion at the same Table of the Lord, would be to wise men a very grateful spectacle."[26] Cotton Mather remained a dedicated Congregationalist to his dying day, but his ecumenical vision added a new dimension to eighteenth-century Congregationalism, pointing toward developments to come.

THEOLOGY

Despite the cultural, political, and ecclesiastical changes characterizing the concluding decades of the seventeenth century and the early decades of the eighteenth, the theology of Congregational divines throughout these years displayed a remarkable staying power. Committed to an "evangelical Calvinism" by inheritance from the first New England generation, the clergy sons and grandsons of the founders remained largely within the bounds of that theological heritage. It has sometimes been alleged by twentieth-century interpreters that the walls of doctrinal defense were in fact breached during this period through a subtle incorporation of an Arminian viewpoint into the Calvinist theology. Although the language remained orthodox, Puritanism was yielding, it has been said, to the pressures of a new theological liberalism by surreptitiously implying that the appropriation of saving grace in reality depended upon the freedom of human choice. Predestination therefore was emptied of its classic meaning, and human effort was accorded an enhanced role in the process of salvation. Without doubt these decades witnessed some theological modifications anticipating larger changes to come. It is incorrect, however, to include Arminianism among them. Congregational divines emphatically criticized Arminianism as found in both English and American Anglicanism and did not begin to experiment with it as a liberalization of their own theology until the time of the Great Awakening in the 1740s. The second and third generations of Congregational clergy remained firmly committed to the central themes of their inherited Calvinism.

Reaffirming the Foundations

Like their Puritan predecessors, these theologians focused their thoughts upon the covenant of grace and understood that covenant as a relationship with God into which one is brought by divine choice and power. To Increase Mather, for instance, entrance into the covenant is by God's subduing and capturing those who are chosen, that the direction of their lives may be reversed and they may be newly empowered by the gift of grace. There is nothing here resembling a contractual agreement between parties as equals, nor is there recognition of such human abilities as could freely accept an offered divine gift. Fallen humanity rebels against God and needs first to be tamed. The source of the problem is the human will, turned inward in self-love, and this must be broken. Inability itself, said Increase, is a product of this fallen will, and the "cannot" protested by some who would hide behind native weakness is in reality a "willful cannot." So the drastic purifying action of God must begin the process of conversion and renewal. God's act, then, leads one to contrition, to humiliation, and finally to the faith that cleanses the soul through receiving the healing graces of Christ. Moreover, life within the covenant continues to be under the preeminence of God. Grace, Increase pointed out, implies superiority of the giver, and the life of the Christian therefore must be one of humility and obedience under God's rule. In it one is conscripted to be a soldier for Christ, who is the "Captain of our salvation."[27]

In the generation that followed, strong emphasis continued to be placed on the unconditioned sovereignty of God. When Cotton Mather discussed the covenant of grace, he stressed primarily its character as an absolute covenant resting upon God's predestining decree. Correspondingly, he minimized the covenant's conditional nature. Conditional covenants, he felt, played into the hands of Arminianism by allowing too great a possibility for human effort as prerequisite for the fulfillment of the covenant conditions. "Our election is indeed absolute," he wrote, adding, "No decree of God is conditional," for such contingency in divine plan would be "derogating to the perfection of God."[28]

In this connection Cotton Mather even downplayed the significance of "preparation" for conversion, a concern so important for many of the founders. Despite the fact that this progressive readying of the soul for the reception of grace was generally seen as God's sovereign work, he feared its being perceived as both a human accomplishment and a claim upon God's favor. Simply to speak about preparation, and particularly to emphasize its necessity, could lead in his judgment to that perennial danger, the introduction of a covenant of works into the covenant of grace. The whole work of salvation is God's act of sovereign grace, and at best one can anticipate it only by an annihilation of the self in such abasement as rejects everything pertaining to claim or effort. One could better think of oneself as a perishing sinner than a prepared one. When rescue comes, it is through God's unconditioned mercy, for free grace does all.

Others likewise interpreted in this manner God's saving work. On the western Massachusetts frontier Solomon Stoddard's powerful preaching stimulated a series of successful revivals, bringing several "harvests" of converts into the church. These conversions were aided, he felt, by the employment of many means, including Scripture, prayer, sermon, baptism, and even the Lord's Supper. But in Stoddard's view all this was the miraculous work of a sovereign God. Like the Mathers, he knew the human will was corrupted and in bondage to sin, free to act for good only if liberated by a captivating work of grace. So he shared their aversion to Arminianism and their affirmation of predestination. Faith was a condition of salvation, but it was fully God's gift and even came suddenly and explosively as God's dramatic entrance into the sinner's experience. The saving work of God occurred by God's unpredictable choice and design.

Meanwhile, in Boston's cultured Old South Church, the revered teacher Samuel Willard conveyed by sermon and lecture an equally Calvinist faith. The tones were gentler and the nuances suggested acquaintance with freshly developing intellectual movements, but the message of unconditioned divine sovereignty was the same. At one point Willard spoke of that sovereignty in terms reflective of the new science of Isaac Newton then becoming known. The entire universe, Willard said, is an interlocking system of causation governed by one efficient cause, and that sole cause is God. The working of God, however, is that of the primary cause acting through secondary causes, each of which has its own nature and action. So in depicting the process of salvation Willard returned to the earlier Puritan concern over a duality of causes, divine and human. There is a human cooperation with God in the progress out of sin and to new life, but it is the cooperation of the secondary cause with the primary agent. The human person acts, but as an instrument of the Spirit. Willard, therefore, could affirm with the others the reality of predestination. The person participates, but only as one through whom the sovereignty of God is at work.

Providence

Within this general theological pattern, however, certain themes came to be stressed more distinctively than in earlier times. First among them was the notion of divine providence acting through nature and human affairs as the expression of God's judgments within history. Divine sovereignty determines not only one's eternal destiny, but also the ongoing events of historical life, and much was made in this theology of those events reflecting either blessings or punishments from God. It was a commonplace of Reformed theology to speak of God's control over all aspects of the created order. There is no contingency in life beyond the reach of God's determining power. God is the Ruler of the universe and the Lord of history. So it was an affirmation of a broadly held view when Cotton Mather wrote, "The great God who formed all things has an absolute dominion over all his works, to do even what he pleases with them all, and it becomes His creatures humbly to tremble, with all possible resignation before His holy sovereignty."[29]

The more specific application of this understanding came especially in the late seventeenth century as the jeremiad preachers spoke the words of present and forthcoming judgment. The fires destroying Boston, the storms ravaging the ships at sea, the spread of smallpox, even the devastation generated by the American Indian uprising were all works of God's omnipotence in punishment of a nation's sins. God's wrath is expressed through God's management of events, both natural and human, and God will continue to exercise this fearful judgment as long as there is need. It may be that some of the painful experiences are brought about by acts of demonic power. Satan works constantly to deceive and destroy. But Satan also is under the ultimate control of God.

This was true, they said, of the terrible infliction of witchcraft upon the Salem community in 1692. That was Satan's work, no doubt, the turmoil and deceit perpetrated by malignant power. When the madness began with the fits and convulsions of several young girls in the community, followed by their accusations of certain local residents as being the spectral agents for their tormenting, there was easy assumption that the accused were witches. Widespread seventeenth-century belief, by both laity and clergy, accepted the possibility of such witchcraft without question. The devil did take on human form as specter or apparition to work his evil, and surely those so represented were his bewitched instruments. As the event developed in Salem, however, an important restraint was applied by many clergy under the leadership of the Mathers. This insisted that though specters worked evil, there was danger in judging the accused simply on the "spectral evidence" given by the tormented. False accusations could be made and the innocent could suffer, which itself would only be another work of Satan's deceitfulness. There must be other corroborating evidence for conviction. Finally the Salem trials were brought to an end by this clerical insistence on caution, though only after twenty executions had occurred. Yet in retrospect even all of this episode of satanic evil was viewed as divine judgment, for Satan himself is under God's control. In the end, therefore, the community was called to days of humiliation, calculated to move the Lord to forgiveness of the sins provoking this wrath.

Joined with this sense of divine judgment was the conviction that God used miraculous occurrences to warn and bless. Among Increase Mather's publications were one dealing with the study of comets and another depicting what he called "illustrious providences." Mather's interest in comets was a part of his general openness to the new science as it probed the mysteries of the natural world, but his interpretation took theological form. Writing in 1682, shortly after Halley's Comet made one of its periodic visits, he concluded that such natural phenomena were used by God as "signs" of impending events. Sometimes they foretell joyous occurrences: a blazing star announced the birth of Christ. More often, however, their message was a warning of coming disaster should there be disobedience to God's commands. God similarly used other unusual occurrences for both warning and blessing. Invisible forces of demonic and divine power lie behind otherwise unexplainable events in the natural world, whether instances of mysterious death or of miraculous rescue. The whole created order is an instrument in the hands of an omnipotent God.

The Saving Work of Christ

Counterbalancing, however, what could have been a terrorizing emphasis in the jeremiad preaching of divine judgment, the theology of these decades also began to focus more prominently upon the comforting role of Christ as Savior. Again this was nothing new in Puritan thought. Christian theology throughout the ages had built its systems around the central affirmation of redemption through Christ's sacrifice, and the Reformed tradition fully shared in that basic conviction. Indeed Puritan theology, with its penchant for the covenantal idea, had early developed an interpretation of this aspect of Christ's work, which it termed the *covenant of redemption*. Although Christ's sacrificial death occurred as an event in human history, this was nevertheless planned and prepared for, it was said, by a covenantal agreement in what might be called "divine history," a kind of prehistory located in the eternal life of God. It was then and there, with foresight of the ultimate need of humanity for salvation from sin, that God and Christ covenanted with one another to bring this to pass. Christ, in this portrayal, committed himself to become the suffering Savior by agreeing to accomplish the redemptive work of the cross. In return, said Thomas Goodwin, an early English Puritan, "as Christ undertook to God, so God undertakes to Christ again, to justify, adopt and forgive, sanctify and glorify"[30] those who are chosen for salvation. So the commitment of God to a saving mercy is a bound commitment, fixed firmly by Christ's commitment to a saving sacrifice. These are the promises of the covenant of redemption.

Although this conviction remained continuously at the heart of the Puritan message, emphasis upon it tended to decline somewhat over the years in relation to other preaching priorities. More immediately related to hearers than the covenant of redemption was the covenant of grace. Theoretically the former made possible the latter. The latter, however, was the personal covenant with God into which individuals were directly called and became, therefore, the major focus for evangelical appeal. Unbelievers were summoned to faith and believers to continuing faith and faithfulness in order that a personal covenantal relationship with God might be entered and sustained. Sometimes, it would seem, covenant became a substitute for Christ as mediator of salvation, a condition further promoted by a searching of one's spiritual and moral life for confirming evidence of one's inclusion in that saving covenant partnership. It is therefore not surprising that in a time of change, when assurance of salvation was less certain and the tendency toward judgmental preaching was strong, attention was increasingly turned to that upon which God's covenant promises themselves rested, the saving

work of Christ upon the cross. Comfort could best come from contemplation of that divine act of redeeming power.

Increase Mather, fervent jeremiad preacher in the 1670s, led the
way in the late 1680s as he began more specifically to "preach Christ"
and find evangelical appeal in proclamation of the covenant of redemption. Surety is to be found not in human obedience, he urged, but in
the obedience of Christ whose commitment led him to the saving
sacrifice. Similarly, others turned to the theme of the saving Christ and
made it more prominent in late seventeenth- and early eighteenth-
century preaching. Samuel Willard declared that in the covenant of
redemption God has "taken off the curse of disobedience from the
believer and laid it upon Christ." John Higginson urged that the controversy between God and New England had been mediated by Christ,
who pacified the anger of God and made "peace between God and us."[31]
But most of all this note was sounded by Cotton Mather, who so
relocated the relationship of the covenants in his preaching as to declare
that the covenant of grace was an "echo" of the covenant of redemption.
Both theologically and psychologically his focus was on the person and
work of Christ. He was overwhelmed by the miracle of the incarnation,
deeply affected by the power of Christ's virtue, and dazzled by the
splendor of Christ's sacrifice. These, he felt, should be the core of
preaching, and the sinner should be urged to "fly" to Christ and "nestle"
under Christ's "wings." Then, by union with Christ, there increasingly
can be "imitation" of him, as one feels "virtue going forth from him" to
empower one's own life.[32] Although all of this had precedent within the
Puritan tradition, these decades witnessed this renewed emphasis upon
Christ's saving work.

New Directions

Despite the fundamentally traditional theology characterizing this
period, certain new views began to appear. Clad still in the garments of
classic Calvinism, their expression was limited and muted, but they
anticipated developments in American thought that were to occur with
the coming of the Age of Enlightenment. Two such themes are of
particular importance: the greater use of human reason in seeking
knowledge of God and the equating of human happiness with the goal
of salvation.

Among the leading Congregational clergy during these years Samuel Willard, more than any other, incorporated these ideas into his preaching and writing. Willard, for example, moved beyond asserting biblical revelation as the sole source of religious knowledge to affirm an independent role for human reason. The human person, he wrote, is a "reasonable creature" with the capacity to interpret the "light of nature," which is grounded in God but visible through the rational pattern in the order of the universe.[33] So the mind can see to a certain extent through the visible to the invisible, discerning something of the nature of God and God's laws, even coming to an awareness of the human violation of the divine moral order and the condemnation it brings. Independent reason can go no further than this, however, for God's compassion and the divine plan for human redemption are disclosed only in the biblical revelation received in an act of faith. Moreover, even the knowledge available through the light of nature was seen by Willard to be the result of God's initiative and hence a form of divine revelation. Yet his views represent the beginning of a natural theology in eighteenth-century Congregational thought. Benjamin Colman shared in this early honoring of reason and the natural. Impressed like Willard by the Newtonian description of the constancy and order of the universe, he concluded that God could be encountered through the marvelous work of creation. Through "reading the vast roll of nature," he wrote, one could sense "the glories of the divine majesty."[34] Yet again this was a limited attainment. Knowledge of God's works of providence and redemption, and even final proof of God's being, could come only in the revelation contained in the Scriptures.

Samuel Willard similarly introduced into New England Congregationalism's God-centered theology an emphasis on the search for human happiness as a valid religious goal. Each person, he affirmed, was moved basically by a natural desire for happiness, and the religious quest must therefore seek that which most completely satisfies. In part this was a recapturing of an ancient Augustinian theme, declaring that lesser goods do not suffice to meet this yearning, for only in God does the restless soul find its rest. The goal of salvation is therefore the communion with God that brings life's deepest joy. Willard, however, also adapted this Augustinian conviction to his Puritan theological setting, and in so doing gave further centrality to the quest for happiness. Puritan thought had customarily identified life's ultimate goal as the glorification of God, an aspiration quite contradictory to dedication to human happiness. But Willard identified the two, maintaining that God can be glorified through this self-fulfillment. In fact, there is even a certain priority to the search for happiness, for it is the beginning of the religious quest. Willard's commitment to this view was brought out particularly in one of the controversial issues of his day, the question of whether one ought to be willing to be damned for the glory of God. A strict Calvinist answer would be in the affirmative. Willard, however, answered in the negative, for such humiliation would be a transgression against the deepest impulses of human nature and correspondingly an affront to the glorification of God found in the realization of human happiness. He wrote, "As happiness is our subjective, so is the glory of God our objective, end; and God has tied these together."[35] Once again, these newer ideas appeared in late seventeenth- and early eighteenth-century New England theology only within the context of a continuing conservative Calvinism. But in succeeding decades they developed a life of their own and contributed to serious theological division among Congregational divines.

POLITY

Although the theological interpretation of Christian faith was subject to only minor stress in this period of the second and third New England generations, a quite different picture appears in the area of church polity. Disagreements were often emphatic and tensions were frequently intense as Congregational leaders sought to define and to establish an appropriate structure for the churches' life in the new times. Continuously these years witnessed differences in judgment with regard to the organizational form and the pattern of institutional relationships that Congregationalism should embody, leading often to areas of serious conflict.

Church Membership

When John Davenport opposed adoption of the Half-Way Covenant in 1662, he did so on the ground that birthright membership in the church was only a provisional and temporary status. His Congregational commitment to infant baptism as a seal of the covenant prevented him from adopting the Baptist extreme of restricting membership exclusively to confessing adults. Yet in this Congregational ambiguity of membership by both birth and rebirth, he clearly leaned in the latter direction. Actually, said Davenport, the baptism of infants did not seal for them a personal membership, for they had been baptized only "by and for the parents covenanting in them."[36] Their membership was "mediate" through their regenerate parents, rather than "immediate" by their own intrinsic, personal possession. This meant that though members, they were not sufficiently members to maintain automatically that status into adulthood. Only by their own conversion could that occur, and without it their initial and tenuous membership would be lost. So in opposing the half-way membership of baptized unregenerate adults, Davenport moved as far as his Congregationalism would allow in defining the church and its membership in terms of personal purity. He would keep a great chasm between the church and the world.

The majority party in the half-way covenant debate, however, would lessen that chasm somewhat by recognizing a continuing validity to the membership of the church's baptized children, even though in adulthood it was not sufficient to provide eligibility for sharing in the Lord's Supper. In the synod decision of 1662 the genuineness of this membership was strongly declared. It begins for these children in infancy, derived from the fact that their parents, "one or both," are in covenant in the church, for under the promise to Abraham a "federal or covenant holiness" is passed on from one generation of God's people to another. It is sealed in baptism, which for Christians is the equivalent to the sealing act of circumcision designated for that purpose in Abraham's day. It is membership in a "particular church," for that is the ultimate locus of visible church life. It is a "personal" membership, not simply a marginalized relationship mediated almost in name only by parental qualification. And it is, above all, a continuing membership that can be forwarded to the next generation if obstacles of erroneous faith or scandalous life have not intervened. Said the synod report: "There is no ordinary way of cessation of membership but by death, dismission, excommunication, or dissolution of the society."[37] This was half-way membership, when confirmed by owning the covenant, but it preserved individuals truly within the discipline and care of the church and, probably most important of all, granted the privilege of bringing their own children to baptism.

There remained, however, the question of full membership within the church and the qualifications and means by which this might be attained. Indeed, beyond those whose half-way membership had been sealed in infant baptism, there were the adults to whom this status increasingly was given in response to their willingness to confess the faith despite lack of conversion experience. The Half-Way Covenant had opened the door of the church more than originally had been expected, posing the issue of the degree to which it should remain closed at the critical point of full communion. Solomon Stoddard, more prominently than any, pressed as early as the 1680s for further reduction in restrictiveness. Having made baptism available in Northampton to all who could affirm Christian faith and were morally sincere, he then wanted the Lord's Supper available to all baptized persons similarly qualified. He would eliminate all distinctions in church membership, once noting that "we never read of communicants and non-communicants in Scripture."[38] Others joined with him in this view, a key clergy supporter in the Boston area being Simon Bradstreet of the Charlestown congregation. But their views of the matter carried them beyond the pale of classic Congregationalism. Stoddard's far-reaching proposal was for a presbyterian-type national church based on God's "public covenant" with the whole people of New England and having authority over all local congregations. Yet this, the vast majority well knew, would essentially eliminate the chasm between the church and the world and signal an end for the church as a local covenanting community of believers.

Congregational leaders therefore continued to search for ways to combine restrictiveness with openness on this matter. That too much openness was becoming dangerous is reflected in Increase Mather's comment that if "the begun apostasy" is not checked, then in a next generation "the most conscientious people will think themselves concerned to gather churches out of churches."[39] So for the most part, "personal relations" remained a requirement for full membership, though with the developing understanding that their content was to be a confession of repentance and faith, rather than a detailing of the experience of conversion, and their forum was to be the pastor alone, rather than the entire congregation. There were, however, many variations. In 1661 the church at Salem eliminated personal relations as necessary for those who had been baptized as children within that congregation, but not until 1771 did it remove this requirement for baptized adults who moved into the town from other communities. The Brattle Street Church in Boston, founded in 1699, never introduced the practice of requiring personal relations, whereas Boston's First Church did not abandon it until 1786. A private confessing of sin and faith was generally permitted for women by the 1640s, but for men it was not allowed in Plymouth until 1688, nor in Boston's First Church until 1756. Meanwhile in the 1720s, Cotton Mather at Boston's Second Church rejected totally the use of public relations because the frightening severity could serve "as a scarecrow to keep men out of the temple,"[40] and even earlier Samuel Willard at Boston's Third Church opposed such narrating before the congregation, because its members, he said, are not appointed to be "the door keepers at the House of God."[41]

The upshot was a double effort to be faithful to the past by preserving in the church a purity of membership that distanced itself from the world, yet at the same time to be open to such modification of the methods, and even the standards, of the past as would effectively adapt to the circumstances of a changing day. Once again the final concern was qualification for receiving the Lord's Supper. On this point the Mathers held firm, Increase insisting on "pure churches walking according to the primitive pattern" and Cotton urging that the "terms of communion" should be identical to the "terms of salvation."[42] Yet times were different, the church was reinterpreting its role in the larger society, and Stoddard's urging of a more open communion was broadly known. So by 1726 Cotton Mather could write that "a great part of our pastors" were welcoming to the Lord's table all the baptized who might desire to come. If any delayed, it would be by "their own choosing to stay till more satisfied in their qualification, than from the churches refusing to admit them."[43] Heredity, orthodoxy of belief, and propriety of behavior were now replacing repentance and regeneration as criteria for communion. In Roland Bainton's phrase, the process was a transformation of "the elect of New Canaan into the elite of New England."[44]

Ministry

Troublesome matters also were encountered as clergy of the second and third generations faced varied practical aspects of their vocation. Much of this related to the continued difference between lay and ministerial understandings of the nature and locus of authority within the life of the local congregations. But several newly developed considerations contributed to both the context and the substance of the tensions.

One thing new for the clergy of the late seventeenth century was the increasing difficulty in obtaining employment. Despite the population growth in the colonies and the corresponding founding of new churches, it quickly developed that there were too many clergy or clergy candidates for the available pulpits. The supply simply outran the demand as immigrant clergy continued to arrive from England and a new generation of ministers emerged from local training within New England itself. For the native born this situation was particularly discouraging, because several of the churches, especially those of prominence, favored the English educated. First Church, Boston, for example, did not install a graduate of Harvard until 1695, more than half a century after the college made its first graduates available for this employment. Other unsettling consequences for the clergy followed from this condition. Because a large number of the locally trained clergy could find positions only in less desirable locations, there was a good deal of mobility among them, some changing positions frequently, especially in their early years. For many, moreover, this meant a delay in ordination, for in numerous instances ordination was withheld until a lengthy trial period had been undergone and qualifications fully approved. Perhaps the most extreme case was that of Moses Noyes, who served twenty-seven years at Lyme, Connecticut, before he was ordained!

Connected with this employment problem was the matter of financial support. Initially the New England clergy were paid by voluntary contributions, either in cash or in kind. Because church attendance was required by law in the colonies' earliest days, it was expected that these freely given offerings would come from church member and nonmember alike. A Massachusetts law of 1635 simply said that "all who are taught in the Word are to contribute unto him that teacheth."[45] Soon, however, tensions arose in many communities where insufficient support was volunteered, a condition sometimes reflecting lay members' dissatisfaction with their clergy but also occurring because of nonmembers' unwillingness to share in these costs. Various remedies were attempted to alleviate the distress, ranging from assessments against those whose voluntary contributions were inadequate to outright taxation of all town residents. Clergy complaints continued, however, because even tax-provided funds were often too meager, at least in the estimation of many who felt that their educational and professional status warranted a higher monetary recognition. In the latter part of the seventeenth century the matter of salary disputes came to be dealt with by means of written contracts with agreed-upon terms of compensation, which clergy held to be a necessary precondition to the "peace and comfort" of their employment.

Tax-provided funds and written contracts with town authorities may have eased the financial burdens of the clergy, but they also contributed to a new area of tension, the desires of townspeople, though nonmembers, to participate in the election to ministerial office of the clergy toward whose salaries they were required to pay. Congregational tradition had limited this voting to males possessing full membership in the gathered church, but pressure now developed to extend the franchise for ministerial election to all taxpayers. Connecticut, with its greater presbyterial inclinations, considered this change as early as the 1660s, completing it in 1708. In the Bay colony the General Court decreed in 1693 that churches must accept the "concurrence" of the towns in the selection of a minister, thereby affirming the dual organization of New England Congregationalism, the church and the "parish" (or "society"), as joint participants in these elections. The situation was therefore created in which clergy were increasingly beholden to an electorate that included many who had no interest, other than financial, in the church.

These tensions, moreover, exacerbated the continuing and more profound problem of ministerial status and authority. The older struggle pitting Brownist against Barrowist views of local church government had never been resolved, and these years actually witnessed its intensification. Although pride unquestionably entered in, most clergy were committed in principle to a dominant ministerial role in the conduct of church affairs. When Solomon Stoddard said that "the elders are to rule over the church and therefore not to be overruled by the brethren,"[46] he spoke for a great many of his Congregational colleagues. Although this conflict between clergy and laity appeared in a variety of forms, one major focus of contention during these years was on voting procedure in a congregation's decision making. Objecting to the "handy" vote in which the minister's upraised hand counted the same as that of any member and in which the majority therefore ruled, the clergy urged the principle of the "negative voice" in which the congregation's majority could be overruled by the pastor's dissent. And often this took the more extreme form of "silential" voting in which the congregation's role was one of acquiescence to the pastor's decision. As early as 1648 the Cambridge Platform of Church Discipline had initiated this procedure by affirming that voiced opposition to the judgment of the elders was "contrary to order and government"[47] and would contribute to disturbance and confusion. More than half-century later a group of Massachusetts clergy expressed again this concern, affirming that "to take away the negative of the elders" would be "to take away all government whatsoever" and "to turn the whole regimen of the church into a pure democracy"—and for many this was the pathway to anarchy.[48]

Many of the laity, however, resisted. Opting for majority rule in the church, they voiced the view that except in preaching, administration of the sacraments, and calling and moderating church meetings the clergy "have no more authority than any particular brother." Some went even further, urging that though a majority of the congregation agreed with the minister, his proposal should not prevail if opposed by "considerable persons," an attempt to transfer control of the church to a small clique of the membership's powerful and elite. But whatever the nature of the resistance, the clergy as a whole came to feel themselves under siege. Even moderate Samuel Willard of Boston complained that throughout the churches one could see "ministers despised, their office questioned, their authority cast off," and "their comfortable supply and maintenance neglected."[49] The conflict was leading toward a new anticlericalism in which both ministerial office and occupant were being deprived of the honor and deference they presumably deserved.

The clergy reaction was often defensive, criticizing lay attitudes and affirming more boldly the special character of the ministerial role. Special sermons on days of fasting and lamentation for the troubles of New England became particular occasions for denunciation of the treatment accorded God's "watchmen," even to the point of portraying this disrespect as a major reason for God's wrath. One line of emphasis in these jeremiads related this to the national covenant between God and New England. The people had broken that covenant through their many sins, generating God's anger, but worst of all they had rejected God's prophets upon whose message restoration of the covenant must depend. The ministers are the covenant's lifeline, said Increase Mather in a sermon on apostasy, and the people must respect them and their preaching as they announce judgment and call for repentance. So even more than other sins, the disdain for God's messengers was occasion for divine wrath. Samuel Willard likened the situation to Israel's strained relations with Jeremiah and Ezekiel. When the people failed to honor Jeremiah's divinely commissioned ministry or to heed Ezekiel's divinely inspired prophecy, God punished them. And this is happening as well in New England, he affirmed, as ministers undertake their "unthankful errand" of warning a headstrong people and receive from them hatred as their reward.

Emerging through this welter of discontent and dispute was an increasingly exalted view of the ministry. Many of the laity had different perceptions, but by and large the ministers of the late seventeenth and early eighteenth centuries, perhaps even more than their predecessors, thought of themselves not as "the mouth and hands of the church" but as "the mouth of God and the hands of Christ." They were God's ambassadors. They had a special rank in the world, and their preaching was ordained by God as a special means of divine grace. Moreover, the sacraments had taken on greater importance in the ministry of grace, and the clergy were their guardians and administrators. Similarly, the clergy continued to assume greater prominence in the conduct of ordinations on the ground that God appointed "spiritual rulers to represent him in this authoritative work," and the further printing of ordination sermons added to the ministerial prestige connected with these occasions. So a high, even exalted, view of the nature and role of the ministry developed despite the conflicts of the times. Azariah Mather spoke of the clergy as "sacred persons, men representing the King." Nathaniel Eells maintained that ministers "officially stand nearer to God than others do." And in 1726 William Shurtleff applied Winthrop's earlier image of New England to the clergy by saying that "the ministers of Christ should remember that in a peculiar manner they are the Lights of the World . . . a City upon a Hill which cannot be hid."[50] Far from hindering its development, perhaps the conflicts of the times even contributed to this lofty conception.

Connectionalism

The conflicts concerning the locus of ecclesiastical authority were also played out in a larger arena. This was the area of interchurch relations, where the issue of ministerial control came to be combined with the issue of the autonomy of the local church. The Cambridge Platform of 1648 had authorized the use of ecclesiastical councils for determining matters where consultation among several neighboring churches might be desired. Such consultation could be sought by a local church or its pastor with respect to matters internal to the life of that congregation—and with this encouragement local churches began to call for assistance in matters such as selection, ordination, and dismissal of a minister, as well as the disciplining of errant members whose offenses seemed to warrant the seeking of this outside help. The power of these councils was purely advisory, for churches basically had no authority over one another, although in extreme situations, where a divided or scandal-ridden church might refuse conciliar correction, the sanctions of "admonition" and even "noncommunion" could be applied. Mainly, therefore, this was a voluntary and cooperative system in which churches were expected to seek and respect the counsel that could come through this larger collaboration.

For many of the clergy, however, the system increasingly failed to satisfy. For example, they found that the majority leadership in the councils was more often in lay than in ministerial hands. Lay delegates generally outnumbered clergy and were chosen not by the clergy but by the congregations. With tension and conflict increasing within the churches concerning the nature and degree of ministerial authority, this imbalance only contributed to restriction of the ministerial role. But further, the councils, from the ministerial viewpoint, simply failed to solve many of the problems with which they were intended to deal. It had been the expectation that councils would be a means for settling disputes within the local churches. The Cambridge Platform had commended them to the congregations for discovering "the way of truth and peace" in times of conflict. Yet the councils summoned for this purpose frequently failed—and largely because they had no compelling authority. If one faction lost in a council, it would often summon another gathering of churches whose inclinations were more favorable. If an entire church disagreed with a council's decision, it might simply choose to ignore it. First Church, Boston, refused the advice of four separate councils in the late seventeenth century. And for less than truly momentous matters the ultimate sanctions would hardly be applied. So the unrestrained exercise of congregational autonomy likewise rendered councils weak in much ministerial understanding.

The remedy, partially achieved in Massachusetts in 1705 and fully adopted in Connecticut in 1708, introduced a greater connectionalism into the life of the Congregational churches. In its full expression in Connecticut, as prescribed in the Saybrook Platform, two instruments were established for "the better regulation of the administration of church discipline"[51] throughout the colony. The first was the "consociation" of churches, one or more in each of the colony's counties, with representation by pastor and two lay delegates from each congregation. Functioning as a council, the consociation had the responsibility not only of effecting mutual assistance among the churches in matters such as ministerial ordinations but also of rendering definitive judgments in matters of dispute and scandal requiring decision and even discipline. No longer were these actions to be merely advisory, but by law they were now held to be binding upon both individuals and local churches. To the advantage of the clergy, the plan also incorporated the principle of the negative voice. The council's judgments, although arrived at by a majority of its members, could be affirmed and applied only with majority clerical approval.

Enhancement of corporate action and of the clergy role also came through the second instrument established by the Saybrook plan. In this arrangement ministers in each county were to form "associations" that should meet at least twice a year for consultation on "the duties of the office and the common interest of the churches,"[52] as well as to enable ministers to police one another with respect to the possibilities of scandal or heresy within the fraternity. They were also to engage in the work of examining and recommending to the churches candidates for the ministry. The latter was a particularly important new function, with pastorless congregations further required to consult with their association, for heretofore little corporate help had been given to or control exercised on the independent churches in their search for clergy.

In Massachusetts, meanwhile, lack of legislative support, plus resistance to the presbyterianizing tendencies of essentially similar polity proposals, had prevented the establishment of consociations, although ministerial associations were encouraged. These, however, were less strictly defined and regulated than the associations mandated for Connecticut. The Massachusetts associations were voluntary in membership and largely fraternal in purpose. As in Connecticut the clergy did examine candidates for the ministry and initiated the practice of granting ministerial license. However, their major activities involved mutual counsel in dealing with problems of discipline in their churches, mutual instruction in matters of biblical interpretation and the faith, and sharing with one another their experiences of prayer and the devotional life. Despite the desire of many Massachusetts clergy for a greater connectional control over the churches, this did not develop as it had with the colony's southern neighbor.

One major reason for Massachusetts' repudiation of the movement toward a more presbyterian polity was the presence and voice of its most eminent spokesman for a congregational form of church government, John Wise. Having objected to the imposed taxation by Andros in the 1690s on the basis of the lack of democratic representation, this pastor in Ipswich moved into the ecclesiastical discussion by emphasizing the same democratic considerations. In the process he enunciated a conception of a local church's autonomy that was to have further influence in American Congregationalism. In 1717 his major writing appeared, a treatise titled *Vindication of the Government of New England Churches*. The vindication, however, was based not on biblical authorization, but on a conviction that "the light of nature" dictates the superiority of democratic government, whether it be in the state or in the churches. Within the state it commends a "compact" form of government that recognizes all persons as free and equal and then joins them democratically into a political order protective of that freedom. Similarly, Wise said, this reasoning applies in the church where democracy can be seen as superior to either monarchy or aristocracy, for here too the light of nature urges that "power is originally in the people." Christ, Wise added, surely was aware of this, and if he "settled any form of power in his church," it must have been that which exposes the members in least fashion to arbitrary measures inflicted by others.[53] So on these grounds, fashioned by reason's perception of natural rights, democracy for Congregationalism and the autonomy of its local churches must be maintained.

WORSHIP

By the time of the third generation in the New England churches another problem had arisen for the Congregational clergy: they had to persuade their parishioners to attend public worship. No longer required by law and likewise affected by emerging religious indifference, attendance at Sabbath services entered into a time of decline. The value of worship needed therefore to be promoted, and sermons such as Solomon Stoddard's "The Inexcusableness of Neglecting Worship" and Benjamin Wadsworth's "Assembling at the House of God" spoke to the problem. High among the clergy's arguments was the necessity of hearing the preached Word. Not only temporal well-being, but eternal salvation itself, depended upon attentiveness and response to the message proclaimed by Christ's ambassadors. Moreover, the ministers said, attendance at public worship was one of the religious duties divinely imposed upon a Christian people, and this was especially true in New England where, more than elsewhere, true churches and sound preaching were found. Thus Timothy Edwards, in a sermon urging this duty, even declared that in the final day of judgment those who neglected that worship would stand condemned before God. Although the character of worship in these years remained generally that of New England's founders, some modifications were introduced. Special added occasions for preaching were developed, covenant renewal was encouraged, and modest changes appeared in Sabbath services and in the nurture of sacramental piety.

Special Days

Among the special or "occasional" days on which communities were summoned for worship were those called, on the one hand, for fasting and humiliation and, on the other hand, for rejoicing and thanksgiving. Days for these purposes in which other activity ceased and preaching was directed explicitly to their special themes had from time to time been a part of Puritan practice in both England and early New England, with Old Testament precedents cited as authorization. The colonies' troubles of the latter portion of the seventeenth century, however, led in New England Congregationalism to greater prominence for these occasions and to their more frequent employment. In accord with the conviction that God's providence governs all events, the days of fasting and humiliation were called in times of real or threatened calamity for a collective acknowledgment of sin and a pleading that God's judgment upon it would cease. Sermons on these occasions were invariably the jeremiads announcing punishment but also pointing to repentance and reformation as the way to restoration. Then as times changed and disaster was averted or its threat declined, days of thanksgiving were declared for voicing gratitude over the divine deliverance.

Some of these occasions for contrition and rejoicing were purely local in nature, expressing the conditions within a given congregation. Others were colonywide in the face of national crises viewed as embodying judgment upon an entire people for violation of New England's covenant with God. Authority for the appointment of these days rested primarily with the churches, exercised through the vote of local congregations responding generally to a pastor's request. On the larger colony level many congregations joined in early times to petition the General Court for declarations of these days, though gradually this power fell more and more into the government's hands. Yet even then many churches continued to vote on keeping those days that the government proclaimed, from which evolved the later practice of silent acceptance, "no one speaking," through simply hearing a reading of the governor's proclamation in Sabbath gathering.

Beyond these occasions dictated by the unforeseeable course of historical occurrences, a scheduled seasonal pattern was developed of spring fasts and autumn thanksgivings. Although Puritans generally resisted observing fixed religious holidays, the yearly rhythm of agricultural life suggested this added development, particularly as it could represent the cycle of death and rebirth experienced in personal piety. The death of the planted seed is like the death of one's sinful being that a flowering may ensue in rebirth to new life. Rejecting classic holy days of the church year, including times of death and resurrection such as Good Friday and Easter, a Puritan reritualizing supplied symbolic substitution through this new focus on nature's periods of death and rebirth.

One additional fixed special occasion for preaching in the New England calendar was the annual observance of election day in the several colonies when local assemblies and colony officials were chosen for the coming year. This civil holiday was of particular importance not only as a recognition of the principle of consent present in colony government but also as a reminder of the divine mission of New England and the special covenant responsibility given to its people by God. So election day celebrations, held in the capital cities, culminated in an election sermon delivered before assembled magistrates, deputies, and clergy who represented the diverse agents of authority in colony life. Beginning with John Cotton in 1634, and after 1640 progressing annually into the eighteenth century, prominent clergy were honored by selection to deliver these messages. The subsequent printing of these sermons made possible their wider influence, as speaker after speaker examined the nature of God's covenanting with New England, explored the role of government under subservience to God's Word, and pleaded with all for a greater covenant obedience to which would be given great blessing. Election sermons were in a sense a "social sacrament," a reassuring sign that New England, if faithful, would continue as a "peculiar people" under the grace of God.[54]

In the course of time weddings and funerals became special occasions for clergy participation and religious observance. Early Puritan practice viewed these events as purely civil affairs with which ministers should not be burdened, though the judgment undoubtedly also rested upon hostility to Roman Catholicism's identification of marriage as a sacrament and its celebration of masses for the dead. Puritan marriages were celebrated by magistrates, and funerals were conducted by townspeople who in silence carried the dead to the grave, accompanied only by the tolling of a bell. It was not until more than half a century had elapsed in New England that Congregational clergy began to officiate at these events, the first prayer at a funeral being offered in 1685 and the first wedding performed by a minister occurring in 1686. Even then the change took place only gradually. With respect to funerals, Cotton Mather noted in 1726 that although in many towns there was prayer "at the house" and a short speech "at the grave," there were still other places where "both of these things are wholly omitted."[55] Eulogies for the dead developed earlier, however, and particularly in the case of prominent persons were included in the Sabbath service following the day of the funeral.

Covenant Renewal

Often connected with the observance of days of fasting and humiliation was the practice of corporate covenant renewal that had been so strongly recommended by the Reforming Synod of 1679. More than simply a time of heroic resolution to reconfirm past commitments, this was an act fully compatible with the mood of the fast day, for self-examination and penitence were broadly recognized as necessary first steps in the renewal process. New loyalty to covenant promise was to be the ultimate outcome, motivated by a reawakened conscience, but Puritan piety knew that such resolve could be mustered effectively only out of honest confrontation with one's sin and the seeking of forgiveness and renewed strength. In this sense the renewal of covenant paralleled one's earlier pilgrimage toward conversion and a first entrance into covenant partnership. Repentance, rather than confident assurance, was its precipitating mood. And this pathway, known by the individual in private experience, must be traveled by the congregation seeking its rebirth in greater fidelity. When the members of Boston's Second Church, served by Increase Mather, renewed their covenant in 1680, they first spoke words confessing their "manifold breaches of the covenant," petitioning for "pardoning mercy" and declaring their "inability to keep covenant with God" except through the help of Christ's indwelling Spirit.[56] The new life of covenant renewal must be the renewed life in Christ.

The actual services of covenant renewal varied from church to church, as did the covenants themselves. Often the covenants were freshly written for these occasions, "enlargements" of the original covenants upon which the churches were founded, bringing them up to date in terms of current circumstances and needs. A report of the covenant renewal in 1705 at Taunton in the Bay colony noted the addition to an earlier covenant of these specifics: "To reform idleness, unnecessary frequenting houses of public entertainment, irreverent behavior in public worship, neglect of family prayer, promise breaking, and walking with slanderers and reproachers of others."[57] Generally the acts of covenant renewal came at the conclusion of an entire day devoted to worship. Neighboring ministers were invited to participate in these occasions and would share with the local pastor in both the prayer and the preaching. When time came for the act of renewal to take place, the method would correspond to the degree of openness in membership and communion recognized by the congregation. At Second Church, Boston, only full communicants participated in the renewed commitment, for all others had yet to make their first covenant declaration. At Plymouth a separate covenant of reformation was written for baptized, but not yet full communicant, adult members of the congregation, and, following the full communicants' reaffirmation, they rose in the service to make their own pledge. At Taunton the enlarged "reformation covenant" was used for all present, assented to first by the "brethren and sisters" who were church members and then by "the rest of the inhabitants" of the community.

The procedure at Taunton points to one further aspect of the practice of covenant renewal, its use in some instances as a recruiting device for the church. When the nonmembers in the Taunton service stood up to give their assent, they also submitted their names in writing to be put on a "list under Christ against the sins of the times." Shortly thereafter, it was noted on one occasion in the pastor's record, fourteen of those persons were "propounded to the church, some for full communion, others for baptism."[58] The renewal service had become a means to encourage further commitment at the differing levels of church relationship. In other places this recruitment by covenant renewal was explicitly connected with half-way membership for adults already baptized, the pledge becoming the equivalent of the qualifying act of "owning the covenant." And elsewhere young people were deliberately included. Realizing the inadequacy of much religious training in the home, some churches restored catechetical instruction and examination by the pastor as preparation for youth's participation in the renewal service. Then, as part of the total community commitment, their acknowledgment of the government of the church and their pledge to live righteous lives would be made.

Sabbath Worship

Despite the polity conflicts and modifications of these years within the churches, there was little change in the week-by-week worship. Congregations gathered to hear the Word and to unite in psalms and prayer, retaining the simple style that had satisfied the founders. Yet two modifications that were to be significant for future development in Congregational worship can be noted.

The first was the dropping of interpolation in the reading of Scripture in worship services, though the movement toward that conclusion was lengthy and somewhat strange. Return to the uninterpreted reading style of earlier Anglican times was initially adopted in 1699 by the Brattle Street Church in Boston, an action that shocked the members of the Boston-Cambridge Ministerial Association who some years earlier had voted against it as unscriptural and unedifying. Increase Mather said that one chapter read with explication will instruct more than would twenty chapters without comment. Meanwhile a different and curious change had occurred in some churches, elimination of the reading of Scripture during the service. The basis for this departure lay in the fact that traditionally interpolation in the Scripture reading had been the responsibility of the teacher, rather than the pastor, in the church's ministry. So with the inability of numerous churches to maintain financially the teaching office, the reading itself was sometimes removed from the order of worship. In the early 1700s, however, churches began to return Scripture reading to the service and to present it in uncommented form. By 1726 Cotton Mather could even insist that to call this a "dumb reading," as Puritans long had done, would be "improper and indecent."[59] Yet resistance continued to both developments. Some churches did not restore Bible reading until the 1760s, whereas the change to uncommented reading was not completed until the nineteenth century was about to begin.

A second modification initiated in worship practice during these years had to do with the singing of psalms and, though seemingly minor in nature, proved highly controversial. Throughout most of the seventeenth century the psalms were sung in New England churches without benefit of printed music. The Bay Psalm Book, which contained the versified texts, had no accompanying musical settings until the 1690s, and the tunes therefore were largely a matter of memory. Only a few simple tunes were sung, and even these, said one report, were so "mutilated, tortured, and twisted" that psalm singing became "a disorderly noise."[60] Reports also spoke of prima donna performances by persons whose individual efforts at ornamentation of the music in the midst of the congregational singing only added to the chaos. Cotton Mather's restrained comment in his diary of 1721 noted that something must be done "to mend the singing in our congregation" that it might "have the beauties of holiness more upon it."[61]

The first step in that direction was taken in 1714 by a pastor, John Tufts, who published a small booklet titled *A Very Plain and Easy*

Introduction to the Art of Singing Psalm Tunes, with Canta, or Trebles, of Twenty Eight Tunes, Contrived in Such a Manner that the Learner May Attain the Skill of Singing them with Greatest of Ease and Speed Imaginable. A second booklet followed, containing additional tunes, now in three part harmony. Quickly a movement developed, led especially by members of the clergy, for use of this printed music in worship. Solomon Stoddard wrote an essay in favor of the reform, and Cotton Mather, anxious to remedy the situation about which he had complained, added his publication, *The Accomplished Singer: Instructions How the Piety of Singing with a True Devotion May Be Obtained and Expressed.* A singing school was established in Boston, with clergy support, to aid in this effort. The third decade of the eighteenth century witnessed growing use in worship of what was soon called "regular singing," that is, singing "by rule" or, as more commonly designated, singing "by note."

Some clergy, however, opposed this change, and strong resistance was encountered in many of the congregations. In part this was simply defense of tradition, but for some it expressed a deeply ingrained fear of movement toward a more liturgical form of worship and further ecclesiastical consequences. One opponent, for example, wrote, "If we once begin to sing by rule, the next thing will be to pray by rule, preach by rule, and then comes papacy."[62] Cotton Mather found it necessary to reply to the related charge that the tunes used in "regular singing" were the same as those used in the Church of Rome. This was incorrect, he said, for the Congregational melodies came from French and Dutch psalmody. But, he added, even if this were true, it would not matter, for "our psalms, too, are used there."[63] Nevertheless, the controversy continued, pitting against one another the proponents of singing by note and singing by rote. The parish of Braintree witnessed a particularly divisive confrontation. There the traditional pastor, Samuel Niles, refused to conduct a service in the meetinghouse when some members insisted on the use of printed music, gathering the others of the congregation in his home for worship and later suspending the offenders from the church. A council representing neighboring churches was called to remedy the situation, but its ultimately unworkable decision was simply for the congregation to alternate in its worship the old and new methods of singing! Other churches experienced these strains as well, and the tensions continued in many places into the middle of the eighteenth century. Finally, however, the use of printed tunes prevailed as hymns were introduced to replace the singing of the psalms.

Sacramental Evangelism

The opening of churches to larger numbers of baptized persons by means of the Half-Way Covenant presented to New England clergy the additional task of assisting these persons to further growth in religious experience and commitment. Half-way membership could be largely a formality, despite its pledge of owning the covenant, and efforts were needed to render it more meaningful and to encourage the next step of qualification for full communion. Evangelical preaching continued to be the primary means toward this end, but clergy increasingly found it advantageous to emphasize more forcefully another aspect of their heritage, the nurture of the spirit through the church's sacraments. In this they developed for several decades what has been termed a "sacramental evangelism."[64]

Focusing on the significance of baptism as a sign and seal of God's covenant of grace with individual persons, New England clergy began offering baptismal sermons relating the sacrament to the gifts extended and the obligations entailed in that covenantal relationship. So closely was this identification developed that baptism in itself was portrayed as essentially a covenant, the baptismal covenant, and the covenantal gifts and obligations were inherent aspects of that sacramental act. Thus, on the one hand, baptism embodied the promise of converting grace and, ultimately, of salvation. One could place confidence in the fact of one's baptism, for it was a means for one's saving good. Years earlier the Cambridge Platform had affirmed that baptized children were "in a more hopeful way of attaining regenerating grace,"[65] but had linked that to their being under the watchfulness and care of the church. Now it would seem as if the sacrament had an efficacy in itself. None would go so far as to declare a bald doctrine of baptismal regeneration in which the water washed away the sin. But baptism, said Samuel Willard, was an "instrument of conveyance" through which the Spirit works. And Cotton Mather held that the "water of baptism" so brings the Christian into fellowship with God that "one more step carries him into heaven itself."[66] A more specific aspect of this general view was that baptism planted within one the seeds of grace, which then could be nurtured into richer life. So baptized, but unregenerate, members were given encouragement in this preaching. Significant benefits could come from the sacrament itself. It was truly a means of grace.

Yet, on the other hand, the baptismal covenant carried with it the obligations for covenant obedience, and its benefits could be forfeited through unfaithfulness. When Increase Mather delivered his jeremiads in the 1670s, he included in his sermons special remarks for the baptized, reminding them of the obligations the sacrament laid upon them and warning them of the dire consequences of breaking that baptismal covenant. And if these obligations had been undertaken by parents for one as a child in baptism, they should be personally assumed as one becomes mature. So when covenant renewal was initiated in the 1680s, the procedure often called upon the youth, as well as the adults, of the congregation to reaffirm the covenant of their baptism. Then in the eighteenth century, clergy increasingly emphasized faithful fulfillment of these obligations as a necessary element in one's pilgrimage toward salvation. It was not that salvation could be earned, nor the doctrine of election set aside, but within that classic framework the sacrament was employed for this further appeal. Cotton Mather said that baptism obligated persons to live as though they were united with Christ.

Increased attention was similarly given to the role of the Lord's Supper in the improvement of piety. Communion manuals were written to provide assistance in mental and spiritual preparation for participation in the sacrament, and new emphasis was placed upon the significance of the experience of communion itself. Always more than simply a commemorative service in Puritan understanding, the Lord's Supper was increasingly commended as a unique place of meeting with a spiritually present Christ. Samuel Willard spoke of this presence as a precondition of sacramental efficacy, for it was by receiving Christ in the communion act that one could partake of the benefits of Christ that the sacrament conveyed. For many, therefore, the communion was an occasion of immense and moving emotion. Increase Mather held that those who received the communion in a loving frame of mind could expect a soul-ravishing awareness of love for Christ and for the church far greater than might otherwise be known. Pastor-poet Edward Taylor's meditations in preparation for communion reflected the intensity of mystical experience that participation in the Lord's Supper could bring. Taylor, pastor at Westfield on the western frontier for fifty-four years, prepared these poetic meditations as private devotions without intention of their publication, but their subsequent discovery has shown how the sacrament became a vital source of his personal piety. In a meditation titled "The Experience," he spoke of the richness of religious awareness found there:

> Oh! that I alwayes breath'd in such an aire,
>   As I suckt in, feeding on sweet Content!
> Disht up unto my Soul ev'n in that pray're
>   Pour'de out to God over last Sacrament.
>   What Beam of Light wrapt up my sight to finde
>   Me neerer God than ere Came to my minde?
> . . . .
> Oh! that that Flame which thou didst on me Cast
>   Might me enflame, and Lighten ery where.
> Then Heaven to me would be less at last
>   So much of heaven I should have while here.
>   Oh! Sweet though short! Ile not forget the same.
>   My neerness, Lord, to thee did me Enflame.[67]

Special concern was felt for the many half-way members of the churches not yet qualified for sharing in the communion, and this posed a problem for the pastors. Some followed Solomon Stoddard, who urged opening the sacrament to all morally sincere baptized persons in the congregation with the conviction that participation in the Supper could itself assist in their conversion. Others, following the Mathers, could not take that direct step, but nevertheless pressed the unqualified to seek the further qualification. Indeed, these pastors said, it is a sin to refrain from partaking of the Lord's Supper, and one's baptismal covenant requires one to make every effort to secure the grace enabling one to avoid that great neglect. Cotton Mather termed it a mocking of God to engage in a renewal of one's baptismal covenant "without seeking the Supper of the Lord."[68] In actuality, this led more and more toward the practice commended by Stoddard, even though the theologies of qualification continued to differ. In most all churches by the 1720s, as Cotton Mather noted, the communion was generally available to all baptized persons who desired it.

MISSION

Although the churches in the second and third generations continued their focus on New England's broad evangelical mission in the world, they also emphasized certain areas of more specific concern in their relation to the social order. Some of these had roots in the time of the founders, but now came into fuller expression.

Education

"When a few scattered and feeble settlements were all that constituted Massachusetts," wrote Horace Mann in the nineteenth century, they "conceived the magnificent idea of a free and universal education for the people." And this innovation, he added, "was the boldest ever promulgated since the commencement of the Christian era."[69] This may be prejudiced praise coming from the great educator, but it reflects a remarkable concern of the earliest New England Congregationalists, which was then continuously improved upon as time advanced. Convinced that all persons should have direct access to the Bible, for it was "one chief project of that old deluder Satan to keep men from knowledge of the Scriptures," and also convinced that sound learning contributes to good citizenship, Puritans in America immediately established schools. As early as 1624 a school for children was established in Plymouth, and in 1634 one of the residents was enlisted in Boston to become schoolmaster of the children there. In 1642 the General Court of Massachusetts required the selectmen of other colony towns to make certain that children in their communities were so taught by parents or others that they could "read and understand the principles of religion and the capital laws of the country." Then more formally in 1647 it legislated that towns of fifty families employ a schoolteacher and those of one hundred families establish a grammar school "to instruct youth so far as they may be fitted for the university." In the 1650s actions establishing colonywide school programs were taken in Plymouth, Connecticut, and New Haven. The intention throughout was that "learning may not be buried in the graves of our forefathers in church and commonwealth."[70] The following decades then saw this effort flourish and bear much fruit. By the middle of the eighteenth century Andrew Eliot declared that "scarce any are to be found among us, even in the obscurest parts," who are unable to read and write.[71] As a further result, various printed materials soon came from the press: psalm books, catechisms, communion manuals, sermons, devotional tracts, newspapers, and, finally, in 1743, a religious periodical, the *Christian History*. Congregationalism had developed a literate constituency.

Accompanying the development of this general public education was the founding of colleges (some later to become universities) for higher learning. Harvard was the first, its planting encouraged in 1636 by a monetary grant from the Massachusetts General Court and its first classes held in Cambridge in 1638. One major purpose of the founding was to provide for ministerial candidates a collegiate training of the sort immigrant Congregational pastors had received in England. In 1643 the college's second president, Charles Chauncy, recalled that "one of the next things we longed for, and looked after, was to advance learning and perpetuate it to posterity; dreading to leave an illiterate ministry to the churches, when our present ministers shall lie in the dust."[72] In 1654 the General Court underscored this concern when it refused to allow Boston's Second Church to ordain Michael Powell, a pious man but lacking academic qualifications, declaring that "if such men intrude themselves into the sacred functions [of the ministry], there is danger of bringing the profession into contempt."[73] Half a century later at Boston's Third Church, Samuel Willard repeated that conviction concerning the importance of ministerial education, noting that although "we do not think the Spirit is locked up in the narrow limits of college learning," ministerial gifts are not ordinarily "acquired in a shoemaker's shop."[74]

Even under primitive frontier conditions Harvard performed this advanced educational task. Hebrew, Aramaic, Greek, and Latin were learned; Scripture was read in the ancient tongues; logic and rhetoric were pursued; William Ames's *Marrow of Sacred Divinity* was memorized for catechetical recitation of basic Christian doctrine; and to bring together biblical knowledge and homiletical usage, the college president provided weekly declamations enabling students to learn how to combine logic and Scripture in refuting heresies and presenting truth. Likewise the spiritual development of ministerial students was encouraged through emphasis on worship and prayer, for Chauncy also had warned that teaching and study alone could not make them "true prophets of the Lord." Generally speaking, however, this collegiate training was not considered sufficient in itself as preparation for ordination and ministerial service. So students for the ministry supplemented their college work with further study of theology, either privately while otherwise employed or under the tutelage of a prominent minister in whose home the candidate would temporarily reside. A great many pastors opened their homes and their studies throughout both the seventeenth and eighteenth centuries to these domestic "schools of the prophets." Yet the college provided the fundamentals of learning necessary for this advanced theological pursuit, and as early as 1660 among the 135 ministerial leaders of the second generation, 116 were Harvard graduates.

Beyond this provision of ministerial training Harvard also began to prepare students for leadership in other aspects of society. This became increasingly true in the early eighteenth century under the administration of John Leverett, who in 1708 became the first non-minister president of the college. Leverett represented a growing liberal wing in the Congregational churches and encouraged a broadening of the college's program, particularly through greater inclusion of the New Learning beginning to emerge in the English universities. Ministerial students continued to be the largest group at the college, but alongside them were future merchants, judges, and magistrates wanting "to be made gentlemen" and preparing themselves for both private careers and public service. Although no major curricular changes in the study of Scripture and doctrine were made, the training of ministers also was affected to some degree by these developments. Study of the new natural science was introduced; historical readings were broadened beyond sacred history to include secular developments, especially the new histories of political liberty; rhetoric was deemphasized and new canons of literary style were explored; and reading of Anglican authors admired for their open-minded tolerance of different religious practices was encouraged. Preparation of clergy in Massachusetts looked not only to the past but also to the changing social and intellectual concerns facing the future.

At the same time many in Connecticut, having sent their sons north to Harvard, now desired that "a nearer and less expensive seat of learning" be established within their colony, and this was accomplished by ten of its Congregational clergy who became trustees in the founding of Yale College in 1701. To some degree this represented a reaction against the growing liberalism at Harvard, for the founders obtained their counsel from the more conservative clergy in Massachusetts. It was Cotton Mather of Boston who secured the original grant for the project from its benefactor, Elihu Yale, and who proposed Yale as the name for the college. Yet the intentions for the school were stated in broad terms in its charter: "For the educating and instructing of youth in good literature, arts, and sciences; that so by the blessing of Almighty God they may be better fitted for public employment both in church and in civil state."[75] The school was to be the servant of the entire community, preparing its students for both sacred and secular vocations, and to that end its further support came from many sources, some from the churches, some from the legislature, and some from private benefaction. Soon Yale College was joined by other church-founded institutions of higher learning in the westward movement of the Congregational churches, representing Congregationalism's dedication to education's importance for effective ministry and good citizenship.

Medicine

In the early eighteenth century, American Congregationalism entered another area of social concern in working out its public mission, that of urging more adequate medical service for community welfare. In this instance the impulse was provided largely by the remarkable talents and efforts of Boston's leading clergyman, Cotton Mather, though supported as well by other members of the city's ministry. Like his father, Cotton Mather was interested in the new science, turning his attention particularly to the field of medicine and even, while a youth, briefly considering the possibility of a physician's career. This interest remained continuous throughout his ministry, and, if anything, became stronger as the years progressed. He kept in touch with the latest developments in English and Continental medical science and referred often to medical matters in his voluminous writings. In 1713 he was elected to membership in the prestigious Royal Society of London, the first native-born American to be so honored, and in the remaining dozen years of his life he sent nearly a hundred communications to the society concerning medical research and discovery. In these Mather not only commented on international medical developments but also shared observations of his own, including the farseeing speculation that "the smoke of tobacco may lay foundations for diseases in millions of unadvised people."[76]

Mather's interest in medicine was integrated fully into the theological and the practical concerns of his ministry. Theologically medicine was understood as one of God's gifts, along with prayer a part of God's healing plan. And in the practical sense its scientific advancement, as well as broad application, must be strongly encouraged as a Christian response to disease and pain. For Mather this was an important form of the life of "do good" that Christian piety should inspire. He was particularly concerned about adequate medical care for the poor, establishing a hospital for the indigent and attempting, though unsuccessfully, to set up a free distribution of medicines for those who were in need. In the broader sense, however, his medical ministry was directed toward public health concerns, advising the community about health problems and through his writings disseminating information about medical remedies often not a part of common knowledge. At times this brought him into conflict with the city's physicians, as in the case of the measles epidemic of 1713. Convinced that many at that time were not seeking the services of physicians, and having lost his wife, three children, and a servant from the disease, he suggested that the doctors distribute directions for its treatment. When they refused, Mather himself issued such a pamphlet on the basis of his own scientific knowledge, justifying it as "a pure act of charity to the poor" who lack doctors' help.

His major conflict with the medical profession, as well as his most important contribution to the advancement of medicine, came a few years later when in 1721 a massive smallpox epidemic struck both England and America. Knowledge at the time concerning the biological nature of the disease was minimal, as was scientific knowledge concerning the possibility of using inoculation as a defense. Mather, however, ventured boldly into both areas. Through intensive searching of the scientific literature, he accepted a primitive form of a "germ theory" by which he comprehended the character of the disease and its transmission, and by further study of materials collected by the Royal Society he learned of inoculation procedures recently practiced in China and Turkey. In addition he had the amazing testimony from an African servant in his own household who had received such an inoculation against smallpox in his native land where it was in common use! Armed with this data when the epidemic became intense, Mather approached the physicians of Boston, urging that they "warily" experiment with this medical procedure for seeking the disease's control. They refused, arguing that inoculation would be dangerous, would interfere with God's providence, and in all likelihood would be a criminal violation of public law.

Mather, however, continued to maintain scientific soundness for this experimentation and finally persuaded one of the city's doctors, Zabdiel Boylston, to undertake it. But when Boylston proceeded to inoculate ten persons, both he and Mather were not only condemned by the other physicians but also made into objects of popular denunciation. Inoculation, it was commonly feared, would infect healthy persons and thereby contribute further to the contagion spreading the disease. At one point the turmoil became so great that a bomb was thrown into Mather's home. But the clergy rallied to Mather's and Boylston's cause. They published a letter in the Boston press declaring the righteousness of the experiment—and thus there developed the strange spectacle of the physicians opposing inoculation and the clergy defending it. Through the controversy, however, Boylston continued his inoculations, and after the epidemic ended Mather gathered all the results to report the experiment's success to the Royal Society. Inoculation as a form of preventive medicine was now introduced to America, and by the time of the American Revolution it was widely used. For Cotton Mather this was a scientific achievement and a significant contribution to a medical ministry that can "do good" for those who otherwise might needlessly suffer.

Poverty

Early Congregationalism shared the somewhat ambivalent attitude toward poverty bequeathed to it by its Puritan heritage. On the one hand, poverty was an affliction sent by God. The Puritan belief in God's sovereignty over all occurrences led to the conclusion that all impoverishment was part of God's plan. That plan was complex, however, and could be read in many ways. Some poverty was punishment for sin. Other poverty was sent by God to the righteous as a test of their faith. And still other poverty came as a blessing, for God knew that possession of riches created greater temptations to worldliness than being poor. In fact, Puritanism often rejoiced over lack of affluence, for if one learned the proper lesson from poverty, it could be no less a path to salvation than could abundance. On the other hand, poverty was also an evil to be moderated and even overcome by compassionate love. The explicit commands of Scripture were to give to the poor, and charity was a confirming evidence of one's justification and right relationship with God. So despite the conflict in attitudes this involved, the Puritan understanding also found a solid place for advocacy of relief for the poor.

Yet not all poor were alike, and New England's laws, following those of the mother country, distinguished between the worthy poor, who could not earn enough to live on, and the unworthy poor, who were able but unwilling to work. For the latter there was little or no compassion. Idleness was a great sin, and its gravity was compounded when the consequence was dependence upon the community for support. By general agreement such malefactors should be required to work and the malingerers should be punished in the house of correction. Particularly undesirable were those who wandered begging from town to town, and laws sanctioned their being whipped and deported. But there were also the worthy poor—widows, orphans, the elderly, the mentally ill, the disabled, and able-bodied paupers who could not find work—and for these persons provisions for help should be made.

In New England practice primary responsibility for poor relief was assigned to the towns, to be supplied through proceeds from taxation. Not always, however, was this a satisfactory solution, for such expenditure was often challenged by taxpayer resistance. Under these circumstances towns sometimes went to great lengths to reduce the number of potentially qualified recipients. Laws were enacted prohibiting residents from entertaining strangers without permission and requiring prospective inhabitants to post bond guaranteeing their financial stability. Indigent persons not legal inhabitants were sometimes "warned out" of the community by its selectmen, an action that relieved the town of financial responsibility if the individuals decided to remain. When the more massive problem of urban poverty was faced in Boston, however, more conscientious and better organized efforts at poor relief were made. An almshouse was built for sheltering the worthy poor, and a workhouse was later constructed for those among them capable of labor who, while residing there, could earn some income through public works.

Public alms, however, needed to be supplemented by private charity, and this added help was provided generally by the churches. One of its facets was the administration of private legacies for poor relief. In England these bequests had been managed through charitable trusts, but in New England they were put into the hands of the churches. Further, the churches used special collections to raise their own funds for relief purposes, and at least in Boston's First Church in 1688 a regular monthly contribution for the poor was solicited. In Boston the churches occasionally aided in the administration of the town's grants to persons who were their own members, adding supplements as need required.

Throughout the seventeenth century, however, the tendency in the churches was to set limits on these acts of charity, focusing primarily on aid to those within their own congregations. But in the early eighteenth century this was abruptly challenged by the influential effort of, again, Boston's leading pastor, Cotton Mather, who devoted much of his amazing energy to providing for the poor. He gave extensively of his own salary to the needy, administered gifts bequeathed for charitable purpose, and promoted all manner of projects to draw others into these labors. He organized societies for good works and developed charity hospitals and schools. Furthermore, the benefits were to be shared by all persons in need, the godly and the ungodly, whether or not they belonged to the household of faith. And through it all he exhorted his community by spoken and written word to join with him in this cause. It is little wonder that one recent historian has written that "no town in Europe or America showed so much concern for its unfortunates as did Boston."[77] But Mather was not alone; increasingly the churches of Congregational New England were finding this more far-reaching compassion for the poor to be an aspect of their mission.

SUMMARY

New England Congregationalists of the second and third generations struggled with the twofold task of being faithful to the basic principles on which their churches were founded and of modifying that heritage to adapt it more adequately to the changes occurring in colonial life. In the process Congregationalism proved to be not an inflexible system, but one sufficiently rooted in the life of the spirit that it could responsibly alter its forms for the sake of relevance in ministry.

One problem faced by the new generations was that of a lessening of religious passion in church as well as in society. Successful adaptation to New World conditions fostered economic progress that, along with increased immigration of those primarily seeking financial gain, brought a growing secularism onto the scene. To some extent the church attempted to restore greater faithfulness by calling dramatically for acknowledgment of waywardness and for new commitment to earlier ways. The many days of penitence in the local churches and the Reforming Synod for society at large gave impetus to this garnering of acts of repentance and covenant renewal. But adaptation was also needed, and this was provided through modifications of earlier rigidity for church membership and reception of the sacraments. As membership requirements were gradually altered for less restrictive admission, requirements for sacramental participation were likewise changed for a more general sharing in salvation's gifts. The Half-Way Covenant's opening of baptism and the Stoddardean opening of the communion kept the church's ministry effective for the many whose faith and religious experience could not quite match that of those who had preceded them.

The new generations of Congregational leaders also faced the problem of growing religious diversity in places where their predecessors had once outlawed all Nonconformity. This was due in part to the boldness of the dissenters who pressed for legitimacy, but also to England's new policy of requiring religious liberty in New England's life. Soon worship in other forms appeared, and the change of heart of Increase Mather and his son Cotton in truly welcoming the Baptists to Congregational Boston represented a further adaptation to changing times. Although it did not yet relinquish its tax-supported advantage in the New England colonies, Congregationalism began shedding its previous exclusivism and prepared itself to move into a more diverse and competitive world.

CHAPTER FOUR

REVIVAL AND REVOLUTION
1730–1800

Life in early New England had never been placid. Even apart from the physical struggles present in creating a new home in a wilderness, the settlers of the first generations faced continuing human problems in shaping their social order. Contending groups struggled with one another in church and state. Neither Puritan religiosity nor Puritan society was a monolithic undisturbed entity—and there were growing numbers unwilling to be advocates of either or both. Yet the conflicts of the seventeenth and early eighteenth centuries were largely contained within limits short of social disruption. Church differences were dealt with in synods, and in matters of state even the severe 1692 charter restrictions imposed by the British were accepted with relative calm.

The last seven decades of the eighteenth century provided a different story, however. These were years of such explosiveness in both church and state as to alter forever the social landscape. In the churches revival burst forth in monumental proportions—the Great Awakening, which momentarily lifted religious fervor to a peak of intensity and permanently contributed to new emphases and configurations in church life. In the state, revolution brought violent military conflict—the War of Independence, which threw off the yoke of British control and led to the creation of the American nation. And both of these, although national movements, had among their complex origins the New England Puritan spirit and its Congregationalism. From Northampton the churches' new spirit spread in the 1740s throughout the Atlantic seaboard. From Boston the surge for political resistance moved in the 1770s to rally all the colonies to the independence cause. Eighteenth-century revivals and revolution, to be sure, were in no way dominated by these denominational and provincial sources, but throughout this period much of American Congregationalism's life was caught up in these movements. In part Congregationalism contributed to them as cause; even more it was changed by their lasting effects.

HISTORY

The Great Awakening

The revivals of religion constituting the Great Awakening of the early 1740s actually had their roots in earlier times. "Puritanism," wrote historian Sydney Ahlstrom, "was itself, by expressed intention, a vast and extended revival movement."[1] Far from being a legalistic system, dominated simply by moral stricture and behavioral regulation, the Puritan pattern emphasized the believer's inner religious experience identified as the healing of sin and guilt by the gift of divine grace. The basis for the life of godliness, in both its outward and inward manifestations, was the miraculous event of personal conversion, and the concerns of theology as well as the efforts of preaching were continuously shaped toward understanding and attaining that end. The Calvinism of Puritanism was an evangelical Calvinism, capable of giving birth to revival. In some "seasons" that revival was more intense than in others, and often long "dry" periods intervened. But even in times of religious decline, the "harvests" could reappear. Solomon Stoddard's parish in Northampton, for example, experienced them successively in 1679, 1683, 1696, 1712, and 1718, as it responded to the vigorous preaching of its revival-minded pastor. Therefore when the Great Awakening occurred in Puritan New England, it appeared within a setting prepared for participation in this new intensity.

Significantly, the first stirring of the new movement was in the parish of Northampton itself, although now under the ministry of Solomon Stoddard's grandson, Jonathan Edwards. It began in 1734, after Edwards had expressed concern for some time over the town's renewed religious indifference and immoral behavior. Tavern frequenting and drunkenness were all too common. The disposition of the town was becoming excessively quarrelsome. There was growing laxity in sexual standards. And, particularly, the young people were offensive in their behavior, as well as inattentive to church and religion. But soon all this changed. It came about in part through Edwards's conscientious pastoral labors, as he consulted young people in their homes about these matters. Much more, however, it came about through Edwards's preaching, as he spoke fervently about sin, punishment, and the need for repentance and faith in the mercy of God. Four sermons at that time on the subject of justification by faith, he latter recalled, proved to be "a word spoken in season."[2] Soon people in Northampton were discussing their eternal destinies, and conversions began to occur. During the winter and spring of 1734–35 this religious zeal rapidly spread. Each Sabbath the meetinghouse was filled, and, wrote Edwards, the worshippers were "from time to time in tears while the word was preached, some weeping with sorrow and distress, others with joy and love."[3] With this religious fervor there came a change in moral behavior, evidenced in new love among the people and termination of the community's glaring sins. Edwards later recalled that this divine work of revival "made a glorious alteration in the town, so that it seemed to be full of the presence of God."[4]

The emotional excitement in Northampton remained at its height for about six months and then began to subside, although a year later Edwards could write that they were still a reformed people. Meanwhile the revival spread to other parts of the Connecticut River valley. Visitors came to Northampton to view the renewal, Edwards was invited to neighboring communities to preach, and soon more than thirty churches throughout the region experienced the fervor that Northampton had begun. But in 1737, almost as abruptly as it had started, the revival came to an end. Edwards immediately recorded its story in his *Faithful Narrative of the Surprising Work of God*, published in London in 1737 and in Boston in 1738, and this document quickly became a link to the much greater movement of revival soon to appear. Read widely in England and America, it provided inspiration in both lands for religious renewal. In America many found in this account a precise and detailed pattern for revival, which they aspired to duplicate. Among the English the account was read by an evangelical Anglican itinerant preacher, George Whitefield, who soon traveled to New England to further the work initiated there.

Although only twenty-four years of age when he first came to New England in 1740, Whitefield was already a widely acclaimed orator, associated with John Wesley and remarkably successful in his evangelistic work. Two years earlier in Georgia he had attracted large audiences during a brief visit to the Anglican churches of that colony, and then upon return to England had taken the revival out of the churches and into the fields where thousands gathered to hear his message. On a further journey to the Middle Atlantic colonies he preached in Philadelphia to great outdoor crowds from the steps of the courthouse, and his words were so effective that even the skeptical Benjamin Franklin was moved to empty his pockets when the offering basket passed by. It was said that Whitefield's voice was so compelling, his ability to clothe words with emotion so perfect, and his style of preaching so dramatic that merely by pronouncing the word "Mesopotamia" he could bring tears to his listeners' eyes! But beyond this, his sermons focused undeviatingly upon the realities of sin and punishment and the promises of forgiveness and new birth. Confronting his hearers with the terrors of damnation and the joys of God's mercy, he used his skills to penetrate to the deepest level of their anxieties and hopes. So his eloquent manner was the vehicle for a message of life or death, and the result was success in religious conversion beyond any measure this country had heretofore known.

Whitefield's first preaching tour in the northern colonies lasted a mere forty-five days, but in it he delivered more than 175 sermons in scores of churches to thousands of hearers. By the time of its completion most inhabitants had heard him preach at least once, and the fervor of revival had spread throughout all of New England. The way had been prepared by Puritan revivals, and, as he noted in his *Journal*, this now was like "putting fire to tinder." His visit to Boston, which lasted ten days, was a time of particular triumph. There he not only filled the meetinghouses but also preached to great multitudes in the open air of the Boston Common. He was enthusiastically received by the Boston clergy, Charles Chauncy's reticence being the only exception, and equally warmly by the students of Harvard College to whom he spoke in Cambridge. Everywhere there was excitement, and at times members of his audience seemed even to be out of control as, according to historian Harry Stout, they "elbowed, shoved, and trampled over themselves to hear of 'divine things' from the famed Whitefield."[5] Included on the tour was a visit to Edwards and the church in Northampton. There again he was eagerly heard, his preaching re-igniting the earlier flame of revival, although Edwards reprimanded him for emphasizing too strongly the emotional responses of his listeners as signs of conversion. At one other point Whitefield disturbed even the clergy who warmly welcomed him, for he was not hesitant to affirm New England's sorry religious state to be the consequence of having had a "lukewarm," or even "unconverted," ministry. "The reason why congregations have been dead," he exclaimed, "is because they have dead men preaching to them."[6] The colleges, he added, were no better, for they relied too heavily on "head knowledge" and ignored the gospel. In the awe surrounding the evangelist's power these charges, for the moment, generated no great hostile response, although later there was a strong negative reaction.

Whitefield was known as "the Grand Itinerant," but there were other itinerants as well who aided in the revival. Gilbert Tennent was one of these and, like Whitefield, came from outside New England and Congregationalism. A Presbyterian pastor turned traveling evangelist, Tennent stimulated revivals in the late 1730s in Pennsylvania and New Jersey and began his tour of New England in 1740 shortly after Whitefield's departure. His rhetorical gifts were not equal to those of his predecessor—Chauncy dismissed him as "an awkward imitator of Mr. Whitefield" who "too often turned off his hearers with mere stuff"[7]— but his successes appeared equally great. However, Tennent disturbed many of the clergy by speaking out, like Whitefield, on the dangers of an unconverted ministry. By the time of his visit many of the New England clergy had begun to develop a more evangelical style of preaching. They not only resented his charges but also suspected his criticisms were an appeal to a residual anticlericalism to evoke popular response. Tennent fell even more out of favor when Boston received a published copy of a sermon he had preached in Pennsylvania that not only warned against an unconverted ministry but also urged persons to leave their congregation and join another, should they believe themselves to be under such unqualified clergy leadership.

Revivalism in New England was stimulated by these itinerants from outside its boundaries. Yet New England depended largely on local leaders as it carried on the enthusiasm of its fresh awakening. In fact, some of the local clergy became itinerants. They were recent graduates of Harvard or Yale who had just lately begun, or were about to begin, their ministries. The appetite of the populace had been sufficiently whetted by Whitefield and Tennent to support a continuing wave of visiting evangelists, and the younger generation now stepped in. Itineracy meant rapid readjustment from the type of ministry for which most New England men had been trained. Yet through apprenticeship to more experienced evangelical preachers (some traveled with Whitefield and Tennent) and through willingness to set aside book knowledge and reasoned discourse for gospel preaching as prompted by the Spirit, they took on their new tasks. For two years, throughout 1741 and 1742, these men journeyed from place to place, presenting a more popular alternative to traditional preaching and keeping the fires of revival burning.

Leadership of the revival, however, was not given over entirely to the itinerants, who often disappeared as rapidly as they arrived and left little but emotion in their wake. A number of the settled ministers allied themselves with the cause, accepting the new emphases and integrating revivalism into the ongoing life of their congregations. Ezra Stiles, a prominent pastor who later became president of Yale, estimated that in 1743 out of the 420 established Congregational clergy in New England approximately 130 could be considered as favoring the new revivalism for their churches. Although this was a minority, it contained many of the leading ministers of the time. In Boston nine of the city's fifteen clergy supported the innovations, whereas three opposed and three were neutral. And among those favoring the revival were such prominent persons as Benjamin Colman at Brattle Street, Thomas Foxcroft at First Church, and Thomas Prince at Old South. But the leading settled pastor in all of New England committed to the furthering of the revival was undoubtedly Northampton's Jonathan Edwards.

The revivalist preaching of Edwards is probably best known through the sermon he delivered in 1741 in the meetinghouse of the neighboring community of Enfield, to which he gave the title "Sinners in the Hands of an Angry God." It was a sermon, like many revivalist sermons, portraying the terrors of damnation awaiting the unrepentant sinner. "The God that holds you over the pit of hell," he declared, "is dreadfully provoked. . . . You hang by a slender thread with the flames of divine wrath flashing about it, and ready every moment to burn it asunder. . . . This is the dismal case of every soul in this congregation that has not been born again."[8] Edwards was not averse to painting the picture in lurid colors to gain the desired effect, and we are told that during the sermon there was "great moaning and crying out" and "the shrieks and cries were piercing and amazing" before finally some "received comfort."[9]

Edwards's preaching, however, involved much more than such

threats. Of the more than one thousand of his sermon manuscripts that have been preserved, less than a dozen are of this nature. Edwards's major contribution to revivalism was his compelling emphasis upon the new spiritual "sense" that is available for those who place their faith in God. He came first to know this in his own conversion experience as a youth, when, he later said, an "inward sweet delight in God" flooded in upon him. It was a "sense of the glory of the Divine Being" so overwhelming that he could only desire to be "rapt up" and "swallowed up" in that God forever.[10] This awareness went beyond cognitive or head knowledge. In a sermon on "A Divine and Supernatural Light," Edwards termed it a "sense of the heart." "There is a difference," he said, "between having an opinion, that God is holy and gracious, and having a sense of the loveliness and beauty of that holiness and grace."[11] It is likely that Edwards was led to stress this awareness not only by his own experience but also by that of his wife, Sarah Pierpont Edwards. A woman of intellectual force and intense spirituality, Mrs. Edwards in 1742 experienced a sense, similar to that of her husband, of being completely caught up in the love and glory of God. In her recollection of the occasion, she told of being melted and overcome by this consciousness of union with the Divine Being. She seemed to float in the brightness of the love of Christ as though carried forward in the beams of the sun's light. Moreover, a mystic sensitivity continued throughout her life as she became truly a "soul mate" with her husband in religious experience. So it is in this light particularly that Edwards's revivalist preaching must be seen. Its major thrust was to encourage an overwhelming awareness of the divine.

Despite the efforts of Edwards and other clergy in supporting the revival, by the winter of 1742–43 the tide began to turn. More open opposition appeared among ministers who heretofore had been neutral or noncommittal. Many had been offended by the charge leveled against them by Whitefield and Tennent that they constituted an unconverted ministry. And now another itinerant entered the scene, who not only repeated with still greater emphasis that accusation but also severely corrupted the meaning of religious revival by his extreme, and even uncontrolled, behavior. James Davenport, great-grandson of the founder of New Haven Colony and pastor of a church on Long Island, was moved by the excitement of revival in mid-1741 to go to New England where for almost two years he carried on the work of a traveling evangelist. From the outset his labors were marked by great hostility to the settled clergy and by bizarre behavior in his preaching to the laity. He claimed to be able infallibly to distinguish the saved from the damned and employed outlandish tactics to bring the latter to a frenzied experience of conversion. "Come to Christ! Come to Christ!" he screamed from the aisle of the church in New London during the first sermon of his evangelistic mission. "Then," says the report, "he went into the third pew on the women's side, and kept there, sometimes singing, sometimes praying, . . . the women fainting and in hysterics. This confusion continued until ten o'clock at night. And then he went off singing through the streets."[12] Scenes like this were repeated time and again. A Boston newspaper account in 1742 said that "were you to see him in his most violent agitations, you would be apt to think that he was a madman just broke from his chains." And with respect to his followers marching down the streets in song, the account added, "They looked more like a company of mad Bacchanalians after a mad frolic, than sober Christians who had been worshipping God."[13] In 1743, again in New London, he reached the final depth in his offensive behavior when, like Savanarola in fifteenth-century Florence, he had his followers cast into a bonfire their fine clothes and jewelry representing "worldly things," followed by all "unsafe" books—in this case the writings of classic Puritan authors!

Davenport's antics, affronting both clergy and church, helped crystallize the growing opposition, especially toward itinerancy. Even apart from the bizarre, the effects of an impermanent and traveling ministry had been seen by many as destructive of stable congregational life. If denied access to the churches, as more and more became the case, that ministry could set itself up in temporary locations for revival services. So as early as November 1741 the Connecticut General Consociation, made up of three pastors and three laypersons from each district consociation, ordered that no minister preach or administer sacraments in a parish not his own without the consent of the settled minister of the parish. This action being ineffective, however, the Connecticut General Assembly passed legislation the following May forbidding itinerancy. The law sought to protect against both native itinerants and those entering the colony from without. For the former, who preached without an invitation from the settled minister and the majority of his church, the penalty was loss of salary paid from tax funds. For the latter, guilty of the same violation, the cost was designation as a "vagrant person" and deportation. In Massachusetts such legal regulations were not possible because of charter restrictions, nor was the desire to restrain the revivals and itineracy as strong. In fact, the majority of Massachusetts clergy in a mid-1743 assembly continued to affirm the "happy and remarkable revival of religion" still occurring, acknowledging only in general terms that "in some places irregularities and extravagances have been permitted."[14]

In Massachusetts the most severe criticism of the whole movement of the Great Awakening came from the pulpit and the pen of Charles Chauncy, minister of Boston's First Church from 1727 to 1787. The grandson of the second president of Harvard College, Chauncy carried on the Puritan intellectual tradition in his ministry to the point of strongly emphasizing the superiority of reason over passion. "The plain truth," he wrote, is that "an enlightened mind and not raised affections ought always to be the guide"[15] in human life. Chauncy did not rule out all emotional experience, but insisted that it must be under rational control. "Light and heat should always go together," he declared, but "if there not be some good proportion of the former, it will turn out to little account, if there be ever so much of the latter."[16] In the revivals, however, that excess of passion was justified by its supporters as the work of the Holy Spirit. But the Spirit, Chauncy urged, works by means suited to the rational character of human persons. This is a divine work of conversion "not in contradiction to, but in an elevation of reason."[17]

Beyond this basic criticism of revivalism's maximizing the role of emotion, Chauncy criticized the revivalists' use of manipulative methods to bring it about. Their frenzied depictions of eternal terrors played indecently upon human fears, he felt, and their further feeding of this by the encouraging of a collective hysteria added the power of mass emotion to the disruption of reflective behavior. "Force is proper to the body," Chauncy said, "reason to the mind."[18] Furthermore, all this giving in to emotion, in Chauncy's judgment, posed immense peril to social stability. More than wrong-headed religion was involved, and Chauncy viewed with fright the threat to settled churches, to a revered ministry, and to ecclesiastical order which the revivals posed. Perhaps his greatest fear, and it remained lifelong, was that evangelical religion would "undo the colony."

Chauncy put these ideas into print in his *Seasonable Thoughts on the State of Religion in New England*, published in 1743. Three years later Edwards published his *Treatise Concerning Religious Affections*, which, though not written explicitly in reply to Chauncy, became revivalism's most learned defense and the most complete exposition of Edwards's views on authentic religion. The main thrust of the treatise was to affirm the significance of emotion for the truly religious life. Edwards wrote that the person who "has doctrinal knowledge and speculation only, without affection, never is engaged in the business of religion."[19] It is ridiculous, he felt, to assume that God can move persons to any alteration in life, especially to a change so momentous as conversion, without deeply arousing the emotions. So this is the work of the Holy Spirit, a touching and transforming of life at the central point of experience, where understanding and will are caught up by new and holy affections.

But by what signs can the genuineness of such affections be known? Edwards concerned himself at this point with the question of evidences, speaking thereby to a major issue in evaluating all revivalism. It may well be, he allowed, that some physical manifestations can occur, for God can work in many ways. But nothing of this nature detected by the external senses can be a certain sign. The pitch of religious excitement, the ability to quote passage after passage of Scripture, the fervent talking about religion, the bodily shaking in religious ecstasy—none of these are sure tests of one's regeneration by God. The surest sign must be internal, the awareness of God's indwelling, the new "sense of the heart." And if there be signs beyond this intuitive assurance, they lie in the moral fruits of the Spirit's presence. Truly gracious affections, said Edwards, promote love, meekness, forgiveness, and mercy. They have their exercise in Christian practice. They are to be seen in a "longing after a more holy heart and the living of a more holy life."[20] For Edwards this constituted true revival.

By the time Edwards's defense appeared, however, the Great Awakening in New England had largely run its course. At least the pitch of emotional fervor had substantially declined, and even such an illustrious itinerant as Whitefield was no longer accorded the reception he had first known. Whitefield's second visit to New England came in late 1744, and although he still had enthusiastic friends providing for him preaching opportunities, he met with protests from many settled pastors and with repudiation from the colleges. The faculty at Harvard issued a "testimony against Rev. Mr. George Whitefield and his conduct," and the authorities at Yale followed with a "declaration" against his evangelistic methods.[21] Yet though the height of the religious excitement had passed, certain consequences of the years of revival remained.

Divisions in Congregationalism

One immediate consequence of the Great Awakening for New England Congregationalism was a division within the ranks of the clergy that, despite efforts at healing, lasted into the nineteenth century. Jonathan Edwards, deeply conscious in 1742 of the chasm between supporters and opponents of the revivals, observed that the ministry was divided "into two armies, separated and drawn up in battle array, ready to fight with one another." Moreover, he concluded, there was no place for "neuters" in this struggle, for "in the day of battle . . . all must be on one side or the other."[22]

From a somewhat longer perspective, however, Edwards proved to be both right and wrong. He was right in noting the intensity of the disagreement among clergy in their theological views and practical methods for furthering the purposes of the church. The clergy were dividing into "New Lights" supporting revivals and "Old Lights" opposing them, as the unifying theology and ecclesiastical order of past generations were being subjected to these new strains. Edwards was wrong, however, in limiting his analysis to this simple distinction. In his view the division in clergy attitudes could be portrayed as a sharp conflict between the forces of "piety" and those of "reason," undoubtedly represented in his mind by his personal disagreement with Charles Chauncy. Furthermore, Edwards charged the Old Light opponents of revival not only with being rationalists in their approach to religious understanding but also with being Arminian in the content of that theology. It is questionable as to whether Chauncy or any of his liberal theological associates had developed that radical an acceptance of the freedom and power of the human will by such an early time, but regardless, Edwards's sharp bifurcation improperly consigned all non-supporters of the revivals to the heretical Arminian camp. Much subsequent interpretation of the clergy division created by the awakening, moreover, reproduced this Edwardsean portrayal of a twofold struggle between pietists and rationalists.

However, it is now known that in the early 1740s a third group emerged in the midst of the controversy, which, not seeking to be merely "neuter," attempted to play a mediating role between the contending points of view. To these persons Samuel Mather, son of Cotton Mather, gave the little-publicized name "Regular Lights." More commonly they came to be known as "Old Calvinists." They sought to retain the basic elements of the theology and ecclesiastical practices of the past while finding some accommodation with the new emphases of evangelism and rationalism in the midst of which they were placed. Their task was complex, for it involved dealing with both the new theological issues raised by the rationalists and the new aspects of ecclesiastical order promoted by the revivalists. But altogether theirs was an irenic effort to keep peace on both fronts, by preventing either ideology or enthusiasm from breaking open the unity of the churches. Because their mediating role moved in these two directions, the Old Calvinists contributed to fluidity in the factional alignments of the clergy, and various shadings of perspective developed in ministerial views. Yet in general terms, the divisions by the middle of the eighteenth century can be seen as encompassing three broad groups among those within the ranks of mainstream Congregationalism. At one pole were the New Light, or New Divinity, people, also known as Consistent Calvinists, represented by Jonathan Edwards and his followers. At the other extreme were the Old Lights, represented by Chauncy and many other liberals developing anti-Calvinist views. In the middle remained the Old Calvinists, whose most prominent representative was Ezra Stiles, and who continued to search for reconciliation. In this task, however, they were not successful. By the second decade of the nineteenth century Old Calvinism had disappeared, and the division between the New Divinity and Liberal movements reached its climax in the Unitarian separation.

A second consequence of the Great Awakening, however, was an immediate rupture in the New England Congregational churches brought about by the revival's excesses in evangelistic fervor. Even the Edwardsean New Light practices were insufficient for some of revivalism's advocates, and in the 1740s and 1750s many withdrew to develop independent churches where a more intense form of religious enthusiasm would be welcome. Some withdrew as individuals from established churches to found new congregations, and in other instances whole churches separated themselves from all previous connections to go their independent ways. Altogether about one hundred such congregations came into being in New England, the movement becoming known as Separate or Strict Congregationalism. Some of these churches had only a brief history, disappearing as fervor declined. Others survived to continue longer in their separation and only after considerable time returned to their former Congregational connection. Still others broke completely from their past by adopting believers' baptism and becoming Separate Baptist churches.

During the course of its existence this Separate movement brought into still greater prominence the alienation taking place in the awakening from many of the accepted patterns of the colonies' church life. By their central emphasis on the transforming power of the Spirit in religious experience, these churches developed a variety of practices quite out of keeping with the ways of established eighteenth-century Congregationalism. Worship was ecstatic, relying heavily on exhortation under the prompting of the Spirit. For this purpose, it was felt, ministerial education was of little value and exhortation by inspired members of the laity might be as effective as that by the ordained. Sermons, moreover, should be delivered extempore, for reliance upon premeditation and preparation could itself lead to a stifling of the Spirit. The role of the sacraments was minimized in worship, as was reliance in general upon all formal devotional practices traditionally looked upon as aids to conversion. God's gift of new birth was understood to be more explosive and sudden in its coming than gradual nurture through use of these disciplines would imply. Polity convictions likewise deviated from the eighteenth-century norm, though in this instance they reflected a return to older and stricter Congregational ways. The Half-Way Covenant was categorically rejected, for the church, it was held, must be a pure body of Christ made up of the saved. And control over local congregations by superior ecclesiastical organizations was likewise renounced, particularly the control by the consociations in Connecticut prescribed by the Saybrook Platform. So with these Separates the principle of local church autonomy was strongly reaffirmed.

Added to the turmoil generated by Separate resistance to accepted ways was the repression with which it was met by both ecclesiastical and civil authority. Although established Congregationalism had gradually moved to a toleration of Anglican and Baptist presence, there was no such acceptance for the Separates. This schism within Congregationalism was dealt with by coercion and restraint. C. C. Goen, a historian of the Separate movement, has observed that "there were very few instances where pastor and church brought the disaffected ones back into the fold through love."[23] The strategy was to tighten controls and apply pressures. In local congregations church discipline was invoked and censures were enforced against members who were behaving in the Separates' "disorderly" ways. Ministerial associations were urged to warn clergy about such persons seeking transfer to their congregations. At Yale College students were expelled for attending Separate meetings or listening to a lay exhorter. Particularly repressive measures were taken by the state, especially in Connecticut where they were politically more possible. Separate sympathizers holding public office were removed from their positions, and members of Separate congregations were fined and imprisoned. A major point of conflict centered on the Separates' refusal to pay taxes levied for the support of the established clergy. Anglicans and Baptists had won some relief from this burden. No such concessions were allowed to Separate dissenters, and in cases of tax delinquency the state enforced the law by confiscation of personal property. As the tensions mounted, the rupture within society that the Separates had initiated was enlarged by those who opposed them.

The French and Indian War

Soon, however, these concerns receded in the face of renewed frontier warfare. In 1756 war in Europe was formally declared between England and France and quickly spilled over onto North American soil to become the final struggle between these two powers for colonial domination in the New World. With the French controlling the settled portions of Canada, New England became particularly vulnerable to invasion. French troops garrisoned in Montreal and Quebec, with the aid of American Indian warriors induced into alliance, could easily attack across the colonies' northern borders, as well as generate conflict as far west as the Ohio valley. So the colonies braced for the warfare ahead.

In the eyes of New England's Congregationalists, moreover, the

French and English conflict involved still greater matters than those of political domination and the identity of the European nation to which the colonies would be subject. The conflict was religious, taking on the dimensions of a struggle against false belief and, in millennial terms, against the rule of the Antichrist. Because France was a Roman Catholic nation, New England Congregationalists feared that its triumph would mean defeat of the "true" church and victory for the papacy. Under France New England would be transformed into colonies whose worship would be through the Mass, whose reverence would be for the saints, and whose loyalty would be claimed by a Holy Father in Rome. Surely the diabolical hand of the Antichrist was here at work—and New Englanders believed that resistance was not simply a defense of the homeland but a part of a cosmic struggle in which malignant power must be overcome by the forces of truth and righteousness. It could not be known for certain whether this warfare would be the final conflict with the forces of the Antichrist, but Armageddon was possible. New England's warriors felt summoned to a crusade.

It was anti-Catholic thinking that underlay the strong ministerial support that developed for the battle. There was, in fact, no pacifism evident among New England clergy until the nineteenth century. Eighteenth-century clergy voiced a vigorous call to arms and un-qualified justification of the military cause. Against Roman Catholic France Old Lights and New Lights joined forces. The theological and ecclesiastical divisions of the past, though not healed, were for the time being set aside. There were two major clergy concerns. One was simply to warn of the horrors of possible defeat. Jonathan Mayhew, preaching in Boston, exclaimed, "Do I see Christianity banished for popery! . . . Instead of a train of Christ's faithful, laborious ministers do I behold a herd of lazy monks, and Jesuits, and exorcists, and inquisitors, and cowled and uncowled impostors! . . . Do I see all liberty, property, religion, happiness changed, or rather transubstantiated, into slavery, poverty, superstition, wretchedness!"[24] That was strong inducement for resistance.

The other major concern was to recall the long-standing belief in New England's role as God's chosen people and to reemphasize the federal covenant under which New England had been granted God's special favor and blessing. During the crisis of war this needed to be observed, for disobedience could lead to military defeat as God's judgment, whereas victory would be God's reward for moral and religious faithfulness. Throughout this crisis the message of divine justice operating in history was preached with the same regularity by which it had been proclaimed in earlier decades. Fast days, with calls for repentance, were observed in times of great peril. Days of thanksgiving, with messages of rejoicing, were observed when the fortunes of war turned toward success. If obedience accompanied resistance, the clergy urged, the divine blessing of victory would be gained.

The war progressed through two phases. During the first two years there were many defeats for the combined British and New England forces. A disheartened Ezra Stiles said in a fast-day sermon that God had permitted the defeats because even the colonies' superior troops needed yet to know the necessity for "the guidance and aid of Jehovah to render their arms successful." Eventually the tide turned and battles were won. Quebec was taken in 1759, and Montreal fell in 1760. Ezra Stiles now declared, "God is giving this land to us who in virtue of the ancient covenant are the seed of Abraham." Edward Barnard explained the work of divine providence in the gift of victory by affirming the presence in New England of "a remnant according to the election of grace of those who feared the Lord and trembled at his word."[25] With the declaration of peace in 1763 the trial was ended. France was restrained, New England's cause was vindicated, and under God's providence the righteous had prospered.

The Anglican Threat

Concurrent with fear of repression by the French was growing anxiety about the intentions of the English. A few years later this took on major political dimensions related to the loss of civil liberties, but in the early and mid-1700s Anglophobia was focused more on the religious sphere. Since the time of Andros in the 1680s the Anglican Church had gained a foothold in the northern colonies and increasingly appeared as a competitive alternative to established Congregationalism. Support for its growth was provided by the British crown, particularly after 1701 when the Society for the Propagation of the Gospel in Foreign Parts (SPG) had been organized. Although the society was initially created to supply Church of England ministers for the largely Anglican middle and southern colonies, its work was soon transformed into a more general missionary program and was extended to New England. By the mid-eighteenth century one-third of the society's missionaries were located in the north and were seeking converts to Anglicanism in almost exclusively Congregational communities.

The attraction of Anglicanism was immensely enhanced in 1722 by the shocking announcement by several faculty members at Yale College of their conversion to the Church of England. Chief among them were Timothy Cutler, the rector, and Samuel Johnson, a tutor. For some time these men had questioned the validity of their Congregational ordination and the rightfulness of their Nonconformity. However, books by an English bishop, included in a gift of volumes from England to the Yale library, helped them to their decision. They now saw ordination in the Church of England to be in the line of true apostolic succession and the liturgy of the Book of Common Prayer to have the orderliness and stability requisite for proper worship. Subsequently they went to England for reordination and returned to important Anglican posts. Cutler became the first rector of Christ Church in Boston and Johnson was named the first president of King's College (later Columbia University) in New York.

In the meantime Connecticut Congregationalism and Yale acted to guard against further defections. The trustees at Yale College voted that henceforth every member of the faculty must subscribe to the Saybrook Confession of Faith, a requirement retained until 1823. Moreover, Anglican students at Yale were required to participate in Congregational worship, and not until 1765 were they allowed to attend the Book of Common Prayer liturgy in an Anglican church nearby. Even then they were warned by Thomas Clap, the school's president, not to "infect the minds of their fellow students with such pernicious errors."[26]

Loss of members from Congregational to Anglican churches increased during the period of the Great Awakening. Although the excesses of revivalism led some New Lights to find greater freedom in the radical Separate movement, it encouraged some conservative Old Lights to move in the opposite direction and find security in Anglicanism. Timothy Cutler reported from his Boston parish that wild revivalism "has turned to the growth of the [Anglican] Church in many places, and its reputation universally."[27] Samuel Johnson added a reason for this by saying that the revivals "occasioned endless divisions and separations, so that many could find no rest to the sole of their feet till they retired into the [Anglican] Church, as their only ark of safety."[28] Anglican clergy had long criticized Congregational polity as being inadequate for the maintenance of ecclesiastical order, and these new aberrations seemed in numerous instances to give validity to the charge.

More serious than the loss of members was the Congregational fear of the establishment of an Anglican episcopacy in America. To realize its fullest potential in the colonies, through adequate supervision of its parishes and the provision of American ordination for its clergy, the Anglican Church, its followers affirmed, must have a resident bishop. Supervision throughout the earlier years had been in the hands of the Bishop of London, but by the 1740s the time had arrived when a change to American leadership needed to be made. In 1749 an effort was launched by the Bishop of London to obtain Parliament's authorization for an American bishop's appointment and consecration. Among Congregational colonists, however, there was a storm of protest, reflecting concern over political, as well as ecclesiastical, consequences. Particularly in New England the words "American episcopacy" became a rallying cry for opposition to this extension of English control. By the 1760s the wave of protest had produced correspondence with dissenters in England to encourage assistance there and a series of meetings between New England Congregationalists and middle colony Presbyterians to coordinate resistance at home.

An American episcopacy could augur badly for both religious and civil liberties in the New World. A bishop of the Church of England was an appointee and servant of the state as well as of the church, joining ecclesiastical and political power. So anxieties were easily generated with regard to the dangers at hand. Many viewed establishing an English bishop on American soil as part of a grand scheme for Parliament's more complete control, even enslaving, of colonial life. It was easy for political leaders to join with church leaders in opposition. John Adams, for one, clearly saw both dangers in this complex intertwining of authorities. The threat of episcopacy, he said, raised great alarm concerning still broader exercise of authority over the colonies by Parliament. But the improper exercise of that authority, which soon developed in unlawful taxation, meant likewise to him that Parliament could "establish the Church of England with all its creeds, articles, tests, ceremonies, and tithes; and prohibit all other churches as conventicles and schism shops."[29] The Anglican threat had a double dimension and contributed strongly to popular feeling on the eve of the colonies' struggle for independence.

The American Revolution

Following the conclusion of the French and Indian War, tension mounted between the colonies and their mother country. Earlier decades of the eighteenth century had witnessed strains created by England's economic exploitation of her American dependencies, particularly through policies controlling colonial trade and industry, and muted protests had been voiced. But now the burden became more onerous. The war with France had been costly, and Parliament resorted to a program of increased taxation of the colonies to recover the loss. Within a period of four years following the declaration of peace it approved, without colonial representation, the Stamp Act, the Sugar Act, the Customs Collecting Act, the Revenue Act, and the Tea Act as sources of revenue from the New World—accompanied, moreover, by a Declaratory Act asserting the supremacy of the British Parliament in making laws for colonial possessions. Quickly more vigorous protests developed, not only against the increased tax burden but also opposing the infringement of colonial liberty in the arbitrary imposition of the levies, and New England began to consult other colonies about their common plight.

In 1770 British soldiers, stationed in Boston, fired on protestors, killing five and generating widespread rage. In 1773 Boston citizens resisted a second Tea Act by boarding British ships and dumping their cargoes of tea into the harbor. In 1774 Parliament retaliated with new laws designed to curb the unrest through authorization of expanded British controls in Massachusetts, including the quartering of additional troops in local communities. To enforce this, the commander of the British armed forces in the colony was installed as the colony's governor. It was now apparent that British authority could not be resisted with impunity, and thought turned from resistance to revolution. A clash with patriots at Lexington and Concord occurred in April 1775, and the second Continental Congress, representing all the colonies, met the following month to prepare for the likelihood of war. A final "Olive Branch Petition" for peace failed when in August the king asserted that all the colonies were in a state of rebellion and authorized British troops to fire on patriot forces at will. War was now inevitable, and on 4 July 1776 the Continental Congress took final political action, declaring the independence of the American colonies from British rule.

Although the movement toward revolution and independence was a political matter, its roots were religious as well as secular. Particularly in Congregational New England was this true, as both the awakened spirit in the churches and a clergy increasingly dedicated to the concern of liberty encouraged popular support for the political struggle. For one thing, the Great Awakening was for many a time of emancipation from certain authoritarian restrictions of the past. The new intensity of personal religious experience under the impulse of the Spirit generated a willingness to engage in different and freer styles of public church life. C. C. Goen's characterization of the revival movement portrays it as a "psychological earthquake" that "reshaped the human landscape,"[30] creating assurance that God's power was so given to individuals that they could resist unwelcome authority and bring about change in their society. Then, as the tyranny of British repression became increasingly burdensome in the economic and political spheres, it was but a short step to transpose this new confidence into acts of political protest. Thus a religious foundation was established, especially through the evangelical emphases of the New Lights, which for many encouraged the commitments constituting revolution.

Even more concretely, the churches' role in the movement toward political independence appears in the influence exerted by the clergy's steady advocacy of the cause of liberty. In one sense the theme had long been a part of the New England Congregational heritage. The founders had come to the new land for the sake of religious liberty, and the forms of government they developed for church and state embodied elements of the democracy that political liberty implies. It is true that those early patterns also had been hedged about by restrictions denying religious liberty to others and so paired political freedom with the need for order that in both church and state the balance was often tipped toward aristocratic rule. Nevertheless, the tradition of honoring liberty was deeply established, and Congregational clergy of the late eighteenth century did not hesitate in their political advocacy to find bold precedent in New England's founding and subsequent history. The voice of the colonies' past cried out for freedom from oppression.

Added to this tradition was further support provided by the

thought of the British philosopher John Locke. In the late seventeenth century Locke developed a theory of government emphasizing the importance of natural rights, the justification of resistance to authoritarian oppression, and a constitutional form based on the free consent of the governed. Puritans in England seized upon these ideas, particularly as related to rights and resistance, to justify the Glorious Revolution of 1688, which resulted in the overthrow of James II and the establishment of a more tolerant order. When Locke's writings made their way into New England in the mid-eighteenth century, they were equally employed to support liberty's cause. Beginning in the 1750s and continuing into the time of the American Revolution, Locke was heavily quoted in New England Congregational preaching. Representative of this was Andrew Eliot's election sermon in Boston shortly after the passage of the Stamp Act in 1765. Well versed in Locke's theories, Eliot portrayed the Massachusetts charter as a contract between the king and the people that could, however, be jeopardized through violation of the popular rights that such a compact entailed. And were that to occur, resistance would be not only a right but also a duty, for submission to tyrannical use of power was itself a crime, an offense against both the state and all humanity.

In the emphases of the Congregational clergy, however, the cause of liberty was more than simply a civil affair. For preachers trained in covenant theology and nurtured on the conviction that New England occupied a special place in God's plan, it was insufficient to base the call for liberty merely on a theory of natural rights. Again in the year of the Stamp Act, Stephen Johnson, leading advocate of liberty among Connecticut clergy, added biblical arguments for the struggle against tyranny, and these soon became a major staple of pulpit discourse. Biblical precedent was found in ancient Israel's loss of its God-given political and religious liberties under enslavement by the Egyptian Pharaohs, leading to God's wrath against the oppressors and bold acts of resistance by the Hebrew people. So too, Johnson argued, was the case with England and New England. If England were to continue her tyranny, she likewise would experience divine punishment. But meanwhile New England must resist, for not to defend her liberties would be to deny her special covenant relationship with God.

As the political situation worsened following the Boston Massacre of 1770, the intertwining of covenant and liberty themes became more intimate and more common in Congregational preaching. Both concerns assumed such great importance that the mention of one almost invariably led to the mention of the other. Not only was the defense of liberty seen as necessary for New England's continuation in the federal covenant, but covenant obedience was preached as the necessary ground for continued receiving of the gifts of liberty. Set in this newer political context, fidelity to New England's special calling remained a central duty, and the pulpit urging was to the twin obligations of resistance to tyranny and covenant keeping. Also embedded in this new emphasis was a tacit transformation in the clergy's conception of the nature of political peril. Earlier generations viewed covenant obedience as a means of maintaining order against the threat of anarchy, but now its goal was containing the threat of tyranny. In no small measure New England was encouraged toward resistance, and ultimately revolution, by the widespread commitment of Congregational preachers to the cause of liberty. James Otis, political leader in the rebellion, termed them "the black regiment" as they carried out their critical role in the struggle.

When by 1775 the situation had progressed to the point of anticipating the necessity for declaring independence and constructing a new government, the clergy of New England took one additional step. They found republicanism, already commended by John Locke, to be a form of government endorsed in the Old Testament. The Old Testament had long provided a model for political government for New England, but the nature of its prescription had been subject to change. In the earliest decades the focus was upon theocratic rule through God's chosen agents. Later, after being subjected to renewed control by the crown, the colonies looked to a modified form of monarchy as seen in David's dynasty. But now attention was turned to the premonarchic period in Israel's history where, it was held, a Jewish republic had prevailed. This was the Golden Age and should be replicated for the present time. A significant announcement of this political view was made in the 1775 Massachusetts election sermon delivered by President Langdon of Harvard College, in which monarchy itself was strongly condemned. Once the people of Israel governed themselves, Langdon said, living solely in dependence on God; but they unwisely demanded a king, and this began their fall into captivity and oppression. So too, he argued, is it with New England. Its people had once governed themselves by electing their leaders, but now their liberties were in grave danger because of the oppression by monarchy. Resistance therefore is essential, as is a return to a government by the people, whose sole monarch must be God.

By 1776 the battle had begun, and Congregational clergy turned still more specifically to the fact of warfare itself. Calvinist theology approved a just-war theory in which a major goal of the conflict must be a vindication of justice. New England pastors had no difficulty in seeing that goal as preeminent in the colonies' military struggle. In a sermon preached shortly after the Declaration of Independence, Peter Thacher listed some of the "lawful" aims of the revolutionaries: to defend the unalienable rights God had given them, to oppose a faithless tyrant, to resist those who would take away the people's civil and religious liberties, to struggle against those who have brought ruin, desolation, and destruction. These being the goals, he added, "it is lawful for us to oppose the armies of George of Britain," for "our cause is a just and righteous cause."[31] Yet according to classic just-war theory, such a war must be fought under the authority of the ruler, and a war of revolution could hardly meet that test. So the clergy pressed their analysis one step further, coming back once again to the theory of the compact as the basis of authority for rule. In effect, they said, the tyranny of the king has so destroyed order that the colonies have lapsed into a primitive state of nature out of which a new and authoritative government can be formed by compact among the governed, lawfully constituted to wage a just war. Joseph Perry's Connecticut election sermon of 1775 identified the act of revolution against tyranny not only as one of opposing the oppressor but also as one of recovering the state.

Church and State

The struggle for political liberty likewise furthered the struggle for religious liberty, and new relations between church and state emerged on the American scene as a consequence of the Revolution. At the beginning of hostilities four of the thirteen colonies—Rhode Island, New Jersey, Pennsylvania, and Delaware—were already committed to a policy of religious freedom. During the course of the war the Anglican establishments in five other colonies—New York, Maryland, North Carolina, South Carolina, and Georgia—came to an end when

English support was withdrawn. Concerted efforts to disestablish the Anglican Church in Virginia were carried on during that time, but final success there did not come until 1786, when the state legislature passed the Bill for Establishing Religious Freedom. The subsequent adoption of the U.S. Constitution in 1788 and its Bill of Rights in 1791 gave further guarantees that religious practices in the new nation would not be subject on the federal level to government requirement or control. Article Six of the Constitution prohibited use of a religious test as qualification for any office under national administration, and the First Amendment in the Bill of Rights declared that Congress shall not legislate any establishment of religion, nor prohibit religion's free exercise. The American struggle for religious liberty had by the end of the eighteenth century achieved considerable success.

Final success, however, was delayed in the three Congregational colonies of Massachusetts, Connecticut, and New Hampshire until well after their statehood had been attained. The long tradition of Congregational domination was too tenacious in these states to be immediately and completely set aside. The struggle was particularly prolonged in Massachusetts. Following the renewal of the Massachusetts charter in 1692, the colony was legally required to grant freedom of worship in accordance with the British Act of Toleration of 1689. From that point on, Anglicans, Baptists, and Quakers developed religious services for their supporters as alternatives to worship in the Congregational churches. Religious worship, however, continued to be supported by public taxes. This generated a new problem of fairness for dissenters, because their taxes were applied to Congregational support. Agitation by Anglicans produced the first change, whereby legislation in 1727 permitted those Anglicans who lived within five miles of their place of worship and regularly attended its services to have their taxes assigned to their minister rather than to the clergy of the Congregationalists. Within the next decade the five-mile requirement was removed, but all else remained. By 1747 this arrangement was set for renewal in ten-year increments.

A slightly different arrangement worked out with the Baptists and Quakers acknowledged their basic objections to the idea of an established church and its power of taxation. Legislation of 1728 granted Quakers and Baptists full exemption from the tax for maintenance of Congregational clergy if they signed a register indicating conscientious scruples against this support and lived within five miles of a meeting-house of their own persuasion that they regularly attended for worship. It was the expectation that they would contribute directly to their own churches. The picture was further complicated during the Great Awakening when the Separate Congregationalist movement arose. Separate dissenters continued to be taxed because they were Congregationalists, though they refused to accept orthodox Congregational clergy. To avoid this taxation, some Separate Congregationalists claimed to be attending Baptist services, giving rise to the accusation that Separates had themselves "dipped to wash away their taxes." To deal with this evasion, the law was revised in 1753 and again in 1758, requiring Baptist church membership, not merely attendance, as qualification for the tax-exemption certificate. To be valid the certificate must be signed by the Baptist minister and three leading members of the congregation. Similar legislation was enacted concerning Quakers, with certifying signatures required from three principal members of the society. In cases where dissenters lived too far from their churches to attend, they were denied exemptions and continued to be taxed for support of the local Congregational clergy.

As religious freedom increased in other colonies during the period of the Revolution, Massachusetts found itself under pressure, especially from its rapidly growing Baptist population, to move toward disestablishment. An effort at conciliation was made in 1779 when the General Court called upon Samuel Stillman, a Baptist minister, to preach the election sermon. But older conservatism reasserted itself and was reflected in the new state constitution adopted in 1780. The constitution did contain a declaration of the rights of individuals to worship according to the dictates of conscience, but it added provisions concerning the state's powers over religious practice. The state could compel the establishment of places of worship at such locations as it felt they were needed. It could continue to compel church attendance, except for dissenters whose churches were at too great a distance. And, especially, it could tax all inhabitants for the support of worship, with the provision that the funds supplied by dissenters, upon proper authorization, be allocated to their own churches. In reality this last stipulation was a step backward, for now certified Baptists and Quakers were required to pay church taxes rather than contribute directly to their own societies. Yet because other dissenting groups were now appearing, this revision was legislated as an instrument for broader control. Although in 1800 Quakers were once again exempted from compulsory taxation, the century ended in Massachusetts with church and state not yet separated and Congregationalism continuing to receive the state's favor. Disestablishment was delayed until 1833.

Developments in Connecticut paralleled those in Massachusetts on these matters, although the legal disabilities of dissenters tended, on the whole, to be somewhat more severe. By virtue of state adoption of the Saybrook Platform in 1708, a closer and more formal relation existed in Connecticut between church and state than was characteristic of the colony's northern neighbor. Although all dissenters suffered in Connecticut, constraints against the Separates were particularly harsh, and change came slowly. In 1770 Separates were finally relieved of penalties they had previously endured for not worshipping according to law, but they were still required to pay taxes for support of the official church. Relief from that burden did not come until 1784 when the state legislature defined its postwar position on religious practice with an Act for Securing the Rights of Conscience. In this act freedom of worship and freedom of existence for dissenting churches were affirmed, but the church tax was retained, a certificate plan for reallocating taxes paid by qualified dissenters was defined, and those who claimed no church affiliation were still to be taxed for support of the "state-church." Final disestablishment in Connecticut did not occur until the writing of a new state constitution in 1818. In New Hampshire it occurred in 1819.

Expanding Frontiers

In 1760 Ezra Stiles predicted that in a century Congregationalism in America would number one million adherents, and although his optimism subsequently declined, he continued as late as 1783 to feel that over the course of time it would outdistance all other denominations in memberships. From the limited perspective of Congregationalism's role in New England his confidence could be understood. At the war's end New England contained 656 Congregational churches, but only 163 Baptist churches, 40 Episcopal parishes, and 20 Quaker monthly meetings.

Yet it is also true that the Revolution had taken a heavy toll on Congregational church life, leading to a generally impoverished condition. Some of the clergy and many of the laity had been wounded or killed in the struggle, and others had been impaired by hardship or sickness. Congregations had been broken up, and a number of church buildings had been burned or otherwise damaged. Homes and places of business had been destroyed, and rebuilding had to be done by persons also burdened with taxes for purposes of public reconstruction. Moreover, church membership had declined, as faith suffered from the inroads of skepticism and the growing cult of reason. In Connecticut no new Congregational churches were organized in the seven years following the end of the Revolution, and only eight altogether from 1783 to the end of the century. In Massachusetts fewer Congregational churches were organized between 1790 and 1800 than in any decade for the previous ninety years. Despite Stiles's optimism, the prospects seemed bleak for significant Congregational growth.

Nevertheless, in the concluding decades of the eighteenth century Congregationalism began moving outward from the limited geographical base it had occupied for more than 150 years. As the now-independent American population followed the western frontier, Congregationalism joined in the migration, initiating what was to become its own transcontinental trek over the next three-quarters of a century. Serious problems of personnel, finance, and ecclesiastical structure emerged in the process, alongside severe denominational competition. But a new sense of mission also emerged, and Congregational churches whose focus had been mainly provincial now began to experience concern for a larger area of responsibility. In the new nation Congregationalism entered a new age.

Settlement in Vermont began in the mid-eighteenth century, particularly when the area provided a major transit route for troops moving northward to Canada during the French and Indian War. Following the conclusion of the hostilities in 1763, its population rapidly increased over the next half-century. Immigration came largely from the New England colonies, and the churches initiated were primarily Congregational. Actually, Vermont's first Congregational church, organized at Bennington in 1762, was of the Separate persuasion, made up Separate Congregational dissenters banding together in migration from several Massachusetts locations. The journey of these people northward was a religious pilgrimage seeking greater freedom in ecclesiastical affairs. With the passage of time, however, the church's more radical views were modified, and it became a part of the larger and more traditional Congregational community. Altogether ten Congregational churches were organized in Vermont in the late 1760s, eleven in the 1770s, twenty-three in the 1780s, and thirty in the 1790s. Congregationalism followed the frontier northward.

Vermont churches, in accordance with what was becoming a Congregational pattern, developed associations of ministers and consociations of churches. The initial plan was closer to the Massachusetts model than to the Connecticut form, although later that changed. As a body binding together all the churches of the area, the Vermont General Convention of Congregational Ministers and Churches was organized in 1796. Congregational interest in education led to the chartering of the University of Vermont in 1791 and the founding of Middlebury College in 1800. Neither of these were denominational institutions, but both were long served by presidents and professors of Congregational affiliation.

Although eastern New York had long been colonized, the opening of New York's western frontier across the Hudson was delayed until the conclusion of the war with Britain. Migration began in 1784, bringing many New England Congregationalists into the new territory. The earliest settlers, however, were widely scattered and were unable to develop or support religious institutions. So as early as 1784, local churches and ministerial associations in Connecticut sent ministers on short missions to supply the frontier's religious needs. When clergy undertook these journeys, their own pulpits were temporarily filled by resident pastors whom the associations provided. In 1788 the General Association of Connecticut organized mission work on a statewide basis, obtaining an act from the legislature which authorized a collection taken up from all Connecticut Congregational churches to finance the plan. The churches responded generously, and the plan was followed with increasing success. In 1798, the association reorganized itself into the Connecticut Missionary Society, received incorporation from the state in 1802, and continued the work under this new voluntary arrangement.

The first church organized in western New York was brought together at Canandaigua in 1790. It appears, however, to have been only a temporary expedient, joining scattered Congregationalists from several communities for worship. The Canandaigua church died out when other churches in those communities were gathered. Several churches appeared in the 1790s, their organization aided by counsel from Jonathan Edwards the Younger, son of the great evangelist-theologian and soon-to-be president of Union College, a school established jointly by Congregationalists, Presbyterians, and Dutch Reformed. From the beginning Congregationalists in western New York worked closely with neighboring Presbyterians, carrying on many united activities, although later this led to serious ecclesiastical difficulty. A significant revival movement developed in 1799 and 1800, contributing to rapid growth among these churches and anticipating the yet more extensive nineteenth-century wave of religious excitement that gave the name "the burned-over district" to this territory.

Further advancement westward was stimulated in the late 1780s and the 1790s when the frontier moved into the vast Northwest Territory, an area ultimately to produce the states of Ohio, Indiana, Illinois, Michigan, and Wisconsin. The territory was established in 1787 by the Northwest Ordinance, a remarkable act of the United States Congress opening the land for settlement and stipulating that it be ruled by principles of government embodying basic concerns for liberty. For the state governments carved out of the territory, the ordinance specifically prescribed freedom of religion and freedom from slavery. These provisions, along with emphasis on the importance of setting aside land for the purpose of education, were proposed by a member of the Massachusetts Congregational clergy, Manasseh Cutler. A man of many talents, Cutler at various times served as a lawyer, judge, physician, and member of Congress, in addition to his fifty-two years as a parish minister. As an active member of the Ohio Company, dedicated to offering new territories to persons impoverished by the Revolution, he successfully lobbied Congress in the late 1780s for the ordinance and the principles it contained. In 1786 he told Congress, "Exclude slavery forever . . . and we will buy your land and help you pay your debts; allow [slavery] to enter and not a penny will we invest."[32] When the Northwest Territory was opened as a slave-free area, Cutler bought one and a half million acres of land for the Ohio Company—at nine and a half cents an acre!

The first migration to Ohio, made up largely of revolutionary army officers and their families, left Massachusetts in December 1787, journeyed southward after reaching the Ohio Valley, and arrived at its destination, soon named Marietta, in April 1788. Religious services were conducted from the beginning, initially by an army chaplain accompanying the group, then by Cutler who visited the colony briefly in the summer and fall, and finally by a young pastor called from the East to bring a ministry not only to Marietta but also to the many scattered settlers now arriving to occupy the Ohio Company's land. Conditions, however, were difficult, and it was not until 1796 that the Marietta Congregational church was organized, becoming the first church to be gathered in the Northwest Territory. With equal concern over the importance of education, the directors of the Ohio Company appropriated money for an academy, and this in the early nineteenth century became Marietta College. In the meantime other Congregational migrations to the Northwest Territory moved into the northern part of Ohio, an area known as Connecticut's "Western Reserve," and their first churches were gathered near the southern shore of Lake Erie just as the nineteenth century began. An historical marker at Marietta now honors the political and religious principles underlying the Northwest Territory, proclaiming that "under the Ordinance of 1787 was established the first government BORN FREE in all the world. Here no witch was ever burned; no heretic molested; here no slave was ever born or dwelt."[33] Earlier Congregationalism could not have made that statement, but the words represent a significant contribution of Congregationalism to American history.

THEOLOGY

The Puritan theology of New England Congregationalism survived its first century in America with very little alteration. Minor modifications of emphasis were made in some of its Calvinist perspectives, and muted intimations of future liberalization appeared, but the theology of the 1720s was not substantially different from that of the 1620s. Much theological energy had been expended during the century, but it was devoted largely to elucidation and refinement of Puritanism's classic views. The mid- and late eighteenth century, however, brought greater ferment to the theological scene. More than one catalyst provoked these new developments. The theological genius of Jonathan Edwards contributed important changes, and his followers sought for decades to "improve" Calvinism still further in consequence of his innovations. But at the other end of the theological spectrum the new emphasis on "rational Christianity" made its impact, dividing significantly the theological allegiances within American Congregationalism.

Jonathan Edwards

In 1750, after twenty-four years of ministry in the church at Northampton, Jonathan Edwards was dismissed for reasons of ecclesiastical differences compounded by local politics. He subsequently accepted the call to a mission to the Housatonic Indians in the village of Stockbridge on the western Massachusetts frontier, a post he served until near the time of his death in 1758. In that year he became president of the College of New Jersey (later Princeton), but died only five weeks after assuming office. The two pastorates at Northampton and Stockbridge not only provided dissimilar settings for Edwards's ministry but also contributed to two distinct periods in his theological labors. In his writings in Northampton throughout the revivals he largely, though not exclusively, chronicled and interpreted the movement of the Spirit in Christian conversion. In Stockbridge, however, he turned his attention to underlying doctrinal concerns, producing major theological treatises on matters such as original sin, freedom of the will, the nature of true virtue, and the end for which God created the world.

Edwards's theology was unique in its blending of two fundamental emphases that had been present in his thinking since the time of his youth. These were a deep-rooted Calvinism, on the one hand, and a philosophical idealism, almost a Neoplatonism, on the other. The former was his theological heritage, and the latter a product of his personal religious experience during his college years. For the young Edwards those years were filled with an awareness of the overwhelming beauty of God, reflected in the beauty of the universe as God's garment and creation. God and universe were intimately merged, portraying in unity the divine glory. So the sovereign God of Calvinist faith was known in the light and warmth of a spiritual ecstacy reaching its climax, at age eighteen, in what Edwards deemed his conversion experience. On that occasion he felt more compellingly than ever before the overpowering presence of the divine throughout all reality. Ultimately this vividness of religious experience undergirded his commitment to revivalism, but it led also to the distinctive idealistic metaphysics that his theology contained.

The latter appeared, for example, in the way Edwards portrayed his understanding of God. Key to this was the idea that God is true Being, but also the source of Being from whom all things continuously flow. The very nature of God, he said, involves the presence of a "diffusive disposition," a disposition to grant that which is God's to that which is other than God. In God there is such abundance of Being, with its beauty and joy, that this richness must be poured forth from the Divine Self. Ultimately God's end in all divine activity is the glory of God's own self. This must be, if God is to be God. But God's action also includes the communication of the Divine Being in self giving. This outpouring is the act of creation which, however, Edwards also identified in Neoplatonic language as emanation. God's Being overflows, as a stream flows from a spring. Aware of the peril of pantheism, Edwards denied simple identity of the world and God. But he affirmed the emanating process as a diffusing of the divine Being and its excellencies. Involved here was the ancient "principle of plenitude," which said that Unity fulfills itself by pluralization. In accord with this, Edwards maintained that it is of the nature of perfection to expand itself in multiplication of its fullness. Thus God as perfect Being is perpetually a source from whom all comes forth.

Using more traditional language, Edwards further affirmed that God, in continuously making the world, gives expression to the divine disposition that is love. This is love first for God's own self, for God is the perfect object to whom love is given. But it is also love for those whom God brings into being. Moreover, said Edwards, there is no incompatibility between these two forms of love. Because creation is an emanation of God, God's love for God's creatures remains God's love for God's own self. Were it not so, God's glory would be diminished. Directed, however, toward human persons, this love is further communication of God's fullness, more specifically, as knowledge, holiness, and joy. These are God's loving gifts to the human mind and heart. God's diffusive activity therefore serves as a continuous source of all that is good.

This same type of metaphysical thinking lay behind Edwards's discussion of ethics, when he explored the nature of true virtue. Far from being simply a moral act, virtue in his judgment was an inward attitude of the heart, a disposition of benevolence toward Being. But this disposition, to be most complete, must be directed not simply toward particular beings as objects of benevolence. Rather, its focus must be on that which essentially is and also is inclusive of all good. It must be a disposition of benevolence to "Being in general," which then is a love for God rejoicing in God's happiness and desiring promotion of God's glory. The opposite of true virtue is selfishness, when one's concern is for one's own desired good. Such attitude resists the love that flows from God's diffusiveness. But love for God does not exclude a love for human persons. Love for others is included in true love for God. But it must be love for others within a love for God, not love for others apart from a love for God. Only in subordination to love for God is love for neighbor justified. In this manner Edwards firmly joined religion and ethics and, as in his Calvinism, made the latter thoroughly God-centered.

While at Stockbridge Edwards likewise turned more directly to his Calvinist heritage, dealing at two critical points with its understanding of human nature. The first resulted in a major treatise on the freedom of the will, in which he developed an analysis influential well into the next century in shaping theological discussion. Critical of Arminianism, particularly as it was being advanced by mid-eighteenth-century English writers, Edwards categorically rejected the view that the will is free to make uninhibited choice for either evil or good. He defended Calvinism's view of the will's enslavement, insisting that the natural will has no power of self-determination. But he also provided a fresh approach to this conviction. Using John Locke's theory of causation, Edwards argued that every event must have a cause and that for acts of the will those causes are in the motives that lie behind the actions. One cannot resist the compulsion of the strongest motive, for it represents in any given situation the greatest apparent good. Hence the choices of the will are as determined as are the events of the physical world, and one labors under "moral inability" to act otherwise. For those not renewed by grace this means enslavement by sin. Yet, Edwards added, there is still a "natural ability" not compromised by this bondage. This is the capacity to act or to do as one wills. The direction of the will is determined, but the ability to act accordingly is one's own, and in this sense one can speak of the will's freedom. Some felt this was a sham distinction. For Edwards, however, it meant that sin was voluntary, despite its necessity, and that the sinner was responsible. This distinction took on great importance in the discussion of the following decades and ultimately provided a theological basis on which evangelism came to rest.

For a Calvinist to speak of an enslaving sinful motive meant, however, to speak of original sin, and Edwards at Stockbridge explored this issue more fully as well. Here again he added something new. Like others before him, Edwards defended the doctrine on the ground of the unity of humankind with Adam. New England's primer had voiced the general conviction that "in Adam's fall we sin-ned all." But Edwards drew upon his view of God as continuous Creator to interpret this in an innovative way. It is not simply a matter of heredity, nor of the whole race having been initially present in Adam. Rather, he affirmed, there is an ongoing unity in humankind maintained by the perpetual power of God. God's unifying power is at work everywhere, in the cohering of separate atoms comprising individual physical objects and in the continuous identities of human persons through their successive moments of experience and change. Similarly there is a solidarity of humankind, sustained by God's ever-active power, through which the descendants of Adam are constituted as one in responsibility with him. Thus Adam's fall, a voluntary act, is continuously shared voluntarily by all humanity, presenting a common human need before God.

Although Edwards brought these innovative perceptions to bear on major theological issues, his general stance was that of classic Calvinism—even of classic Puritanism. The sovereignty of God was a dominant emphasis in his thought, as was the theme of justification by faith for the elect. These ideas were often cast, moreover, into the form of covenant theology. Edwards published no systematic treatment of the covenant idea, but his sermons reflected its significance for his thought, as did his treatise, *A History of the Work of Redemption*. The story of redemption was the story of a broken covenant of works replaced by an invincible covenant of grace. It was the story of God's binding commitment to send the gifts of the Spirit to those who were God's chosen. It was the story of God's promise to grant even the covenant condition of faith requisite for the receiving of these gifts. Edwards knew and spoke the covenant language of his Puritan predecessors. His theology, therefore, was predestinarian as well as evangelical and carried within it the paradox of divine sovereignty and human freedom that Puritanism throughout had affirmed.

New Divinity

The theological work of Jonathan Edwards, combined with his New Light approach to evangelism, brought into being a theological movement distinct from the older Calvinism and generally known as the New Divinity, or, more broadly, the New England Theology. Beginning slowly in the mid-eighteenth century through the work of Edwards's close ministerial associates, this movement steadily gained support until it became, by the early part of the nineteenth century, the dominant theological form in American Congregationalism. Although based, like the thought of Edwards, upon the main themes of Calvinism, the New Divinity was committed also to making "improvements" on this heritage. Often these changes seem minute from a modern perspective, and historians have frequently charged this effort with being so overburdened with technical distinctions as to give birth to one of the more arid periods in theological history. But the theology was also pastorally oriented, tied to the concerns of revival and Christian responsibility. Its main proponents in the eighteenth century were pastors giving lengthy service to their parishes: Joseph Bellamy at Bethlehem, Connecticut, for fifty-two years; Samuel Hopkins at Great Barrington, Massachusetts, and Newport, Rhode Island, for a total of fifty-nine years; Stephen West at Stockbridge, Connecticut, for sixty years; John Smalley at New Britain, Connecticut, for sixty-three years; and Jonathan Edwards the Younger for a total of twenty-nine years at New Haven and Colebrook, Connecticut. Energies in the late 1700s were turned less to revival and more to revolution. But in the early 1800s the New Divinity was revitalized in still other hands to become the foundation for America's Second Great Awakening.

Although Jonathan Edwards's followers did not attempt to perpetuate the great theologian's metaphysical interests, they took certain of his theological views and developed them to meet the needs of the changing times. Among these, the most influential for the evolving of their theology was Edwards's emphasis on the voluntary character of sinfulness and holiness. Theologians of the New Divinity were increasingly concerned to urge the role of human responsibility for sin and salvation. This in no way led them to support the Arminianism Edwards so strongly opposed, but in accord with the implications of both the revivals and the revolution, these theologians placed larger stress on the person as an acting agent, obligated and accountable. Although they continued to affirm, as Calvinists, the doctrines of divine sovereignty and predestination, they spoke emphatically of human freedom and responsibility. This led to further variations from tradition, as well as to their gradual modification of Edwards's views.

One place of differentiation was in their interpretations of original sin. Edwards had rejected all explanations imputing Adam's sin to his descendants without their being personally involved as acting agents. His solution had been to develop a concept of the oneness of the race through God's power in which each person necessarily participated in the act of the progenitor. For Edwards's followers, however, this was a speculative supposition and an inadequate affirmation of responsibility. They felt impelled to make it more certain that the sinner's enslavement to sin was itself a result of the individual's own action. Some, like Samuel Hopkins, denied the distinction between original and actual sin, maintaining that all sin was actual. The very origin of sin for each individual was, according to this view, in that person's own act. Hopkins said that "all sin consists in sinning"[34] and that the descendants of Adam participate in his sin only to the extent that "they approve of it, by sinning as he did."[35] John Smalley criticized earlier interpretations that made Adam's sin responsible for the sinfulness of the race by saying that these explanations are "rather calculated to ease the conscience" by "casting all the blame back on the first sin only."[36] He argued that all sin results from the sinner's own voluntary exercise of the will, even the sin that leads initially to one's corrupted condition before God. Although Edwards had said essentially the same thing, these followers now "improved" it by making it more emphatic and precise. Joseph Bellamy added that "the more unable to love God we are, the more we are to blame,"[37] for that inability itself is the consequence of a voluntary act.

The New Divinity theologians further pursued the idea that sin was voluntary by applying more forcibly Edwards's emphasis on "natural ability" as found in his discussion of the freedom of the will. Although they fully affirmed fallen humanity's "moral inability" to overcome self-love apart from the regenerating gift of God's grace, they also stressed the natural ability that remains to act in accordance with one's motives, whether evil or good. Intent upon magnifying human responsibility, New Divinity theologians pressed in two directions the significance of this native power of choice. For one thing, they said, it leaves the sinner with no excuse for not obeying God's law. Bellamy declared that the law is "exactly on a level with our natural capacities" and therefore, as far as those abilities are concerned, all humanity is "capable of a perfect conformity" to it.[38] So the fact of natural ability increases the sinner's blame and need for repentance. But additionally, natural ability increases the possibility of repentance, because the sinner has a natural capacity for turning to God. This conclusion had practical, as well as theological, significance. Whereas earlier Calvinism in its denial of any ability had often counselled the sinner's passive waiting for God's initiating act, the preacher's call could now be made for immediate repentance. New Divinity theologians opened the door more fully to the validity of the evangelistic appeal that revivalism embraced.

Yet why this sinful world in the first place? God was not the author of sin, for sin was a voluntary human act; then why did a perfect and powerful God allow it to enter? As Edwards's followers probed this question, they developed an additional distinctive conviction for the New Divinity. This world, they declared, is the best possible of all worlds, made so by the fact of sin's presence. Edwards's doctrine of divine benevolence provided a basis for this affirmation. The goal of God's benevolence is the achievement of the greatest good for all creation, a good that must involve awareness and experience of God's redeeming love. Were there no sin, the fullness of God's nature could not be known. Therefore, wrote Bellamy, sin is "a necessary means of the greatest good."[39] This did not mean that sin is itself a good, nor that sin is the direct and efficient means of the greatest good. But sin was permitted, even decreed, that it might provide the occasion for God so to act as to achieve the highest good. This was the wisest of all possible plans to secure the goal of God's benevolence.

For New Divinity leaders the Edwardsean view of divine benevolence likewise required revision of the doctrine of atonement through the death of Christ. In Calvinist theology the satisfaction theory had long been employed to explain Christ's sacrifice. Christ's death was offered for the elect, satisfying for them the justice of God by paying the penalty for their sins. But in the light of the larger goal of God's benevolence this was now found to be too limited an interpretation of the meaning of the cross. The highest good of the created order demanded a broader understanding of atonement, and the New Divinity theologians developed this in what came to be known as the *governmental view*. God's world, they said, is governed by God's law, and its highest good comes through an upholding of that law and government. The law requires punishment for sin, and Christ's death serves this purpose. However, rather than serving directly as substitutionary penalty, it provides a sacrifice equivalent to what would be that penalty if it were to be exacted. This act, therefore, maintains the honor of the law and vindicates the rightness of God's government in accordance with it, removing thereby the impediment of unsatisfied justice to the granting of forgiveness. Moreover, it is a sacrifice offered for all humanity, satisfying the general justice of God, rather than a distributive justice limited to select individuals. So the atonement is general in scope, having universal applicability. Yet this did not mean universal salvation, for New Divinity theology was still predestinarian in its basic foundation. Although Christ's death was sufficient for all, the saving benefits of that atonement were bestowed only upon those elected for such destiny by God's sovereign act.

The Liberals

Concurrent with this development of a modified Calvinism by the theologians of New Divinity there emerged a movement to reject Calvinism altogether in the interest of a more liberal theology. Early liberal leaders were again members of the Congregational clergy, located in this instance mainly in eastern Massachusetts. Most prominent among them in the eighteenth century were Lemuel Briant, whose brief ministry in Braintree was ended by an early death in 1754; Ebenezer Gay, who served as pastor at Hingham for sixty-nine years until 1787; Jonathan Mayhew, who ministered at West Church in Boston from 1747 to 1766; and Charles Chauncy, whose sixty years at First Church in Boston came to an end in 1787. Although this movement was in no way as extensive as that of Jonathan Edwards's followers, it set the stage for that flowering in the second and third decades of the nineteenth century resulting in the Unitarian separation from Congregationalism.

Fundamental to the liberal movement was its emphasis upon the role of reason in religious understanding. A preferred term for this new outlook was *rational Christianity*. Although Puritanism had always accorded human reason a place of significance in the work of theology, that was reason restored from a fallen condition by grace and committed to the limited task of interpreting the content of God's revelation. Influenced, however, by English philosophical movements celebrating the greater independence of human reason as an unblemished gift of creation, critics of orthodoxy now began to assert the power of natural reason itself to discover and authenticate religious truth. For one thing, God's ways in nature could be discerned by the inquiring mind and made a basis for knowledge of the Creator. Earlier in the century Samuel Willard and Benjamin Colman had developed views along these lines, but their steps toward a natural theology remained fully subordinate to the authority of a theology founded on divine revelation. Among the "rational Christians," however, that restriction was abandoned, and reason in fact became the judge of revelation. Chauncy spoke of eternal and immutable truth to which human reason had access and to which all claims of revelation must conform. And Gay added that though revelation may make somewhat clearer the things reason has discovered, any claims of revelation that are absurd by rational standards must be rejected as untrue.

This meant that God's own actions complied with the reign of reason in the government of the universe. God governs in an orderly and predictable way, dealing rationally with human persons who are themselves rational creatures. At a practical level this conviction led to the liberals' opposition to the Great Awakening, for revivalism encourages the disorderliness of extreme emotion. Theologically, moreover, this view denied God the arbitrariness of a sovereign will and thus undercut a major tenet of the dominant Calvinism. These are consequences of the basic confidence that reason rules in divine life as well as human.

God's rational rule of the universe, said the liberals, is directed primarily by God's goodness or, as Chauncy frequently phrased it, by God's benevolence. The latter term was employed also by the Edwardseans for identifying God's nature. And although, like the Edwardseans, the liberals affirmed that God had created the best of all possible worlds for the serving of God's benevolent purpose, the two theologies were far apart in portraying the nature of that purpose and the manner in which the world related to it. For the Edwardseans the world was best because it included sin, which made possible the redeeming love of God and thereby contributed to God's glory. For the liberals the world was best because it was created for the furthering of human happiness and was ordered in all its aspects to achieve that end. Mayhew acknowledged that this also could be interpreted as contributing to God's glory. But the emphasis had shifted in a substantial way. Human happiness was the goal of God's benevolence, and God's glory was itself contingent upon that realization. A different focus had emerged for rational theology. Not only were God's acts accommodated to the requirements of human reason, but God's purpose was defined by human aspiration. Rational Christianity gave more central attention to the human person in reaching its understanding of the ways of God.

The liberal focus on humanity was supported, if not generated, by a more optimistic view concerning the moral potential of human nature. Liberal theology was ultimately Arminian in its affirmation of an uninhibited freedom of the will for moral choice and in its confidence concerning the use of that freedom. It rejected the doctrine of original sin, for in a world where sin is voluntary and each individual is by nature a morally responsible agent, it is impossible for one person to be charged with either the guilt or the corruption of another. Actually, even the fall of Adam, though punished by condemnation to suffering and death, was less a fall than a failure to rise. In creation Adam was made not perfect, but perfectible, and his sin was an unwillingness to improve to that goal. Similarly all humanity was created with the possibility of perfection and charged with the obligation to realize that potential. Such perfection was not necessarily an easy matter. Chauncy saw it complicated by the fact that the suffering and death brought on by Adam's sin have been perpetuated for all humanity, making the world a testing ground for the attainment of virtue. But there is moral capacity to resist all temptation and to move toward perfection, and liberal theology rested its confidence on that conviction. Briant said that Christianity is "the sincere, upright, steady and universal practice of virtue," and Chauncy added that when one's human capacities are used for this purpose, one "may attain to the moral likeness of God."[40]

For the liberal theologian salvation was a moral achievement. Other matters were indeed involved. There was an atonement through the death of Christ, which liberals, like the Edwardseans, interpreted in governmental terms. There was forgiveness of sins. And there was God's assisting grace. Yet salvation was more a matter of self-improvement than a radical transformation wrought by God. One grows into salvation by responding to the moral instructions of Christ, the supreme Teacher sent chiefly to make plain the ways of righteousness and to provide a perfect example of obedience to God's will. "Conversion" was a gradual process of growth in virtue, and "new birth" represented the fuller attainment of those desirable qualities cultivated through moral development. The major focus was on human capacity and human accomplishment. Briant wrote, "It is the righteousness of the saints that renders them amiable in God's sight."[41]

Rational Christianity viewed this as part of God's plan for human happiness, for there is joy in virtue and in the communion with God virtue brings. But Chauncy took a further, more radical step. If God's goal for humanity is its happiness, Chauncy argued, that must be intended not only for life's brief span but also for eternity—and ultimately it must be granted to all persons because, he said, "the blessed God stands in the same near and tender relation to the whole human race."[42] Chauncy concluded that eternal salvation is universal. Such a view, however, was unorthodox beyond any possibility of receiving a calm hearing. Chauncy knew this, and for some three decades he shared these thoughts with only a small circle of like-minded friends. In the 1750s he did put them into a manuscript titled *Salvation for All Men*, but he waited until 1784 to release it for publication, and even then did so without his name attached. The storm of controversy that it generated justified his caution.

Despite Chauncy's effort to resolve the issue of ultimate salvation by declaring God's promise of universal human happiness, he encountered, though in somewhat different guise, the age-long problem of harmonizing divine sovereignty and human freedom. The freedom humanity possesses means that some might forever fail in the moral development requisite for ultimate happiness. Yet God not only desires this happiness for all humanity but also "authoritatively wills it."[43] Chauncy tried to mitigate the problem by accepting the existence of a hell of suffering and then reinterpreting that suffering as reformative and temporary rather than as penal and eternal. There the wicked could learn and mend their ways. Yet the issue remained, for not all might do so. In the end Chauncy simply held that a benevolent God will grant final salvation for all persons.

POLITY

Throughout American Congregationalism's first century considerable thought and energy were given to matters of church organization and function, focusing concern upon the nature of the church, its membership, its ministry, and its manner of structuring its institutional life. The core ingredients of this polity had been carried to early New England by the founders of these churches and remained largely intact through the years. Yet as Congregationalism matured in its new setting, its polity required refinement in theory and modification in practice. Thus much early effort in New England was given to a fuller definition and shaping of the Congregational way. By the mid-eighteenth century, however, this intensity of attention had largely subsided, replaced by other demanding matters, and, apart from brief provocation by the Great Awakening, issues concerning church organization did not reemerge as primarily important until another hundred years had passed.

Church Membership

The major polity issue brought to general attention by the events of the Great Awakening was that of qualification for membership within the local church. American Congregationalism had long agonized over this question. The purist approach of the earliest days had called for a recounting of one's personal experience of conversion, along with a profession of faith and the supporting testimony of scandal-free living. The church was a community of the saints—and though saints could also be sinners, they were forgiven sinners whose basic life direction had been radically altered by the powerful working of God's grace. So far as could be determined, these were the elect, and only they were qualified to constitute the church and to avail themselves of its sacraments. But changes occurred, notably by gradual modification of the requirement for witnessing to an experience of conversion and then by development of the Half-Way Covenant and its related Stoddardeanism opening the door to the church's sacraments for any who appeared morally sincere and committed to live by the faith. Through these changes the church relinquished some of its earlier restrictive character and was brought into closer identity with the world.

One result of the Great Awakening, however, was a renewed confrontation with this issue and at least a partial return to the earlier, more exclusive way. The aim of the revivals was the conversion of the unregenerate, and this intensive emphasis on life-changing Christian experience led to protest against the more lenient practices then current in the formation of the church. The Separates were the most vehement in their reaction. Their dedication to the principle of the church's purity led them to withdraw and set up their own congregations with membership strictly limited to the "saved." Their major objection was to the "graceless" community life that characterized a congregation when admission into intimate church fellowship was granted to those who could not testify to a personal experience of grace. In the light of the widespread practice of granting baptismal privilege and the Lord's Supper to members who claimed no conversion, the Separates' condemnation was also against the desecration of sacramental holiness occurring within the impure church.

This protest against lax membership practices was not limited, however, to those who withdrew. More important for its greater impact on the future of Congregationalism was the critique of membership criteria made by the New Light movement coming out of the Great Awakening. Jonathan Edwards was again a leading voice. In his criticism of half-way membership he complained that a dead formalism had come to characterize the owning of the covenant. It was simply a meaningless step taken when persons, who had long neglected religious duties, became parents and petitioned for church membership in order to have their children baptized. And where testifying to conversion was still a prerequisite for admission to the Lord's Supper, this was often done by a stereotyped recounting lacking any reference to a personal experience of God's saving grace. Thus, Edwards said, "true disciples of Christ are obliged to receive those as their brethren and embrace them in the highest acts of Christian society, even in their great feast of love, . . . whom yet they have no reason to look upon otherwise than as enemies of the cross."[44] At the same time Edwards criticized the Separates for their extreme behavior, charging them possessed by a "lunatic" spirit. Edwards's goal was not to withdraw but to inject greater piety into the churches. Yet on the question of requirements for church membership and participation in the sacraments, he identified very closely with the Separates.

In 1750 Edwards encouraged the Northampton church to return to the older practice of a stricter qualification for the communion. As a consequence, though also for his attempt to enforce punitive discipline on some of the church's youth, he was dismissed from his ministry by the congregation. Many Congregational clergy, such as Ezra Stiles's Old Calvinist moderates, disagreed with Edwards on this issue. The year before his dismissal Edwards published his *Humble Inquiry*, advocating more selective membership and communion. At the urging of the clergy moderates, Solomon Williams, minister at Lebanon, Connecticut, prepared a reply. The moderates differed with Edwards not on theology but on application. Both felt that the church should admit none but "visible saints," nor should any others be eligible for the communion. But they differed over which visible criteria could be relied on to determine genuine inward saintliness. Edwards insisted that those who received communion should be able to share a personal relation of conversion. This might be offered untruthfully, he allowed, but the lack of such relation would contribute to yet greater uncertainty. If persons "do not pretend to have any oil in their vessels," he asked, "what cause can there be to trust that their lamps will not go out?"[45] For the moderates, however, moral behavior was enough indication of inward grace. Williams wrote that morally sincere performance of outward duties should be viewed in charity by the church as "the product of the great inward duties of love of God, and acceptance of Christ." Persons so acting could then be accepted as "real saints."[46]

As the eighteenth century moved on, the New Divinity people sustained Edwards's judgment on this matter, whereas Old Calvinist moderates gradually lost ground and by the end of the century disappeared. Some Old Calvinists joined with the liberal movement, where Chauncy was affirming a yet more open approach to church membership and reaffirming the old Stoddardean view of the Lord's Supper as a converting ordinance. The majority of Congregationalists, however, ultimately adapted to the New Divinity evangelicalism and soon became participants in the Second Great Awakening. As a consequence the Half-Way Covenant was completely ignored by the beginning of the nineteenth century. But some uncertainty remained concerning at least the manner of a personal relation, thereby carrying the membership question into another generation.

Local Autonomy

Another consequence of the Great Awakening's recall to a more restrictive understanding of church membership was a renewed emphasis on the autonomy of each congregation. Again the Separates led the way. The earlier part of the eighteenth century had witnessed a growth in connectionalism, particularly in the system of consociations and associations mandated for Connecticut by the government's adoption of the Saybrook Platform. The Separates rejected this without equivocation. For them the local congregation of pure saints should in no way be subject to control by outside authority, least of all by agencies established by the state. God's power was given to the elect, first as individuals under the control of the Spirit and then as local churches composed of the saints. The established ecclesiastical order had no divine commission and therefore no authority over local congregations. Ultimately, in Congregational fashion, the Separates did develop advisory councils drawn from representatives of neighboring churches, and by 1781 they had set up in Connecticut a statewide convention for their denominational activity. Yet all of this was organized in such a way as not to contravene local church autonomy.

For the main body of New England's Congregational churches, however, the path toward resurgent emphasis on local autonomy was more complicated. Regional and political, as well as ecclesiastical, factors interfered, contributing to uncertainties and conflicts along the way. This was particularly true in Connecticut, where New Divinity leaders, upon gaining control of the colony's ecclesiastical agencies, used them to protect their Calvinism against erosion in local churches. By the mid-1750s Joseph Bellamy's Litchfield Consociation persuaded the Connecticut General Association to affirm a Calvinist confession of faith that could be used to overcome Arminianism in the local congregations. It also attempted, though this time unsuccessfully, to form a general consociation that would have final judicial authority over all ecclesiastical disputes. Again, in the late 1750s, the New Haven Consociation, controlled by the New Divinity, acted in a major confrontation to overrule the ordination of a liberal candidate called to a ministry within its jurisdiction, despite authorization of the call by the local church supported by an advising council from neighboring churches. Elsewhere in Connecticut, however, pastors of the New Divinity, perhaps because of the Separates' influence, resisted the Saybrook system and sought to return to the Cambridge Platform, where they found a greater sense of freedom for the local church. Altogether, therefore, the Connecticut picture was mixed, with significant movement toward resolution delayed until the Saybrook Platform was quietly dropped from the colony's laws in 1784.

The situation was different for the New Divinity in Massachusetts, where no legal system of supracongregational authority prevailed. In Massachusetts conflict focused mainly on the relation of neighborhood councils to the local church. By tradition these councils were summoned at the option of local churches to provide assistance in decision making on weighty matters. Yet while called for that purpose, the extent of their authority had never been precisely defined. On the one hand, they were simply advisory; on the other hand, their advice was to be received with "reverence and submission." In time disagreements arose, particularly in instances of the selecting or the dismissing of pastors by local churches. Protective of the ministry against rash decisions by local congregations, the Massachusetts clergy in 1773 strongly urged seeking a council's recommendation in the choosing of a minister and the unqualified abiding by a council's decision in cases of conflict surrounding dismissal. Especially in the latter case, they argued, great disservice can be done to the clergy if, in the heat of controversy, congregations have complete freedom to act. The laity, however, disagreed, unwilling to give up their autonomy on so crucial a matter.

But the most persuasive voice in this dispute was that of a member of the clergy who agreed with the laity. Nathanael Emmons, a minister of the New Divinity, was called to the church in Franklin, Massachusetts, in 1773, where in fifty-four years of service he championed the cause of local autonomy. An advocate of "pure democracy" for Congregationalism, he spoke for equality of pastor and members within the local congregation and for such independence of churches in their interrelations as would permit none to violate the freedom of any other. There is, he said, no divine authority for church councils, and all ecclesiastical power is lodged in the local congregations, which are subject only to Christ. Emmons's polity views tended on the whole to be extreme in their hostility to any cooperative endeavor, and not all were fully adopted. But his outspoken advocacy for the rights of a congregation contributed immeasurably to the enhanced emphasis given to local autonomy by the end of the eighteenth century.

Laity

A further effect of the Great Awakening upon Congregationalism appears in the enhanced role of the laity in the life and worship of the local church. Again this was particularly true for the Separates, for whom the revivals became a leveling experience, reducing the gap between the ordained and the unordained. With major emphasis in worship placed upon evangelistic exhortation by the gifts of the Spirit, the Separates saw less reason for a class of educated and set-apart clergy and more reason for using the talents of any persons whom God empowered to preach. Thus in the early 1740s lay exhorters began to share with local clergy in public pleadings for repentance and conversion. Some even became itinerants for the cause. In their confrontation with the establishment Separates made it plain that they would prefer an uneducated lay exhorter to an educated, "unconverted" preacher, for the former provides a greater sense of the presence of God.

Resistance in established churches to this breach of tradition was vehement. Even prorevival clergy were appalled. Benjamin Colman characterized the lay exhorters as persons who, having "sprung up like mushrooms in a night, in the morning thought themselves accomplished teachers" called by God—and the general clergy complaint was that this lay preaching was "contrary to Gospel order and tends to introduce errors and confusion into the church."[47] However, despite their rejection of such lay activity on the part of the Separates, the majority churches of the Great Awakening became more open to lay recognition and responsibility. Jonathan Edwards defended diligently the traditional, even sacerdotal, understanding of ordained ministry received from his Puritan heritage, but at the same time credited the laity with being the prime movers of the revival. Through their responses, their prayer groups, the contagion of their "testifyings" to personal experiences of conversion they functioned as "instruments" for the mighty work of the Spirit. When Edwards wrote on the revivals he rarely mentioned the local ministers under whom these occurred, but focused rather on the ordinary people used by God to effect the ongoing plan of redemption. Edwards acknowledged that a prime aspect of the awakening was the freeing of the laity from a role heavily weighted toward subservience to a clergy-dominated order. Those awakened by the Spirit were energized to assume greater personal responsibility for their own religious condition and that of their churches.

The clergy themselves, in a negative way, also contributed to the laity's assumption of a more active role. Inheritance of a long Barrowist tradition of ministerial control had led the "Standing Order" to a pattern of clergy arrogance that alienated many lay people. Furthermore, the effectiveness of ministerial leadership had been reduced by the intense clergy conflicts on matters of theology and church practice during the Great Awakening. Thus psychologically as well, whether in revivalist or nonrevivalist churches, the laity were prepared to claim a more active place in the conduct of church affairs. Churches rescinded the privilege of the "negative voice," which had given clergy a veto over laity in decision making. The role of lay officers in the church was enhanced, and congregations as a whole achieved liberty to be "watchmen" over their ministers in the conduct of their profession. Slowly a Brownist form of church government replaced the Barrowist, bearing out Ezra Stiles's confidence that "common Christians" were "good judges" in ecclesiastical affairs.[48]

One additional aspect of this trend led to the more active participation of women in church life. In Jonathan Edwards's written descriptions of the revivals several accounts of women's conversions appear, and their testifyings are duly recorded. Moreover, when on one occasion Edwards illustrated God's use of lay leadership, he found an Old Testament example in Deborah, who led the Hebrew men of Meroz to victory over the Canaanites. In his exposition of the incident Edwards noted that when some of the men refused to follow Deborah because she was a woman, they were punished by God!

One woman who exemplified these changes was Sarah Osborn, a member of the First Congregational Church in Newport, Rhode Island. Converted during the Great Awakening, she increasingly over the next several decades found ways to use her commitment and talents to further the work of revival in her local church. In 1741 she took over the direction of a young women's prayer society, an activity she continued until the end of her life. In 1765 she initiated a revival in an unusual way, by allowing a number of slaves to attend family prayers in her home on Sunday evenings. Within a year more than three hundred persons, both African American and white, were coming to her house each week for religious gatherings, and in 1769, though religious fervor in Newport had declined, these prayer groups continued to meet under her supervision. When men joined these groups she knew that she was pressing the acceptable boundaries of feminine behavior and deliberately took steps, as she said, "to avoid moving beyond my line." But religion, she also observed, was "the chief business" of her life. When pressed by a neighboring pastor to conserve her strength and use her leisure for more womanly pursuits, she curtly replied, "Needlework overpowers me vastly more than the duties I am engaged in." In 1770, according to Ezra Stiles, a neighboring pastor in Newport, she exercised "great influence" in her congregation's choice of Samuel Hopkins as its new minister, a further testimony to her remarkable leadership in church affairs.[49]

WORSHIP

During the course of the first two centuries of Congregationalism in America, fewer major changes occurred in the area of worship than in any other aspect of its life. A typical order of service around the year 1800 would have been the following:

Blessing
Psalm or Hymn
Scripture Reading
Prayer
Anthem
Sermon
Prayer
Psalm or Hymn
Blessing

The pattern of simple worship employed by the first generation of New England churches continued largely to prevail. Important changes did occur in the music of the service, and the content of preaching was altered to some extent as it adapted to the newer theological and political climate of the times. But generally speaking, the inherited character of worship remained relatively undisturbed. Even such a formerly contentious issue as the manner of reading Scripture was quietly resolved in local churches according to practical and personal considerations. In Exeter, New Hampshire, after going some time without an independent Scripture lesson in the Sabbath service, the church voted in 1777 to restore the reading, though without interpolation. Some protested the latter qualification, but not for the classic reason of opposition to the "dumb reading" of Anglican practice. Their complaint was that in the winter it became very cold in the meetinghouse and, they said, it would be more comfortable to sit by their own fires where they could read as understandably by themselves the Scripture otherwise heard in church. So they asked that either the Scripture reading be dropped again from the service or the pastor explain what he reads. The latter modification was approved, and in 1780 interpolation was incorporated into the worship at Exeter. Subsequently, in New England practice as a whole, the manner of Scripture reading was simply left to the pastor's option.

Music

For approximately the first century and a half in New England the singing of congregations in worship was limited to use of metrical paraphrased versions of the psalms, and during the first half of that period the music itself was restricted to a few simple memorized tunes. The texts came largely from the Bay Psalm Book published in 1640, to which musical notations were added in the 1690s. The printing of melodies, and then harmonies, led to a half-century controversy between those who would sing by rote and those who would sing by note, but during that period there was growing dissatisfaction over the texts themselves. Other paraphrases of the psalms were developed, culminating in the 1758 revision of the Bay Psalm Book by Thomas Prince, pastor of Old South Church, Boston, who aspired to a closer approximation to the original meaning of the psalms and to a greater poetic sophistication and beauty. But times were changing, and Prince appended to his revised Bay Psalm Book a collection of hymns that, in his description, were "not versions of the Scriptures, but pious songs derived from them, by Dr. Watts and others."[50]

Isaac Watts, a Congregational minister in England, made the most significant contribution to all church music in the eighteenth century, first through his exceptionally literate paraphrases of the psalms and then through his equally excellent creation of texts for hymns. Although these were written and published in England early in the eighteenth century, they did not become generally available in America until the time of the Great Awakening. In 1741 his psalms were published by Jonathan Edwards in Boston and his hymns by Benjamin Franklin in Philadelphia. The first to appeal were the psalms texts, for they continued to be based directly on biblical passages. These were quickly adopted by many churches as a replacement for the Bay Psalm Book. But by the 1750s churches began to turn to the hymns, despite the fact that the texts, unlike the psalms, were "uninspired." After all, Prince had included them in his publication. The adoption of hymns, however, was more gradual, as indicated by the 1761 vote of First Church, Boston, where it was agreed that the psalms should be supplemented by such of Watts's hymns "as our reverend pastors shall think proper" and "as soon as it can conveniently be done."[51] Nevertheless, by the end of the century the singing of hymns had largely replaced the singing of psalms in Congregational worship.

The more general acceptance of singing by note, first for the psalms and then for hymns, led in time to choirs. At first choirs were simply to assist in the improvement of congregational singing. In the 1761 vote at First Church, Boston, the importance of reviving "the spirit of singing in this church" was acknowledged, and to that end it was concluded that "a number of the best singers among us" should be asked to sit together "in some convenient place in the meetinghouse." Other churches followed this precedent with even more specific designation of location, the congregation in Hollis, New Hampshire, for example, voting in 1767 "that those persons that have taken pains to instruct themselves in singing may have the two fore seats below on the men's side."[52] The change from the old practice of lining out the psalms to the new choral leadership in congregational singing did not, however, take place without resistance, even conflict. In the church at Worcester, for example, both methods were followed for a while in a rather incongruous mixture, until in 1779 the impasse was broken when the choir simply oversang the precentor! By the 1780s the further expectation that choirs provide anthems had developed, and by 1800 these were generally included in public worship. The early choirs in the New England churches usually sang in four parts: soprano, counter-tenor, tenor, and bass, with the melody sung by the tenor. The soprano was included for women, although in some cases women were not yet admitted to the singing societies that supplied members for the choirs, in which case their part was taken by men in falsetto or by boys.

Music in Congregational worship was originally unaccompanied vocal music, but gradually musical instruments were introduced. Al-though a variety of instruments were enjoyed in private life, it was long felt that their use in worship was biblically prohibited. The Brattle Street Church in Boston was offered an organ in 1713 by a wealthy Boston merchant, but declined the gift. The organ was later accepted by the Anglican King's Chapel. The first known record of an organ in a New England Congregational church appears in Ezra Stiles's diary of 1770 where he noted that a two-hundred-pipe instrument had recently been set up in the church at Providence. However, he designated it "an innovation of ill consequence."[53] Fifteen years later Charles Chauncy reluctantly agreed to the installation of an organ at First Church, Boston, for, according to Stiles, Chauncy knew that his congregation would have one "before his head was in the grave." By 1798 half a dozen organs had been placed in Massachusetts churches. Actually, the first instrument used for accompanying singing in Congregational worship was the bass viol, introduced in the mid-1700s, and near the end of the century other instruments were added. In Salem the clarinet and the violin were first played in worship in 1792 and the flute in 1795. Shortly after the turn of the century, congregational singing in Boston's Park Street Church was supported by flute, bassoon, and cello.

Preaching

As in many aspects of American Congregationalism in the latter half of the eighteenth century, the style and content of preaching were affected significantly by the period's two major occurrences, the revivals and the Revolution. Earlier preaching in the New England churches had tended to find a balance between appeals to the head and to the heart. The appropriate doctrines were drawn from the text, and the applica-tions or "uses" called for committed response. But in the period of the Great Awakening a more significant differentiation appeared between the two, leading to sharply contrasting styles of preaching. Although many of the moderate Calvinists remained faithful to the older Puritan preaching tradition, major deviations to both the right and the left were brought on by the conflicts over revivals. Those who resisted revivals turned more and more to an appeal to the intellect; the style of their sermons was "rationalist." Those who promoted revivals directed their efforts to the realm of emotion, which generated commitment; the style of their sermons was "evangelical."

Rationalist preaching flourished among the theological liberals, located in eastern Massachusetts and trained at Harvard, who felt that because religion was reasonable, it must be thoughtfully explained. Great care was given to preparation for this preaching. Sermons were written out in full-length manuscript, with much attention paid to literary quality. They were usually read from the pulpit verbatim. Andrew Eliot noted the importance of this practice, for if it is neglected, he said, the preacher is in danger of "delivering many things that are crude and indigested."[54] Earlier Puritan practice also had called for extensive written preparation, but only brief notes were taken into the pulpit. To the complaint that the new reading of sermons constituted a lifeless form of preaching, the liberals replied that clear understanding of the gospel was essential as preparation for the reception of grace and the fulfillment of duty. For rationalist preaching a restrained form of delivery was commended. Eliot said that ministers should strive to "deliver themselves with decency," attaining to "a good elocution and an agreeable behavior in the pulpit."[55] In the mid-eighteenth century this type of preaching generally appealed to urbane congregations aspiring toward a more refined and sophisticated social status, especially in the Boston area. It also contributed to a cultural elitism dividing New England Congregationalism.

Evangelical preaching of the period had a different purpose and a different style. Seen as a means whereby the Holy Spirit brought sinners to repentance and conversion, it aimed its appeal more at the passions where conscience could be touched, anxieties generated, yearnings stimulated, and life-and-death decisions made. Methods varied, from the early boisterous harangues of the itinerants to the less-extreme manners of moderate New Divinity preachers, who were college trained at Yale and motivated to continue the revivalistic appeal even after the intensity of the Great Awakening had passed. The preaching of

Jonathan Edwards can be seen as a prototype of this style. Edwards emphasized strongly the moment of delivery in preaching. The thought must be carefully prepared, but the manner of presentation must be such that the Holy Spirit can work through the words and touch the human heart. This did not require theatrics, but it did include an earnestness in speaking worthy of the seriousness of the occasion. It also required such flexibility in relation to the prepared sermon as to allow for the Spirit's continued inspiration. When Edwards entered the pulpit, he took with him a brief outline of his intended sermon and then, as the situation warranted, gave way to spontaneity. Edwards's style, moreover, encouraged the use of imagery to touch the emotions. Rather than simply relying on reason, he turned often to visions that could generate sensations of either fear or joy. The visions of hell served one purpose in leading to repentance. But Edwards frequently employed the image of a divine light that could draw one into union with God and to a sensing of the beatitude of eternal salvation. This more refined appeal to the emotions was then perpetuated by the preachers of the New Divinity who followed. Joseph Bellamy and Samuel Hopkins had lived with Edwards as students, adopting his preaching style as well as his basic theology, and they in turn became mentors of another ministerial generation. They continued the tradition that emphasized an experiential saving knowledge of God imparted by the Holy Spirit through evangelical preaching.

Preaching in the latter part of the eighteenth century was also significantly affected by the political struggle and rhetoric of the American Revolution. This was particularly true of the "occasional" sermons preached on the many special days designated for worship when discussion of public issues assumed primary importance. And as the conflict with Britain neared its breaking point, public issues became subject for "regular" Sabbath sermons as well. John Adams's fervent appeal to "let the pulpits thunder against oppression" was well heeded by New England Congregational clergy.

Several types of special occasions called forth this patriotic preaching. First there were the election days, when the annual election sermon was preached before colony leaders. This was a time for dealing with the issues of responsible government and the cause of liberty. Certain other occasions were observed with greater frequency in local communities. There were artillery election days, when local company officers were chosen, and other days honoring or sending forth the militia. There were fast days calling for sober reflection and repentance, often in the face of political or military peril. There were days of thanksgiving when peril had been reduced or victory gained. All these days were occasions for the preaching of patriotic sermons, and ministers were expected to speak out concerning the great political questions of the day. The clergy's impact on New England's thinking about revolution came considerably through such patriotic preaching on public days.

Even "regular" preaching, however, was not immune to consideration of political ideas. The main concern of Sabbath preaching was the message of salvation, directed primarily to the individual's personal relationship with God. Ministers saw themselves principally as "physicians of the soul," charged with speaking to the wounded in spirit by proclaiming the gospel of grace. But preachers knew that spiritual liberty and civil liberty were intertwined, for the covenant with God was personal and social, and faithfulness in this world was not detached from beatitude in the next. Moreover, God's judgments pertained to all of life, and God's providence governed both individual and corporate destiny. So within this understanding national sin and national hope deserved a place in the weekly preaching of salvation. Particularly when the political struggle became intense and war was about to begin, regular sermons focused explicitly on the crisis. In such times the providential deliverances of New England's past and the divine promises for its future became the basis of hope in the midst of conflict. A new millennial theme also appeared, portraying the struggle for new political order as part of a foreordained plan by which God was bringing forth Scripture's long-prophesied eternal kingdom. This preaching therefore coordinated with the message of personal salvation the more comprehensive affirmation of corporate destiny generated by the crisis of the Revolution.

Democratization of the Meetinghouse

Throughout the first century and a half of its history New England Congregationalism incorporated the class consciousness of colonial society into its house of worship. Seating for Sabbath services and other occasions of worship was assigned according to criteria heavily weighted toward prestige and social rank. Monetary worth and age were primary considerations for obtaining the most desirable seating locations, but political and social prominence were influential factors as well. When a new meetinghouse was completed in Northampton in 1737, it was voted that the order of priority in qualifications for seating was (1) wealth, (2) age, and (3) persons' "usefulness but in less degree."[56] The responsibility for assigning seating was put into the hands of a seating committee, often composed of the selectmen of the town and the elders and deacons of the congregation. Because assigning seating was a highly sensitive task and members of a committee could be tempted to show favoritism to one another, a second committee was generally appointed to seat the seating committee!

Originally seating in New England meetinghouses was on bare benches, the men placed on one side of a central aisle and the women on the other. In time enclosed "pews" sufficient in size to include several worshippers were built by individuals for personal use. Their locations, often around the perimeter of the room, were also assigned by the seating committee, and in these instances wealth and size of subscription to the cost of the meetinghouse were the sole factors considered. The development of pews, however, brought a major social change in seating for worship. Wives and other female relatives sat with men in these family enclosures. In some instances, in accordance with their family's standing, children were also given seating there. Most children, however, were assigned gallery seats, along with the African Americans and American Indians in the congregation.

This procedure for seating in worship was passively accepted in most places until the middle of the eighteenth century. Disapproval was more often against the specific assignments made by the committees than against the system itself. To deal with such complaints some towns sought to mollify the discontent by designating certain inferior locations as equal in dignity to those that were more desirable, an act known as "dignifying the seats." The new sense of democratization in society, prompted by both the Great Awakening and the political struggle for liberty, led in time, however, to disenchantment with the entire system. In the town of Acton, Massachusetts, in 1757, those who disapproved of the system proposed that the favored seats closest to the pulpit be assigned to the town's leading sinners, for they needed most to hear the minister's words! Later that suggestion was withdrawn on the ground that it would make the work of the seating committee even more difficult if it had to name those who would be so identified! A final rejection of the class-conscious system was achieved, however, only gradually. In Massachusetts the towns of Needham and Amherst abolished it in 1771, Manchester in about 1780, Stow in 1790, Weston in 1791, Framingham in 1794, Newton in 1800, and remnants of the system were still operating in some places well into in the nineteenth century.

MISSION

The Congregational churches of New England continued in the eighteenth century to be concerned predominantly with internal matters related to their own health and holiness. Nevertheless they developed greater outreach toward and ministry in their surrounding communities. As involvement in the struggle for civil liberties and the independence of the nation broadened Congregational vision, other larger concerns likewise appeared.

Attitude Toward Slavery

In 1638 the first African slave was brought to New England, the beginning of what for a century and a half was to be a profitable business enterprise conducted by Massachusetts and Rhode Island slave traders. The slaves traded by these merchants were generally sold to the British West Indies, the Spanish territories, or the plantation colonies of the American South, although some were retained in New England for local labor. The numbers of the latter were never particularly large, but by 1775 there were approximately 16,000 African Americans in a New England population of about 660,000.

Slavery, however, was conceived and practiced in New England somewhat differently than in other locations. Legally, the New England slave occupied a position between that of a plantation slave and an indentured servant. This was due to the Congregational effort to follow a Hebrew model based on the Old Testament for the holding and treatment of slaves. Following Scripture the slave was treated as property and recognized as a person. As property, slaves could be bought, sold, and transferred by wills as parts of a personal estate. As persons, however, slaves were members of the master's family and possessed certain common rights under the law. New England slaves lived with their families and conformed, as their families did, to the prevailing religious and social norms. They were called "servants" rather than "slaves." Furthermore, slaves in New England often served for a limited time, following which freedom was gained. Some of New England's African Americans were "freedmen"; others were bound. Yet because of their race, those freed were usually at greater economic and social disadvantage than those who remained enslaved. Paradoxically, emancipation in New England was more oppressive than bondage, pointing toward later discriminatory practices.

Throughout the seventeenth and early eighteenth centuries slave merchants in New England carried on their trade without serious opposition. Although in 1700 a layperson, Judge Samuel Sewall in Boston, published a small tract, *The Selling of Joseph*, advocating the abolition of slavery, this was quickly answered and came to no effect. Somewhat earlier Rhode Island had passed a law limiting involuntary servitude to a ten-year period, and slightly later Connecticut passed legislation to guarantee the care of slaves after they were no longer able to work. Most of these efforts accomplished little. Even the venture of some Boston selectmen, when they promoted the immigration of "white servants" in order, as they said, "to put a period to negroes being slaves," had little impact.[57]

Clergy attitudes during this period showed accommodation to the system, with some concern to ameliorate the cruelties of the master-slave relationship. Even Cotton Mather, who devoted much energy to improving conditions for African Americans, owned at least three slaves. In 1706 his parishioners presented him with the gift of Onesimus, who, when freed in 1717, was replaced by Obadiah. And a brief time earlier, according to Mather's diary, the household acquired Ezer, "a new negro servant (a little boy)."[58] Mather's concern for African Americans, however, represented a new development. In 1693, in response to requests, he founded a "Religious Society of Negroes," a prayer and discussion group, and in 1717 he established a charity school for African Americans and American Indians that aimed at the development of literacy so they could read and understand the Scriptures and catechism. Mather also helped develop charity hospital facilities, but his concerns were more for the soul than for the body.

Of great importance to Mather was the conversion and baptism of slaves. There had been little interest in this during earlier generations, and as late as 1680 Governor Simon Bradstreet reported to London that no African Americans had ever been baptized in Massachusetts. Reasons for this were economic and social. They included reduction of a slave's work time because of religious activities and the danger of encouraging a sense of equality that could impair the master-slave relationship. There had also been the fear that conversion and baptism would lead to the loss of slaves and ultimately to the end of the slavery system. English settlers in America, unlike Spanish, French, and Portuguese colonists elsewhere, accepted the tradition that Christians should not enslave Christians. For them conversion and baptism meant emancipation. Cotton Mather argued against this view. He pressed for slave evangelism and urged in 1694 the enactment of a law denying manumission to be a consequence of baptism. Mather's quarrel was not with slavery, but with lack of concern for the salvation of the slave.

New England support for abolition, however, began to develop in the second half of the eighteenth century. Nathaniel Appleton, a Congregational layperson, contributed to this when, in 1767, he published his *Considerations on Slavery*. Writing with moral indignation, Appleton first described the horrors of the slave trade and the cruelties inflicted upon slaves, urging the case for abolition on purely human grounds of compassion. No economic gain from this merchandising of human flesh can compensate, he declared, for such inhumanity and pain. Then he added another thrust by denouncing, possibly for the first time in America, the hypocrisy of slavery during a time when white colonists were engaged in a struggle for liberty. It would be better, he said, if "while we are preventing the chains being put upon us, we are knocking them off from those who already have them on."[59]

Clergy joined the cause, and in 1776 Samuel Hopkins, New Divinity pastor at Newport, Rhode Island, published his *Dialogue, Concerning the Slavery of the Africans*, a tract of immense importance for shaping Christian abolitionist thinking. When Hopkins began his ministry at Newport in 1770, he confronted a thriving slave trade, generally supported by the church people of that city. Hopkins was not yet an abolitionist, but he saw great evils in slave-trading practices, and for the next six years he preached frequently against them. By 1776, however, his thinking crystallized into the conviction that the system of slavery itself must be abolished. For Hopkins the ethical ground on which this finally rested came from the New Divinity theology and its doctrine of "disinterested benevolence." This benevolence is the sum of all holiness, and its practice is action in accordance with the nature of God. Such action should therefore be extended to all persons, particularly the poor, the needy, the downtrodden, the slaves. By uniting this divine mandate for disinterested self-giving with his abhorrence of slavery's evil, Hopkins led the way toward a more dedicated Christian abolitionism.

One consequence of this abolitionist theology was the formation of several antislavery societies. The earliest society was founded in 1775 in Philadelphia. It disappeared during the war but was reborn in 1784. The New York Manumission Society was established in 1785 and used Hopkins's *Dialogue* as part of its campaign literature. Hopkins founded a society in Rhode Island in 1789, and a Connecticut society came into being in 1790, headed by Ezra Stiles, then president of Yale. Meanwhile legislation in the New England states moved toward abolition. In 1780 slavery was outlawed in Massachusetts by its new constitution. In 1784 Rhode Island acted to phase out slavery by decreeing that all children born of slave parents subsequent to that year would be free at the age of twenty-five. In 1789 Connecticut outlawed the slave trade and in 1797 acted to provide for the gradual abolition of all slavery. Clergy leadership and popular will joined to bring New England into the abolitionist camp by the end of the eighteenth century.

One exceptional expression of this progress was the ministry of Lemuel Haynes, the first African American to minister to a white congregation and, so far as is known, the first to be ordained in North America. Haynes, born in 1753, was the abandoned child of a white mother and an African-American father. Until he reached the age of twenty-one he was bound out as an indentured slave. His owners, a devout church family in Granville, Connecticut, saw to it that he was brought up exposed to a contagious Puritan piety. Haynes was baptized, joined the church, and determined to enter the ministry. Following the revolutionary war, in which he served in the army, he read theology at night and did farm work by day. Later, in accord with prevailing practice, he studied with local Congregational pastors, supporting himself by teaching school. Finally in 1780 he was licensed to preach and was ordained in 1785 after being called to be pastor at Torrington, Connecticut. In 1788 he accepted a call to the church in West Rutland,

Vermont, where he served for thirty years. Later ministries took him to Manchester, Vermont, and then, at the age of sixty-nine, to Granville, New York, where he served for another eleven years until his death in 1833. After his death the *Colored American* claimed that he was "the only man of known African descent who has ever succeeded in overpowering the system of American caste." Among his personal friends were Richard Skinner, one of Vermont's strongest antislavery governors, and Stephen Bradley who introduced into the Senate the bill that abolished the slave trade in the United States. Haynes's life stands as a remarkable representation of the ways in which Congregationalism grew in insight and courage around this difficult issue.

Missionary Outreach

The mission program for American Indians, initiated in the mid-seventeenth century by Thomas Mayhew and John Eliot, was severely interrupted by the onset of the King Philip's War in 1675. During the fifteen months of the struggle, many of the Praying Indians from Eliot's communities fought with the settlers against their former allies, but the ultimate effect of the hostilities was a significant reduction in the mission program. Following the war New England colonies developed new American Indian policies designed to ensure the safety of whites. The number of Praying Indian villages was reduced from fourteen to four, and American Indian groups were confined to their traditional lands, an early form of reservation. At the same time many American Indians began a westward migration, and by 1750 their population in the New England colonies had greatly declined.

Mission efforts, however, continued. In 1723 Solomon Stoddard in Northampton questioned "whether God is not angry with the country for doing so little towards the conversion of the Indians."[60] As a result, interest in this work was renewed. Meanwhile Presbyterians in Scotland turned their mission concerns toward America through their Society for Propagating Christian Knowledge, and by 1730 a cooperative program of American Indian evangelization was developed by Presbyterians and Congregationalists for western Massachusetts, New Jersey, and Pennsylvania. A major outpost for this missionary activity was the village of Stockbridge, Massachusetts, to which Jonathan Edwards was called as pastor in 1751. Its American Indian mission station had been in existence for more than twenty years at that time. The life and work of David Brainerd, a young missionary in this cooperative program who worked among American Indians in New Jersey as well as Massachusetts, had a particularly significant impact on New England Congregationalism. His career, carried on with dedication in the midst of much hardship and illness, lasted only four years, but its influence on others was immense through the publication of his *Journal* by the sponsoring Scottish society and his memoirs and diary by Jonathan Edwards. Through the reading of these records many individuals in the late eighteenth and early nineteenth centuries were led to commit themselves to missionary vocations. Brainerd, engaged to one of Edwards's daughters, died in Edwards's home while the latter was still pastor in Northampton.

One further eighteenth-century program for American Indians developed in Lebanon, Connecticut, under its pastor, Eleazer Wheelock. He launched a plan to bring American Indian young men into a boarding school where they would live with a group of white missionaries who would learn their language from them. At the end of their studies both American Indians and white evangelists would be sent out among the American Indian groups. In 1754 property for this purpose in the town of Lebanon was donated by Joshua Moor, and Moor's Indian Charity School was established. In the 1760s two of the school's graduates went to England and, with the help of George Whitefield, obtained substantial financial support for the project. Desiring a new location and also incorporation, Wheelock secured a college charter for an institution at Hanover, New Hampshire, in 1769. When the school moved there the next year it was renamed Dartmouth College after the Earl of Dartmouth, a patron of the enterprise in England. The purpose of the college remained unchanged during its early years, the evangelization of the American Indians through the education of youth and the training of missionaries for the American Indian people.

During the revolutionary war missionary concerns were largely subordinated to the military and political causes, and following the war their efforts were directed toward the needs of the expanding frontier. Yet New England Congregationalism was, in reality, ill equipped for this venture. Although it was the largest religious denomination in

New England, it had become weakened during the period of the Great Awakening and the Revolution through the rise of other church groups and through secularization of the society. It continued to suffer from the theological divisions brought on by the conflict between evangelical and rationalist views. Its churches were still tied to state governments, not yet freed from the strictures of establishment. And perhaps as handicapping as anything else, its strong emphasis on local autonomy for individual churches left it without a workable central organization to give direction and support to a mission program.

Yet in spite of these limitations, the Congregational churches of New England were emboldened to transport their ministry as the nation moved west. In part they followed their own people migrating into new territories, but they also felt called to evangelize the unchurched who joined the exodus seeking adventure and fortune. Contributing to the Congregational boldness was the widely affirmed motivation of "disinterested benevolence" preached by the clergy of the New Divinity. Congregationalists were inspired to undertake missionary careers not only by the examples of David Brainerd and others but also out of their conviction that the vocation itself could be a significant avenue for this selfless love.

Among the New England states Connecticut was best prepared to initiate this work because of its ecclesiastical organization developed earlier through the Saybrook Platform. From the mid-1780s on, therefore, it sent local pastors out on four-month trips as missionaries. They were paid $4.50 as weekly compensation, and an additional $4.00 per week was allotted to hire supply ministers for the pulpits they left vacant. By 1798 a total of twenty-one pastors had completed a term of this missionary service. Their successes led that year to the founding of the Missionary Society of Connecticut, charged with soliciting funds and recruiting personnel for more organized missionary outreach. Its first missionary, David Bacon, went to the Western Reserve in "New Connecticut" in 1800, followed by Joseph Badger in 1801. In 1799 the Massachusetts Missionary Society was founded, and between 1801 and 1807 missionary societies were organized in all of the remaining New England states. For American Protestantism as a whole the nineteenth century became the "great century" of domestic and foreign missions, with many denominations sharing in the movement. Congregationalism, because of built-in limitations, experienced obstacles in its work, but ultimately its efforts brought much success. By the beginning of the nineteenth century the mission movement was under way.

The Mission of America

American Congregationalism from the time of its beginnings saw God's providential hand in the discovery of New England and in the role for which it was destined in the divine plan. The "city on a hill" was called to be a model of pure church and society, leading nations to a millennial completion of human history in which God's rule would be supreme. In the eighteenth century this view was continued and even intensified as theologians found signs to give it support. Moreover, an emerging nationalism broadened it and joined to it the political aspirations of the times. There emerged an American millennialism in which the entire nation was "God's new Israel," providentially chosen and under God's guidance for divine duty and destiny.

No single theological view dominated this development, but eighteenth-century Congregationalism contributed broadly to furthering millennial faith. In Jonathan Edwards's understanding, the millennial kingdom was an earthly realm characterized by the reign of Christ in human hearts. It would be a time of great holiness, when "vital religion shall everywhere prevail," as well as "great peace and love." The nations will "be knit together in sweet harmony," and all humanity will "be united in one amiable society."[61] As the great work of God's spirit, it would witness revival of piety in the slumbering churches and profound experiences of redemption and new life. But that, in Edwards's judgment, was occurring in the revivals of his day. He saw the Great Awakening as the beginning of the millennium soon more fully to come and, by God's providence, commencing in America. Ezra Stiles also shared this basic expectation, but he read different signs. In Stiles's view the coming of the millennium depended especially on the cleansing of the church. The church needed to be reformed according to the "apostolic model" of purity and autonomy in the local congregations. Stiles believed this was occurring in the ecclesiastical developments of his day, and thus he too could sense the foretaste of the millennium. It would not come immediately, but, by God's providence, it was beginning in America.

By the end of the eighteenth century America had therefore replaced New England in popular religious thinking as God's chosen land. This identification became even more pronounced as political developments led toward stronger national consciousness. Also millennial destiny and duty took further shape as secular considerations were applied. For example, the success of the military struggle was seen as God's "wonderful work," and the imagery of the future contained the language of civil liberty as much as of the reign of Christ. Yet underneath it all was the religious conviction that America was "God's New Israel," charged to be a "light to the nations" and providentially destined to be an instrument in history's final consummation. Leaders of state and church shared a conviction expressed by John Adams that the United States of America had been brought into being by God's providence for "the illumination of the ignorant and the emancipation of the slavish part of mankind over all the earth."[62]

SUMMARY

Two major occurrences dominated the last two-thirds of the eighteenth century for American Congregationalism. One was religious and the other political, but there were similarities in their effects. Both movements claimed immense energies from laity as well as from clergy, and in this process they contributed to a leveling in the relationship between pastor and people. This was a reversal of an earlier trend in the churches of American Congregationalism, for their first century had created a Standing Order of clergy who exercised roles not only of preeminence but also of exaggerated authority.

The first movement was the Great Awakening, a time of revivalism that convulsed much of New England with the emotions of intense religious experience. An almost complete leveling occurred in the extreme Separate segment of this awakening, for classic clergy qualifications were largely ignored and lay exhorters readily replaced the ordained. Yet within the main body of Congregationalism there was also a leveling consequence, for the common denominator of salvation experience eroded the significance of hierarchy and bound all together in a more closely knit community of the redeemed. Roles in church government were altered in conformity to this awareness, as lay voices were more prominently heard.

The second transforming occurrence was the American Revolution. Its leveling effect continued the process of democratization. Laity and clergy were common warriors in the cause, and the call to arms itself carried the message of liberation. In prerevolutionary preaching the somewhat abstract message of Christian liberty and the more concrete summons to political liberty were so interrelated that each implied the other. No longer was there summons to urge Christian liberty as the occasion for submission to some form of human authority, for faithful covenanting with God meant seeking political freedom from oppression. The Congregational churches, therefore, came out of the Revolution with a stronger sense of the meaning of democracy, even as applied to their own institutional life.

Beyond involvement in these two decisive movements, Congregationalism by the end of the eighteenth century stood at the edge of much that was to occupy its future. In those years it developed its first ventures in home missions, its first experimentation with theological liberalism, and its first commitments to the eradication of slavery. This was both a time of formation and a time of transition leading to a vital nineteenth century.

CHAPTER FIVE

EXPANDING HORIZONS
1800–1870

In 1827 a friend of Lyman Beecher wrote concerning the noted evangelist and social reformer, "Dr. Beecher says he would rather live in this day than in the meridian splendor of the millennium."[1] This comment may reveal as much about Beecher's unbounded energy and love of life as it does about the nature of the times, but without doubt the times themselves offered great appeal not only to Beecher but also to countless others who saw great opportunities to labor for advancing the rule of God.

For America the early half of the nineteenth century was a time of "looking forward." The nation's independence had been achieved, its destiny was more clearly discerned, and whether defined in secular or religious terms, an appealing future lay before it. The sheer magnitude of the land itself was awesome, with a frontier that pushed steadily westward to the shores of the Pacific. Always there was a new territory to be settled, a new community to be founded, even a new state to be added to the growing union. But for Beecher and others in church leadership, the potential in the human landscape was equally awesome. Challenges heretofore unknown lay before them for taming the frontier's atheism and lawlessness with a Christian call for faith and righteousness.

It was a time of "expanding horizons," and not least was the church's emphasis on moving forward. Evangelism became a major concern, and revivalism continuously dominated the religious scene—in the East as well as in the West. Similarly, the gospel's advancement through missionary programs claimed much of the church's energy, with first domestic missions and then foreign missions developed and steadily pursued. Still again, the cause of righteousness required moral reforms and called forth organized societies in large numbers to meet these needs. The early nineteenth century was a time for pioneers who

advanced frontiers in faith and faithfulness to match the nation's enlargement. In consequence the churches prospered. At the century's
beginning but one person in fifteen claimed Christian allegiance,
whereas at midpoint it was one in seven. Thanks to both evangelistic
effort and increasing immigration, church membership grew in those
decades from 365,000 to 3,500,000. The great tragedies of the time
were slavery and the Civil War. In the end, however, the slaves were
freed, the nation reemerged from its self-inflicted carnage, and the
churches survived to begin anew. Through the course of these years
Congregationalism surrendered its colonial numerical preeminence,
outstripped on the frontier by the Presbyterians, Baptists, and Methodists. But its contributions outweighed its numbers, and its ecumenicity,
its intellectual creativity, and its social sensitivity both aided the
period's development and pointed to advances yet to come.

HISTORY

Politics and Disestablishment

With the opening of the nineteenth century an item of unfinished,
largely unwelcome political business remained for New England Congregationalism. Despite the separation of church and state achieved for
federal practice in the new nation's Constitution and the widespread
matching of that freedom of religion in the independent practices of the
middle and southern states of the union, New England continued to
cling to remnants of its earlier establishments. Changes had been made
throughout the decades surrounding the American Revolution, and the
disadvantages experienced by non-Congregational churches in New England were considerably reduced. In many New England states, however, orthodox Congregationalism still enjoyed a tax-favored status,
along with the accompanying prestige of being recognized as providing
the official religious expression for community life. As a consequence it
faced increasing opposition.

The protests continued to come from non-Congregational churches,
but the opposition also assumed larger political dimensions. As the
clash of political philosophies took shape in the new nation, Congregational clergy almost unanimously committed their support to the
Federalist party. Its Hamiltonian advocacy of a somewhat elitist form of
American government appealed to the clergy's traditional conservatism

concerning political authority. This political view stood in contrast to the alternative of a Jeffersonian Republican program emphasizing a more egalitarian democracy. Although democratic procedures were by no means rejected, Ezra Stiles's concept of a "democratical aristocracy" represented more adequately the Congregational clergy's long-held view. Moreover, Jeffersonian democracy had come to be painted in lurid colors, as containing radical elements from abroad dangerous to church and social order. And so, fed by fears that this newer politics was grounded in a deistic philosophy antithetical to the Christian faith and was an agency that might re-create in America the social excesses of the French Revolution, the Congregational clergy of New England rejected Jeffersonian Republicans. When Jefferson ran for the American presidency in 1800, Timothy Dwight, president of Yale, led the attack against him in Connecticut, asking if Jefferson should be elected so that "we may see the Bible cast into a bonfire . . . [and] our sons become the disciples of Voltaire or our daughters the concubines of the Illuminati."[2]

An even more specific reason for Congregational clergy opposition, however, was the fact that Jeffersonian Republicans favored disestablishment for the New England churches. In this the liberal politicians were supported by the Baptists and the Episcopalians, long opposed to state favor for Congregationalism, and also by the Methodists newly appearing in New England. As early as 1802 these political and religious forces began to unite in Connecticut. That process reached its climax in 1816 with the formation of the Fusion party, also known as the Toleration party, described as a union of all those in the state who "detested political Congregationalism." This consolidation of disestablishment power led to rapid success. In 1816 in Connecticut the penalty for nonattendance at church was repealed. In 1817, with election of the Fusion party candidate as governor, further modification of the tax discrimination against non-Congregationalists was enacted. Finally in 1818 a convention summoned by the legislature replaced the old colonial charter with a new constitution, which declared that "the exercise and enjoyment of religious profession and worship, without distinction, shall be forever free to all persons in this state."[3] Disestablishment for Connecticut was complete.

The process was more complicated and protracted in Massachusetts. Again the political conflict was between the Federalists-Congregationalists and Republicans-dissenters, but in the early decades of the nineteenth century control often shifted from one group to the other. In 1811 Republicans in power approved the Religious Freedom Act undercutting Congregational monopoly in church tax support, but reaction against it returned Federalists to office in the following election. In 1820 the Congregationalists and their political allies controlled a constitutional convention, but by 1823 Federalism had essentially disappeared from the political scene.

Moreover, along with the changing of politics, a division developed within Congregationalism that contributed to the final dissolution of the establishment. This conflict between those Congregationalists who favored Unitarian and those who favored Trinitarian views was originally theological in nature. But when in the 1820s local congregations divided over the issue, the struggle was expanded to include a legal contest for control of church property and other assets. After state court action gave preference to the liberals, Trinitarian Congregationalists reversed their former position and, in the early 1830s, allied themselves with non-Congregational dissenting churches and radical politicians in opposing the idea of a religious establishment. On the other side, Unitarians continued to support the existing governmental system that had provided them with legal favor. In 1833, however, a constitutional amendment for disestablishment was submitted by the Massachusetts legislature to the people, and it was subsequently ratified by a vote of approximately ten to one.

When Congregationalism in New England came finally to accept disestablishment, it did so not merely as a necessity to which it was driven, but as an arrangement advantageous to the health of the churches. Lyman Beecher's reflection on the transformation was typical. Beecher, like so many others in New England, fought diligently in the early years of the century to preserve the favored position of Congregational churches and their ministry. But disestablishment, he later affirmed, was "the best thing that ever happened" to those churches, for "it cut [them] loose from dependence on state support" and "threw them wholly on their own resources and on God." And as for the ministers, he added, some may say that they now "have lost their influence," when actually "by voluntary efforts, societies, missions, and revivals, they exert a deeper influence than they ever could by queues, and shoe-buckles, and cocked hats, and gold-headed canes."[4]

The Unitarian Separation

If disestablishment was a painful process, so too was the early nineteenth-century conflict over Unitarian views and the final division it precipitated among the churches. The roots of this struggle extended back into eighteenth-century theological disagreements between Massachusetts' liberals and Edwardseans, but those earlier relations were more argumentative than disruptive. By the early 1800s, however, not only did the theological gap widen, but also control of the ecclesiastical establishment, particularly in the Boston area, began to shift more and more into liberal hands.

The first significant confrontation brought on by this tension occurred in 1803, when death of the incumbent vacated the Hollis Professorship of Divinity at Harvard, a major position for the training of Congregational clergy. Conservatives, led by Jedidiah Morse, minister at Charlestown and an overseer of the college, urged appointment of an orthodox Calvinist to the post, but instead the selection was of a well-known liberal, Henry Ware. When Morse sought to have Ware's beliefs formally examined before his induction, the college's corporation replied that such a testing of his creed would be "a barbarous relic of the inquisitional power, alien alike from the genius of our government and the spirit of the people."[5] Ware took office in 1805, and within the next few years several additional liberal appointments to the Harvard faculty were made. The school, though Congregational, had become an adversary of orthodox Congregationalism. In fact, when Morse took the matter public with a tract titled *Are You of the Christian or the Boston Religion?*, he was answered by a lay member of the corporation in a work titled *Are You a Christian or a Calvinist? Do You Prefer the Authority of Christ to that of the Genevan Reformer?*

One action of the conservatives was to found another school for the training of clergy. For them this was significant not only because it provided Massachusetts a Calvinist alternative to Harvard for the educating of church leadership but also because it united the two existing streams within New England Calvinism. On the one hand, there were the New Divinity people, now known as Hopkinsians, who had long desired an institution to perpetuate their "improvements" of Calvinism and their interest in revivalism. On the other hand, there were Old

Calvinists, who desired a school with greater emphasis on the pre-Edwardsean tradition. Although each had been planning independently to found its own institution, encouraged by Jedidiah Morse they together seized on the Harvard crisis and in 1808 founded Andover Theological Seminary. The preservation of Calvinism was guaranteed by a requirement that all Andover faculty affirm a special orthodox creed based on the Westminster Shorter Catechism. And the united nature of the effort led to two key appointments—Leonard Woods, a Hopkinsian, and Eliphalet Pearson, an Old Calvinist—both in the area of theology. Soon Andover attained a leading role in preparing pastors and missionaries for Massachusetts Congregationalism.

In 1809 Park Street Church was organized in Boston in a further attempt to counteract the growing liberalism in the city's religion. Dedicated to Calvinism and revivalism, the congregation in 1811 called Edward Griffin from the Andover faculty to be its pastor. His sermon, titled "On the Use of Real Fire in Hell," gave the church's location the name "Brimstone Corner"! Among the other churches in the city, however, only Old South remained conservative. As liberalism spread throughout the first decade and a half of the 1800s, the liberals continued to look upon themselves simply as dissidents within the Congregational fold. No attempt was made to use the term *Unitarian*. Actually, the term, as it had been applied earlier to Joseph Priestly in England, represented a much more radical theological view than New England liberals embraced, particularly with respect to their understanding of the person of Christ. American liberals resisted classic Trinitarianism but were reluctant to follow Priestly and describe Christ in merely human terms. They sought a middle way.

In 1815, however, Morse forced the issue by republishing an English document describing American liberalism as "Unitarian." He likewise called upon Congregational conservatives to break off communion with those among them holding this heretical point of view. Once the term was applied to the American movement, theological debate quickened to define more precisely the nature of American Unitarianism and its difference from Trinitarian orthodoxy. Responsibility for this task was assumed by William Ellery Channing, Boston's leading liberal pastor. Channing published a brief response to Morse in 1815, and in 1819 he delivered an ordination sermon on "Unitarian Christianity," which became a theological manifesto for the liberal faith. Dealing with more than the Trinitarian issue as it related to the person of Christ, Channing developed a systematic treatment of major themes in the new theology. With lines more precisely drawn and the term *Unitarian* more freely applied, the next step was institutional separation.

That development was stimulated in 1820 by a decision of the Massachusetts Supreme Court. Two years earlier a vacancy had occurred in the ministry at First Church, Dedham. As in most Massachusetts communities, responsibility for calling ministers was shared by the church, made up of qualified communicants, and the parish, made up of qualified town voters. Normally the church would initiate the process by selecting a candidate and then seek concurrence from the parish. In this case, however, presumably because the parish was liberal and the church orthodox, the parish acted on its own, called a liberal to the position, and summoned an ecclesiastical council that endorsed the choice. The church responded by denying the validity of the election. It convened a different ecclesiastical council that declared the proceedings of its predecessor irregular. It then withdrew from the parish, claiming for itself the church's name and property. Legal proceedings followed, leading to a Massachusetts Supreme Court decision in 1820 rejecting the protests of the church and awarding the property to the parish. The court declared that "the only circumstance which gives a church any legal character is its connection with some regularly constituted society." This meant that power over all civil matters related to the church belonged to the parish. Indeed, the court further ruled that "as to all civil purposes, the secession of a whole church from the parish would be the extinction of the church."[6] In such an instance the parish could then organize a new church that would inherit its predecessor's name and use of property.

After this decision the institutional separation of Unitarians from orthodox Congregationalists proceeded quickly. Lyman Beecher, who moved to a ministry in Boston in 1826 to combat Unitarian "infidelity," glumly described the Unitarians' success by declaring that "they sowed tares while men slept and grafted heretical churches on orthodox stumps."[7] In a few years 120 Congregational churches became Unitarian. Most of these were in the Boston area, for the separations involved urban-rural as well as theological differences. Of these departing churches, thirty-nine were liberal congregations that made the change voluntarily and without division. The remaining eighty-one, however, lost their names and properties in liberal parishes by forced deprivation or by voluntary secession of orthodox groups within them. In these cases the orphaned remnants had to begin anew if they were to preserve their Trinitarian Congregationalism. Formally the denominational separation into Unitarianism and Congregationalism became complete in 1825 with the founding of the American Unitarian Association.

The Second Great Awakening

In the midst of these struggles over disestablishment and denominational division, however, the vital life of Congregationalism was preserved, as seen in its worship, its preaching, and particularly its openness to the renewing freshness of revivalism. Once again evangelistic concern became a dominating feature in the life of Congregational churches, through participation in America's Second Great Awakening. Like the first awakening, this new wave of religious enthusiasm was interdenominational, involving Presbyterians, Baptists, and Methodists, along with Congregationalists. It also, like the first, became nationwide in its reach and, despite intensive concentration on the frontier, led to an evangelization of the East as well as of the West.

Yet there were differences between these two major periods of religious renewal. Although the nineteenth century saw the origin and use of emotionally charged "camp meetings" in frontier revivalism, the general tone of religious feeling within the churches tended more toward moderation than hysteria. In its Congregational phase it largely avoided emotional excesses and at one early point was even characterized as being like the falling of a "gentle rain." Moreover, nineteenth-century revivalism looked beyond personal conversion in a manner not characteristic of the eighteenth century. In the new awakening a social agenda supplemented individual agendas, and converts were summoned to live out their new births specifically in programs of moral and social reform. Voluntary organizations for this purpose blossomed, and the energies of new and renewed Christians were poured into monumental commitments for improving the nation. Pursuing this wider course, revivalism of the early nineteenth century flourished uninterrupted for more than forty years, with Congregationalism a fully engaged participant.

Occasional revivals occurred in local New England churches throughout the 1790s, but the Congregational phase of the Second Great Awakening began with the renewal of religious fervor at Yale College in 1802 under the inspiration of its president, Timothy Dwight. When Dwight was called to this office in 1795 he inherited a student body toying with deism and quite indifferent to Christian faith. Thomas Paine's *Age of Reason* had appeared the previous year, and its skepticism became popular on the Yale campus. The Yale college church was almost extinct, one report indicating that as late as 1800 its membership included only four among the undergraduate students. But Dwight, who was a grandson of Jonathan Edwards, met the situation head on. In frequent addresses he spoke out against deism in all its forms. He invited student discussion, and when the seniors proposed the question "Whether the Scriptures of the Old and New Testaments are the Word of God," he heard their arguments and forcefully replied. As minister of the college church, he presented his own theology in an extended series of eloquent sermons repeatedly offered in a four-year cycle over the course of the twenty-two years of his presidency. The results were remarkable. Beecher may have been guilty of rhetorical exaggeration when he described them by saying that "all infidelity skulked and hid its head,"[8] but by 1802 revival was well under way, with about one-third of the student body acknowledging conversion. Benjamin Silliman, a member of the faculty, declared, "Yale College is a little temple; prayer and praise seem to be the delight."[9] Subsequently there were fifteen different periods of revival at Yale from 1800 to 1840, and this revivalism also spread to other colleges to become a significant feature of the Second Great Awakening.

The awakening within Congregationalism, however, occurred mainly in the churches, where many local pastors and occasional traveling evangelists played leading roles. At the outset a major figure was Asahel Nettleton, trained at Yale under Dwight's presidency and ordained as an evangelist in 1811. Campaigning in the churches of Connecticut and upper New York, Nettleton carried on the Dwight tradition of earnest, but sober and nonflamboyant, revivalism. Not attracted to mass gatherings, he focused his work on small towns and local congregations. Moreover, Nettleton directed his preaching chiefly to the intellect rather than to the emotions, and supplemented this by means of frequent intimate discussions with individuals and small groups. Theologically he was an Edwardsean, strongly emphasizing human inability and viewing revivals as initiated solely by the work of God. In both method and theology he represented a conservative type of Congregational revivalism that, despite its modest success, was soon replaced by styles more in keeping with the enthusiasms of the times.

No person was more influential in that development than Lyman Beecher, a pastor whose local ministry served as the launching pad for far-flung evangelistic enterprises. Beecher also demonstrated the trans-denominational character of nineteenth-century revivalism, serving Presbyterian as well as Congregational churches during his ministerial career. His major Congregational parishes in Litchfield, Connecticut, and Boston became centers for widespread revivalist work. In theology Beecher joined those who, without abandoning Calvinism, liberalized it. He followed the theology of Nathaniel W. Taylor, professor of divinity on the Yale faculty, who found a way to incorporate a recognition of freedom of the human will more fully into Calvinist thought. While serving a Presbyterian church in the 1830s, Beecher was accused of Arminianism because of this view and was subjected to a heresy trial by conservative Old School Presbyterians. Eventually he was acquitted of the charge. Yet this concern for human freedom undergirded his newer evangelism and gave theological validation when he appealed to the unconverted to take the initiative in striving to come to repentance and faith.

In several other ways Beecher influenced Congregational revivalism. For one thing, his preaching broke from traditional forms, and its extempore mode became an avenue for "logic on fire." His pulpit battles with infidelity and moral evil were fought with verbal eloquence and emotional power. Furthermore, Beecher recognized the need for organizational skills to forward the revival movement. It was his suggestion that local pastors cooperate with one another in their evangelistic effort, preaching in each others' pulpits under an agreed-upon plan. Thus while in Connecticut, Beecher fostered the spread of revivalism through a program of "systematic itineration" in which local clergy, rather than outsiders, became the itinerants providing fresh inspiration to local congregations. Finally, Beecher viewed revivals as instruments not only of conversion, but of moral reform. For this he poured energy into organizing and nurturing voluntary societies of church people committed to programs for personal and social righteousness. When in 1812

Beecher joined with others in founding the Connecticut Society for the Reformation of Morals, he simply began a lifelong effort to find ways in which the converted could also become the committed, encouraged into organized activities for human well-being.

Congregational revivalism of this period was further shaped by another great evangelist, Charles Grandison Finney, whose influence and distinctive style led to him being called "the father of modern revivalism." In 1824 Finney began his ministry as a Presbyterian, but later he found greater freedom in the polity of Congregationalism. Under both denominations, however, his evangelistic work was largely that of an itinerant, carrying the gospel to the cities of the East and to the western frontier. Philadelphia, Boston, and New York became centers for Finney revivals in the 1820s and 1830s, along with the freshly settled communities of upstate New York and the Old Northwest. In 1835 he accepted appointment as professor of theology at newly founded Oberlin College in Ohio and for several years combined college teaching with conducting revivals in the East. Later he became president of Oberlin, a position he retained for fifteen years until his retirement in 1866. During this period he was also pastor of Oberlin's First Congregational Church.

Even more than Lyman Beecher, Charles Grandison Finney found the Taylorite theology, with its emphasis on human ability, congenial to his evangelistic method. Throughout his ministry Finney emphatically urged direct personal responsibility for initiating the process of conversion. One of his most famous sermons was titled "Sinners Bound to Change Their Own Hearts." A powerful preacher whose homiletical style personalized the call to repentance and conversion for each hearer, Finney adopted some controversial "new measures" whereby the evangelistic process could be encouraged and brought to completion. Chief among them was the "anxious bench," a pew at the front of the sanctuary where those who were struggling for conversion might sit while the preacher and others sought more directly to "pray them through" to the saving experience. In the intensity of the Finney revivals sinners were prayed for by name, and even women from the congregation were encouraged to take part.

Finney's new measures also included innovations in the manner by which revivals could be initiated, and Finney methods adapted well to growing urban environments. "Holy bands" of church members were sent into the community to identify and create interest. Inquiry sessions, cottage meetings, and prayer circles followed, bringing seekers together in more intimate settings. The "protracted meeting," with several consecutive evening revival services, enabled a local congregation to achieve cumulative effect. In the early years of Finney's ministry some of his new measures were condemned as extreme. In those years Beecher said that if Finney ever came to New England he would meet him at the border and fight him all the way to Boston! However, the differences were confronted in 1827 when Nettleton and Beecher met with Finney, and in 1831 Beecher welcomed Finney to Boston with open arms. Finney justified his innovations by writing that when God "has found that a certain mode has lost its influence by having become a form," then God "brings up some new measure which will BREAK IN upon their lazy habits, and WAKE UP a slumbering church."[10] Like other leading nineteenth-century evangelists, Finney believed that revivals led to reform and that all touched by grace had an obligation to take part. "Every member must work or quit," he said, for there are to be "no honorary members."[11] When the slumbering church is truly awakened, its members will find many tasks to perform.

Voluntary Societies

Out of this upsurge of Christian commitment came the "voluntary society," a distinctive element in the early nineteenth-century church. Although the societies that developed in these years represented a variety of interests and functions, they shared certain common characteristics. First, they came into being not by some official church action but by the initiative of concerned individuals responding to a recognized need. Even after voluntary societies were taken into church sponsorship, voluntary support remained crucial for their success. Further, each group was committed to a single cause and found its strength in a unity of focus and purpose. The American Bible Society's affirmation that "concentrated action is powerful action" represented this view and plan. Finally, these societies reached out beyond denominational divisions to pool broader Protestant efforts to meet particular needs. Some ecumenical organizations, especially in the field of missions, eventually reverted to denominational status, but others continued throughout as agencies of ecumenical cooperation.

The earliest of these organizations involving Congregationalists were societies dedicated to foreign and domestic missionary outreach. A campus revival at Williams College in Massachusetts in 1806 initiated interest in carrying the Christian message abroad, and shortly thereafter a small group of students, calling themselves the Brethren, joined in commitment to the task. Their decision was reached in a dramatic moment, in the "Haystack Meeting," when praying together in the lee of a haystack during a rainstorm, they resolved to engage in a mission "to the heathen." Remaining together for professional training at Andover Theological Seminary, three of these students joined with additional Andover graduates in 1810 to seek help from Connecticut clergy for furtherance of their plan. The clergy responded with favor and, along with several ministers from Massachusetts, elected nine clergy and laity as a self-perpetuating body to establish the American Board of Commissioners for Foreign Missions (ABCFM). Chartered by the Massachusetts legislature and given financial support by Connecticut and Massachusetts churches, the board in 1812 sent its first five young men, accompanied by the wives of three, on a mission to India. The board welcomed participation by non-Congregationalists, and soon representatives of the Presbyterians, the Dutch Reformed Church, and the Associate Reformed Church were included on the governing body. Ultimately, however, the development of Presbyterian and Reformed mission boards led each of these groups to withdraw. By 1870 the ABCFM was an exclusively Congregational organization.

Domestic missionary concerns emerged among New England churches even earlier, as local and state organizations sent out pastors for the establishment of churches on the frontier. For many years these "home" missionary societies operated independently of one another, but by the mid-1820s there was desire for consolidation. The catalyst once again came from dedicated students. In 1825 several Andover seniors committed to domestic mission, along with a member of the faculty, formed a "Society of Inquiry" to bring to the attention of the churches the possibility of creating a national home missionary body. Nathaniel W. Taylor, among others, was called upon to study the matter. The result was an interdenominational gathering of 126 clergy and laypersons in New York in 1826 that brought into being the American Home Missionary Society (AHMS). The United Domestic Missionary Society, founded by the Presbyterians and Dutch Reformed in 1822, was incorporated into this new organization, and the New England Congregational societies became AHMS auxiliaries for regional promotion. As with the ABCFM, however, Presbyterians and Dutch Reformed gradually withdrew for their own denominational work, and by 1860 the AHMS was predominantly Congregational. In 1893 its name was changed to Congregational Home Missionary Society.

Missionary work in the Protestant churches in early nineteenth-century America was further served by a group of voluntary societies devoted to education. More broadly ecumenical than either the ABCFM or the AHMS, these organizations received the generous support of Congregational laity and clergy, many of whom shared in their founding. In 1816 the American Bible Society was established, bringing together regional Bible societies already existing in several New England and Middle Atlantic states. Its sole task was to distribute a Bible "without note or comment" to each home that did not possess one. Much credit for the founding of this group belongs to Samuel J. Mills, one of the Andover students initiating foreign missions but unable to make the journey overseas. From 1812 to 1814 Mills made extensive missionary trips along the western frontier. He returned conscious of its appalling religious needs and began campaigning vigorously for a national body to distribute the Scriptures. At the founding interdenominational convention of the American Bible Society Lyman Beecher also played a leading role. Over the years the society achieved remarkable success, reaching homes throughout the entire nation and also expanding its distribution of the Bible to other destinations around the world.

Equally dedicated to mission through education was the American Tract Society. Established in 1825, its origins were Congregational, the New England Tract Society having been developed eleven years earlier. All sectarian distinctiveness was subordinated to a larger ecumenical purpose, however, when members of several Protestant denominations joined with it and declared their intent "to publish and distribute such tracts only as shall inculcate those great doctrines in which they all harmonize."[12] This was not an easy task in the face of many denominational differences. Nevertheless the success of the organization was outstanding. In addition to more than two hundred tracts dealing with theological and ethical themes, it published the fifteen-volume Evangelical Family Library and the twenty-five-volume Religious Library of great Christian classics. It also published a widely circulated paper, the Christian Messenger. The materials of the society were distributed by colporteurs who traveled into the remote areas where no churches were yet founded and who worked on the eastern docks distributing tracts to immigrants as they first entered America.

Two additional organizations involved Congregationalists in active support of mission through education. The American Education Society (AES) came into existence as a national organization in 1826, a continuation of the American Society for Educating Pious Youth for the Gospel Ministry established in Boston in 1815. The sole task of the American Education Society at its beginning was that of financially aiding qualified students for the church's ministry, and the work was interdenominational, shared particularly with the Presbyterians. By midcentury, however, the Presbyterians had their own organization, leaving the AES to the Congregationalists, and the society's responsibilities were also expanded to include general financial aid to the denomination's colleges and seminaries.

The American Sunday School Union, founded in 1824, was also a vehicle of American Protestant churches for educational mission. Local Sunday schools first appeared in England in the 1780s as a means for the churches to provide both elementary education and religious training for indigent children. Developed in America in the next decade for its religious function, the movement grew and was furthered by local and state societies in many parts of the nation. When a national society was organized, it brought together persons from a wide range of Protestant denominations: Baptists, Congregationalists, Dutch Reformed, Episcopalians, German Reformed, Lutherans, Methodists, Moravians, and Presbyterians. The American Sunday School Union was distinctively a lay movement, with a constitutional provision that no member of the clergy could ever be an officer. It focused on founding Sunday schools, largely in areas where no churches yet existed on the western frontier, and the publication of materials for educational programs. Although denominations eventually developed their own Sunday school and publication societies, cooperation was maintained with the national organization and much benefit was derived from its pioneering labors.

In addition to these voluntary societies dedicated to missions and education, new nondenominational organizations arose to support causes of moral and social reform. The American Temperance Society was established in 1826, The American Anti-Slavery Society in 1833, and the American and Foreign Sabbath Union in 1843. Throughout these years other organizations, dedicated to the causes of peace, prison reform, the elimination of prostitution, and the struggle against poverty, arose. Congregationalists, both as individuals and as churches, were deeply involved in these enterprises.

The proliferation of voluntary societies constituted what has been called the "benevolent empire," the flood of projects and programs flowing from the revivals and inspired by the evangelists' conviction that one is "saved for service." Many of these national societies were further drawn together by "interlocking directorates" giving greater cooperation to their efforts, and among the leaders Congregationalists, both lay and clergy, played a prominent role. Voluntary societies, so significant in these decades of the early nineteenth century, were testimony to the optimism of the time and to the conviction that the task of the church was not simply to convert individuals but also to remake the social order.

Plan of Union

Even earlier than the founding of the interdenominational American Home Missionary Society, New England Congregationalists began cooperative work in domestic missions with the Presbyterians. For many years in the latter part of the eighteenth century close relations had existed between Presbyterians and Congregationalists, particularly in Connecticut. In the 1790s, for instance, delegates from the Congregational General Association in Connecticut and the national Presbyterian General Assembly were welcomed as voting members at each others' meetings, and it was natural that this intimacy should evolve into joint missionary activity. In 1800 a proposal for such effort was made by Jonathan Edwards the Younger, then a Presbyterian General Assembly delegate at a meeting of Connecticut's Congregational General Association. Negotiations between the two bodies led to the adoption of the Plan of Union in 1801. Although initial Congregational authorization came only from Connecticut, other New England state associations accepted the arrangement—Vermont in 1801, New Hampshire in 1810, Massachusetts in 1811, and Maine in 1828.

The intent of the plan was to promote the cooperative founding and administration of churches on the advancing frontier. Three possibilities were envisaged: Congregational churches served by Presbyterian pastors, Presbyterian churches served by Congregational pastors, and churches of mixed membership served by pastors of either denomination. In the two former cases the churches would conduct their affairs according to their chosen polities, and any dispute between church and pastor would, with mutual agreement, be referred to the association or the presbytery of which the pastor was a member. Failing an agreement, the dispute would be heard by a joint council made up equally of representatives of the two denominations. In the case of mixed churches disputes of any nature would be heard by a standing committee of the communicants, with the right of appeal permitted in the case of Presbyterian members to the presbytery and in the case of Congregational members to "the body of male communicants of the church." It was further agreed that a member of the standing committee could be seated on the presbytery with all the rights of a ruling elder of the Presbyterian church.

There can be little question about the intended fairness of this plan. Nor can there be doubt about its usefulness, especially during the early years of its operation. On the frontier it brought together into mixed churches scattered Congregational and Presbyterian families in areas where an insufficient number of either existed for the formation of a denominational church. It also made possible a more effective employment of the clergy. Moreover, the plan contributed a sense of cooperation to frontier missionary labors over against growing sectarian competitiveness. After 1826 it was administered through the agency of the American Home Missionary Society.

Yet serious difficulties were generated by the Plan of Union, and at its demise in 1852 it was declared by Congregationalists to have been a disaster. The main charge at the time of its termination was that it had been used by Presbyterians as a means of denominational conquest. The plan, Congregationalists complained, had been employed to capture what should have been Congregational churches by making them into Presbyterian churches. One distressed Congregational leader estimated the number of such losses at two thousand. That figure has subsequently been judged excessive, but without question the operation of

Why?

the plan, particularly in western New York and Ohio, was greatly to the advantage of the Presbyterians. At the time of the plan's termination another Congregational leader declared forcefully, "They have milked our Congregational cows, but have made nothing but Presbyterian butter and cheese."[13]

It would be wrong, however, to blame dissatisfaction upon the terms of the plan itself or upon its abuse by Presbyterians. No doubt the Presbyterian governance system was more tightly structured than the Congregational and held churches more firmly in its grasp. Whereas, for example, a local church could by a majority vote of its members leave a Congregational affiliation and become Presbyterian, it could leave Presbyterianism only by a unanimous vote of its members and the consent of the presbytery to which it belonged. However, historical analysis has produced ample evidence of Congregationalism's own complicity in its failure to achieve the degree of growth that might have been expected from this missionary venture. Nearly a century ago Congregationalism's most renowned church historian, Williston Walker, wrote knowingly concerning this. "The fault," he said, "was chiefly Congregational."[14]

One major factor in the slow progress of Congregationalism was the feeling in New England that the polity of Congregationalism was less qualified than that of Presbyterianism for establishing and ordering churches in the unruly West. Congregational polity was for stable communities rather than for those still being formed on a yet undisciplined frontier. Some said that the polity was "too democratic." One Congregational observer also noted that it was necessary "to put some screws upon the organization of churches."[15] This attitude was startlingly revealed at midcentury in an autobiographical reflection by Asa Turner, founder of Congregational churches in Illinois and Iowa in the midst of Presbyterian pressure and one of Congregationalism's most successful missionaries to the West. Looking back twenty-two years to the time of his westward migration, he declared, "I was taught when I went out of New England I must be a Presbyterian. I had never in my life heard a sermon on our church polity and had never seen a line in print on the subject. . . . The blame is that New England fathers have not taught their own children."[16] In the early 1830s Professor Moses Stuart of Andover Theological Seminary did in fact note that at that time nearly one-half of the school's graduates had become Presbyterians.

Other factors were also at work in Congregationalists' culpability for their loss. For one thing, they often succumbed to geography's seductive role. Congregational pastors on the frontier longed for companionship with other clergy and often found it most available in the already existing presbyteries of Pennsylvania. Moreover, with pastors joining these neighboring presbyteries, the more feeble Congregational associations were absorbed into the Presbyterian structure. The Accommodation Plan of 1808, supplementary to the Plan of Union, made it possible for an association to become a part of a Presbyterian synod, while permitting its local churches to remain Congregational in name and internal practices. As a result strong and independent Congregational associations were late in developing in many areas. It was not until 1834 that the General Association of New York was formed, while that of the Western Reserve was delayed until 1836. Finally, Congregational growth was retarded due to the suspicion with which many in the New England churches viewed western theological developments, influenced by Finney and his Oberlin colleagues. Arminianism appeared a genuine danger, but was less likely to be found in the more solid orthodoxy of the Presbyterian church.

Yet Presbyterianism itself was not that firm in its orthodoxy and by 1837 had divided into an Old School defending classic Calvinism and a New School open to more liberal views. The Old School, suspicious of the newer trends in Congregational thought, repudiated the Plan of Union, leaving only the New School to cooperate with the Congregationalists. Meanwhile, dissatisfactions concerning presumed Presbyterian imperialism mounted, and Congregationalism began to develop a greater sense of confidence in its own ability to be a polity adequate to the challenges of the frontier and of the growing nation. So when an emerging national consciousness among Congregationalists led to a convention attended by representatives of their churches nationwide, both the time and the mood were right for a termination of the Plan of Union. The meeting was in 1852 in Albany, New York, and the vote, though urging that "Congregationalists and Presbyterians exercise toward each other that spirit of love which the Gospel requires,"[17] nevertheless put this specific plan to rest.

Following the Frontier

At the 1847 annual meeting of the American Home Missionary Society Horace Bushnell, influential eastern Congregational pastor and theologian, spoke concerning dangers faced by the churches on the western frontier. One danger was "Romanism," for burgeoning immigration was bringing new Catholic inhabitants, and the Roman Church was viewed as an autocratic power seeking domination in the New World. However, said Bushnell, there was a still greater danger, which he termed "barbarism," an "ignorance, wildness, and social confusion" creating a land "without education, law, manners, or religion." And, he added, if this were to prevail, "Romanism, bad as it is, will come as a blessing."[18] Without doubt life on the frontier created conditions often adverse to the "civilizing" process. It had the instability of persons constantly on the move. One missionary wrote that the migrants "might almost, like the Tartars, dwell in tents; everything shifts under your eye," and another reported being "struck by the unsettledness of the people," which "unhinged them for life."[19] Lack of the restraining influences of a stable society could allow primitive conditions to encourage primitive behavior. Two British visitors from the English Congregational Union reported that the American frontier "revived all the irregularities of the Corinthian Church, as though they had been placed on record to be copied, not avoided."[20]

Yet the missionaries and evangelists were hopeful with respect to the West's prospects for the future. In 1835 Lyman Beecher moved to Cincinnati to become president of Lane Theological Seminary and expressed his feeling concerning the frontier in lectures entitled *A Plea for the West*. Although he fully recognized the perils of western America, he also proclaimed its potential. "The capacity of the West for self-destruction, without religion and moral culture," Beecher wrote, "will be as terrific as her capacity for self-preservation, with it, will be glorious."[21] He made his "plea" for eastern aid, because the West cannot do it alone. No people, not even New England, he noted, has ever in one generation dealt with the problems of the wilderness and at the same time developed the institutions of civilization. But when the latter are at last created in the West, particularly in their religious and moral dimensions, then great good for the whole nation will ensue—for, wrote Beecher, "the religious and political destiny of our nation is to be decided in the West. . . . The West is destined to be the great central power of the nation."[22]

Not all easterners shared that vision, and despite the enthusiasms of seaboard revivals western missions were given only modest support. The American Home Missionary Society became increasingly pressed for money and personnel. It constantly searched for committed young clergy willing to found and serve western churches in spite of the society's meager contributions to their salaries. The AHMS policy was to provide one-fourth of the amount deemed necessary to support a missionary minister and family, and this generally was an annual stipend of no more than one hundred dollars. Moreover, this also meant that where small churches involved only a few interested, but scattered, persons in an undisciplined community, the congregation's obligation to provide the balance of a living wage often could not be fulfilled. The home missionary program was a struggling enterprise.

One significant way, however, by which Congregationalists overcame the problems of instability and inadequate support was through group or "colony" migration. Asa Turner was a major promoter of this movement, urging that groups of families migrate together, sometimes accompanying home missionaries to their new locations. By this means, he felt, they could transport their more stable institutions, "fixing the character of the towns, spreading the moral power of New England, and effectually aiding to save the West."[23] In 1830 Turner began his frontier ministry by leading a group of twenty persons to the founding of a church in Quincy, Illinois. Eight years later he was called to be pastor of a similarly transplanted group in Denmark, Iowa. In the latter instance a committee had been sent out from New England in 1836 to select the site, stake the claims, and lay out the town. Then in 1838, after the arrival of the others, a church of thirty-two members was formed, sufficient to call an AHMS pastor to a stable ministry.

So despite frustrations and encouraged by successes, Congregationalism, with the help of the American Home Missionary Society, followed the frontier. From western New York and the Western Reserve, which later became part of Ohio, the movement continued on into the upper Midwest. From the 1830s through the 1850s Congregational churches were planted in Illinois, Michigan, Wisconsin, Iowa, Minnesota, and finally on the West Coast.

Actually, Congregational missionaries had been sent by New England societies to Illinois as early as 1814, but due to the influence of the Plan of Union their work had led to Presbyterian churches. Even the church founded by Asa Turner in Quincy, Illinois in 1830 opted first for Presbyterianism, and not until 1833 did it become Congregational. The first Congregational church established in Illinois was founded in the town of Princeton in 1831 by a "colony" from Northampton, Massachusetts, that had emigrated as a body. Congregational polity spread slowly in Illinois because of Plan of Union influence, and it was not until 1851 that a Congregational church was organized in Chicago. Enthusiasm for the early work in Illinois was supplied especially by the "Yale Band," a group of Yale theological graduates who, while still at college, had chosen that area for their mission.

Congregationalism first appeared in Michigan in 1824 through the arrival of Isaac Ruggles, a frontier pastor from upper New York who had resisted there the pressure of the Plan of Union to lead his church into Presbyterianism. Ruggles settled in Pontiac, but worked throughout the surrounding area and by 1833 had established eight Congregational churches. In 1831 he was joined by John Pierce, another strongly convinced Congregationalist, commissioned by the AHMS but urged by the society to establish Presbyterian churches as more fitting for the frontier situation. Pierce replied that because Congregational polity was adequate for the primitive times of early New England, "it would not be less so to the new settlements of the West."[24] By 1840 three Congregational associations had been formed among Michigan Congregational churches. A large number of these churches were made up of people from New England who had come by way of New York after the opening of the Erie Canal in 1825. As in Illinois, some had migrated in "colonies" to their new locations.

The first Congregational missionaries in Wisconsin were sent to the area's American Indian inhabitants prior to the coming of white settlers. This was done by the American Board of Commissioners for Foreign Missions, for at the board's beginning American Indian missions were under its control. Prominent among these in early Wisconsin was a mission to a colony of Stockbridge Christian Indians, removed from their Massachusetts home by the United States government and transferred to the Midwest. They brought with them their church organization, served by a lay leader. In 1827 the ABCFM sent Jesse

Miner to be their missionary pastor, followed in 1829 by Cutting Marsh, who remained their minister for another nineteen years. In 1841 the church affiliated with the joint Congregational and Presbyterian state organization in Wisconsin and maintained its existence until early in the twentieth century.

The leading early Congregational missionary to white settlers in Wisconsin was Stephen Peet, who arrived in 1833 to become pastor of a newly founded church at Green Bay. In 1839 Peet toured Wisconsin extensively for the AHMS to survey the possibilities for church growth, and shortly thereafter became its agent for missionary expansion. By 1851 the AHMS had aided 121 missionaries in Wisconsin assigned to Congregational and Presbyterian churches, but there were only ten churches in the state that had become self-supporting. Throughout these years in Wisconsin the Plan of Union was only partially observed—that is, no mixed churches were permitted. All churches were required to identify themselves as either Congregational or Presbyterian. But in 1840 the two groups were united in the Presbyterian and Congregational Convention of Wisconsin, which became a presbytery to Presbyterians and an association to Congregationalists. Gradually, however, the Presbyterians withdrew, and in 1884 the organization became the Wisconsin Congregational Conference.

Congregationalism first crossed the Mississippi in 1836 when Asa Turner, still located in Illinois, made a tour of inspection in Iowa and preached to early settlers there. Two years later a church organized at Denmark, transplanted as a colony from New England, became the first Congregational church in the state, with Turner called to be pastor. In 1839 Reuben Gaylord arrived as an AHMS missionary and established Iowa's second Congregational church in Danville. Meanwhile the Presbyterian churches founded at Burlington and Dubuque changed to Congregationalism. Although the Plan of Union was functioning, Congregationalists were showing more optimism and taking more initiative than earlier, and by 1840 the Congregational Association of Iowa was organized. Congregational strength was further increased in 1843 by the arrival of the "Iowa Band," a group of theological graduates from Andover who selected Iowa as their place of mission. Seven of the band and two others were ordained by the Denmark Association, which itself had been created by a division of the state into two Congregational associations only two days earlier! New England polity was rapidly taking hold, and Iowa in the 1840s and 1850s led the Midwest in what has been termed a "Congregational Renaissance."

The first mission to white settlers in Minnesota was the work of AHMS missionaries in 1849 who followed Presbyterianism. In 1850, however, Charles Seccombe, a Congregationalist commissioned by the society to serve at St. Anthony, refused to join a presbytery and give up his Congregationalism. In consequence he gathered a congregation in 1851, which became the First Congregational Church of Minneapolis. Another AHMS Congregational missionary, Richard Hall, extended the work of Seccombe, and by 1858 there were thirty Congregational churches organized into the Minnesota General Association.

The period of the 1830s through the 1850s also witnessed the extension of Congregationalism to the West Coast. Missionary interest in the Far West began in 1833 when a letter was published in a Methodist missionary magazine telling of a visit to St. Louis two years earlier by four American Indians from the Oregon Territory seeking the white man's "Book of Heaven." Although they did make the journey, their religious motive is now judged to have been spuriously attributed to them by the letter's imaginative eastern author. Nevertheless, missionaries were quickly dispatched, first by the Methodists and then, for the Congregationalists and Presbyterians, by the ABCFM. In 1836 two Presbyterian missionary couples sent out by the board reached the Oregon Territory. They were Dr. and Mrs. Marcus Whitman, he a physician, and the Reverend and Mrs. Henry Spalding. In the next few years they were joined by several others, with Congregationalists among them, totaling eight workers in the Oregon mission by 1846. In addition to his missionary activities, Dr. Whitman became a statesman to defend the United States possession of the Oregon Territory against the British. This was accomplished in a trip back to the Congress in Washington in the winter of 1842–43. The Whitman mission among the American Indians, however, ended in tragedy. In 1847, when American Indians were being afflicted by some of the diseases brought by incoming white settlers, a rumor spread that Whitman was poisoning the native population. In an uprising Dr. Whitman, his wife, and several other workers were killed. As a result, the Indian mission was closed. Congregational churches, however, had been established among white settlers from 1844 onward, the first being a church at Oregon City founded by the Congregational missionary pastor, Cushing Eels. In 1848 Oregon's General Association of Congregational Churches came into being.

In that same year gold was discovered in northern California. By 1849, when the discovery became nationally known, a rush to the Pacific began. Although home missionaries were sent immediately, it was difficult for the churches to keep pace. By the end of 1849 there were an estimated 100,000 people living in California, served by twelve Catholic priests from the Spanish missions and thirteen Protestant clergy, only one of whom was a Congregationalist. The Congregationalist was Joseph A. Benton, who had come as a chaplain for a mining company and had organized a church in Sacramento. At that point, however, Congregational and Presbyterian work was thoroughly interrelated in California. For example, the First Congregational Church of San Francisco was founded in 1849 by Timothy Hunt, a Presbyterian chaplain to the city. Soon, however, the American Home Missionary Society sent other Congregational missionary pastors, along with Presbyterians, although work in the mining communities did not substantially begin until the fervor of the search for gold had begun to decline. Gradually in the 1850s, particularly after the termination of the Plan of Union in 1852, California representatives of the two denominations drew apart. As Congregational churches developed, the General Association of California was organized in 1857 to provide companionship and coordination for Congregational work. Cordial relations remained between the two denominations in California, but each developed its own churches and identity.

Education

Forward movement on the frontier included a continuation of Congregationalism's long-standing commitment to education as important for an informed electorate and an enlightened church. For children and youth strong support was given to the development of public schools despite the poverty in frontier life. In 1853 Horace Bushnell defended public education over against the parochial school system being introduced by Roman Catholicism. "Here we take our stand," he said in an address on "Common Schools," for these schools constitute "a great American institution, . . . one that is inseparably joined to the fortunes of the republic."[25] Of course these public schools, in a Protestant nation, were themselves evangelical in orientation. Within the Congregational churches Sunday schools flourished, using materials provided by the interdenominational Sunday School Union founded in 1824 and the denominational Sunday School Society created in 1832. Education for children and youth remained a priority matter.

Eventually the frontier needed colleges, and many were organized by Congregationalists as they moved across the nation. In 1834 Oberlin College was founded in Ohio and rapidly became a center of both strength and controversy within the Plan of Union churches. A pioneer among colleges, it advocated innovative views in education, theology, and social reform. Under the presidencies of Asa Mahan and Charles Grandison Finney it minimized classical education in the interest of that which it deemed more practical, opened its doors to women and African Americans, developed a radical theological emphasis on the possibility of human "perfection," and committed itself with unusual intensity to the abolitionist movement in the struggle against slavery. For these strong positions it was suspect in orthodox Congregational circles for many years, but ultimately its graduates were fully welcomed in church and society.

As the frontier moved westward, additional colleges were founded in the newly populated states. Illinois College, developed by the Yale Band, was established in 1835, and in the same year Marietta College opened in Ohio. In 1847 members of the Iowa Band contributed to the organizing of a college in Davenport, which later moved and became Grinnell. In Wisconsin Beloit College was founded in 1846 and Ripon College in 1855. The Congregationalists in Michigan established their college at Olivet in 1859, and those in Minnesota founded Carleton in the town of Northfield in 1866. Similarly, colleges were founded by Congregational pioneers in their early years on the West Coast. Pacific College came into being in Oregon in 1854, and only one year later Congregational clergy in California developed the collegiate institution that ultimately became, in Berkeley, the University of California. In 1865 developments in the Midwest brought into being Washburn College in Kansas and Berea College in Kentucky. From the time of their beginning in New England until 1865, Congregationalists had founded twenty-five colleges. This interest in higher education, however, was no Congregational monopoly. In the early nineteenth century the founding of church colleges was on the agenda of all major denominations, and Congregational numbers were more than matched by Baptists, by Methodists, and especially by Presbyterians.

As colleges met the needs of New England and the advancing frontier, seminaries also were developed to provide clergy for the churches. In the East Congregationalists had lost Harvard to the Unitarians, but they retained Andover, which had been organized in 1808, and Yale, which, partly in discontent over Andover's conservatism, developed its Divinity School in 1822. Further, Bangor Theological Seminary was founded in Maine in 1816, in part to provide theological training for students who had not completed a full course of collegiate study, and at Hartford the Theological Institute of Connecticut came into being in 1833 as a conservative reaction to the more liberal Taylorite theology of Yale. In moving westward Congregationalists organized three additional seminaries by 1866 to meet regional needs. In 1835 Oberlin Theological Seminary was opened as a department of Oberlin College, encouraged by the enrolment of a group of students who had withdrawn from the Presbyterian Lane Theological Seminary because of its objection to their abolitionist views. Chicago Theological Seminary was incorporated in 1855 and opened to students in 1858. Dedicated to the Midwest's educating of its own clergy, its board of directors and board of visitors were chosen by triennial conventions of ministers and lay delegates from Congregational churches in the area west of the Ohio River and east of the Rockies. Beyond the Rockies Congregationalists acted to meet the need for a seminary in the Far West, particularly in rapidly growing northern California. The founding meeting for Pacific Theological Seminary was held in Sacramento in 1866, where, despite the unwillingness of other denominations to participate and the meagerness of their own resources, Congregationalists decided to move ahead. The school opened in 1869 in San Francisco with four students and Joseph Benton as its sole faculty member. Later it moved to Oakland and then to Berkeley, became interdenominational, and was renamed Pacific School of Religion.

In the early nineteenth century Congregationalists also provided leadership in education for women. Prior to that time even elementary and secondary education had been severely limited for young girls. In Boston, for example, girls were not permitted to attend public schools until 1790 and only in summer months until 1822. Private academies therefore were essential to offer basic education to girls and also to serve as preparatory schools for young women when collegiate studies became available to them. One of the first was the Litchfield Female Academy, organized in 1792 by Sarah Pierce and attended in the early 1800s by Lyman Beecher's daughters, Catherine and Harriet. In exchange for their education Beecher provided religious instruction for the school. In 1821 Emma Hart Willard, a descendant of Thomas Hooker, opened a girls' boarding school. Ultimately locating in Troy, New York, it became the first endowed institution for women's education. Sarah Porter, daughter of one of the founders of the ABCFM, established a day school for young women in 1843 in Farmington, Connecticut. These and others opened educational doors long closed. One frustrated attempt had been Prudence Crandall's school for young African-American women in the early 1830s in Canterbury, Connecticut. Harassed by the community and opposed by both civic and church authorities, Crandall was forced after a short time to abandon her project.

Oberlin College was a strong center for women's education from the time of its founding in 1834. At first it admitted women students with restrictions. In 1841, however, women began graduating from the "full course," rather than from the shortened literary course to which they had been limited. Oberlin women graduates entered into public life in many areas, inspired also by the college's distinctive religious and moral ideals. The first woman to be ordained to Christian ministry, Antoinette Brown Blackwell, a Congregationalist, received her theological training at Oberlin.

Women's higher education was significantly advanced in 1837 when Mary Lyon founded Mount Holyoke Seminary (College) in South Hadley, Massachusetts. A devout Congregationalist and a former student and teacher in female academies who had long struggled against poverty in obtaining her education, Mary Lyon determined to establish a college that would rest on Christian foundations and be open to women of all economic conditions. By combining manual labor with the program of studies, she was able to set the board and tuition price for a term of ten weeks at sixteen dollars! Through its educational success and the outreach of its alumnae, Mount Holyoke provided stimulus for the founding of other women's colleges in the nation. Furthermore, more than fifty women trained by Mary Lyon became missionaries, founding colleges for women in Turkey, Persia, and South Africa.

National Denominational Consciousness

In the 1830s and 1840s, as Congregationalism continued its movement into the West, a new and growing awareness among its leaders began to take hold. The frustrations of the Plan of Union led to renewed recognition of the distinctive strength of Congregational polity. In fact, the difficulties in founding and sustaining Congregational churches in the new territories highlighted the need for national, not simply regional, structures. Thus when pleas from the churches of the West arose seeking assistance, eastern Congregationalists responded with a newly developed national denominational consciousness.

The first major gathering giving visible structure and program to this rising Congregational awareness took place in Albany, New York, in 1852. It was the first meeting of representatives of American Congregationalism as a whole since the Cambridge Synod of 1648. Invited by the General Association of New York, 463 clergy and lay delegates representing Congregational churches in seventeen states met to confront the problems and opportunities facing them in the new times. The most significant decision made during the Albany Convention was the unanimous agreement to terminate the Plan of Union as it still functioned with the New School Presbyterians. In that action Congregationalism was set free to develop on the frontier its own churches and ministries. The vote, however, was in no way a move toward a narrow and competitive sectarianism. A resolution also adopted unanimously by the Albany Convention declared disavowal of "all merely sectarian zeal," adding that the one and sole object of Congregationalism was to promote "in the freest and most efficient manner the world's salvation in Jesus Christ."[26]

Other decisions also affected Congregational work on the frontier. Of particular importance was the vote to raise fifty thousand dollars to assist the congregations of the West in the construction of church buildings. Genuine sanctuaries for worship were needed, they agreed. Lyman Beecher's plea in the discussion had been, "If you want to get martins about your house, you must put up a martin box. It is meetinghouses, too, that we want, rather than log houses."[27] Thus the commitment was made, with the recommendation that on the first Sabbath of the new year all pastors of Congregational churches preach on this matter and an offering in each church be taken. As a result, by early 1853 almost sixty-two thousand dollars were raised for building frontier churches, and the American Congregational Union (later renamed Congregational Church Building Society) was established to sustain this effort. Further resolutions supported the work of the American Home Missionary Society and urged congregations to encourage young persons toward ministry "in view of the alarming disproportion between the increase of our population and the increase of Ministers of the Gospel."[28] Finally, the Albany Convention spoke directly to tensions disrupting relations between Congregational churches in the East and West. Declaring that charges against the West as harboring "heresy in doctrine and disorder in practice" were too vague to need specific refutation, it urged a closer connection between Congregationalists of all regions, suggesting that delegates from the East attend meetings in the West, so that future misunderstandings might be avoided.

No provision was made at Albany for a continuing national structure or even for additional national meetings. Within a few years, however, the need for a new gathering became apparent. By 1864 not only did earlier actions aiding the frontier require continued attention, but also new concerns had surfaced among the churches. The Civil War meant that many slaves in the South had been freed, exposing serious needs and opening up new opportunities for educational and religious mission. Moreover, a national Congregational consciousness produced pressure for more precise denominational definition and identification. More than two hundred years had passed since the Cambridge Synod of 1648 defined Congregational polity, and nearly that many had elapsed since the 1680 Savoy Declaration last clarified and set forth Congregational belief. In the meantime important developments had occurred in both practice and faith. Therefore, at the instigation of many of the state organizations, a second national gathering of representatives of Congregational churches was called. It met at Old South meetinghouse in Boston in 1865 and took for itself the name National Congregational Council. Its 502 lay and clergy members came from twenty-five states and included fourteen persons from foreign countries, largely representatives of Congregational unions in Canada, England, and Wales.

Delegates from the churches were chosen through state organizations and represented the approximately 275,000 members and 3,000 ministers then constituting American Congregationalism.

The National Congregational Council continued the supportive work of the Albany Convention for meeting the needs of the western, and also now southern, frontier. It was reported that in the thirteen years since the 1852 gathering, 427 meetinghouses had been built in the West, at a cost of $149,298, with national funds subscribed for that purpose. But with need for another four hundred buildings, the council voted an additional goal of $200,000 to be raised from the churches. For "evangelization of the West and South" the council commended the work of several nondenominational benevolent societies, suggested a goal of $750,000, which collectively they should raise to extend their efforts, and pledged its cooperation in this fund raising as continuation of Congregationalists' large role in the societies' support. In addition, churches were urged again to encourage able and dedicated young men, "the choicest of our sons," to prepare for ministry. One Iowa delegate declared that his state needed forty new ministers but that only one seminary graduate was available—and complained further that when one of these "Iowa-made" ministers shows his competence, "the long arm" of New England "reaches out and picks him up from his six hundred dollar church and finds him a two thousand dollar church in Massachusetts and makes him a Doctor of Divinity!"[29]

Despite such complaints, there was little or no disagreement on these practical needs. Issues of polity and faith, however, took considerable more time and discussion. A comprehensive description of Congregational church polity modeled after the Cambridge Platform of Church Discipline, along with a concise "epitome," was presented to the National Congregational Council by a preparatory committee. Although these were received with much agreement, serious differences surfaced between leaders in the East, who stressed the local church's independence, and those from the West, who valued the importance of cooperative agencies and even some measure of control over the congregations. In the end it was agreed to adopt only a brief substitute statement emphasizing both the independence and the communion of churches, along with a rejection of any hierarchical conception of ministry. The preparation of a longer statement was referred to a committee that would act after the council ended. Seven years later that committee completed its report and published the statement of Congregational polity known as the Boston Platform.

Problems also arose in agreeing upon the Declaration of Faith, although a theological statement was voted before the council closed. The chief issue in extended discussion was whether or not the prevailing theology within Congregationalism should be described as *Calvinist*. In the two proposed faith statements placed before the council this term had been used, and discussion showed that it was agreeable to a large majority. Professor Edwards Amasa Park of Andover represented this view when he declared, "We are Calvinists, mainly, essentially, in all essentials of our faith."[30] But *Calvinism* was variously understood, and some felt that use of the term was impolitic and could lead to misunderstanding. When no resolution of this impasse was in sight, a dramatic rescue was achieved through the ingenuity of Alonzo H. Quint, a Massachusetts pastor and one of American Congregationalism's outstanding mid-nineteenth-century leaders. As chair of the business committee, he prepared and submitted a substitute Declaration of Faith as the council, by prearranged schedule, traveled to Plymouth for a meeting at "Burial Hill" celebrating the memory of the early Pilgrims buried there. The writing was so hurried that the final lines were prepared on the train to Plymouth, with Quint's tall hat as his table! But the writing and the setting led to council harmony. Although the term *Calvinism* was not used, the faith conveyed in earlier Calvinist confessions and platforms was "substantially" reaffirmed. In addition, the statement affirmed both the basic Congregational polity of "our Puritan Fathers" and the ecumenical commitments of present-day Congregationalists who "extend to all believers the hand of Christian fellowship."[31] Thus, with but two dissenting votes, the Burial Hill Declaration was adopted in 1865 by the National Congregational Council and became an important part of the historic documents of American Congregationalism.

Slavery, Emancipation, and Reconstruction

Casting a shadow over this religious fervor and expansion during the first half of the nineteenth century was the dark cloud of slavery—and the struggle to remove it. Emancipation efforts began in the late 1700s, and by 1830 enslavement of African Americans had largely disappeared in the North and a moderate antislavery movement had developed in the South. At that point, however, southern attitudes hardened, particularly as the invention of the cotton gin increased the value of plantation slavery for a growing cotton-driven economy, and slave uprisings began to create unrest. Furthermore, southerners resented the increasing intensity of the northern campaign for emancipation. Protestant churches were torn apart by the struggle, resulting in northern and southern divisions within the Methodists, Baptists, and Presbyterians. Spared this tension because they had so few churches in the South, Congregationalists supported the antislavery cause.

The major agency for Congregational participation in the abolitionist movement was the American Missionary Association (AMA). Founded in 1846 through the union of several earlier antislavery organizations, the AMA was another of the nondenominational reform societies, but its main membership and support came from Congregationalists. Prominent among its founding groups was the Amistad Committee, formed in 1839 in defense of a group of African slaves. While being transported in a slave ship, the *Amistad*, the slaves mutinied, killed the ship's captain and many of the crew, and attempted to sail back to Africa. Betrayed by the navigators they pressed into service, they ended up captured by the U.S. Navy in Long Island Sound, jailed in New Haven, and brought to trial for murder. Students and faculty at Yale Divinity School rallied to their support, and the Amistad Committee, made up of prominent citizens, was created to aid in their legal defense. In 1841 the case reached the U.S. Supreme Court, where, with former president John Quincy Adams serving as defense attorney, the court's judgment set the captives free. Subsequently they were returned to their homeland accompanied by two missionaries who initiated through their aid an African mission program. With other antislavery groups participating, this union of abolitionist and missionary activity led in 1846 to the founding of the American Missionary Association "for the propagation of a pure and free Christianity from which the sins of caste, polygamy, [and] slave-holding . . . shall be excluded."[32] Thoroughly interracial, it included many African Americans among its leaders and members.

Congregationalists channeled much of their antislavery effort through this agency. From its beginning many of its workers were Oberlin graduates. It was commended to Congregational churches by their state organizations and the National Congregational Council. Ultimately the American Missionary Association came to be exclusively a denominational organization, adopted into the Congregational mission structure. But antislavery sentiment in Congregationalism also found other avenues of expression in the 1840s and 1850s. Revivalists, led by Finney, emphasized commitment to abolition as a consequence of conversion. Congregational colleges took up the cause and encouraged aid to "contraband" slaves fleeing for freedom. And above all else there was the remarkable novel *Uncle Tom's Cabin*, written by Harriet Beecher Stowe in 1852. Lyman Beecher's daughter, Stowe was introduced to the struggle against slavery when her father was president of Lane Theological Seminary, and she became a strong advocate of the abolitionist movement. Her novel, though not unfriendly to the South, portrayed dramatically the evil of slavery and became a unique instrument for touching the nation's conscience. Historian Sydney Ahlstrom declared that "Harriet Beecher Stowe was sure that God wrote the book—and in a way this was so, for no author was ever burdened with a more driving sense of Christian moral fervor."[33] The book's sale ran into millions, and its wide acceptance caused Congress to break a two-years conspiracy of silence on the subject of slavery. However, it took a tragic war and a courageous president to bring the institution of slavery to an end.

On 1 January 1863, at approximately midpoint in the Civil War, President Lincoln issued the Emancipation Proclamation. Although this was a strategic war move against the South, applicable only to slaves in the Confederacy, it opened the door to the legal abolition of all slavery in the United States. That occurred upon the war's conclusion in 1865, when, with the adoption of the Thirteenth Amendment, all of America's 3.5 million slaves were finally set free. However, the gradual attainment of freedom by African Americans during the war, as the Union armies advanced, and their final emancipation at its end left an appalling human need. Essentially an entire people were set adrift, with little qualification to make their own way in society. Federal government efforts to "reconstruct" the South floundered badly through inept planning, carpetbagging corruption and greed, and the resurgence of the power of white supremacy and intimidation. Political participation for African Americans, momentarily obtained, was quickly lost, and hopes for economic gain ended in large-scale poverty. The dozen years of Reconstruction have been called "the Tragic Era."

Congregationalism's attempt to assist in meeting this massive need was directed through the American Missionary Association and centered largely on providing opportunities for improved education. The 1865 National Congregational Council in Boston recommended that $250,000 of the churches' commitment to benevolent societies be given to the AMA, and more than this was raised. Initially the AMA's focus was on elementary education. Throughout much of the South it had been illegal to teach a slave to read, and the level of illiteracy was high. Thus even while following Union armies across the southern states during the latter stages of the war, the AMA developed elementary schools and began basic teaching. As early as 1863 it had eighty-three teachers in the field, and by 1870 this number had increased to more than five hundred. With the end of the war, more advanced schools were added, including the founding of several colleges: Berea College in Kentucky (1865), Fisk University in Tennessee (1867), Talladega College in Alabama (1867), Tougaloo University in Mississippi (1869), Straight College in Louisiana (1869), Atlanta University in Georgia (1869), and Tillitson Collegiate and Normal Institute in Texas (1876). AMA funds were also used to assist in developing Hampton Institute in Virginia and Howard University in Washington, D.C. In addition the AMA contributed substantially to the founding of African-American churches in the South, many of these becoming Congregational.

Severe opposition was encountered by AMA missionaries and teachers. They were targets of the hostility of the Ku Klux Klan, as well as of the ridicule of others who objected to the provision of education for African Americans. One pastor in Mississippi declared, "*Hic, haec, hoc* will be the ruin of the African."[34] Actually, the education provided was not classical. Beyond rudimentary subjects, it emphasized homemaking, agriculture, and industrial arts, along with study of the Bible. Even the colleges in the early years had limited and practical curricula. But the ventures were a good success, due not in the least to the skill and dedication of the underpaid teachers, mostly from the North, who gave of themselves to this mission. Two-thirds were women, and of them one of their students later wrote, "These women left their homes, their friends, [and] their social ties. . . . Their courage, their self-sacrificing devotion . . . were their pass keys to the hearts of those for whom they came to labor. . . . Their monument is builded in the hopes of a race struggling upward from ignorance."[35]

THEOLOGY

Although the Declaration of Faith adopted at Burial Hill in 1865 captured broad theological accord within mid-nineteenth-century Congregationalism, its affirmations were sufficiently general to encompass continuing theological differences. Designed to be ecumenical in nature, it emphasized confessing "with the whole church" a common human sinfulness, a remission of sins by Christ's expiatory death, a deliverance from the power of sin by the Holy Spirit, and a final judgment leading some to eternal life and others to everlasting punishment. It likewise affirmed the Scriptures as the divinely inspired source of religious truth and stressed the importance of the organized church, its ministry of the Word, and its sacraments of baptism and the Lord's Supper. Within this framework the controversial views of Nathaniel W. Taylor, Charles Grandison Finney, and Horace Bushnell could all find acceptance, but it was exactly the theologies of these men that constituted the theological ferment of this period. The declaration, however, did uphold a Trinitarian understanding of God, thereby ruling out the Unitarian view of God and Christ held by William Ellery Channing and other liberals, dissidents within Congregationalism in the early years of the nineteenth century.

William Ellery Channing

When Channing in 1819 delivered his sermon on "Unitarian Christianity," he enunciated with clarity the liberals' criticism of orthodox Congregationalism and also the nature of their own theological reconstruction of the Christian message. At fault, he held, was the doctrine of the Trinity, along with certain other ideas related to this understanding of the nature of God. Channing's complaint against Trinitarianism was its presumed repudiation of the unity of God. It may be noted that Channing did not acknowledge the intent of classic Trinitarianism to affirm paradoxically "one God in three persons" but chose to focus only on the latter half of that description. Therefore, he said, the doctrine of the Trinity subverts the unity of God by talking of "three infinite and equal persons," each having "his own particular consciousness, will and perceptions," and each performing a different role in human redemption. But "there is one God and one only," he urged, "one being, one mind, one person, one intelligent agent." This is "God the Father," and "with Jesus we worship God the Father as the only living and true God."[36]

Similarly, Channing emphasized the unity of Jesus Christ. In his judgment the Trinitarian depiction of Christ as a divine person who entered into a human life led to a "two being" Christology that sees in Christ two minds, "the one ignorant and the other omniscient," as well as two wills and two sets of perceptions—and this, he said, is "an enormous tax on human credulity." Channing did not acknowledge the classic Christology of orthodoxy that spoke of Christ as having "two natures in one person," preferring to focus only on the duality of "beings" present in the Incarnation. Thus in his answering and summary statement, Channing declared, "We believe that Jesus is one mind, one soul, one being, as truly one as we are, and equally distinct from the one God."[37]

Channing's criticism of orthodoxy went further, however, focusing as well upon the doctrine of salvation. In his judgment the God of the Trinity was a vengeful deity who demanded the death of his Son as satisfaction of divine justice, making possible the merciful freeing of sinners from punishment. But, Channing insisted, it is not Christ's death that makes God merciful. Rather, God as "Father" is merciful and sends Christ in love to be humanity's Savior. Although Channing's Christology was not very precise, Christ was seen as a superhuman, but not divine, being to whom God commits this mission. It is Christ's task, by his teaching and example, "to effect a moral or spiritual deliverance" of humanity, that is, to rescue persons from sin and its consequences and "to bring them to a state of everlasting purity and happiness." Christ was sent to deliver humanity from sin itself, rather than simply from its punishment. Channing asked, "Why pluck the sinner from hell, if a hell be left to burn in his own breast? Why raise him to heaven, if he remain a stranger to its sanctity and love?" So salvation is a process of spiritual development and growth in virtue, and Channing believed that even in earthly experience one could progress to "the perfect life." This occurs indeed by the aid of God's Spirit, but grace is in no way irresistible, and by God's Spirit is meant "a moral, illuminating, and persuasive influence" to which persons in freedom can respond. For Channing this was the "reasonable" way of understanding the biblical message over against some of the "irrational" doctrines of Calvinism. At this point, therefore, Channing's reconstruction of Christian theology continued what earlier liberals within Congregationalism had already affirmed.[38]

Nathaniel W. Taylor

In the early nineteenth century, however, the mainstream of Congregational theology came from the Edwardsean tradition through the interpretations of the New Divinity. But this New England Theology was not monolithic, and differences soon appeared within it. One major place of dispute centered on the age-old question of the relationship of divine and human action in the religious and moral decisions of human life. The paradox of divine sovereignty and human freedom had long been perplexing, although for Calvinists the balance generally shifted toward greater emphasis on the irresistible power of God. In the late eighteenth century New Divinity theologians such as Hopkins and Bellamy affirmed the voluntary character of sin but still kept it within a context of absolute divine sovereignty. Likewise faith and love were for them the gifts of irresistible grace. No genuine doctrine of human freedom was found there. Moreover, in the early nineteenth century Nathanael Emmons carried this perspective to the point of explicitly affirming divine dominance in human choices and actions. By way of explanation he developed his "exercise" theory of human behavior. Although there are human exercises of the will that can be called voluntary, he argued, these are in fact shaped by the exercises of God's will that "creates" them. Emmons wrote, "Moral agents can never act, but only as they are acted upon by a divine operation."[39] There is human volition, but whether for sin or virtue, it is always produced by God.

In contrast to Emmons's exercise scheme was the "taste" scheme of human behavior advanced by Asa Burton, which portrayed persons as characterized by a certain condition or relish of the soul, a taste for either evil or good, a set of motives out of which human action flowed. Burton, a Congregational pastor in Vermont, published a major treatise supporting this view in 1824. He identified the "taste" with the heart and called it a "feeling faculty" producing human decisions and deeds. He wrote, "The appetites of the heart are the principles of action, which set all the wheels in motion. . . . Take these away and men would not be agents, and good and evil could not be imputed to them."[40] Yet there was still no genuine human freedom advanced by Burton, for the human will was subject to the taste's control. The sinner was limited by the "moral inability" of the will, which Edwards had earlier argued controlled behavior, even as did gracious affections for those of a regenerated heart. The main difference between Edwards and Burton was that Edwards spoke only of the understanding and the will in the human psyche, incorporating affections of the heart into the will, whereas Burton viewed such feelings as a third faculty along with the other two. But for Burton the taste determines the volitions, and so the result was the same.

Nathaniel W. Taylor, whom historian Sidney Mead calls "a Connecticut liberal," began to break through this necessitarianism in his description of human religious and moral acts. Taylor's liberalism built upon the Edwardsean tradition, and he considered himself a faithful advocate of Calvinism, but his interpretation opened the door to greater understanding of human freedom. Accepting Burton's threefold psychology of understanding, taste, and will, Taylor considered the will an efficient agent in human action. Taste, or "sensibility," is merely neutral ground through which the will can be reached by the gospel appeal for faith and love. The freedom of the will to respond was expressed by Taylor's insistence that the will possesses "power to the contrary." It acts under no necessity from controlling motives, but could under the same circumstances make a choice opposite from that actually made. Yet, as a Calvinist, Taylor also believed that the will does not act alone. God is at work. The manner of God's work can never be understood, but its fact makes for certainty of action according to God's plan. Therefore Taylor's liberal Calvinism held both conclusions together as compatible. He wrote, "If any two things are consistent, certainty of action, and freedom of action, are consistent." His final descriptive statement on this matter, a phrase he urged time and again upon his followers, was "certainty with power to the contrary."[41] Taylor refused to compromise either the sovereignty of God or the genuine freedom of each human person.

But what about original sin? As a Calvinist, Taylor was forced to face that issue along with the corresponding question of human depravity. Some conservatives believed that he had given in to the Unitarians by emphasizing so strongly the reality of human freedom. Taylor denied this charge and spoke of the moral depravity of the race. For Taylor, however, moral depravity was not a condition received by imputation or inheritance from, or even by participation in, Adam's original sinful act. The depravity of each person was his or her own, wrought at the earliest possible moment by wrong choice. Although Taylor denied the control of the will by those affections or motives that constitute one's sensibility, he did not minimize their influence. Indeed, he said, experience, as well as Scripture, reveals the lower impulses to be so strong that, apart from the saving influence of grace, persons in the appropriate circumstances will inevitably, though not necessarily, sin. This sinning will begin as soon as those persons become moral agents, that is, as soon as in infancy or childhood they are able to sin. Although depravity is universal, it is freely chosen. In treating original sin, Taylor insisted that every infant or child had "power to the contrary," even though it was never employed.

Through grace, however, the evangelist can appeal to other motives within human nature and lead a convert to regeneration. The appeal is made particularly to one's "self-love." Taylor's use of this term created difficulties, because Hopkins used "self-love" to mean the sin of selfishness. For Taylor, however, self-love meant the desire for happiness, and this can be approached through both the understanding and the will. Presented as the only satisfying fulfillment of self-love's desire, the gospel's promises can lead, under the influence of the Holy Spirit, to the free decision to conversion. The new life in Christ is wrought by the Holy Spirit, but only as it is freely chosen to be one's greatest treasure. No one, Taylor said, will ever be converted in the "state of inaction."[42]

Taylor's emphasis upon the reality of human freedom to determine one's destiny led to a different perspective from that of the New Divinity on the nature of God's moral government. New Divinity theologians had maintained that God, through the exercise of sovereign power, could prevent the existence or continuance of sin in human life, but that sin was permitted as a necessary means for the greatest good. The argument was that sin was essential for there to be redemption. Taylor, on the other hand, denied both of these assertions—and he did so on the ground of free agency. First, if human freedom is real as God's gift of creation, then the good government of God could not deny that freedom by arbitrarily preventing its use even for evil. And second, although it is true that God permits sin, it is not sin itself that contributes to the greatest good, but rather the freedom to choose, of which sin is a consequence. God's gift of freedom, which can also lead to holiness, is necessary for the greatest good of humanity. Only such unconstrained moral agency, in Taylor's judgment, makes this the best of all possible worlds. From his post as Yale's professor of theology, Nathaniel W. Taylor taught and wrote out of this influential liberalization of Calvinism. His views were soon called the "New Haven Theology."

Charles Grandison Finney

Even more than Taylor, Charles Grandison Finney, evangelist of both the East and the West, modified the faith of the past, stretching his inherited Presbyterian and Congregational theology almost beyond the point of any Calvinist identification. In his *Autobiography* Finney described his evangelistic method of preaching. He wrote, "Instead of telling sinners to use the means of grace, and pray for a new heart, I called upon them to make themselves a new heart and spirit, and pressed the duty of immediate surrender to God."[43] Charles Hodge, conservative Calvinist theologian at Princeton, called this a "new Pelagianism" because of its naïve optimism concerning the freedom and ability of the human will to attain to salvation. Finney, in turn, labeled Calvinism an old "fiction" and rejected the assumption that the will was enslaved to sin and morally unable to act otherwise in response to the gospel's call for repentance, faith, and obedience. He wrote that the sinner's "cannot" is his "will not," for "the will is free . . . and sin and holiness are voluntary acts of mind."[44]

Yet the Holy Spirit, in Finney's judgment, is also essential in the transition from sin to holiness. Finney's theology was no simple moralism. Wherever gospel truth is proclaimed, the Holy Spirit is present, working within the mind and the conscience of the sinner to create deeper awareness of the nature and threat of sin, as well as clearer understanding of the promise of forgiveness and new life. But the Spirit did not, as it had been understood in earlier evangelism, create a "miracle" of conversion. Finney declared that conversion is not a miracle, for it is simply the "result of the right use of constituted means." The means encompass the persuasive activities of the evangelist and the Holy Spirit and include exciting the emotions of the sinner with respect to the need for a change of heart. Finney believed that people "are so sluggish, there are so many things to lead their minds off from religion and to oppose the influence of the gospel that it is necessary to raise an excitement among them till the tide rises so high as to sweep away the opposing obstacles." But when this is done, conversion through persuaded free choice is a natural event. In fact, the connection between the proper use of means for a revival and a revival itself "is as philosophically sure as between the right use of means to raise grain and a crop of wheat." Conversion and revival will occur when people are persuaded "that they ought to give themselves to God and vote in the Lord Jesus Christ as the governor of the universe."[45]

One additional aspect of Finney's theology distinguished it from the prevailing Calvinist, even Taylorite, theology of mid-nineteenth-century Congregationalism. This was Finney's conviction that, with the continuing help of the Holy Spirit, the Christian can in this life attain perfection. Because Finney was joined in perfectionist theology by his Oberlin faculty colleagues, this affirmation made many Congregationalists uneasy and led some to question the value of an Oberlin college education. Yet in those years Finney's "perfectionism" was largely misunderstood. Rather than being a renewal of antinomianism, in which perfection, through the overwhelming presence of the power of God, was a blissful state of mystic communion, Finney's view remained faithful to his basic understanding of human life and its conversion. He argued that sin and holiness cannot coexist in one's life, because both require an ultimate choice, for self or for God. Moreover, the duty laid upon one in the gospel for unqualified surrender to God asks nothing that is beyond attainment for the human will aided by the Holy Spirit. Therefore, Finney concluded, although such perfection may not yet be reached, the Christian can properly hope for its coming in this present life. For Finney the preaching of the doctrine of perfection was a means for stimulating earnest Christian purpose grounded on confident hope.

Horace Bushnell

Still greater theological ferment, however, was created within Congregationalism by its mid-nineteenth-century pastor of North Church, Hartford, Horace Bushnell. An innovative and liberal thinker, often opposed for defying theological convention, Bushnell pioneered by opening new approaches in several areas of theology. In the 1840s

Bushnell began questioning the heavy dependence of the churches upon revivalism as their means of leading persons into the commitments of Christian life. Revivalism, in his judgment, was too individualistic, too separated from the organic social connections in life where friends, family, and church provide context and help as vehicles of grace. Revivalism takes every person as if he or she exists alone, presumes for each a hostility to God, and then looks for "some sudden and explosive experience in adult years" to bring reconciliation. This, Bushnell complained, makes religion "a kind of transcendental matter, which belongs on the outside of life, and has no part in the laws by which life is organized." It makes religion "a miraculous epidemic, a fireball shot from the moon."[46] But God, he insisted, does not normally work that way. Rather, God works most often through life's organic relations, particularly in bringing children to religious maturity through a gradual process. Bushnell developed a doctrine of "Christian nurture," which held that the Christian influences of the home and the church lead a child to grow up into the commitments of faith and love, unable to look back and find a time when he or she was not a Christian. The church, he said, must live by growth, rather than by conquest. Ultimately this understanding concerning religious development became a basic axiom for the Christian education movement.

Bushnell's convictions concerning Christian nurture, however, raised further questions in the minds of many about his view of human nature. How could he acknowledge sin, and particularly original sin and human depravity, if he could suggest that a child might develop, without conversion, into a Christian? And was this development not simply a natural process of educing a good presumably innate in the child? Bushnell vigorously denied these charges. There is sin, for Adam fell and, because humanity itself is an organic whole, the malignant consequences of that sin are propagated from one generation to another. Bushnell wrote that Christian redemption is no "self-culture," nor simply a "scheme of ethical practice." Rather, "it is a salvation, a power moving on fallen humanity from above its level, to regenerate and to save." Yet human depravity is not total, for in each person "there is a susceptibility to good, . . . which may be appealed to by what is right and holy."[47] Although Bushnell was accused of being a Unitarian in his view of human nature, on the matter of sin and salvation he stood closer to his inherited Calvinism.

In his understanding of the way of salvation, Bushnell contributed to theological developments on the role of Christ and the nature of the atonement. His theology at this point was especially shaped by his keen appreciation of Christian experience. Theology must relate to life, and the life of the Christian was preeminently one of experiencing the overwhelming goodness of Christ. Bushnell spoke about "Christed" persons who had been transformed by awareness of Christ's humility, selflessness, and love—and he himself had been deeply moved by a mystic vision in which, he reported, "I have seen the Gospel."[48] This was the "Gospel of the Face," that is, of the face of Christ who, as divine Mediator, captures allegiance through the attraction of his moral power. Bushnell particularly applied this in developing his "moral influence" view of the doctrine of atonement. Rejecting all "substitutionary" and "governmental" interpretations in which Christ's death was seen as changing the attitude of God, he urged that contemplation of that death has a powerful healing effect upon those who find within it Christ's total self-giving in "vicarious sacrifice." Said Bushnell, "There is a cross in God,"[49] which Christ reveals by taking unto himself at Calvary the sins and pains of the world, and the power of that cross can change the human heart. Bushnell's message of salvation was thoroughly Christ-centered. In fact, the only complaint of his congregation about him was that he preached Christ too much! And he replied that this was not "a fault to be repented of, for Christ is all and beside him there is no gospel to be preached or received."[50]

Bushnell's emphasis upon religious experience as a basis for theological reflection led him to his most innovative and far-reaching contribution to the development of Christian understanding. This concerned the inadequacy of language to convey fully the meaning of Christian awareness and the need to liberate theology from the rigidity of dogmatic expression. Human words, he believed, are frail conveyors of the life of the Spirit, earthen vessels that represent only inexactly what they seek to portray. Here Bushnell reflected a Platonic view that words are but shadows of divine things, no more than symbolic of reality. Moreover, he said, when theologians use those "faded metaphors" as though they were precise depictions of religious truth, they engage in a logic-chopping that creates a lifeless theological endeavor. He once wryly suggested that should such thinkers encounter Moses' burning bush they would be inclined to analyze the flame and put out the fire! Thus rather than encase dogmatic propositions, the words of religion must speak "poetically" of that which transcends human thought. They must be a response to ultimate reality reflecting wonder, awe, and reverence. Bushnell did not feel, however, that this skepticism about religious language should lead to an outright rejection of all creeds. Words and creeds convey partial truth, and Bushnell felt he could accept many creeds in interrelationship. "When they are subjected to the deepest chemistry of thought," he said, they become "elastic" and run "freely into each other." But one must remember their inherent limitations, for "the poets are the true metaphysicians."[51]

POLITY

When the National Congregational Council of 1865 came to a discussion of polity, it received from a preparatory committee a thirty-one page document proposed as a mid-nineteenth-century replacement of the equally lengthy platform adopted by the Cambridge Synod of 1648. Although the basics of the churches' polity had remained constant, changes had occurred over the more than two centuries intervening, and it was thought desirable to describe the current form of government in considerable detail. In the discussion, however, the council discovered that the polity of Congregationalism was still evolving, for differences in both theory and practice prevented agreement. With the larger reconciling task referred to a continuing committee, the council limited its formal approval to three broadly stated points deemed "distinctive of the Congregational polity." They provide a frame within which some of the more specific developments of the period can be placed.

Local Church

The first principle, said the council, is "that the local or Congregational church derives its power and authority directly from Christ, and is not subject to any ecclesiastical government exterior or superior to itself."[52] In the late eighteenth century there had been a renewal of emphasis upon the local church's autonomy, which carried over into the early decades of the nineteenth century. Local autonomy was particularly urged when Congregationalism, in the midst of the struggles perpetrated by the Plan of Union, sought to establish its own character in contrast to that of its Presbyterian partner.

Nathanael Emmons, who in the late 1700s had been autonomy's major proponent, lived until 1840 and continued throughout out his latter years to uphold this point of view. In fact, his position took an extreme form in its skepticism about all ecclesiastical structures beyond the local congregation. Concerning councils he wrote that in any modification of local autonomy, they are "vain and useless because they have no divine authority at all." And when efforts were made to develop a general association in Massachusetts, he voiced opposition with the pungent broadside: "Associationism leads to Consociationism; Consociationism leads to Presbyterianism; Presbyterianism leads to Episcopacy; Episcopacy leads to Roman Catholicism; and Roman Catholicism is an ultimate fact."[53]

Such strong stress on local autonomy was reminiscent of that of John Wise a century earlier, when he opposed the Massachusetts Proposals of 1705. Yet there was a difference. Wise based his conclusion on political reasoning. Ecclesiastical democracy had the same roots as political democracy, namely, natural rights of the individual and the consent of the governed. Emmons, on the other hand, was critical of pure democracy in public life and based his ecclesiastical democracy on theological grounds. Christ, Emmons said, is the sole Lawgiver of his church and has granted independence to each local congregation of believers, consigning to it and it alone the authority and power to carry out his mandates for church life. And throughout this period, when local autonomy was lauded, it was theological, rather than political, reasoning that prevailed. Parallels might be drawn between secular democratic government and Congregational church government, but the warrant for church government was divine.

In 1864 a manual of Congregational polity identified the principal powers of the local church to be those of (1) electing its own officers, (2) admitting or excluding its own members, (3) forming its own creed, (4) regulating the details of its own worship, and (5) independency. One notable omission, from the perspective of later Congregational practice, was the power of managing its own property and financial affairs. This was because many mid-nineteenth-century Congregational churches continued the double "church and ecclesiastical society" organization of earlier times. In this arrangement the church, made up of communicant members, was responsible for matters of the religious life, whereas the society, which also included nonmember contributors from the community, took care of the property and financial administration. This pattern continued in many New England churches, despite the fact that disestablishment and new laws made it possible to dissolve the society and turn over to the church the care of temporalities. Even some new churches on the western frontier were organized in this double way.

The nineteenth century saw a lengthy dispute on this matter. In 1860 H. M. Storrs, writing in the *Congregational Quarterly*, called the ecclesiastical society a "needlessly cumbrous appendage, . . . an evil" and declared, "We want simplicity. No merchant would keep two sets of books when one would do."[54] But the problem was more than one of simple bookkeeping. As in the time of the Unitarian separation, conflicts between church and ecclesiastical society caused strains in the choice of a minister, as well as in the financial provisions for the church's support. The 1864 manual, therefore, contained a section entitled "How to Incorporate a Church." In incorporation the church's members would be the legal corporators, owning the meetinghouse and financing the program, though delegating certain responsibilities to elected trustees. Yet the same manual, published in Chicago, also provided a "proposed constitution" for an ecclesiastical society and a "proposed compact" between the society and the church.

Admission to church membership continued to be based on what the 1864 manual termed "credible evidence of piety." Although membership no longer required profession of a conversion experience, "evidence of piety" was to be determined, except in special cases, through examination before the congregation in which "one's religious history and present Christian experience" were explored and one's consent to the church's Confession of Faith and its covenant obtained. Also, if persons desired to join by transfer from other evangelical churches, it was "the right and privilege of the church to seek acquaintance with the Christian life of such applicant members by asking for a narrative of their religious history."[55] In all cases the church's affirmative vote was required. Similarly, the church was required to vote letters of dismission and recommendations for transfer to other specified churches. Letters seeking only general dismission and recommendation would not be granted, for they could be presented to churches deemed heretical. The voting, in all instances, continued to be exclusively an adult male privilege. In 1865 Henry M. Dexter, one of nineteenth-century Congregationalism's most influential leaders, not only ruled out voting by "youthful members" as unacceptable, but added that "female voting" is against Congregational historical usage, against Scripture, and against reason.[56]

Cooperation among Churches

The second polity principle upheld by the Boston council of 1865 was "that every local or Congregational church is bound to observe the duties of mutual respect and charity which are included in the communion of churches with one another; and that every church which refuses to give an account of its proceedings, when kindly and orderly desired to do so by neighboring churches, violates the law of Christ."[57] Here, as in the past, the fine line between autonomy and expected cooperation appeared. Although in Congregationalism's beginnings government-summoned synods had played an important role, the major means of cooperation among local churches had been through neighborhood or vicinage councils. Yet as noted earlier, these councils often failed to serve the purpose for which they were called, especially when expected to be agents for solving disputes or disciplining churches or pastors. This lack of effectiveness, as well as the councils' purely occasional meeting and ad hoc composition, rendered them unsatisfactory in the eyes of many as the major means of weaving the autonomous churches together into effective working unity. Congregationalism needed something more, particularly for its churches in the expanding West where congregations were scattered, mutual reinforcement was needed, and problems of ministerial quality and church discipline were pronounced. In the early eighteenth century Connecticut had developed its own somewhat presbyterian connectional pattern, and gradually other areas of the country worked out ways to strengthen and sustain their churches' cooperative relationships.

For the clergy a sense of this cooperation had been achieved in early New England through the development of ministerial associations, voluntary organizations of clergy meeting for mutual help and enrichment. Later these groups added ecclesiastical functions by licensing candidates for the ministry and regulating ministerial standing. Similar voluntary gatherings, though without ecclesiastical functions, also came into existence for the churches, some in the late eighteenth century but more in the nineteenth. These assemblies were generally termed *church conferences*, although they were also known in various regions as *unions*, *conventions*, and in a few cases *associations*. The terminology in this period was not standardized. These meetings usually originated in counties or districts, with district conferences later being combined into state bodies. In this unification Maine led the way with the founding of its General Conference in 1826. At the beginning, however, these organizations, whether district or state, had no ecclesiastical functions. Their main objectives, as described in Thomas Upham's report of 1829, were to offer united prayer, extend Christian acquaintance, provide mutual instruction, render aid to feeble churches, and supply strength to individual Christians for the religious life. Many persons, wrote Upham, came away from these assemblies declaring, "It was good to be there."[58]

By the middle of the nineteenth century there slowly evolved out of these organizations a new structure, district gatherings frequently called an *association of churches*. More carefully organized than the church conferences, they were made up of lay and ministerial delegates from the area's local churches and were designed to establish a more effective working relationship among the neighboring congregations. Constitutions were adopted, areas of responsibility were defined, and common tasks were undertaken. This was not done without opposition. Defenders of local autonomy feared the emergence of unwelcome authority and the erosion of the separate congregations' liberties. Supporters, however, expressed confidence that the new organizations could combine "the greatest liberty and the widest unity."[59] Growth was slow, and it was not until the late nineteenth century that district associations were fully accepted. As associations gained recognition, they began also to accept responsibility for certain ecclesiastical functions, such as ordination and the holding of ministerial standing. Ultimately, enlarged into associations of churches and ministers, they became a major component in the twentieth-century organization of American Congregationalism.

The nineteenth century also saw the establishment of organs of national cooperation through the Albany Convention (1852) and the Boston National Congregational Council (1865). But both of these were ad hoc gatherings, and it was not until 1871 that a permanent structure emerged.

Ministry

The third polity principle of the 1865 Boston Council was "that the ministry of the gospel by members of the churches who have been duly called and set apart to that work implies in itself no power of government, and that ministers of the gospel not elected to office in any church are not a hierarchy, nor are they invested with any official power in or over the churches."[60] Two aspects of ecclesiastical democracy, as related to clergy, were affirmed. First, an assertion was made that within the local congregation an essential equality, with respect to church government, exists between the clergy and laity. In 1826 Nathanael Emmons described the minister as a "mere moderator" when it came to the matter of voting and governing within the local church.[61] This confirmed the trend that had developed throughout the eighteenth century, whereby lay participation and responsibility replaced clerical domination in church affairs.

At the same time the sacred role of the minister was not denied by this egalitarianism, for members of the clergy were seen as "ambassadors of God," called by God in special manner to their vocation, and given divine authority to proclaim the Word. To some extent vestiges of a sacred clerical order remained, as can be seen in an 1848 polity manual's view that ordaining persons for ministry "is properly committed to ministers and should not be undertaken by others, except in cases of such extreme necessity as knows no law."[62] But the nature of ministry had changed. The minister of the nineteenth century was no longer a part of a theocratic establishment, allied with the state and seen as a guardian of public order. The minister was a member of a profession employed by a local church to serve its religious needs. Authority, therefore, rested less in the office and more in the qualifications of the person called to fulfill the office's tasks. One consequence of this shift was an equalization of rights between clergy and laity.

The second form of ecclesiastical democracy expressed in the council's polity statement declared equality within the ordained ministry itself. Congregationalists had long held to this view, based on their biblical rejection of hierarchy, and the Congregational manuals of the mid-nineteenth century reaffirmed the term *bishop* as used in the New Testament to be simply another designation for the office of pastor. However, a new development began to occur in Congregational understanding of ordained ministry. Heretofore ordination was limited to those called to the ministerial office of pastor or teacher in the local church. Even the first missionary to the American Indians, John Eliot, was given authority for his mission through ordination as pastor to a local church of white settlers serving as his base. But with the development of domestic and foreign missions in the early nineteenth century, ordination was expanded to include those going out as missionaries unattached in their work to any particular congregation. And eventually churches ordained to other church-related, but not pastoral, callings. Although that expansion was discussed by the 1865 council, no action was taken concerning the specific forms it might assume. The council simply urged that those forms too must be included in the equality of ministry that Congregationalism affirms. There is no hierarchy, nor can these nonparochial ministries impose themselves in any way upon the local churches.

Mid-nineteenth-century Congregationalism witnessed another and quite remarkable instance of equality in ministry, the breakdown of its historic male exclusivity through the first ordination of a woman to clergy office. However, this was not achieved, nor even recognized, by national council, but came about through the boldness of a strong candidate and a local congregation. Within Congregationalism this ministry had only brief duration, but it nevertheless was the beginning of a significant movement.

Antoinette Brown was the child of a pious Congregational home in upper New York state. When she was five in 1830, her father was converted through the revivalist preaching of Charles Grandison Finney, and four years later she confessed her faith and joined the church. From an early age Brown had aspirations for education and ministry and in 1845 entered Oberlin College. After completing the college course in 1848, she began theological studies. Despite Oberlin's openness to admitting women for collegiate work, Brown experienced resistance in her theological program, never being fully accepted along with male students as a candidate for its degree. A major aspect of the problem was the centuries-long conviction that the Apostle Paul prohibited women from speaking in church and therefore banned their entrance into ministry. Finney, however, was cordial to Brown and encouraged her speaking. And when President Asa Mahan read a paper she had written reinterpreting the Pauline injunction in a manner favorable to women, he had it printed in the *Oberlin Quarterly Review* as a basis for discussion. Nevertheless, when Brown completed her studies in 1850, she was denied a degree and participation in the commencement. She was finally awarded a master of arts degree in 1878, and in 1908, in recognition of her career, she was granted the honorary degree of doctor of divinity.

For three years after leaving Oberlin Brown lectured publicly. In 1853 she was called to become pastor of the First Congregational Church of Butler and Savannah, New York, and following Congregational practice, the local church ordained her for that ministry. Her ordination service had an ecumenical dimension. It was held in a Baptist church because the Congregational building was too small, and the sermon was preached by a Methodist minister. Appropriately his text was Galatians 3:28: "There is neither Jew nor Greek, bond nor free, male nor female, for you are all one in Christ Jesus."

However, Brown's ministry in New York did not last long. Her theology was more liberal than that of her parishioners. On one occasion she refused to adhere to a mother's request to preach hell and damnation to the woman's dying but unconverted son. Troubled by this theological disparity, she resigned from her pastorate. Moving to New York City, she did social work in the city's slums and prisons, then met and married Samuel Blackwell in 1856. As a wife and mother Brown rarely appeared in public life for the next several decades. Yet her talents were employed in study and in writing, as she explored extensively the growing tensions between science and religion. Finally she returned to ministry in the Unitarian denomination and founded All Souls Unitarian Church in Elizabeth, New Jersey, which she served until her death. Mid-nineteenth-century Congregationalism was not able to hold this talented and liberal woman, but the denomination can look back with pride in its role in her early training and ministerial birth.

WORSHIP

When Horace Bushnell described the Sabbath services in his home church in rural Connecticut during the early nineteenth century, he characterized them as being largely intense intellectual exercises. There was in them, he said, "too little of the manner of worship," for those present "think of nothing, in fact, save that which meets their intelligence and enters into them by that method." The New Divinity worshippers "have digestion for strong meat," welcoming a diet of "free will, fixed fate, foreknowledge absolute, Trinity, redemption, special grace, eternity." And the result, he added, was that "if they go away having something to think of, they have had a good day."[63] This may be a somewhat exaggerated characterization, for in the days of Bushnell's youth Timothy Dwight's prompting of a new awakening was widespread and the revivalism that Bushnell later protested was getting under way. But the characterization stands in contrast to what followed. Worship throughout the first half of the 1800s ceased to be simply an exercise of the mind, appealing instead to all of human experience.

When the 1865 Boston council discussed worship, it highlighted two considerations. First, worship is an act of adoration and praise. It is "God's due," and therefore "it is essential that every Church render a pure and acceptable worship before the throne of Divine Majesty." The council lamented that this type of reverence was too often absent, noting that, indeed, to worship God in this manner one must be "in love with infinite excellence" and, like the saints, be so filled with a sense of the holiness of God that one's "feelings burst forth" in expressions of praise. But second, if this ideal is little attained, then the very practice of worship in the life of the church should be a means toward such "edification of its members in the divine love" as can lead toward that end.[64] Sabbath services have in this sense a clear pragmatic value, and in this imperfect world their function is to edify—that is, to lead persons not only in mind, but also in heart and soul, to a level of experience that transcends the mundane and is fulfilled in the glorification of God.

Sabbath Services

In the judgment of the 1865 council, all elements within the regular weekly gatherings for worship should contribute to this goal.

There is power of edification in the direct words of Scripture as heard in worship—"records of the divine dealings, breathings of penitence, prayer, and thanksgiving, and the story of redemption"—and particularly in "an expressive reading, which re-clothes the sacred words with their original life." But here the council's report longed for even more, commending the congregations' "chanting" of the Psalms as ancient songs of the church, for "it requires the strength of a great multitude to bear into our hearts the weight and sense of these words of God." The council grieved that this "is no more in use among us." Nevertheless, there is much value in other congregational singing, and the council spoke of the "mighty power of edification and persuasion" found in hymns that "our churches and their schools have only begun to realize." Such music, it suggested, was particularly valuable as an instrument of evangelization, for it could bring heretofore unchurched children into the Sunday school and their parents into the sanctuary.[65]

This developing hymnody tended largely toward the gospel hymns of the nineteenth century. Within Congregationalism an early example appeared in the work of the evangelist Asahel Nettleton. Dissatisfied with Isaac Watts's *Psalms and Hymns* as "too formal and lofty for evangelical use," Nettleton first prepared his *Village Hymns*, a collection of popular hymn texts, and then his *Zion's Harp*, which added appropriate music to the words. Many other hymnals followed, one of the most unusual being that of Lyman Beecher's son and late nineteenth-century popular preacher, Henry Ward Beecher. In 1855 he published his *Plymouth Collection of Hymns and Tunes*, which he claimed were "wide enough in range to be used by any evangelical church." The music was drawn from secular as well as religious sources, one of the tunes being the popular political ditty "Tippecanoe and Tyler Too."[66]

Public prayer in worship was likewise edifying, said the council, particularly "when one man of fervent and devout spirit leads the multitude, in words, which, with his tones, are the birth of a moment—the breathing of the Holy Ghost." This was in keeping with the Puritan tradition, a call for spontaneous, rather than for prewritten, prayer. It was also a call for committed and converted ministry, for such prayer can be offered only by one who is "habitually in communion with God." Thus when these conditions occur, the council added, this prayer serves an evangelistic purpose, for "the spirit of devotion may spread, like leaven, from soul to soul, till all be leavened."[67] Although the council spoke of public prayer as though it were a male prerogative, it is significant that efforts were made to allow and encourage a role in such prayer for women. Finney encouraged this in his early revivals when sinners were prayed through to conversion by both men and women from the congregation. And a report from New Hampshire shortly thereafter noted how the Rockingham Association of Churches affirmed that a prayer meeting can be made more of a power in the church by "the propriety of females taking part by speaking and leading in prayer."[68]

But most fully, said the council, the purpose of edification in worship is fulfilled by gospel preaching, through a sermon conveying with maximum forcefulness the message of the Word, appealing to mind, heart, and will and becoming the instrument of revival. Within Congregational practice in the first half of the nineteenth century, characteristics developed that differentiated this preaching from its own past and from the more extreme exhortations of many frontier revivalists. Congregational revival preaching contained extensive use of the Bible and earnest appeals to the gospel's call for repentance, but it was not camp meeting "Bible thumping." Flavel Bascom, an American Home Missionary Society pastor in Illinois, recalled a sermon of the latter sort that he had heard given by a backwoods preacher. After having stated his biblical text, the preacher never referred to it again, but roamed through the Scripture quoting passage after passage as one word suggested another. Thus, said Bascom, the speaker went "bellowing and blowing through the Bible," without shedding any more light on the passages quoted than the "roar of artillery does upon the Declaration of Independence."[69]

Congregational preaching in the early nineteenth century retained the intellectual sobriety of its Puritan biblical and homiletical roots. In a report to the 1865 council, preaching was described as a setting forth of the revealed truths of God's law and gospel "in their manifestation of the glory and government of God, in their relations to each other, and in all of their applications to the duties of men and the salvation of sinners."[70] That was a majestic task, tied closely in purpose and content to the commitment of the earlier generations.

Yet there was a difference. Donald M. Scott has noted that by the mid-1800s "the structure and language of the sermon, how it operated as a rhetorical event" had changed.[71] The sermon of the 1600s was formal and stylized, with emphasis upon idea and argumentation. It proceeded under specific "heads," opening the text in terms of its biblical setting, dividing the text by extracting from it the appropriate doctrines, and then applying the text in its various uses for the spiritual pilgrimage. The sermon of the 1800s, however, was more a means of personal address, with a broadened language often drawn from the minister's personal experience or from situations of contemporary life. In the mid-1800s Henry Ward Beecher used what he termed "home-bred" words of a daily vocabulary that "we heard in our childhood" and that "store up in themselves the sweetness and flavor that makes them precious."[72] Biblical imagery was still important, but sermons were less a form of technical argument and more one of edification, fusing idea and feeling in an appeal for the hearer's response.

The appeal of the preaching was augmented by the appeal of the preacher. The message and the medium became more intertwined, the preacher undertaking to represent himself as friend of sinners and sympathetic agent for the declaration of the love of Christ. The prophet of judgment, distant from his hearers, was less evident than the caring companion who shared the struggles and anxieties of his people—and thereby preached what Beecher called the "living Gospel," which took root within the inner confines of the preacher's life. This meant that the preacher himself needed to be a model for holiness, out of whose experience empathy and compassion could be discerned.

One additional consequence of focusing on the preacher, and of revivalist preaching in general, was a new type of church architecture. Earlier Congregational worship took place in colonial-style meeting-houses, with narrow sanctuaries and large "tub"-type pulpits, capped with their high sounding boards, which gave a special note of authority to the sermons, regardless of the individual speaker. In the nineteenth century sanctuaries became auditoriums, sometimes embellished in neoclassical style, fitted with front platforms and small desklike pulpits to accommodate more naturally the personalized preaching style of the speaker. Organs and choirs became the backdrop, located at the rear of the platform, and there was generally a place up front for a song leader to lead the hymns. Not only were new churches built this way, but older meetinghouses were converted to this plan. Worship as revival preaching and gospel song shaped and reshaped nineteenth-century Congregational architecture.

Sacraments

Congregational worship continued to include administration of the sacraments of baptism and the Lord's Supper, but again changes in emphasis occurred. The "sacramental evangelism" of the early eighteenth century waned by the early nineteenth, and the sacraments themselves became subordinated to the compelling influence of revivalism. In the process the sacraments lost their objectivity as God's acts and were viewed more in terms of their subjective value as occasions to enhance religious experience. The symbolism of "spiritual renewal" in baptism and of "spiritual union" in the Lord's Supper was not forsaken, but the reference points of the symbols changed over time. Less individually and theologically perceived, the sacraments emphasized the social contexts for the religious development of the baptized and the religious experience of the communicating faithful. A pragmatism that valued worship as a human means for religious edification within the church was applied to the church's sacramental life.

Charles Hambrick-Stowe has pointed out that although earlier Congregationalism viewed baptism as related first to God's covenant with the church and later to God's covenant with individuals, in the nineteenth century baptism was viewed primarily within the context of the family. This was true among both liberal and orthodox Calvinists in the early decades of the 1800s. Because for Nathaniel Taylor there was no original sin as universal inheritance from Adam, infant baptism was not a sign of remission but signified God's promise to nourish the child's spiritual growth. God's promise involved the child's total upbringing, and the focus shifted to the family as the context and instrument for such accomplishment. Taylor followed his Yale mentor, Timothy Dwight, who denied any regenerative power for infant baptism and limited the sacrament to children of believers because the latter alone could provide the home environment essential for this religious development. Among more orthodox Calvinists, Leonard Woods, professor at Andover, affirmed original sin, yet he joined in this changing emphasis because he disparaged baptism as merely an outward rite in comparison to the power of conversion. For him the significance of infant baptism was in its consecrating children to God and in its inspiring of parents to provide that home environment that might ultimately contribute to revivalism's goal, the conversion of the sinner. By the mid-1800s Horace Bushnell had developed further the liberal view by minimizing conversion and stressing Christian nurture in the home as the more important contributor to Christian life. Henry Ward Beecher graced infant baptisms with sermons on parental responsibility for training children for service to God and church.

The role of social experience was likewise prominent in mid-nineteenth-century discussions of the Lord's Supper, replacing the earlier objective sacramental emphasis of the Calvinist interpretation. The Supper became a memorial meal where the experience of the union of communicants with Christ, and through Christ with one another, was most important. The Boston council cited the Lord's Supper as an occasion of grace "in which all ages join and all disciples remember their only Lord."[73]

Departure from classic Calvinism's interpretation of the Lord's Supper was emphatically deplored in 1846 by John Williamson Nevin, professor at the German Reformed Mercersburg Seminary in Pennsylvania, in his book *The Mystical Presence.* Nevin criticized the subjective "modern Puritanism" of Timothy Dwight and others in Congregational, and also Presbyterian, views of the sacrament, which had lost sight of Calvin's sense of the real, though spiritual, presence of Christ as nourishment for the faithful at the table. This difference of perspective is important not only historically but also because the Reformed Mercersburg theology eventually combined with continuing strains of nineteenth-century Congregationalism in the 1957 formation of the United Church of Christ. In the mid-nineteenth century, however, Congregationalists found meaning in the Lord's Supper largely in the unifying experience of a memorial. In its celebration they gathered near the foot of the cross and forged a corporate companionship of Christians grateful for the redeeming sacrifice of Christ.

MISSION

Emil Brunner, twentieth-century theologian, once said that the church is to mission as fire is to burning. He was speaking of the church in the ideal sense, for in the real world this has rarely been true. Yet the analogy has a certain appropriateness for early nineteenth-century Congregationalism. Driven by the energies of revivalism and channeled through the programs of voluntary societies, Congregationalists and their churches of those decades reached out in marvelous ways to serve and influence life outside their meetinghouse walls. Their areas of concern for extended mission were largely continuous with those of the late eighteenth century, but the settings broadened and the commitments became more systematically sought and directed. Congregationalism contributed to the period's "expanding horizons" through its undertaking larger responsibility in the wider world.

American Indian Missions

The earliest missionary efforts of American Congregationalists had been directed toward American Indians, and the work of Thomas Mayhew, John Eliot, David Brainerd, and Jonathan Edwards made a limited, though significant, impact. With nineteenth-century national expansion, however, the opportunities became greater, as well as more complex, and Congregationalists leaned upon their newly born agency, the American Board of Commissioners for Foreign Missions, for coordinated action. Justification for use of this foreign mission arm lay in the fact that American Indian groups were dealt with by the federal government as independent nations in their treaty arrangements. Involvement of the government, however, added to the complexity. On the one hand, it provided benefit. Many denominations, including Congregationalists, profited from the Civilization Fund established by Congress in 1819, which allocated federal monies to church mission boards for assisting their work with American Indians ("Christianizing" and "civilizing" were deemed a common process). On the other hand, the federal government's violation of treaties and its arbitrary relocation of American Indians from better to poorer lands offended missionary consciences and sometimes led to conflict.

The American Indian work of the ABCFM began with a mission to the Cherokees in Tennessee in 1817, where the first station was named Brainerd in memory of that dedicated eighteenth-century missionary leader. In 1818 a mission called Eliot was established among the Choctaws in Mississippi, and in 1821 one named Dwight followed in Arkansas, again among Cherokees. Throughout the next decade the work spread rapidly, with missions added in Georgia and South Carolina, and the western frontier entered through pioneering projects in New York, Ohio, and Wisconsin. In each area multiple stations were created, schools established, churches founded, and a stable community life encouraged. But in the 1830s federal and state governments began efforts to move the American Indian population westward to lands beyond the Mississippi River, and difficulties followed. Some missions were given up in the process of relocation, whereas in others attempts were made to resist. The ABCFM opposed a proposal to move the Cherokees from Georgia to Oklahoma, carrying a defense of Cherokee sovereignty into Congress and the U.S. Supreme Court. In 1832 the Court decided for Cherokee independence, but President Andrew Jackson ignored the decision and ordered the Cherokees relocated, saying, "John Marshall has pronounced his judgment; let him enforce it if he can." In the process Samuel Worcester, an American Board missionary to the Cherokees, served fifteen months of hard labor under sentence by a Georgia court for his part in the opposition.

Although such setbacks were experienced by the American Board in its American Indian missions in the early 1830s, advances were also made, and these were continued in many midwestern and western states throughout the following decades. One such venture prior to the Civil War was the mission in Minnesota to the Santee Indians, a branch of the Dakotas, itself a branch of the Sioux. The Santees were first visited in 1834 by two Congregational laypersons from Connecticut, the brothers Samuel and Gideon Pond, who had been moved by revival experiences to undertake a preaching mission to the American Indians. Two years later Samuel went back to Connecticut, studied for the ministry, obtained a commission from the ABCFM, and returned with these qualifications to continue his Minnesota work. From the outset the Ponds also taught agricultural skills to stabilize the American Indian communities.

In the meantime the American Board sent additional missionaries to the Santees. Thomas Williamson arrived in 1835 and Stephen Riggs in 1837. They established a school, a church, and an ongoing mission program. Riggs and Williamson served this mission faithfully for more than a quarter of a century, developing a translation of the Bible and other religious literature in the Dakota language and aiding in the creation of a farm economy. In 1862 all this progress was disrupted and the program put to serious trial. When a war-pressed federal government was unable to provide the food subsidies promised, an uprising broke out among the Santees. Many settlers and American Indians were killed and vast numbers of warriors imprisoned. But in prison, through the ministry of Riggs, Williamson, and native converts, a Christian remnant was preserved to become the nucleus of a restored community. In 1866 the federal government moved the Santees to a reservation in Nebraska. There, under new indigenous leadership tested by prison experience, the Santees developed a strong Christian community extending well into the next century.

By 1870 the federal government had moved all American Indian groups to lands west of the Mississippi, and shortly thereafter the ABCFM, concentrating exclusively on its program overseas, released the last of its American Indian missions to the care of the American Missionary Association, already deeply involved with African Americans.

Foreign Missions

Congregational involvement in foreign missions began with the founding of the American Board of Commissioners for Foreign Missions in 1810 and its sending of five missionaries to India in 1812. Although early setbacks were faced, including resistance by the British East India Company and the loss of two of the group to the Baptists, a small mission station was established in Bombay in 1813. Even before word of that success was received, however, the board moved ahead. By the time of its annual meeting in 1812, the ABCFM had enlarged itself from nine to twenty-four corporate members, representing no longer merely two, but eight, states, and had identified four different fields of missionary activity for its future work.

Although the work proceeded slowly in the first decade of the board's existence, it advanced more rapidly in the 1820s and 1830s. By 1850 the ABCFM had mission stations literally around the earth. The four types of missionary activity led to the following American Board-sponsored missions during the first half dozen decades of the agency's life: (1) Missions among "peoples of ancient civilizations." The India mission established in Bombay in 1813 was followed by others in Ceylon (1816), Madura (1834), Madras (1836), and Arcot (1851). Working interdenominationally with Presbyterian and Reformed groups, the ABCFM transferred the Arcot mission to the Dutch Reformed Church in 1857. A mission in Siam was established in 1831.

China was entered with missions at Canton (1830), Singapore (1834), Amoy (1842), Foochow (1847), Shanghai (1854), and Peking (1854). The first mission in Japan was developed in 1869. (2) Missions among "peoples of primitive cultures." In 1820 missionaries were sent to the Sandwich (Hawaiian) Islands, a program turned over to the indigenous Hawaiian Evangelical Association in 1863. Missions in Sumatra and Borneo were begun in 1833. Africa was entered with work in Guinea (1833), South Africa (1835), and Gabon, West Africa (1843). In 1870 the latter was transferred to the Presbyterian board. (3) Missions among "peoples of the ancient Christian churches." This was work among the Armenians, Greeks, Bulgarians, Syrians, Assyrians, and other Christian minorities in the Ottoman Empire, initiated as early as 1820. By this effort it is evident that a broad Christian ecumenism, according validity to Eastern Orthodoxy, had not yet developed among Congregationalists. (4) Missions among "peoples of Islamic faith." This mission was begun in Turkey in 1820 but was addressed to all Islamic peoples of the Near East, including large Arab, Persian, and Turkish populations.[74]

Inspired by the revivalism of the early nineteenth century, the chief goal of ABCFM missionary activity for the first several decades was simply the saving of souls from eternal damnation. It was so defined by the board at the outset in 1811 and in 1834 reaffirmed with the statement that "the preaching of the Gospel, by the living voice" is "the great business of our missionaries," whereas "other labors directly aimed at the amelioration of society should always be kept strictly subordinate."[75] In the late decades of the 1800s educational, medical, and agricultural missions, through the prodding of missionaries themselves, gradually began to gain recognition from the board as having their own significant value.

In the earliest years of foreign missions it was felt that unmarried women should not be sent out as missionaries. The first such appointment, that of Cynthia Farrar to Bombay in 1827 as superintendent of women's schools, was an exception to the rule. She served there until her death in 1862. The exception was made because the board had heard of the success of British women already serving as missionaries in India. In succeeding decades the board also was influenced by letters from missionary wives from all parts of the world telling of the desperate condition of women and girls in non-Christian cultures and asking for female help. So by 1868 the board had forty-two single women serving abroad in missionary positions, located in Turkey, Syria, Persia, South Africa, India, China, and the Sandwich Islands. These appointments were further stimulated toward the end of the nineteenth century when the Congregational Woman's Boards of Missions provided substantial financial aid to support women missionaries for foreign work among women and children.

Domestic Missions

Although American Indian and foreign missions were a large part of early and mid-nineteenth-century Congregational missionary concern, Congregationalists also spent great effort to save souls and build churches on the expanding western frontier. Christianizing the West, indeed Christianizing all of America, became a dominating passion. Congregationalists participated in this domestic crusade alongside other Protestant denominations, producing the Evangelical Alliance committed to winning the nation to religious conversion and fidelity. The whole land, it was hoped, could be brought to evangelical Protestant commitment. Not only did the religious disinterest of the frontier and its often accompanying "barbarism" need to be combatted, but Protestants wanted to stop the threatening advances of Roman Catholicism carried by European immigrants into both eastern and western urban life. The goal was a Protestant America.

For Congregationalists structures to support this mission were the Plan of Union and, later, the American Home Missionary Society. The difficulties encountered in the Plan of Union with the Presbyterians, combined with Congregationalism's initial reluctance to advance itself as a polity appropriate for the frontier, led to statistics suggesting that Congregationalism's contribution to this evangelical mission was negligible. Whereas in 1800 Congregational churches in America outnumbered those of other evangelical denominations, in 1860 Methodists had 19,833 churches; Baptists 11,221; Presbyterians 5,061; and Congregationalists 2,234. Other, newer denominations had also appeared on the scene.

Congregational contributions, however, went beyond numbers in terms of impact upon the educational and moral maturing of society and the theological and ecumenical progress of the Christian church. And while in the light of the magnitude of the task the AHMS long struggled for adequate funds and personnel, the domestic mission did not lack the churches' endorsement. One particular aspect of this was the considerable financial support provided by the women of New England Congregational churches who organized Female Cent Societies to underwrite the projects of the AHMS. By contributing their pennies above and beyond their families' support of the church, and by recruiting large numbers of donors, the women kept missionaries at work on the western frontier.

Furthermore, commitment to domestic mission remained clothed in the garment of millennial theology. Prevailing evangelical thought insisted that a converted and Protestant America could lead to God's final triumph. And a Christianized America would be a model bringing the rest of the world to Christ and to salvation. Although newly developed foreign missions would play a significant role, evangelists continued to hold that the biblically prophesied millennium would begin with the American nation. The long-nurtured New England covenant hope of being God's chosen people remained, perpetuated as the hope for a Christianized America.

Moral and Social Reform

A Christianized America, nineteenth-century evangelists believed, would be not only a converted nation but also a reformed nation in moral and social behavior. As the voluntary societies were organized, therefore, many were devoted to reform causes. Congregationalists participated in this variety, but their major interests focused on the causes of temperance, Sabbath keeping, and the eradication of slavery.

Throughout the colonial period the consumption of alcohol was not a serious issue in church or society. By the nineteenth century, however, the situation had changed. The use of alcohol had greatly increased, and secular and religious groups recognized its medical and moral dangers. In the Second Great Awakening the revivalists made alcohol a major issue, strongly inveighing against the evils of intemperance. The first temperance society was formed in 1808, and by 1830 there were more than a thousand local temperance organizations in the United States. The American Temperance Society began in 1826 as a national organization, building from grass-roots support. In 1840 a society was formed of reformed drinkers who had signed a total abstinence pledge, and within a few years its membership numbered half a million. As government got involved, Indiana enacted the first local option law in 1832. In 1851 Maine became the first state to legislate total prohibition.

Congregational participation in the temperance cause was inspired initially by Lyman Beecher, who in 1812 submitted a report to the General Association of Connecticut recommending the ending of all drinking at ecclesiastical meetings, the urging of church members to cease all selling, buying, or use of "ardent spirits," and the formation of temperance societies to aid in this purpose. Other Congregational evangelists also took up the cause. Finney, for example, singled out intemperance as an object of special concern, and his view was quite uncompromising. Ministers and churches, he said, should "cast out from their communion" those members who "continue to drink or traffic in ardent spirits." By this means, he believed, the churches could do away with "the death-dealing abomination."[76]

Congregationalists and their churches, in the East and the West, allied themselves with the crusade. In Maine the General Conference championed the cause of temperance, declaring year after year that the use of and traffic in liquor constituted an immorality inconsistent with church membership. When the Maine Liquor Law was enacted, the conference rejoiced and committed itself to the law's support through parish education and through "taking the spirit of Christ into politics"[77] by commending candidates who would uphold the law. In 1838 the Illinois State Association recommended total abstinence, along with political efforts to secure statewide prohibition and a measure to make it a penal offense for any candidate for public office to attempt to secure votes by giving drinks to voters. The Congregational church at Du Page, Illinois, wrote total abstinence into its rules for membership. Similar concern was expressed on the national level when the 1852 Albany Convention urged all ministers and churches to favor in their states and territories legislation patterned after the Maine law. This was needed in order that "redemption from one of the most demoralizing and desolating evils with which we are afflicted"[78] could be accomplished.

The Puritan tradition deeply honored the Sabbath as a day of worship and rest, and there was no diminution of this reverence among later Congregationalists, who participated in the Sabbatarianism that

generally characterized American evangelical churches. Harriet Beecher
Stowe valued the Sabbath's sacred sense of quiet. She wrote, "To the
devout the effect was something the same as if the time had been spent
in heaven." When Horace Bushnell visited Cuba in 1855, he was
shocked by its use of Sunday for continuous work and wrote home to his
wife, "How different from the hallowed peace and the almost heavenly
riches of our own Christian Sabbath!"[79]

Civilization, however, was fast despoiling that heavenly peace.
Throughout America the Sabbath was increasingly violated by private
work and by public activity. Stage coaches, boats, and later the railroads
ran as public conveyances on that day, and even the government transported mail on the Sabbath. A nationwide protest began as early as
1811, and in 1814 seventy-three petitions were sent to the House of
Representatives on the matter, one of them written by Lyman Beecher
for the Connecticut General Association. Finney likewise joined in
protesting the government's misuse of the Sabbath, fearing that with
the mails running and the post offices open this could lead to court
sessions and legislative meetings on that day. "And," he wrote, "what
can the church do, what can this nation do, WITHOUT ANY SABBATH?"[80]

In 1843 the American and Foreign Sabbath Union was organized
to bring together an interdenominational movement to preserve
"Sabbath-keeping." Justin Edwards, a Boston Congregational pastor
who had been a leader of the temperance campaign, was chosen to be its
executive. The next year the National Sabbath Convention was held,
presided over by Congregationalist John Quincy Adams. For decades in
the first half of the nineteenth century Congregational churches and
their state associations made the preservation of the Sabbath one of their
major social concerns. A church in Ohio declared that collecting hay or
grain on the Sabbath, or using the day for unnecessary travel or for
visiting friends, was a "violation of Christian duty." The Illinois State
Association declared that "capitalists holding property in railroads,
stages, and steamboats by which the Sabbath was desecrated were guilty
of violating the spirit of the Fourth Commandment."[81] The conference
in Maine urged setting aside a day for fasting and prayer "in view of the
profanation of the Sabbath."[82] Congregationalists tried to preserve their
long-standing Sabbath tradition.

The antislavery movement, as earlier noted, claimed strong commitment from Congregationalists. Individuals, churches, associations,

mission organizations, and the national Albany Convention all joined in the condemnation of American slavery and in the hope for the liberation of the slaves. Yet the issue was not a simple one, and opinions varied over the question of how this momentous social change could be achieved. The major point of division was between those who favored a gradualist approach, seeking the eradication of slavery through the power of persuasion and religious conversion, and those who favored "immediatism," seeking abolition through head-on confrontation employing legislative and other direct means. In this dilemma Congregationalism was split, sharing with the whole antislavery movement the perplexing question of how to remove such a pervasive evil from the social fabric.

An early effort to alleviate some of the distress of slavery was through the organization of the American Colonization Society in 1817. Its plan to return slaves to their native Africa was first proposed by Samuel Hopkins in 1776 and finally put into action by the society as a voluntary program available for free African Americans and others who could be emancipated through appeal to the consciences of their masters. A colony was established in Liberia, and in 1821 the first emigrant ship, carrying eighty-nine African Americans, arrived at Sierra Leone. Throughout the 1820s and 1830s Congregational support focused upon colonization, led by Leonard Bacon, distinguished pastor in New Haven. The plan of the society fitted well into Bacon's gradualist approach to resolving the slavery issue, a view he continued to promote for some years. For Bacon there were evil and good slaveholders. The important thing was to convert the evil slaveholders and appeal to the consciences of the good. But those good masters, who motivated by the law of love see their slaves as persons rather than as property, had the responsibility to educate their slaves before freeing them. Bacon thus joined the concern for the amalgamation into society of freed slaves with the concern for emancipation. In time Bacon and others gave up on colonization, for it simply did not work. Their gradualist emphases continued, however, up to the time of the Civil War, fueled by fear of social disruption and the breakup of the nation.

The more radical "immediatist" view was introduced dramatically in 1831 by William Lloyd Garrison, who in the first issue of his famous paper, the Liberator, declared slavery to be a sin that must immediately be brought to an end by granting slaves full citizenship rights. In 1832 he organized the American Anti-Slavery Society, which affirmed all slaveholding to be a grievous sin and demanded its immediate abolition. By 1838 more than a thousand auxiliary societies to this movement had been developed. Although Garrison rejected the church for its temporizing, he gathered much church support. Bacon countered the call for immediacy by urging the "immediate duty of emancipation" as against the "duty of immediate emancipation," but Garrison's verve and intensity swayed many to the more radical approach. From this point on Congregationalism struggled with the tension of the two approaches to the one goal of eradicating slavery.

Most Congregational evangelists felt this dilemma. A major exception was Theodore Dwight Weld, member of the dissident abolitionist student group leaving Lane Theological Seminary for Oberlin, who, along with his wife Angelina Grimke Weld, became a tireless campaigner for the immediatist cause. Lyman Beecher, however, was pulled in both directions, though he was strongly antislavery. When Garrison asked for Beecher's help, Beecher responded that Garrison must first give up his "fanatical notions."[83] Charles Grandison Finney advocated a more aggressive abolitionism and also was bolder in action. While serving a church in New York, he excluded slaveholders from communion on the ground that slaveholders were not Christians. But Finney's preaching on emancipation saw it chiefly as a consequence of conversion, leaving an impression of moderation. This angered the radicals, leading to a withdrawal of financial support for Oberlin by one of its liberal New York benefactors. Weld, however, came to Finney's defense, a clear indication of the basic depth of Finney's commitment to immediate abolition.

Congregationalism anguished over the method of reform through the 1850s. In a few instances this led to division in local churches. At Andover, Massachusetts, the Free Congregational Church was organized by radical abolitionist dissenters from South Church. The First Congregational Church of Chicago came into existence in the same manner. After 1846 the American Missionary Association, upholding the more radical antislavery sentiment, became a catalyst for further change. It criticized the American Home Missionary Society for continuing to support missionaries to churches that allowed membership and offered communion to slaveholders. It also attacked the American Board of Commissioners for Foreign Missions for accepting contributions from slaveholders and for refusing to condemn the institution of slavery. In both instances its influence was felt.

State and national organizations of the Congregational churches likewise struggled with these tensions. The General Conference of Maine, after years of supporting colonization and advocating prayer as a main means for emancipation, took steps in the 1850s to criticize the U.S. Congress for opening up new slave territory in Kansas and Nebraska and to approve the American Home Missionary Society's new position of withholding financial aid from slaveholding churches. In the West, which showed an earlier openness to more radical views, Michigan's General Association in 1844 described slavery as a heinous sin and recommended that its churches cut off all communion with other churches allowing slaveholder membership. In 1853 the Michigan General Association registered its protest against the Fugitive Slave Act and affirmed its intent to disobey the law should any slaves fleeing their masters come into the custody of Michigan churches. The Albany Convention was similarly concerned. Its vigorous debate in 1852 prepared the way for the next decade's more decisive stand by the American Home Missionary Society against recognizing or aiding slaveholding churches. When the National Congregational Council met in Boston in 1865 the Civil War had ended, but in its reflection the council affirmed the war to have been "the judgment of Heaven upon slavery," which prepared the nation, so it believed, "for profounder convictions of Christian truth and larger effusions of the Holy Spirit."[84]

SUMMARY

The melding of the American colonies into an independent nation, along with the opening of the frontier for western expansion, led American Congregationalism to step beyond the limits of its colonial origins and to face new challenges and opportunities. In the process it entered more thoroughly into the larger interdenominational stream of American church life, losing thereby its earlier status of preeminence, but gaining the experience of participating with others in the more-inclusive task of Christianizing all America.

Throughout the first several decades of the nineteenth century Congregationalism contributed much to the intensification of religious and moral energy characterizing the beginning of the new national experience. As a leader in the Second Great Awakening, it provided preachers of power for revivalism's rebirth and pioneers in advocacy of moral causes to deal with society's ills. Out of this came not only new enthusiasm in the churches but also the work of nondenominational voluntary societies to energize campaigns of social reform. The most critical cause of the mid-nineteenth century was that of the eradication of slavery, and here Congregationalists played a significant role through the work of both its seasoned leaders and its college youth.

Congregationalism's new posture likewise led it into a home missionary program for sending clergy and establishing churches on the western frontier. In one sense this did not lead to denominational advancement, for in the Plan of Union Congregationalism lost many churches to its stronger Presbyterian partner. But throughout these years Congregationalists assumed a disproportionate position of leadership in many areas. Although Congregationalism rejected the radical Unitarianism arising in some of its New England churches, it fostered throughout the decades the gradual liberalization of Calvinist theology for much mainstream American Protestant thought. It affected the development of American higher education by founding and nurturing colleges and seminaries in its westward movement. Its declared ecumenical interests led the way to larger cooperation among the denominations on the frontier. And its early commitment to foreign missions developed an agency that served as forerunner for more extended nineteenth-century efforts toward world evangelization. Congregationalism in these decades broke out of its more circumscribed past to become a force in an expanding nation.

CHAPTER SIX

AN ERA OF PROGRESS
1870–1920

Historian Martin Marty has characterized the late nineteenth and early twentieth centuries in America as a "complacent era."[1] This is an apt designation—but only to the extent to which it was intended. The period's complacency lay in its broad indifference to emerging social problems, particularly the problems of poverty and human degradation, widely generated by the urban growth and the economic injustices of the times. Despite the strong antislavery commitments and other moral concerns of preceding decades, the conscience, even of the churches, seemed little touched by the plight of the new underclass in the nation's life. Only near the turn of the century did a few prophetic voices, several of them Congregational, speak out for applying the Christian message to society's economic ills in what became a "social gospel." For the most part the age, in facing those problems, remained an era of complacency.

From a broader perspective this age was also an "era of progress." America in earlier decades had pursued expanding horizons, and from 1870 to 1920 it continued the progress then begun. Westward expansion was completed, and the remainder of the forty-eight contiguous states became part of the federal union. Marvels of invention contributed to an industrial revolution that developed means of manufacture, transportation, and communication far beyond any earlier dreams. Fortunes were made in the railroads, in mining, and in the manufacture of steel, making cities into teeming centers of new industry. The United States emerged as a world power, strong in its own defense and willing to embrace distant territories as imperialist "protector." America was fast coming of age.

This was also a time of progress for the churches. Throughout the land their memberships continued to increase—not only in aggregate numbers, but even more significantly in proportion to total population.

317

Church membership was 15 percent of the nation in 1850; it more than doubled to 36 percent in 1900 and more than tripled to 50 percent by the early 1920s. Congregationalism, though no longer one of the larger denominations nationally, shared in this growth. These decades were also an era of progress for Congregationalism in other ways. Foreign mission projects, begun in the early nineteenth century, reached a point of high fruition. A national structure took permanent shape and allowed for more coordinated effort among the churches. Ecumenical commitment found new fulfillment in interdenominational cooperation. An openness to advanced intellectual life enabled Congregationalists to play a leading role in shaping the period's new and more liberal theology. Through this forward movement, moreover, the inevitability of continued progress toward society's perfection became a center of religious confidence and hope. In this "era of progress" even those who deplored the current moral complacency looked forward to the certain coming of the earthly kingdom of God.

HISTORY

National Consciousness Fulfilled

At Albany in 1852 and at Boston in 1865 ad hoc gatherings of Congregational lay and clergy representatives from churches around the nation temporarily met Congregationalism's need for achievement of national identity and for cooperative effort in carrying out common tasks. Neither of these meetings, however, left a structure, or even a plan, to sustain a permanent national organization for the Congregational churches. Within a few years, therefore, efforts were undertaken to bring this about. The catalyst was the national Pilgrim Memorial Convention held in Chicago in April 1870 to celebrate the 250th anniversary of the landing of the Pilgrims at Plymouth, for one of its enacted resolutions called upon the state associations of Congregational churches to work for the formation of a permanent national body. Led by Ohio, state groups quickly set about the task, laying the plans, determining broad support from the churches, and issuing a call to a founding meeting. In November 1871 in Oberlin, Ohio, the result was the formation of the National Council of the Congregational Churches of the United States.

As the National Council adopted its constitution, it took several steps to define its nature and function. Members, divided between laity and clergy "as nearly equally as is practicable," were representatives of local churches, initially specified as one delegate for every ten congregations. Each recognized benevolent society and theological seminary had one delegate, with voice but no vote. Meetings were projected for every three years, with new officers elected at each session. Only those charged with record keeping and correspondence would function through the interim. The council existed "to consult upon the common interests of all the churches," particularly with respect to evangelization and the united development of resources, and "to express and foster" the churches' "substantial unity in doctrine, polity, and work."[2]

The constitution also stated the limitations of the National Council as an agency within the polity of historic Congregationalism. Recognizing the "inalienable right of each church to self-government and administration," it affirmed that "this National Council shall never exercise legislative or judicial authority, nor consent to act as a council of reference."[3] However, on this issue of permissible council actions early disputes occurred. Although acknowledging the importance and usefulness of a national organization, some Congregationalists, anxious about possible violation of local congregational autonomy, sought to restrict the council's functioning.

Within the first decade two forms of protest arose. In 1877 an overture from the General Association of New Jersey charged that by "meeting statedly, to give advice in denominational matters" the National Council was acting in a manner "subversive of Congregationalism."[4] It argued that the council should be summoned only in emergencies to deal with limited issues prompted by particular occasions. The question was whether a national council should be modeled after a Congregational neighborhood council, called only at a time of need to deal solely with the problem on which advice was sought. The National Council denied that it was a council of that sort and, in effect, stated that it had a right to meet regularly and advise more broadly based on its constitutional mandate "to consult upon the common interests of all the churches" and to "foster their substantial unity."

In 1880 another approach was taken by the General Association of New York, which urged that the National Council could promote unity among the churches more effectively by limiting its actions to discussion of issues, and not voting upon them, thereby removing "the possible danger of separation and division." The council could act like a "conference of churches," a type of district gathering enjoyed by many in the nineteenth century, which stressed discussions and devotions rather than decisions. Actually, this issue had already been addressed in 1871, when the term *conference* was rejected in favor of *council*. In 1880 the intent of that earlier selection was sustained. Defending its use of voting, the council affirmed that there are issues before it on which the common mind needs to be known and no other method exists "to collect that agreement than the old simple way of voting yea or nay to the topic before us."[5] And in an added tour de force the National Council noted that the General Association of New York had itself engaged in a vote to bring this matter to national attention! So the National Council defended its procedures against the charge of eroding Congregational local autonomy and continued its program of fostering the common interests of the churches.

In succeeding years further steps were taken to strengthen the National Council and to structure it more adequately for its task. A critical council session in the process was the Kansas City meeting in 1913 that produced a revised constitution and an improved national organization. Responding to forty years of council history, the 1910 gathering at Boston authorized the Committee of Nineteen to develop plans for increasing the council's effectiveness. Widely representative of the churches (apart from the absence of women!), the committee of lay and clergy members spent three years analyzing correspondence with churches, district and state organizations, benevolent societies, and all parts of Congregationalism. Proposals were developed, circulated, and revised in the light of critical review. Extended public hearings were held for discussion and revision at the Kansas City meeting itself. At the end of this careful democratic procedure the committee's recommendations were adopted by the more than 750 delegates with but one dissenting vote.

The new constitution continued to protect against violation of local church autonomy, but it strengthened the National Council, enabling it to play a larger role in the denomination's life. The council's purpose was expanded to include cooperation with all mission organizations related to Congregationalism, as well as promotion of the work of the churches "in their national, international, and interdenominational relations." Meetings of the council were increased to every two, rather than three, years to keep it in closer touch with ongoing developments. An executive committee was created to carry on the business of the council between meetings, and the offices of moderator and secretary were redefined to give them more responsibility during interim periods. Words of caution limited the authority of the moderator, who although commissioned to represent the council at ecclesiastical gatherings throughout his tenure, was informed that "all his acts and utterances shall be devoid of authority" and shall have "only such weight and force as inhere in the reason of them." But altogether the council became a more continuous and ongoing institution for providing assistance to the churches' common work. Chief among the new tasks was coordination of the mission program. The Commission on Missions was established to correlate the work of the separate Congregational missionary societies to avoid duplication and to secure "the maximum of efficiency with the minimum of expense." With these steps Congregationalism expressed more explicitly its growing consciousness of national unity and responsibility.[6]

The New Sciences

Two major scientific movements coalesced in the late nineteenth century to encourage radical developments in American Protestant theology. First came the theories of geological, and then biological, evolution, which called into question the accuracy of the biblical account of creation. The Genesis portrayal of a six-day creation seemed absurd to mid-nineteenth-century scientists, who saw millions of years of the earth's gradual development disclosed in its rock formations and the fossil record they preserved. The renowned Yale geologist, Benjamin Silliman, tried to reconcile these divergent views by interpreting the Hebrew word for "day" to mean an extended period of time. Although his argument eased the tensions for some, the conflict between scientific discovery and biblical literalism remained.

Far more shattering to orthodox biblical understanding, however, was the theory of biological evolution and, particularly, its conclusion with respect to human origin. Although these matters had been probed earlier in the international scientific community, the publication of Charles Darwin's *Origin of Species* in 1859 and his *Descent of Man* in 1871 set the issue. Again the biblical account of creation was contradicted, for instantaneous creation of animal species was denied by the affirmation of their evolution through natural selection over great lengths of time. The biblical account was even more startlingly challenged by the assertion that the human race was a product of primitive animal progenitors.

This new view of human origin raised other troubling theological questions concerning human nature. It threatened orthodox affirmations concerning the existence of a first Adam, his creation in the image of God, and his fall into sin affecting his successors. Central themes of Calvinist theology were undermined, as well as the authenticity of the biblical story. The crises in religious thought precipitated by the theories of evolution were indeed severe, and Congregationalists were caught in the midst of them.

Along with these developments in natural science, there was a growing movement in the science of historical study, particularly as applied to the ancient documents of the Bible. The Bible had long been looked upon as a divinely dictated, and therefore inerrant, volume conveying God's revelation to humanity. In the late nineteenth century, however, biblical scholars began to study the Bible by use of literary-critical techniques applicable to any historical document. By the process of "lower criticism" changes were made in the biblical text itself, and its accuracy was steadily improved. Scholars examined thousands of Hebrew and Greek manuscripts containing variants in Old and New Testament texts, reconstructing the Bible's original wording. Corrections in translation were also made to reflect new linguistic knowledge.

Even more significantly, the process of "higher criticism" was used to study the biblical documents within the context of their historical origins. Traditional authorships of biblical books were questioned, and several books were judged to be layered compilations joining segments from varying historical and cultural periods. Elements of myth were found in historical accounts, contradictions were noted in records coming from different sources and periods, and other questions of literal accuracy arose. As a new sense of its human origins and fallibility grew, the Bible was valued as a significant record of human religious experience and faith, the story of both Hebrew and early Christian growing awareness of God and accompanying sensitivity to God's will. The Bible was God's Word, filtered through human comprehension and understanding.

The impact of the new scientific and biblical scholarship on American Protestantism was immense, and by the beginning of the twentieth century most Congregational colleges, seminaries, and clergy had adopted new liberal perspectives. Reaction to Darwin's views on biological evolution was cautious at first, even within the scientific community. However, acceptance was greatly assisted when Asa Gray, a distinguished botanist on the faculty at Harvard University and lay member of First Church (Congregational) in Cambridge, not only supported the major portions of Darwin's theory on scientific grounds but also spoke to the theological issue of evolution's threat to a doctrine of divine creation. Gray urged that Darwin's theory actually strengthened the doctrine of divine creation by expanding the range of God's creative activity into the whole evolutionary process. Gray's point was strengthened when George Frederick Wright, a Congregational pastor at Andover and later professor of science and religion at Oberlin, joined with him in 1876 to publish a volume of essays commending Darwin's basic views.

Soon other Congregational theologians and clergy expressed support. In the process, however, one aspect of Darwin's theory was changed. Darwin postulated an evolution from lower to higher species through a process of natural selection worked out through the "survival of the fittest." But this struggle of "tooth and claw" seemed inappropriate to God's way of working, and in its place evolution was viewed, in the religious interpretation, as energized by the "arrival of the fittest." Through God's creative activity, evolution's religious defenders argued, there appeared at critical points in biological history new species that speeded evolution on its upward way. With this understanding, Congregational leaders joined in celebrating the marriage of science and religion and its direction toward a more modern faith.

As early as 1872, in the Lyman Beecher Lectures on Preaching at Yale, Henry Ward Beecher spoke of the advances of science and warned the Divinity School audience about the danger of "having the intelligent part of society go past us." "The providence of God," he said, "is rolling forward in a spirit of investigation that Christian ministers must meet and join." Later, in 1882, he declared himself to be "a cordial

Christian evolutionist."[7] In 1886 Theodore Munger, pastor of North Church in New Haven, urged thankfulness for existence, "however it came about," and cautioned that "[we] not deem ourselves too good to be included in the one creation of the one God." By the century's end Washington Gladden, Congregational pastor and social gospel pioneer in Columbus, Ohio, summarized the maturing faith of many Congregational leaders by calling evolution "a most impressive demonstration of the presence of God in the world."[8]

Acceptance of the scientific theory of evolution required, however, a companion liberalization in interpretation of the Bible. Congregational leaders moved in this direction slowly, recognizing that questioning biblical inerrancy was an emotionally difficult and publicly hazardous matter. Some years later Washington Gladden recalled that when he was a Massachusetts pastor in 1875, the Massachusetts Congregational clergy, though accepting the new biblical scholarship, were nevertheless shaken by it and still had "great timidity" in commending it "in the hearing of the public."[9] In his subsequent ministry in Ohio, however, Gladden became one of the effective popularizers of the new approach to biblical understanding. In 1891 he published a volume titled *Who Wrote the Bible? A Book for the People*, which received wide circulation and was warmly praised for interpreting higher criticism in a manner helpful to the laity of the churches. Others also took up the task of reinterpreting biblical authority. Theodore Munger urged that the Bible is "not a magical book, . . . not a diviner's rod."[10] Rather, he said, it must be read in "a more natural way" as subject to the normal laws of literary development. In this sense, he added, "it is not a revelation, but it is the history of a revelation." Henry Ward Beecher concurred by noting that "it is the human race that has been inspired; and the Bible in every part of it was lived, first, and the record of it made afterwards."[11] As early as the 1880s Congregational leaders were replacing the old with the new in their manner of viewing and honoring the biblical message.

Also in the 1880s this confluence of ideas led to development of the New Theology. Although this theological movement was promoted in several denominations, Congregationalists were once again among its major leaders. To the names of Beecher, Munger, and Gladden can be added those of George A. Gordon, minister at Old South, Boston; Lyman Abbott, Beecher's successor as minister at Plymouth Church, Brooklyn; Newman Smyth, minister at Center Church, New Haven;

and William J. Tucker and Egbert C. Smyth, members of the theological faculty at Andover. Through their work the new liberalism was expanded theologically to make a decisive break with the Calvinism of Congregationalism's long heritage, a step dramatically represented at Andover when its faculty was no longer required to consent to a Calvinist creed! Based on optimism concerning human capacity for goodness and concerning God's immanent and directing presence, the New Theology shifted major emphasis from personal redemption from sin to social progress leading toward the coming of the Kingdom of God. The new sciences opened the way in the late nineteenth and early twentieth centuries for a notably different theological form of confidence and hope.

A Changing Social Order

The changing social character of the late nineteenth century also called upon Congregationalism to adapt and respond. It was a period of immense population growth. Whereas the early 1800s saw gradually increasing European immigration to America, the floodgates were opened after the Civil War. From 1870 to 1920, more than 26 million immigrants entered America and the nation's total population tripled, from approximately 35 million to more than 105 million by 1920. At first immigrants came largely from northern and western Europe, but by 1890 the tide of immigration shifted to peoples mostly from Europe's southern and eastern nations. In addition, a smaller number of immigrants from China and Japan settled on the West Coast. America's "melting pot" was a reality.

As population increased, immigrants settled in the nation's cities. Earlier immigrants had spread out to work the rich farmlands of America, but by the late nineteenth century immigration centered in metropolitan areas. Cities provided major opportunities for industrial employment and permitted ethnic groups to retain a sense of solidarity. Furthermore, as farmers felt increasing economic stress due to decreases in agricultural prices, they left their farms in the late nineteenth century to find better jobs in the city. Urban America exploded. In 1870 approximately 20 percent of the American population lived in cities; by 1900 the urban population had increased to 40 percent. In the three decades from 1860 to 1890 major eastern cities, such as New York,

Philadelphia, and Baltimore, more than doubled in population, while younger cities in the west grew rapidly. In 1890 Chicago was the second largest city in the nation, having more than a million inhabitants, and urban populations were fast concentrating in St. Louis, Cleveland, and Detroit. The melting pot was becoming largely metropolitan.

The urban growth of America harbored both promise and peril. Lyman Abbott observed that "every city has been a Babylon, and every city has been a New Jerusalem . . . and it has always been a question whether the Babylon would extirpate the New Jerusalem or the New Jerusalem would extirpate the Babylon."[12] For some, without doubt, the cities were at least approximations of a New Jerusalem. Rapid industrialization made them prosperous centers of manufacturing, commerce, and banking. Large profits from many industries had created concentrations of money and power. The urban elite lived with all the accoutrements of success, and even their costly churches became symbols of material gain. Yet for many others cities were a new Babylon, alien lands of tears and trouble for the dispossessed. The rise of cities led to the growth of urban poverty, with its accompanying evils and tragedies. Overcrowded beyond the capacity of factories and housing to handle, cities faced acute problems of unemployment, congested tenement living, slum conditions, and the distorted human relations that such circumstances can bring. And most often, from the churches' perspective, cities became desert lands devoid of religious faith, as religion got lost in the midst of social struggle.

The problem of urban poverty was further exacerbated by the reigning philosophy of the late nineteenth century concerning industry, labor, and economic life. Drawing upon an unqualified laissez-faire capitalism, urban leaders simply applied Darwin's "survival of the fittest" theory to the economic struggle and the acquisition of wealth. Andrew Carnegie, a highly successful entrepreneur in the steel industry, wrote an article entitled "Wealth," published in 1889, in which he justified the uninhibited competitive character of a wealth-producing manufacturing system that rewards those of talent and energy who lead their industries to success. Although this system also creates extreme social inequality, in which some may even be impoverished, it is a price society must pay for the overall progress the system brings. Carnegie, a devout church member, added his belief that Christian responsibility should lead wealthy persons to share their wealth through philanthropy. But economic success, by the competitive process, was the primary goal.

As this laissez-faire economic system became the driving force in late nineteenth-century American industry, it intensified economic inequality and led to social disruption. The chief victim was the laboring class, both the unemployed and the employed. The average worker was depersonalized, treated like a commodity, and alongside all other commodities labor was subject to the laws of supply and demand. Thus with workers plentiful and competition keen, wages and working conditions remained insensitive to human need. Child labor was common, sweatshops hired women for a pittance, and men in heavy industrial labor were overworked. Steel workers were at their tasks twelve hours a day and seven days a week for barely subsistence pay.

Not surprisingly, labor unions came into being. The Knights of Labor began in 1869 and the American Federation of Labor in 1886, but they were strongly resisted and in the early years accomplished little. A mood of desperation prevailed for labor, particularly in the railroad and steel industries, leading to strikes and violence. In 1877 a strike against the Pennsylvania Railroad, following a 10 percent cut in wages, precipitated mob action and bloody battles, and struggle continued for railroad workers over the next several decades. In 1894 a strike against the Pullman Company, precipitated by a 25 percent wage reduction, brought federal troops and the imprisonment of many labor leaders. In 1892 a wage cut at a Carnegie steel plant led to a strike and plant shutdown. The strike was broken by state militia, and the plant reopened with nonunion labor. Industrial turmoil characterized these decades.

Churches viewed these developments from a conservative distance. Particularly in the earlier stages of the struggles clergy voiced little or no sympathy for labor. Instead churches gave theological support to a social Darwinist view of economic life and moralized the reason for existence of rich and poor. Drawing on the doctrine of providence, clergy affirmed that business success resulted from Christian living and that poverty was a punishment for sin. God has need of rich Christians and blesses them for their continued contribution to society's economic progress. Moreover, rich Christians engage in significant moral acts when they provide the charity needed to sustain the impoverished. The poor, however, have no one to blame but themselves for their miserable state. In this land of riches and opportunity any decent and ambitious person can move toward success. Henry Ward Beecher, theological liberal but political conservative, put it strongly: "No man in this land suffers from poverty unless it be more than his fault—unless it be his sin. . . . There is enough and to spare thrice over; and if men have not enough, it is owing to the want of . . . industry, and frugality, and wise saving."[13] With respect to strikes, the clergy attitude was equally condemnatory. Many feared that strikes could lead to anarchy and socialism, but even short of that peril most clergy argued that they should be met with police repression. After the Pullman Company strike the Congregational religious press urged that the strike leaders be punished with life imprisonment. In the words of historian Henry May, this period witnessed "a massive . . . defense of the social status quo."[14]

In these years labor itself, apart from its Roman Catholic immigrant members, largely rejected the church and made its reasons clear. When in 1885 Avory H. Bradford in Montclair, New Jersey, asked labor groups by questionnaire about their nonattendance at church, the answers denied that their indifference was due to "unbelief in Christianity as taught by Christ," but affirmed it to be caused by "unbelief in Christianity as practiced by the churches." Washington Gladden made a similar inquiry in Columbus, Ohio, in 1886, learning that many workers remained aloof from the church because of economic injustices suffered at the hands of their churchgoing employers. One respondent wrote: "When the capitalist prays for us one day in the week, and preys on us the other six, it can't be expected that we will have much respect for his Christianity." The alienation, especially from the successful mainline Protestant churches, ran deep in the 1870s and 1880s.[15]

Gradually the clergy conscience began to change. A new "social gospel" movement emerged out of a growing sensitivity to the pain of society's injustices, encouraged by the liberalism of the New Theology then coming into favor. Prophetic voices first spoke out in the 1880s, and by the 1890s many were witnessing to a new moral mandate implicit in Christian responsibility. Washington Gladden was one of the most influential of the advocates of the new outlook, but other Congregational leaders—Egbert Smyth, William J. Tucker, Newman

Smyth, Lyman Abbott, Josiah Strong, Charles M. Sheldon, and George D. Herron, to name but a few—were among them. Later, in the early 1900s, the heaviest burden of leadership was assumed by a Baptist, Walter Rauschenbusch.

Many earlier moral causes were carried forward into this freshly generated activism, but the catalyst and overriding consideration was that of justice for labor. The social gospel movement as a whole was convinced that the biblical promise of redemption was for the healing not only of the individual but also of society. The Kingdom of God, toward which all must move as ultimate human destiny, was to be a redeemed social order. God had revealed the pattern for that redemption in the moral teachings of Jesus, and Christians were called to an ethical responsibility for healing social as well as personal relations. The New Theology's confidence in the human capacity for goodness and in the immanent working of God allowed the social gospel to combine a call to the exercise of justice with great optimism concerning its outcome. There was hard work ahead, but the work would be accomplished— perhaps even in the present generation.

As the twentieth century dawned, social gospel leaders among Congregationalists found increasing support through the National Council of Congregational Churches. In 1889, when Washington Gladden addressed the council, he met with a hostile response. In 1904, however, he was elected moderator for the following triennium and in 1907 delivered a much-lauded moderator's address on "The Church and the Social Crisis." Additional papers presented at the 1904 and 1907 sessions show rapidly expanding Congregational concern about the labor issue. Meanwhile, beginning in 1901, the Committee on Industry had been at work for the council, gathering data and encouraging interest among state associations and local churches in Christian resolution of industrial problems. By 1910 Gladden's term *applied Christianity* was in common use. It was also in 1910 that the National Council endorsed the Declaration of Principles for labor relations prepared by the newly founded Federal Council of Churches. Social gospel concerns were now fully part of the national Congregational agenda, and the council committed itself to "seeking to lift the crushing burdens of the poor, and to reduce the hardships and uphold the dignity of labor, . . . a cause which belongs to all who follow Christ."[16]

City Evangelization

Although painfully aware of the alienation of the laboring class from the churches in the concluding decades of the nineteenth century, Congregationalism, along with other Protestant denominations, sought to win unchurched city dwellers to Protestant faith. New immigrants flooded the cities in large numbers, many of whom either lacked or soon lost earlier church identity. It was a new opportunity for mission. The National Council of Congregational Churches spoke out about the cities, giving urban issues greater attention than was accorded the rural and village ministries long supported in the mission program. The cities more and more embodied the potential in America, and urban problems demanded attention. The manner of care, however, was unclear, and the efforts of the National Council during this period reflect new developments in the church's understanding of the nature and purpose of evangelism itself.

At the National Council meeting of 1874, Congregationalists considered the question, "How can the Gospel be most efficiently preached to the masses?" In somewhat startling fashion the speaker concluded that large and inexpensive assemblies must be built in the cities, for the masses cannot either dress sufficiently well or pay the high pew rents necessary to hear the preaching available in the cities' costly churches! Lack of money and wardrobe keep them from the possibility of conversion! But underlying this analysis was the assumption that evangelism could best be carried on as it had been in the past, through preaching in large gatherings seeking the persuasion of many. Finney's successes were a matter of recent memory, and Dwight L. Moody, his successor in public revivalism, was currently reaping harvests of conquests.

Dwight L. Moody was important for Congregationalists not only because as a young shoe clerk in Chicago his active religious work began while a member of the city's Plymouth Congregational Church, but also because his later nondenominational evangelistic crusading was accorded strong Congregational support. At the 1877 meeting of the National Council Samuel E. Herrick, a Congregational pastor, spoke appreciatively of the months-long Moody revival in Boston earlier that year. At the 1889 National Council meeting, a committee chaired by Lyman Abbott commended Moody as "the most successful evangelist of our time."[17] Moody's customary strategy was to conduct his services in a large urban tabernacle, built specifically for this purpose and financed by contributions from the business community. To many this appeared an excellent way to reach "the masses." And yet from a single denomination's perspective this was inexpedient. Moreover, in the course of time Moody's social conservatism turned his revivalism more and more into a program for the middle class.

By the mid-1880s, therefore, Congregationalists had a new inner-city mission plan, drawing upon cooperative effort from all their churches in a given urban area. Many Congregational churches were no longer "downtown," for they had followed their more affluent members to the outer edges of the city, but they could work together on this common task. The effort began with the formation of the Chicago City Missionary Society in 1882, composed of pastors and lay representatives of Chicago's Congregational churches. During the course of the next two decades similar Congregational organizations were established in twenty-five other cities. These city missionary societies focused on gathering Sunday schools and organizing congregations for development into new churches. Prior to this time city missions had been only transient preaching centers or agencies to distribute gifts of charity. Now, however, effort was turned to the creation of more permanent and committed constituencies. Local neighborhoods were the key, and those who lived together were encouraged to worship together. With the aid of the city missionary society, local communities constructed new church buildings in which this worship could take place. Nor was this work limited simply to the inner city. By 1898 the Chicago society had organized fifty-five Congregational churches in the city and its environs. Evangelism no longer focused exclusively on conversion. It nourished community.

Furthermore, this work of evangelism, it was believed, should be increasingly in the hands of lay leaders. When the National Council's Committee on City Evangelization reported in 1892, it urged that "what is needed is THE MINISTRY OF THE WHOLE CHURCH TO SAVE THE WHOLE COMMUNITY."[18] Lay men and women should be trained, as either paid or volunteer workers, for the tasks of home visitation, Bible reading and interpretation, Sunday school teaching, and even evangelistic preaching. The committee rejoiced that training schools, such as the Moody Bible Institute, were becoming available to make this possi-

about true

ble. Congregationalism thus began to draw upon its laity more fully for its evangelistic work of new church growth.

Another movement emerged out of inner-city evangelization, the development of the "institutional church." The genius of the institutional church was that it offered many activities beyond worship to engage communities in wholesome relationships. Using large buildings, with gymnasiums and other public facilities, it offered athletic programs, music societies, concerts, lecture series, dramatic productions, sewing classes, day nurseries, and other social services. Large institutional churches were first developed in the 1870s in several denominations, and by 1900 these inner-cities churches numbered more than 170, many of them Congregational. Some critics questioned the "churchliness" of these institutions. In 1895, however, the National Council endorsed their methods and affirmed them to be "timely" expressions of the divine "regenerating power in human life."[19] Yet their successes were sporadic, and in time their costliness led to their decline. In 1898 a report to the National Council added the "social settlement" to the agencies for city evangelization. Although Congregationalism commended these centers of dedicated persons living together in the heart of the slums and providing services and facilities for the impoverished, the report carefully refrained from identifying them as "church." Under church sponsorship, however, they carried into their communities the evangelistic work of Christian ministry.

During the next two decades, however, changes in the nature and focus of evangelism occurred within Congregationalism. City evangelization became church extension and was finally incorporated into a broader program of home missions. A new Commission on Evangelism was created, with a purpose to stimulate evangelism within the churches, rather than beyond them. The intent was still to recruit new members for existing churches, but the focus was on internal nurturing in congregations so that they might reach out to achieve their goals. By 1919 the commission provided detailed recommendations to the churches for a program directed toward the growth of their Sunday schools, the strengthening of pastors' training classes for church membership, the reclamation of absentee members, the development of prayer circles within the congregations, the training of selected lay persons to assist the pastor in a Lenten recruitment campaign, the use of special services during the Lenten season, and finally the celebration of an "Easter ingathering," whereby new members joined the church. Also included was the recommendation for the use of a new daily home devotional booklet, *The Fellowship of Prayer*. By 1921 the commission was renamed the Commission on Evangelism and Devotional Life.

Threats to a Protestant Nation

In 1885 Josiah Strong, pastor of Central Congregational Church in Cincinnati, published under the auspices of the American Home Missionary Society a book titled *Our Country*. Focusing on the problems faced by America, and particularly by its cities, the book rapidly became a best seller and, in the words of Henry May, was "the *Uncle Tom's Cabin* of city reform."[20] The cities, it affirmed, were the vital center of American life, but their health was jeopardized by many perils, not the least of which was the economic injustice bringing great wealth to the few and poverty to the many. Josiah Strong was one of the early proponents of the social gospel, and his writing significantly advanced that concern.

Strong, however, also sounded another note, emphasizing the evangelical belief in a Protestant American nation as God's chosen instrument for developing the kingdom of righteousness. But this national "manifest destiny," Strong believed, was endangered by the perils of the times. Two forces in particular appeared as threats to a triumphant Protestant America. The first was Roman Catholicism, growing rapidly within the cities through immigration from European Catholic nations. Actually, fear of Roman Catholicism far antedated Josiah Strong's late nineteenth-century expression of concern. As early as the 1820s anti-Catholic feeling developed among Protestant groups, based upon the seemingly superstitious character of Roman Catholic religious practices and the fear that allegiance to the pope would undermine American political democracy. There were acts of violence against Catholic institutions in the 1830s, when a convent was burned in Massachusetts and riots broke out in Pennsylvania. By the 1840s and 1850s anti-Catholic political opposition organized by developing the Order of United Americans, which later became the Know-Nothing party. It was committed to keeping Catholics out of public office. Throughout this period many Congregationalists, such as Lyman Beecher and Horace Bushnell, joined in identifying Roman Catholicism as a danger to the institutions of American life. Lyman Beecher's powerful *Plea for the West* viewed Catholicism as a particular threat to the development of the frontier, bringing antidemocratic practices into the area destined, in his judgment, to be the new heart and strength of the nation.

Anti-Catholic fear was scarcely abated by the 1880s. Josiah Strong wrote in 1885 about the "irreconcilable difference between papal principles and the fundamental principles of our free institutions."[21] For Strong the heart of the problem was the Catholic denial of freedom of conscience. Catholic piety asked for the placing of one's conscience, whether for one's beliefs or actions, under the control of the church, which in Catholic lands was literally the religion of the state. But this, Strong said, is an absolutism of both church and state quite out of accord with the republicanism of America. Strong also noted that this absolutism included denial of free schools, which "are one of the cornerstones" of American government. With this he touched a matter of urgent importance for his time. In 1887 the American Protective Association was organized, in part to resist public funding for Catholic parochial education. In 1889 the National Council of Congregational Churches took determined action on this matter, voting not only to resist such public funding but also to defend public education as important for American unity and to criticize parochial schools as "a menace to the best interests of our country."[22] Anti-Catholic attitudes continued among many Congregationalists well into the twentieth century. In 1897 Washington Gladden, who was more irenic, considered this hostility to be "one of the most melancholy signs of the times."[23]

In Josiah Strong's judgment there was also a second threat to a Protestant America, namely, the presence and growth of Mormonism, found especially in the area of the western mountains and the Southwest. The sanctioning of polygamy, Strong noted, was the most striking feature of Mormon practice and that by which it was publicly best known. Yet polygamy, he felt, was only a lesser issue, and ultimately it would yield to an outlawing by the United States government. The real problem was Mormon autocratic political power. In Strong's understanding the authority structure within Mormonism was as imperious and threatening to democratic procedures as was that of Roman Catholicism. It had a priesthood claiming absolute dominion over all aspects of its adherents' lives, and the priesthood itself was ultimately subservient to one man, the church's president, "who is prophet, priest, king, and pope" and "not one whit less infallible" than the one who wears the Roman tiara. The Mormon leader even "outpopes" the Catholic ruler by claiming conversation with God and reception of "new revelations direct from heaven." It was, however, the Mormon president's temporal power that was most threatening, for by planting Mormon colonies throughout the West, Mormons were moving toward the establishment of an "earthly empire" antagonistic to American institutions and Protestant faith. Strong feared that a Mormon representation in Congress from new Mormon states in the West would have dire consequences for American life.[24]

Sharing fears of growing Mormon strength, and particularly distressed by the nature of Mormon religious beliefs and practices, Congregationalists of the National Council devoted a portion of each of their sessions throughout the 1880s to evaluating the peril and seeking to stem its advance. Their main opposition came through an educational program initiated in 1879 and consistently supported throughout the following decade. Carried on in Utah and New Mexico by the National Council's New West Education Commission, the program provided elementary schools and advanced academies as an alternative to the Mormon education that dominated public schooling. The commission's schools were open to non-Mormon and Mormon pupils alike, and during their years of operation a proportionately large number of Mormons attended. These, however, were also religious schools, staffed by missionary teachers who brought a Protestant perspective forcefully into the instruction. It was a missionary program, because counteracting Mormonism was a missionary task. Other denominations, particularly the Presbyterians, carried on similar work, and throughout the 1880s an increasing number of non-Mormons migrated to these areas. By 1889, therefore, the National Council heard an optimistic report concerning a reduction of Mormon power, and in that year it merged the New West Education Commission into the larger work of the American College and Education Society.

Growing Diversity

The American Protestant nation, which Josiah Strong and others hoped to create for the coming of the Kingdom of God, was also to be white and Anglo-Saxon. Strong wrote concerning the America of his time, "It seems to me that God, with infinite wisdom and skill, is here training the Anglo-Saxon race for an hour sure to come in the world's future."[25] More qualified than any other people for embodying the divine final destiny, Anglo-Saxons, he believed, will gradually dispossess, assimilate, and mold other races until they have "Anglo-Saxonized" all humanity. For Strong the American church is called to be a white Anglo-Saxon Protestant institution driven by a mission to bring redemption to both America and the world.

History, however, did not meet his expectation. Strong's Congregationalism in the late nineteenth century was largely a WASP institution, but the realities of the times led to a growing diversity. One addition, growing out of the Civil War, was the African-American church. Actually, a few African-American Congregational churches had come into being in New England in the early nineteenth century. The first was the Dixwell Avenue Congregational Church in New Haven, founded in 1820, followed in 1833 by the Talcott Street Church in Hartford and in 1843 by the Fourth Congregational Church of Portland, Maine. There were also occasional African-American members in otherwise white congregations. But the major effort at gathering African-American Congregational churches came through the work of the American Missionary Association following the Civil War.

The earliest activity of the AMA in the South occurred during the war and was directed to setting up schools and providing education for slaves as they gained their freedom. Day schools and night schools were established for elementary education and vocational training, and then colleges to promote more advanced knowledge. But AMA missionary work was evangelical as well as educational. Many Sunday schools were developed for religious instruction, and finally churches were organized for worship. At the outset these African-American Congregational churches were located near the colleges, where ministerial leadership was available. The first such church was founded in 1867 in Atlanta, under the ministry of the Rev. C. W. Francis, who had come from Yale to be a professor at Atlanta University. Also during that year an African-American Congregational church was founded adjacent to Talladega College, newly established in Alabama. Others soon followed where leadership from college faculties could be obtained.

In succeeding years, however, the growth and increase of African-

American churches was made possible by African-American leadership trained in religion departments at the colleges, which then became seminaries preparing persons for ministry. Although Bible instruction was given in all the AMA schools throughout this period, religion departments for more advanced religious study were established at Fisk, Talladega, Tougaloo, Straight, and Atlanta. For the next half-century these institutions trained ministers for several denominations, though particularly for African-American Congregational churches. Other AMA schools sent students for ministerial training, and the ministerial students were encouraged to go out and found mission Sunday schools and churches even before they graduated.

By 1895 there were 143 African-American Congregational churches in the South with approximately 9,500 members, and the Sunday schools claimed some 17,000 pupils. However, considering the fact that the African-American population in the South numbered about 7 million at that time, this was only a small fragment of the whole. Baptists and Methodists made up a far larger portion of African-American church members, and the plain fact was that Congregationalism suffered numerically in the South as it had in the rest of the nation. But the type of Congregationalism introduced into the South was never really capable of obtaining widespread reception in the culture then prevailing. In the analysis of A. Knighton Stanley, the AMA was interested in reaching the African-American "intellectual elite," reasoning that the potential leadership found there would exert the most effective influence on moral and cultural development in the South. African-American Congregational churches therefore became, in Stanley's judgment, "strongholds of the rising Black bourgeoisie." Their Congregationalism was a transported New England Congregationalism, "cities set upon a hill" to "inculcate and encourage order and propriety, and an intelligent form of worship." This meant, Stanley further concluded, that "the Puritan preacher and the Pilgrim moralist came to the South, the land of poetry and song, as an incomplete manifestation of the Body of Christ," to seek a place among a differently inclined southern people.[26] But even their limited progress provided a new racial component within American Congregationalism.

Diversity also appeared in late nineteenth-century American Congregationalism through the appearance and then later absorption of immigrating German Congregationalists. Although a few German converts to Congregationalism had come to America directly from Germany and set up churches before 1860, the larger migration of Congregationalists of German descent had lived in Russia for decades until they were forced to leave in the 1870s and 1880s. Congregationalism appealed to these former Lutherans because it was less dogmatic, stressed local church autonomy with lay participation, and emphasized a heartfelt piety leading to an experienced regeneration. Historian William G. Chrystal points out that lay prayer meetings were "at the center of their lives," occasions when they "sang, read scripture and offered testimonials that spoke of fellowship with God in Jesus Christ."[27] When restrictions on their political and religious freedom began to occur in 1871, these people brought their Congregationalism to America and settled in the Midwest and the West. In 1878 in Crete, Nebraska, German Congregationalists founded a seminary, in conjunction with Congregational Doane College, to train their ministers. In 1883 they organized the General Evangelical Church Assembly of German Congregationalists to unite the work of individual churches.

Close contact with American Congregationalism developed quickly. George E. Albrecht, a native German but English-speaking Oberlin graduate and former American Home Missionary Society pastor in Iowa, became superintendent of the new organization of German Congregational churches. The training of pastors shifted to the Chicago Theological Seminary, which established a foreign department offering courses in German as well as in Scandinavian languages. Superintendent Albrecht attended the meeting of the National Council of Congregational Churches held in Chicago in 1886. Meanwhile, the German school at Crete moved to Iowa and then to South Dakota. In 1916 it joined with the German department of Chicago Theological Seminary to become Redfield College Seminary and later the School of Theology of Yankton College. Finally in 1927 the National Council formally incorporated the German churches into the main stream of American Congregationalism by recognizing their uniting organization as equivalent to a state conference in Congregational structure. By the mid-1930s German Congregationalists numbered 193 churches and more than 22,000 members within American Congregationalism.

Three other ethnic groups in the late nineteenth century enriched the growing pluralism of American Congregationalism. Congregational contact with the people of Armenia began in 1831 through the work of the American Board of Commissioners for Foreign Missions. Initially it met considerable opposition from the Turkish Ottoman Empire and the Eastern Orthodox church. There were severe political persecutions in the 1870s, but by that time sufficient seeds had been sown to encourage some of the Armenian refugees fleeing to America to organize themselves into Congregational churches. The first group founded the Armenian Congregational Church of the Martyrs in Worcester, Massachusetts, in 1881. Soon other Congregational churches and some Presbyterian churches were organized by survivors of the persecution, all being bound together by an Armenian Evangelical Union. A close-knit ethnic identity persisted among these churches until the late 1940s, when the Armenian language was finally given up as the language of worship. By the 1950s fourteen of these churches had become a part of American Congregationalism, although they continued to maintain their allegiance to the Armenian Evangelical Union.

Chinese immigrants began arriving in America in the early 1850s, first as miners responding to the California gold rush and then as workers employed to build the railroads. Although initially welcomed, the Chinese were gradually subjected to increasing hostility. In 1882 the Oriental Exclusion Act severely limited their immigration and prohibited their becoming naturalized American citizens. Further legislation throughout the early twentieth century added to these restrictions, including a prohibition against Chinese laborers bringing their wives to America. Meanwhile attempts were made by the churches to blunt this hostility, along with efforts to educate and to evangelize. The American Missionary Association, starting in 1869, focused on establishing schools for basic education for Chinese residents, and Congregational churches began to organize Chinese Sunday schools. The major leader in this work was William C. Pond, Congregational pastor in San Francisco and later superintendent for Chinese work in California for the AMA. Under Pond's leadership the first Congregational church for Chinese was founded in San Francisco in 1873, and over the course of the next several decades Pond was involved in the development of forty-nine missions to the Chinese people. Most Chinese missions, however, lasted for only brief periods of time, and by 1921 just nine remained. Ultimately three strong, self-sustaining Chinese churches, in San Francisco, Berkeley, and San Diego, emerged out of this mission program to become a continuing part of American Congregationalism.

Congregational work with Japanese immigrants to the West Coast began in San Francisco in the 1870s, but it was not until the turn of the century that it began to show significant results. In 1899 the Congregational Home Missionary Society initiated a mission program for native Japanese in America and, like the American Missionary Association earlier, called upon William C. Pond to help in its development. Although two mission points were established in Utah and a church was founded in Seattle, the main focus of the work was California. Half a dozen churches were developed in the Los Angeles area, one in the state's center in Fresno, and two in the San Francisco area. In 1909 Pond was elected superintendent of these Japanese Congregational churches, and during his administration several were able to become financially independent of the mission program. Their Japanese-language ministry was secured from Japan and Hawaii, and lay members took on large responsibility for the churches' activities. In the 1920s these churches became a bulwark against the anti-Japanese hostility that expressed itself particularly in state legislation prohibiting Japanese land owner-ship and American citizenship. However, the greatest trials for the Japanese and their churches came in the early 1940s, when at the beginning of the Second World War all persons of Japanese ancestry were evacuated from their homes on the West Coast and interned, largely in desert camps, until the war's end. Upon the refugees' return, denominational executives urged Japanese congregations to merge with neighboring white congregations. Proud of their heritage, however, seven of these Japanese Congregational churches resumed their independence and, along with a newly established Japanese church in Chicago, continued as a distinct ethnic community within American Congregationalism.

The Role of Women

With the closing of the nineteenth century and the opening of the twentieth, women began to find somewhat greater opportunities for public service within the Congregational churches. The progress was still slow, as evidenced by the fact that as late as 1921 only 15 percent of the delegates to the nineteenth meeting of the National Council were female and no woman had yet been elected to its Executive Committee. But female initiative was thrusting some doors open, and a slow movement toward recognition and responsibility was developing.

A major area for this progress was within the denominational mission program. There the leadership of church women came to play an increasingly significant role. From the beginning of Congregational missionary work in the late 1700s and early 1800s, local church women, first with their "female cent societies" and then with their "ladies' associations," generated enthusiasm and material support for mission projects. By the late 1860s this support took more specialized administrative forms through four regional woman's boards of mission organized to assist the development of the missionary program overseas. In 1868 the Woman's Board of Missions (WBM) was organized in Boston and the Woman's Board of Missions of the Interior (WBMI) in Chicago. Five years later the Woman's Board of Missions for the Pacific (WBMP) was created in California and the Woman's Board of Missions for the Pacific Islands (WBMPI) in Hawaii. Although the American Board of Commissioners for Foreign Missions remained the denominational agency through which overseas missionaries were commissioned, placed, and supervised, women through these boards became more closely involved.

For example, the woman's boards directed their support entirely to unmarried women missionaries committed to work with young girls and women on the foreign field. The need for single women was exceedingly great, and the American Board had not been able to meet the demand. The woman's boards stimulated recruitment of single women for these missionary assignments, and in 1920 forty-seven of the seventy-three persons commissioned were women. The woman's boards selected the women missionaries, after which the American Board acted to commission and supervise them. But most of all, the woman's boards maintained full independence in raising and administering funds for these missions to women and children. An enterprising network of local auxiliaries and district branches covered each of the regions, and intensive campaigns brought successful funding for the program. The women encouraged giving that would not otherwise have been available for the American Board, and their efforts were marked by success. In 1919 the women raised almost $400,000, contributing an additional one-third to the American Board's resources for that year. This double effort for missions lasted until 1927, when the woman's boards gave up their independence and were incorporated into the American Board.

Throughout these years women also were finding more opportunity for religious training and professional employment as non-ordained workers in local Congregational churches. Interest in such professional possibilities dated to late nineteenth-century programs of city evangelization, in which the contributions of lay workers for home visits, Bible teaching, and other forms of outreach were so effective. Many of these workers were women, and it became increasingly apparent that some structure should be established by which Christian women, and especially young women, could be prepared for this and other forms of church work. While exploring this concern in the early twentieth century, Congregationalism considered briefly the possibility of instituting a deaconess movement, patterned after an earlier German Lutheran model, in which trained and committed women would live together in communities from which they would go out to perform various social and church services. American Lutherans, Episcopalians, and Methodists were experimenting with this pattern, and momentarily a Congregational plan was developed for a deaconess home in Illinois. The National Council meetings of 1901, 1904, and 1907 heard reports and considered this prospect, but ultimately set it quietly aside.

An alternative, however, commended itself strongly: the religious training of women, either in seminary or in a special institute, for employment as lay workers in the churches. Admission of women to seminary courses had long been severely restricted, but as early as 1895 the National Council praised Hartford, and in 1901 Chicago, for steps taken to accept women students. A special institute had been developed in Cleveland, which in 1907 also received the council's praise. The major Congregational institution for this educational purpose, however, was the Congregational Training School for Women. Founded in 1909 in Chicago by Florence Fensham, a remarkable woman who had taken courses at Chicago Theological Seminary and had earlier developed the coeducational Christian Institute using seminary faculty as instructors, it focused upon women's training for church employment. Graduates often became "church assistants" or "parish workers," terms representing a variety of educational, social, and secretarial duties. By 1915 the National Council noted the presence of 125 women parish workers then in the churches and voted to include their names and locations on a special page in their yearbook. By 1921 the council reported that, with some men also now serving as parish workers, the total number had reached nearly three hundred.

Far less progress was made by women throughout these years in relationship to ordination. The meager results can be seen in a report made to the National Council in 1921. In 1919, it noted, there were 5,695 ordained Congregational ministers, of whom sixty-seven were women. Among the latter, only eighteen served independently as pastors of churches, fourteen were in joint pastorates generally with their husbands, and fourteen were in religious education or some other form of employ as church assistants. The employment of the remaining twenty-one could not be determined. But more telling than the numbers was the commentary. The reporting commission declared that so far as it was aware, "no scandal or seriously unpleasant incident has grown out of the ordination of women in our denomination," the service of these women "is for the most part a quiet, inconspicuous service," and therefore it does not "appear at present to offer to our denomination any serious problem." The report added, "We do not discover any marked tendency to increase the proportion of our women pastors."[28] Women's ordination and ministry had a long way to go.

Interdenominational Cooperation

When the 1865 Boston National Congregational Council adopted the Burial Hill Declaration, it expressed not only the central convictions of its faith and polity but also its sense of Congregationalism as but one part of the worldwide unity of the Church of Christ. "We are but one branch of Christ's people," it said, adding its belief that the many denominations that hold a common Christian faith "are sacredly bound to keep 'the unity of the spirit in the bond of peace.'"[29] This attitude toward other Christian churches was further affirmed in 1871 when the National Council of Congregational Churches came into being. After adopting its constitution, the gathering at Oberlin immediately accepted the Declaration on the Unity of the Church. In this statement the council expressed its desire "to promote the growing unity . . . among the followers of Christ" and to do its work "in friendly cooperation with all those who love and serve our common Lord."[30] From its beginning the National Council committed itself to an ecumenical mission. Throughout the next half-century it remained conscious of this goal, consistently maintaining in its agendas matters involving interdenominational relations. Ultimately three areas of major concern developed, and by the beginning of the twentieth century were combined in the work of the council's Committee on Comity, Federation, and Unity.

The subject of comity was first broached in 1874 when a secretary of the American Home Missionary Society spoke to the National Council deploring the denominational competition faced in establishing churches on the home mission field. He noted that when the AHMS was the home mission agent for several denominations, it could prevent these rivalries by refusing to sustain a competitive pastor in a field already being served. But, he added, with each denomination now having its own missionary organization, "this check is removed, the spirit of sectarian propaganda is intensified, and can push its schismatic and wasteful schemes with little restraint." There is "a waste of ministerial labor and charitable funds," but even more "a great waste of moral power," for the spectacle these churches present to the world "is not specially fitted to recommend the gospel of Christ."[31] Although little positive result was immediately obtained, the council became increasingly engaged in seeking amelioration of this problem. Its major effort, initiated in 1886, was to decentralize the issue and to urge the Congregational state conferences and associations to establish comity committees for consultation with similar bodies from other denominations in situations requiring comity restraints. During the next two decades the council received reports of at least limited successes achieved in different sections of the country. In 1898 it heard a detailed description of a program in Maine, where an interdenominational commission had been established, drawing into cooperative mission agreements Baptist, Free Baptist, Methodist, Christian, and Congregational churches. Because of the commission's enforcement of firm comity principles, the report said, many rural churches had survived and were supporting themselves rather than "struggling hopelessly for subsistence and leaning heavily upon outside missionary aid."[32] Similarly in other sections of the country, the report stated, this denominational restraint by comity was being accomplished, with Congregationalists as active participants.

During these years, however, the National Council also looked toward more complete forms of cooperation among the churches than might be found in simple comity arrangements. In 1892 two resolutions with far-reaching implications were passed. The first commended in general terms the growing "spirit of fraternal union among Christian people of every name" and urged support of "the increasing tendency of Christians of different branches of the church to join hands" in common effort. The second was more specific and favored the creation of "a federation without authority, of all bodies of the Christian churches, as soon as the providence of God shall permit."[33] As a consequence of this action, a process was initiated that sixteen years later led to the organization of the Federal Council of the Churches of Christ in America, a federation binding in cooperative action thirty Protestant denominations embodying eighteen million persons. With the development of the plan for the Federal Council completed by 1905, the National Council voted its approval of Congregational membership in 1907, and Congregationalists played an important role in the Federal Council's founding meeting in Philadelphia in 1908. The ecumenical hopes of Boston in 1865 and Oberlin in 1871 were being more and more fulfilled.

Less immediate success, however, was attained in the third area of common effort, that of the organic union of Congregationalism with other denominations. Nevertheless, the National Council undertook explorations and even negotiations throughout these years, despite being met almost unexceptionably with frustration. The first exploration was authorized by the National Council of 1886, an inquiry into the possibility of union with the Free Baptists, whose theology and polity, though not baptismal practice, were similar to those of Congregationalists. But the discussions were unproductive and approach to the Free Baptists was never renewed. A revived interest in promoting organic union occurred in 1895 when the council voted a set of general criteria for church union to be proposed to all evangelical churches. The council recognized that no "speedy corporate union" could be attained, but expressed the hope that a process of growing together in mutual acquaintance and cooperative activity might begin to prepare the way.[34] In these discussions the Christian Convention was named particularly as a possible future union partner for Congregationalists. That union did ultimately occur—thirty-six years later, in 1931.

The most intense efforts at organic union prior to the 1930s took place, however, in the first decade of the twentieth century. The National Council meetings of 1904, 1907, and 1910 gave much attention to an attempt to bring the Congregational churches, the Methodist Protestant Church, and The United Brethren in Christ into a single denomination to be called The United Churches. Negotiations were carried on for several years by committees of the three denominations, resulting in 1907 in the publication of a detailed plan titled "Act of Union." The plan was approved that year by the National Council, with the recommendation that the conferences, churches, and benevolent societies of the denomination accept this corporate union. But the effort failed. The National Council's discussion had revealed reservations on the part of some of its members concerning the adequacy of the plan's protection of local congregational autonomy, and this contributed to a tension in the negotiations that ultimately brought them to an end. The National Council tried to restore the negotiations in 1910, but to no avail. In 1917 the Commission on Comity, Federation, and Unity reported explorations being made jointly by authorized committees of Congregationalists and Disciples of Christ concerning possible future union, but no action was taken, and formal interest subsequently subsided. Congregationalism's only concrete advance in church union throughout these five decades came in 1887 and 1888, when a small group of Congregational Methodist churches in Georgia and Alabama were quietly absorbed into Congregationalism. The Congregational Methodist Church had been organized in 1852, composed of Methodist congregations desiring more democracy in church government than Methodist episcopacy allowed. Attracted to the polity of Congregationalism, several of these congregations simply joined the Congregational associations in their respective locations, becoming fully recognized Congregational churches. No merger was required on the national level. Despite the disappointments in efforts to achieve interdenominational mergers, Congregationalism in these decades showed a commitment to church union that was to continue strongly into the years ahead.

Crusading Wars

Gaius Glenn Atkins, Congregational pastor and historian, noted in 1932 that the first decade and a half of the twentieth century in America could be remembered as "the Age of Crusades." "The people," he said, "were ready to cry 'God wills it' and set out for world peace, prohibition, the Progressive Party, the 'New Freedom' or 'the World for

Christ in this Generation.'"[35] This enthusiasm also embraced belief in divine sanction for the armed conflicts of the time and readily interpreted such wars as crusades by which America continued to live out the responsibilities of its manifest destiny.

The Spanish-American War of 1898 was seen in that light and was fully endorsed by the churches as the means by which American power could liberate and improve oppressed peoples. Although American economic aspirations were unquestionably involved, national indignation against Spain's refusal to grant independence to Cuba was the war's primary cause. Prompted by the sinking of an American battleship, the *Maine*, in the Havana harbor in 1898, as well as by unsubstantiated reports of Spanish atrocities, war with Spain was quickly declared. The war, however, soon expanded to become more than simply a crusade to save the Cuban people, moving onward to other Spanish possessions, even in the far Pacific. When it ended, following Admiral Dewey's destruction of the Spanish fleet at Manila Bay, America came to possess the Philippines, Guam, and Puerto Rico, as well as having set Cuba free.

For the Protestant churches of America the victory over Spain and the liberation of the Spanish colonies was not only the triumph over an oppressive nation but also an opportunity to reduce Roman Catholic influence over what had been its captive peoples. Congregationalism shared fully in welcoming this divinely given opportunity. Lyman Abbott, a leading voice among Congregationalists at the close of the nineteenth century, declared after the victory, "We do not want more territory, but God does not permit a choice. Events are stronger than men. We have entered upon a new phase of our National life." So he advocated protectorates over the colonies that Americans might provide for them "free" (non-Catholic) churches and schools. This he called "the new imperialism—the imperialism of liberty." Moreover, he said, this fulfillment of American destiny in the education of "a childlike people such as the Filipinos" was a "noble stage in the development of human brotherhood." Even more it was, in Abbott's judgment, a destined part of the earth's evolutionary process, directed by God, "the Infinite and Eternal Energy from which all things proceed."[36]

The blessing of war as a necessary instrument of progress was no less characteristic of the attitude of American churches nearly two decades later, with the outbreak of the First World War in Europe. In the intervening period in America a peace movement had begun to take hold. As Robert Handy points out, "The American Peace Society doubled its membership; The Federal Council supported the cause of peace, and an interfaith Church Peace Union was founded in 1914."[37] Yet when war came, attitudes began to change, and by the time of America's entrance into the conflict in 1917, the support of almost all the churches was again given to the war cause. Once more it was a crusade, this time "to make the world safe for democracy." And so uncritical was ecclesiastical endorsement that denominational statements at times even perpetuated the extreme expressions of government wartime propaganda. With little qualification the churches proclaimed the Allied military cause to be a holy war. American involvement was a step toward further fulfillment of her divine destiny.

Again Congregationalists shared this view. Lyman Abbott, then retired as a pastor but active as a writer and editor, wrote a book in 1918 titled *The Twentieth Century Crusade*. Its central thesis was that "a crusade to make this world a home in which God's children can live in peace and safety is more Christian than a crusade to recover from pagans the tomb in which the body of Christ was buried"—and the war was part of that modern crusade. Upon publication Abbott wrote to his close friend, former president Theodore Roosevelt, "This book affirmatively . . . contends that our participation in this world war primarily for the sake of the people whom most of us do not know, furnishes a striking evidence of the power of Christianity, and the extent with which its spirit has pervaded the nation." Elsewhere he wrote that because the Allied armies are fighting for peace, "they might as well bear on their banners the inscription, 'Blessed are the peacemakers, for they shall be called the children of God.'"[38] Abbott's successor in the Brooklyn parish, Newell Dwight Hillis, carried the military endorsement even farther, preaching a vindictive hatred of the Germans and calling for their being "cast out of society." Only a few raised tentative voices questioning the violence of it all, and they were harassed, as Congregational leaders rallied to the war cause.

THEOLOGY

The fifty-year period from 1870 to 1920 witnessed more drastic change in the theology of American Congregationalism than did the entire two hundred and fifty years preceding it. Earlier changes had been lesser modifications within the general pattern of historic Calvinism, but in the late nineteenth century the Calvinist structure itself gave way. On the one hand, certain of its central doctrines were abandoned or radically reinterpreted. Henry Ward Beecher wrote forcefully concerning them: "The chapters of the Westminster Confession concerning decrees, election, reprobation . . . I regard as extraordinary specimens of *spiritual barbarism.*" Or again: "The whole theory of sin and its origin . . . is hideous, it is horrible, it is turning creatures into a shambles and God into a slaughterer."[39] On the other hand, the constructive work of theology also was redirected. Theology acquired other bases for support than an infallible Scripture, it became "modern" in adapting to new discoveries in the advancing sciences, and it developed an optimism based as much on human capacity for goodness as on divine exercise of power. Altogether theology became more "humane." In many respects the melody line of the old gospel remained, but, transposed, it was that gospel in a new key.

Critique of the Old Theology

In 1908 George A. Gordon, Congregational pastor in Boston, looked back on the past several decades and analyzed the weaknesses of nineteenth-century Calvinism in an article titled "The Collapse of the New England Theology."[40] Several characteristics of that Calvinism, said Gordon, led to its decline. For one thing, it suffered from an unqualified traditionalism, a limitation of thought to ancient concepts, a failure to engage in face-to-face contact with current problems of human existence and "to interrogate the vast and tragic reality at first hand." The New England Calvinist system was composed of inherited abstract beliefs, remote from contemporary religious consciousness or intellectual discovery as sources for new insight and understanding. Any efforts its theologians expended at modification of doctrines simply "tinkered the ancient scheme, while God's great growing world was speeding forward heedless of their poor categories." The presumed improvement of the doctrine of atonement by development of the governmental theory was an instance, in Gordon's judgment, of this remoteness of theology from life. The new theory took no account of the direct awareness of the "fatherly love" of God, but simply perpetuated the ancient supposition that God requires "to be appeased by some offering, propitiated by some costly sacrifice . . . before he can lift into hope a penitent child." Or again, use of the Edwardsean distinction between the natural and moral ability of the human will illustrated, in Gordon's view, this artificiality in theological construction. Rather than representing a genuine and experienced freedom of choice in the face of good and evil, this theological distinction became simply an apologetic device to save consistency in the theological system. But the justification of God's eternal decree of nonelection of some on the ground that natural ability left them with no excuse for their sin was judged by Gordon to be a "wretched riot of dialectical unreality."

Underlying this bondage to a theological system often arid and irrelevant was what Gordon termed its "restricted use of human reason." By this he meant the limitation on the use of reason to the things of the natural world and correspondingly the banning of reason from evaluating the claims of biblical revelation. The infallible Bible had been the rule and guide for shaping the theological system. Reason occasionally was given some play, but in the last analysis was always restrained by an authoritative book. Gordon noted that "it is not edifying to see Edwards in the full movement of speculation suddenly pause . . . and lug into his argument proof-texts from every corner of the Bible." The Calvinist theology of New England was not an expression of a free mind. But for Gordon human insight should not be so restricted in the making of theology. God's presence is in human life, in its thoughts and feelings, and this presence must be read and expressed in theology's words. The role of reason, Gordon believed, is not separate from the role of revelation in developing an understanding of God. The Bible itself can be read as the story of human life that God filled with divine presence. Calvinist theology failed, however, by denying to reason these broader explorations.

Even more, Gordon affirmed, the old theology collapsed because of deficiencies in its content. Its central doctrine of divine sovereignty, he said, carried within itself a "fatal contradiction." This appeared when applied to the fact of human sin and its origin. Either the fall was an act of human freedom denying sovereignty, or God's decree included the fall and its consequences, thus denying sovereign love as the character of God. Similarly, the contradiction appeared when applied to God's dealing with human sinfulness, by granting the gift of grace to some but not to others. Gordon declared that "nothing is more melancholy than the perpetual see-saw" between decree and depravity, nor than that between the sovereignty of a God of love and the arbitrary damnation of a vast portion of humankind.

The old theology, moreover, was deficient in Gordon's judgment by its serious omissions. In its abstract character it failed to emphasize the moral potential in human life and allowed itself "to be outgrown in ethical ideas" by more progressive thinking in society. And because an understanding of divinity must arise out of a sense of the best that is known in humanity, the older theologians were unable "to read the character of the Eternal in terms consonant with an enlightened conscience." In particular, they failed to make central in their understanding of God the supreme morality disclosed in Jesus Christ. Yet it was Christ, the "highest man," who represented God's moral nature most fully to human consciousness. Thus the older theology, by neglecting that insight, lacked a Christlike God.

The New Theology

When Lyman Abbott spoke of evolution as "God's way of doing things," he expressed a conviction lying at the heart of the New Theology. However, it was not Abbott's idea, nor that of his companion theologians, to repudiate by this affirmation the historic Christian tradition concerning creation, sin, and redemption. In their understanding the biblical faith, with its gospel of salvation, remained basic for the church's continued conviction concerning God and God's way. Abbott wrote in 1892 that the evolutionary mode of interpretation not only preserves the historic faith but also presents it "in a purer and more powerful form."[41] Both the purpose and the progress of human life become clearer through this new perception of the way of God's working.

Although Darwin wrote about "the descent of man," tracing human origin back to its prehuman sources, his Christian interpreters preferred to emphasize the direction of ascent, with evolution representing the upward course of ongoing life. By this means of development the lower leads steadily into the higher and moves onward toward the highest. Henry Ward Beecher declared that the human person "is made to start and not to stop; to go on and on, and up, and onward, steadily emerging from the controlling power of the physical and animal condition in which he was born . . . ever touching higher elements of possibility, and ending in the glorious liberty of the sons of God."[42] The theory of evolution not only provided an explanation of the world's past, but gave confidence for a continued progress toward the best in times yet to come.

For these Christian evolutionists the key to a theological explanation of such history and hope was the affirmation of the immanence of God. Theodore Munger declared that evolution helped Christian theology "regain its forgotten theory of divine immanence in creation."[43] God's creating cannot be limited simply to past event, but is ongoing process by virtue of the divine presence ever at work. Secular evolutionists had recognized the need for affirming some "resident force" impelling the evolutionary process, and for Christian evolutionists that force was the God of biblical faith. God works out the divine designs in natural history and human history. When Washington Gladden discussed Darwin's view of biological evolution, he added his Christian interpretation concerning the impelling force: "We say that it is Nature, but it is truer to say that it is God. It is a natural world, in every force of which God is immanent."[44] And God likewise was immanent in human nature, increasing a divine presence in human life as it is lifted toward more perfect ends. But in this case, among human persons, there can be resistance to the divine urging and goals.

Despite its optimism, therefore, the New Theology had to take account of the fact of sin. There was human impediment to progress that needed to be overcome. Yet the explanation for sin was generally fitted into the evolutionary framework. Either rejected or ignored by these theologians was the idea of a first Adam whose fall from original righteousness was inherited as original sin by his descendants. Lyman Abbott declared, "Adam did not represent me; I never voted for him."[45] Rather, the answer to the question of sin's origin was generally found in humanity's animal ancestry. Munger said that human existence involves a mixture of brute and spiritual tendencies, giving to each person the capacity to rise or fall. As a result, there is not a single or original fall, but a succession of falls in human experience whenever animal tendencies dominate. Lyman Abbott concurred, noting that in such yielding to one's animal nature, one "descends from his vantage-ground of moral consciousness to the earthiness out of which he had begun to emerge."[46]

The remedy for sin, however, was found by these theologians in a basically optimistic view of human nature, as well as in an emphasis on the immanent presence and working of God. For one thing, the process of evolution had already brought humanity to the point of spiritual sensitivity and moral capacity. The human will possesses marvelous freedom to act in accord with highest moral standards and stands ready to respond in varied circumstances to the prompting of God's desires. Even more, the process of evolution continues to move humanity to higher levels through God's immanent presence and power. Although persons may from time to time fall through a "slipping backward," this was never, in the view of Newman Smyth, a "fall out of evolution." Rather, evolution "moves on through the fall and beyond it," in a process of "creative and redeeming love." Abbott described the process in this way: "The individual man is partly the animal from which he has come, and partly the God who is coming into him; but God is steadily displacing the animal."[47] So in evolution God triumphs over sin.

The triumph comes through the saving work of Jesus Christ. But no classic doctrine of atonement is found here. Christ is God's supreme point of entry into humanity, and through his example and influence he leads humanity into fuller expressions of divine life. The cross should be viewed in this manner, for, said Abbott, it illustrated the highest form of self-giving, a suffering for others. Christ saves by attracting persons to loyalty to his way, and this is grace, the grace that leads to new life. Gladden does not hesitate to use traditional theological language for this. First there is *conversion*, in which one makes up one's mind to follow Christ, then there is *regeneration*, in which one has begun truly to love Christ and to serve him. Both involve a co-working. No one, said Gladden, can any more be converted without the aid of God's Spirit, nor regenerated without concurrence of one's own will, "than he can see without light or breathe without air."[48]

The task of the Christian is to labor for a life that follows Christ. In its most popularized form within the New Theology this demand for discipleship was presented by a Congregational minister and author, Charles M. Sheldon, in his 1897 novel *In His Steps: What Would Jesus Do?* The story was of members of a congregation who were challenged by their pastor to attempt for a year, in every undertaking, to act in a manner they thought would have been the manner of Jesus' acting under such circumstances. When several accepted the challenge, the story portrayed their application of this criterion to their separate lives.

Embellished further by several romances, the novel was widely read, attaining ultimately to publication of several million copies and translation into more than twenty foreign languages. But the Christ-centered ethic prevailed in the thought of the New Theology in a more conventional manner as well. A distinction was made between the religion *about* Jesus and the religion *of* Jesus, and the theologians of the movement minimized the speculative elements of the former in favor of the more comprehendible and normative character of the latter. As the "highest man," Jesus set the path for all humanity in its upward ascent toward the goal for which it is destined by God.

That goal was social as well as individual. The New Theology stressed strongly the solidarity of all humanity and thus became a theology for the social gospel. It was not enough to think of salvation merely as personal, for it must be conceived as pertaining to the whole social order. For Washington Gladden particularly, this was the imperative for Christian thought, and the final end of all human and divine endeavor was the coming of the Kingdom of God. Because the Kingdom encompasses all of human life, this meant that the line often drawn between the secular and the sacred must be erased. Rather, the line should be drawn between good and evil, and all the institutions of secular society should be considered of sacred worth in their need for redemption. It is not enough to convert individuals and then to view their trade and politics as exempt from the life of the Spirit. Christ came to save the world in its totality, for it is, in all its aspects, the work of divine creation. Therefore the ultimate goal is not even the purification of the church, as had often been held in the past. The church itself must serve the larger goal, which is the coming of the Kingdom. This will be a spiritual Kingdom, pervaded by Christ's love, but it will also be a social fact. And, said Gladden, that Kingdom "would come tonight, with power and great glory" if all persons could only "believe the simple truth that the way of Jesus is the way of life."[49]

Yet all this must be seen within the New Theology's larger framework of a doctrine of evolution. In the last analysis, in Abbott's view, the consummation of redemption is the consummation of evolution. It is "the consummation of this long period of divine manifestation" that will not be completed "until the whole human race becomes what Christ was, until the incarnation so spreads out from the one man of Nazareth that it fills the whole human race, and all humanity becomes an incarnation of the divine."[50] The process is under way and requires the commitment and labor of the moment, but from the longer perspective, Abbott believed, all this ultimately will come to pass by the immanent presence and power of God.

Official Formulations of Faith

Throughout this period of theological transformation within Congregationalism, two official formulations of faith were developed through the work of the National Council of Congregational Churches. One came near the beginning of the period and the other near the end. Their differences reflect the changes in theological outlook that had occurred in the intervening time.

The first formulation was the Commission Creed of 1883. After the National Council was founded in 1871, desire developed for a new expression of common faith. The Burial Hill Declaration of 1865 was still young, but it had been a hurried compromise statement prepared in the midst of theological dispute and for many did not state with sufficient clarity the major doctrinal positions widely affirmed within the churches. Therefore by 1880 the National Council agreed to undertake the task of developing a new creed for Congregational use. Its method, however, was to authorize a commission of twenty-five members to prepare such a document for release by the commission itself, with the understanding that this statement would simply "carry such weight of authority as the character of the commission and the intrinsic merit of their exposition of truth may command."[51] Three years later the creed was completed and released.

In accord with the desire for greater doctrinal detail, the creed contained twelve compact paragraphs, each being an exposition of a major area of Christian belief. Intended by the council to be not simply a reaffirmation of former Congregational confessions but a statement taking into account theological developments of more recent times, the creed represented the liberalization of Calvinism that had occurred by 1880. There was no mention of predestination. Human freedom and responsibility were affirmed. Knowledge of God may come through the works of nature and the prompting of conscience in addition to the revelation in Scripture. As to the authority of the Scriptures, the new developments in biblical studies were hinted at, though not directly affirmed. Yet basically this was a conservative creed. Its structure perpetuated the traditional outline of classic Christian beliefs, with emphasis on the means and process of personal salvation. Moreover, among the doctrines included were several as yet untouched by modernity: original sin, Christ's atoning death, and everlasting punishment.

The second formulation was the Kansas City Statement of Faith of 1913. When the National Council's new constitution was adopted that year, a new statement of faith was included in its preamble. Thirty years after the publication of the Commission Creed the council acted again to "set forth the things most surely believed among us." Although the preamble began by declaring allegiance "to the faith which our fathers confessed, which from age to age has found expression in the historic creeds of the Church universal and of this communion," the new statement clearly reflected the still-greater liberalization of theology that had occurred. The older pattern of tracing a personal pilgrimage from sin to salvation was abandoned, and the theme of personal redemption was only briefly mentioned by a reference to Christ, "who for us and our salvation lived and died and rose again and liveth evermore." The statement instead, in the mood of the social gospel, mainly emphasized the churches' striving to know God's will, to walk in God's ways, and to labor for justice, peace, and human "brotherhood." It then ended with its vision and faith for the future, expressed as the transformation of the world into the Kingdom of God, the triumph of righteousness, and life everlasting.[52] There was no mention of evolution, but the tone and the optimism were of the New Theology. Washington Gladden called it a "noble Confession of Faith" and declared, "We can write that on our banner and go forth . . . to conquer."[53]

POLITY

With the formation of the National Council of Congregational Churches in 1871 the main components of the Congregational organizational structure were in place and their roles within it essentially established. The basic unit was the local church, autonomous in handling all matters pertaining to its faith, worship, and congregational life. In situations requiring decisions of major importance, as in matters of ministerial leadership or church discipline, the local church was nevertheless expected to seek and hear seriously the advice of neighboring churches called together in vicinage council. At the same time other agencies of cooperation had come into existence, district associations of churches and ministers and, in some cases, at least the beginnings of state organizations. To those the National Council added the broader dimension of nationwide cooperation. Beyond this pyramidical structure there were the several autonomous benevolent societies, all now claiming a Congregational identity and receiving Congregational support. The structure was in place, but Congregationalism continued to welcome an evolving polity in which adjustments within the structure could still be made.

Local Church

One matter of continued concern related to the local congregation was the advisability of perpetuating a companion ecclesiastical society as the church's business partner. Although this had been an issue of some dispute earlier in the nineteenth century, attention paid to it on the national level reached a high point in the 1870s. Many New England churches were still yoked with their societies, even though the latter were now voluntary organizations no longer mandated by law. Similar arrangement continued as an option in the founding of other churches across the nation. So under the urging of Henry M. Dexter, who vigorously opposed the dual structure of church and society (or "parish"), the 1874 meeting of the National Council called for a study and a report at its next session. The report on "The Parish System," presented to the council meeting of 1877, was the most comprehensive statement ever printed in council minutes, covering eighty-eight pages and examining exhaustively the history of and recent experience with this unique form of church organization in Congregationalism. In general the report favored continuation of ecclesiastical societies, although only in an arrangement whereby the society's supervision of property and handling of finances would in no way impinge upon the freedom of the church to conduct by its own design its religious ministry. No decision on this issue was reached in the council session, however, and the succeeding council of 1880 inherited the task of conceiving how this ideal limitation of financial power might be achieved!

When the 1880 National Council meeting dealt with the matter, it became clear that no common mind could be reached. Wholly apart from the commendation or condemnation of the system that might be read from past experience, a new view emerged questioning whether secular administration of church affairs could ever be isolated from spiritual accountability. The earlier report wanted to separate the two, lest the church's "devotional meetings be converted into business meetings." The new argument urged that management of church property and "the pledge of salary to the minister and the fidelity with which it is discharged" are not simply business matters, for they too will "affect seriously the spiritual interests of the church."[54] Finally, the issue was simply set aside and never reappeared on a council agenda. In subsequent decades, however, the growing practice was for churches to incorporate in order to qualify themselves to handle their financial affairs on their own. By 1916, when William E. Barton's broadly accepted manual *The Law of Congregational Usage* appeared, it contained a section of instruction titled "How May a Church Free Itself from Relations with a Society?" Although a number of New England churches did retain their traditional societies, this dual structure became more and more a relic of times past.

Gradual modification of past ways also occurred in the practices of local churches concerning church membership. In 1886 a report to the National Council described the tests for admission commonly employed at that time. Two types were noted. The first test was doctrinal and required statements concerning the "fundamentals of Christian faith," which would show knowledge of such areas of belief as the Trinity, the work of Christ, the way of salvation, the sacraments, and the awards of final judgment. The second test was of experience and referred to personal awareness of sin and grace and to quality of personal life. With regard to the latter, the report declared, "Our standard has been high. While there is local laxity, probably it may be assumed true of our churches at large that they would decline to receive as members, persons who insist upon the liberty to dance, to play cards, to attend the theatre and the opera, to engage on the Lord's day in employments which are not works of mercy or of necessity, to indulge in any use of intoxicants as a beverage."[55] The earlier rigor was retained, with nineteenth-century Protestant mores now generally enshrined in Congregational membership tests. Candidates were carefully examined, sometimes by the congregation and always by its committee. Admission was by the congregation's affirmative majority vote, the franchise being granted in most churches by this time to both female and male adult members.

Barton's description in 1916 of admission to church membership discloses continuities, but also changes. In the early twentieth century admission continued to require the congregation's approval, but the conditions for acceptance were less specific in their demands. Applicants, in Barton's telling, were "propounded" (that is, publicly named from the pulpit) to the congregation a week or more before the vote was to be taken, thereby giving time for the objection of any member who might find a candidate unsuitable. Prior approval of the candidate had been given by an examining committee, although Barton noted that "it will often occur that a committee will require little assurance beyond the testimony of the pastor." The greater modification, however, occurred with respect to tests to be administered, whether by committee or pastor. In Barton's description, the basis for church membership customary for the time was "credible evidence of Christian character, confession of Jesus as Savior and Lord, and the acceptance of a covenant to walk with the members of the church in Christian love."[56] Although local churches could differ from one another in their membership conditions, the "acids of modernity" had been at work. Personal commitment remained supremely important for admission to membership, but the details of requirements in doctrine and morals could not be so precisely defined as earlier generations had assumed.

Associations and Conferences

In the evolution of organizations for mutual support and cooperative working among the local churches, the simple matter of name identification required attention. Spontaneous emergence of district and state bodies throughout the nineteenth century occurred without regard to standardization of nomenclature, and in 1907 the National Council acted to urge clarification. By that time, it was reported, 133 of the district organizations were called associations, 129 were conferences, 10 were conventions, and 4 were consociations. On the state level, thirty-seven of the bodies were known as associations, four were conferences, four were conventions, while two were state ministerial bodies also called associations. The council's recommendation was that the term *conference* be used for the state organizations and the term *association* for the district bodies. Compliance was rapid, and by the succeeding council meeting of 1910, almost all the organizations, both state and district, were employing the new names.

Throughout the course of this period the district associations (also called *local associations*) increasingly came to be major agencies for the work of the churches. Having begun modestly in the early and midnineteenth century as simply gatherings of persons from neighboring churches for consultation and spiritual enrichment, they became structured organizations with lay delegates and ministerial members, representative of the participating churches and authorized by them to carry out designated common tasks. In this development the performance of common tasks came gradually to include the exercise of certain ecclesiastical functions. An important moment in this regard was again the meeting of the National Council in 1907, where recommendations for standardization of associations' responsibilities were made. It was urged by the council that associations become the agencies for ordination, replacing neighborhood ecclesiastical councils for this purpose, that they become the organizations holding the ministerial standing of ordained clergy, and that they be made the final authority in maintaining the register of ministers and churches in good standing. Further, the council recommended in a general way that "larger recognition be given to the place of local associations of churches as a conciliar body to act in cooperation with the state and national organizations in the interest of the churches."[57] Although some hesitance was expressed concerning abandoning ordination by vicinage council, the associations readily accepted their new roles. In 1909 Charles S. Nash, who had served as chair of the council's Committee on Polity, declared that by virtue of this enlargement of function the association had become "our pivotal fellowship body."[58]

During this period state conferences likewise began to develop into their more permanent form. Because this required extended organizational changes, it became a lengthier process and was not completed until the early 1930s. At the beginning of the twentieth century the organization of Congregationalism on a state level generally consisted of two elements. One was a modest "state association," limited often to an annual meeting, a few committees, and the keeping of statistics on the churches. The other was a "state home missionary society," which had a paid executive and sufficient income to carry on a program of founding new churches and aiding others not yet capable of self-support. Many felt that an integration of these activities was desirable, not only achieving coordination in a state's Congregational work but also giving as much emphasis to nurturing the state's existing churches as to their further extension.

In the early 1900s the movement toward such centralization began simultaneously in five western and midwestern states: Northern California, Michigan, Nebraska, Ohio, and Wisconsin. In 1907 the National Council added its encouragement. Among its recommendations were that state conferences be established as legally incorporated bodies, that they be led by superintendents and such boards as needed, that they act in cooperation with local churches and their associations, and that they "provide for and direct" both "the extension of church work" and "the mutual oversight and care" of all self-sustaining and missionary churches.[59] With the direction clearly set, the states individually organized the new conferences along these lines.

Some questioned state superintendency as an introduction of hierarchy. One effective answer, however, had already come in an address by Joseph H. Chandler in Wisconsin on "Undeveloped Resources of Congregationalism." Referring to the apostle Paul's comment about Apollos's watering where Paul had planted in the development of the apostolic churches, Chandler declared that Congregationalism was weakened because it had no Apollos! So a superintendent in each state was needed, and most among the concerned did not dispute either the role or the title. In Northern California in 1908, when the position was created, the title *superintendent* was chosen over its alternative, *conference missionary*. Always, in the establishment of these state conferences, the continued autonomy of the local church was affirmed. But by means of the state conferences a stronger agency of cooperation was developed within the structure of Congregationalism.

Ministry

From the time Congregational churches began to move westward on the expanding frontier they experienced difficulty in generating both a sufficient number of clergy and a consistency in the quality desirable for clergy leadership. The minutes of the National Council in the 1880s and 1890s contain frequent reports and resolutions with respect to these problems. Although the denomination's colleges produced many fine graduates who turned to ministry and the Congregational seminaries across the nation provided for them an appropriate theological education, their numbers were insufficient. As a consequence, a number of Congregational churches called to their ministry persons of uncertain qualification. Some were clergy from other denominations less inclined to insist on educational standards, some were earnest Congregational lay men who had gifts of oratory but little opportunity for academic training, some were "stray preachers" who wandered about and seized opportunity when churches were in need. Meetings of the National Council sought to devise remedies for this problem through encouraging intermediary helps, such as correspondence courses and summer institutes in theological training, independent reading programs leading toward ordination, and selected admission to theological schools of persons without college degrees. Yet none of these, nor all of these together, was sufficient to guard against the unqualified ministries that continued to appear and afflict Congregational churches.

Although this was a very practical matter to be dealt with by improvement of recruiting and educational efforts, it also became a polity matter having impact upon ecclesiastical procedures. As the problem increased in the late nineteenth century, a major question developed concerning the adequacy of ad hoc ecclesiastical councils to qualify persons for service as Congregational clergy. Traditionally both ordination to ministry and installation into a specific ministerial position had been the work of vicinage councils made up of lay and clerical representatives of neighboring churches summoned by the church seeking ministerial leadership. The intent had been to recognize that, despite the autonomy of the local church, Congregational ministry was more than a local affair, for its quality was a matter of concern for the denominational churches-at-large. Control by council could provide broader perspective and offset any tendency toward local aberration in evaluation of persons for these sacred tasks. Yet in the passage of time even the adequacy of councils for this purpose was questioned. For one thing, the assembling of such councils was difficult in the expanding West, with its often scattered churches. But further, the councils' ad hoc nature created uncertainties. Lack of continuity from council to council could lead to difficulty in generating and sustaining common standards. Even more, councils were subject to manipulation because they consisted of arbitrarily invited churches. A charge recorded in the National Council minutes of 1886 noted that "picked" councils could become "packed" councils.[60]

With the development of the more permanent associations of churches and ministers as agencies of Congregational cooperation, it became desirable to rely upon them for steadier standards and more careful control. Thus, as previously noted, ordination was placed increasingly in the hands of the associations following the National Council recommendation of 1907. The practice of installation, however, presented a more complicated set of issues. The installation of a pastor by a council was an act that, in early New England terms, established a *settled ministry*. Those called to ministerial posts but not installed were designated *acting pastors*, with the implication that as yet there was no commitment to permanency in those ministerial relationships. Actually, installation involved a double guarantee. On the one hand, it conveyed the council's assurance to the church that the candidate's qualifications were adequate. On the other hand, it gave security to the pastor against arbitrary discharge by the congregation, for breaking an installed ministerial relationship required the approval of neighboring churches through a council of dismissal. But as the nineteenth century progressed, first the former guarantee, and then the latter, were questioned and set aside, as practices changed with regard to installation to ministerial office.

A report to the National Council meeting of 1880 showed alarming statistics. Of the 3,674 Congregational churches, only 898 had settled pastors. Among the remainder, 1,893 had acting pastors, 200 were served by licentiates or clergy from other denominations, and 683 had no pastor at all. The report revealed the shortage of Congregational clergy as well as a declining interest in the use of installation in establishing the pastoral relationship. Whereas earlier in the century a much higher percentage of clergy had been installed, churches were increasingly abandoning the practice—and a major reason, it was reported, lay in the fear of loss of autonomy through being subject to a dismissal council.

This situation stirred several responses. Some felt that the distinction between *pastor* and *acting pastor* carried in the yearbook was really invidious, for it reflected less the qualifications of the clergy than the fact that congregations were reluctant to bind themselves to installation's guarantee. Others sought to find a middle ground between conciliar endorsement and permanent commitment by proposing the use of *recognition* by assembled council. The recognition of an ordained minister called to a new post would entail the same examination and approval of ministerial qualifications as would installation, but without requirement of a dismissal council if termination were to occur. In fact, it was voted in 1886 to make a yearbook distinction between pastors who were endorsed by councils of either installation or recognition and those whose calling to a church's ministry had been submitted to no council at all. But beyond these adjustments there remained the larger question of whether or not ad hoc councils were really the best instruments for endorsement of a candidates's qualifications for ministerial service. Finally, as in the case of ordination, it was urged that installation or recognition be an act of the association. In some instances vicinage councils continued to be used for these functions, but the greater emphasis was placed upon the approbation of the association as an ecclesiastical council when requested by the local church to meet this need. In the process, however, the use of installation continued to decline. Churches favored the practice of recognition, in which the association's endorsement and welcome were gained for the incoming pastor without commitment to its overseeing termination if that were to occur.

Benevolent Societies

By the early twentieth century seven benevolent societies were recognized by the National Council as agents for carrying out the mission of the denomination. Six had come from earlier times: the American Board of Commissioners for Foreign Missions, the American Missionary Association, the Congregational Home Missionary Society, the Congregational Church Building Society, the Congregational Education Society, and the Congregational Sunday School and Publishing Society. To these a seventh had more recently been added, the Congregational Board of Ministerial Relief. Some had been interdenominational in their origins, but now all were limited to serving Congregational needs and lived by Congregational support. Throughout their individual histories, however, these societies had been independent organizations, self-perpetuating in structure, and autonomous in handling their own affairs. As a consequence, two polity issues arose. The first dealt with the relation of the societies to the churches, the second with the relation of the societies to one another.

In the 1880s Congregational leaders began to raise questions about the incongruity of mission organizations soliciting and spending the churches' money without the churches being represented in any way in the decision making by which the programs were developed and administered. A leading voice in the protest was that of A. Hastings Ross, a Michigan pastor, who claimed that the rise of the voluntary (and independent) societies was an abnormality within the growth of Congregationalism and that this must be rectified through making the societies more accountable to the churches. "We affirm," he said, "that representation in controlling missionary and benevolent work is in exact harmony with our principles, . . . while closed corporations and voluntary societies are contrary thereto."[61]

A hope for such representation of the churches in the administration of the societies was expressed by the meeting of the National Council of 1889, but there was no quick realization. However, a dramatic conflict occurred in the early 1890s when the American Board, through its Prudential Committee, insisted on disqualifying candidates for missionary appointments who did not hold to the committee's more conservative theological views, even though those candidates were acceptable to the councils and the associations that ordained them. Finally, in 1893, the American Board relented on the theological issue because of heavy protest, and also it opened up its corporate membership to some degree to persons named to it by the churches through their associations. In similar manner in 1902, at the urging of the National Council, the Congregational Home Missionary Society expanded its ruling body to include some church representation. A more complete resolution of this polity issue was delayed, however, until the Kansas City National Council meeting in 1913. In the major transformation of national structure accomplished at that time it was decided, the benevolent societies agreeing, that all voting members of each National Council would be voting members of the boards of all the mission organizations. Other board members would also be elected by the different societies, but by this overlap of membership with the National Council, the churches would be significantly represented in guiding their mission programs. And this, from Ross's point of view, would be proper Congregationalism.

The second concern was that of so relating the independent benevolent societies to one another that their total program could be carried on more efficiently and economically. Although desire for this goal was expressed at the founding meeting of the National Council in 1871, the process of bringing it to realization was again lengthy. Over the next four decades, however, progressive steps were taken leading to agencies of cooperative consultation, the coordinating of schedules for common annual meetings, closer and more integrated relations with district associations and state conferences, and the development of the Apportionment Plan and Together Campaign for soliciting and distributing mission funds. Then in 1913 a further integrating of mission programs was accomplished when the reorganization of the national structure included the development of the Commission on Missions. Representing the benevolent societies, the Woman's Boards of Mission, and the National Council, this agency was made responsible for "advisory supervision" of the work of the societies. Although the societies remained distinct, they were now brought into this closer and more efficient relationship with one another.

WORSHIP

In 1886 the Minnesota General Association submitted a memorial to the National Council requesting the naming of a council committee to give "thought and study to the subject of proper methods of expressing worship." Although the association recognized "the right of every Congregational church to determine its own form of worship," it believed that great benefit could come to all the churches from such a study and recommendations.[62] In responding to that request, the council began a series of committee projects, developed intermittently over the next three decades, designed to bring about what it termed "improvement of worship."

Sabbath Services

The first report was made to the National Council at its next session, in 1889, and included a survey of existing worship practices as well as suggestions for enrichment. The main elements of the "old" order of Sabbath morning worship, the report said, remain largely in place: invocation, hymn, Scripture reading, prayer, notices, hymn, sermon, prayer, hymn, and benediction. But, it noted, in recent years many additions had been grafted to this "parent stem." Reporting on fourteen hundred replies to questionnaires sent to Congregational churches, it described the following current practices: to open the service, 913 churches now use the doxology, 61 use a Scripture sentence or call to praise, and 64 place a psalm chanted by the congregation either at or near the service's beginning. Within the service, 1,016 use a responsive reading from Scripture, 993 include an anthem by a choir, 941 gather an offering in a manner constituting a "religious exercise," 538 recite the Lord's Prayer in unison, 365 sing the Gloria Patri, 59 employ written prayers, and 49 include a reading of the Apostles' Creed. In some churches there are also regular readings of the Decalogue, or of the Beatitudes, or of the gospel summary of the divine law, though none of these are common practice. Finally, the report coyly added, "Two churches, as a relief from the strain of attention and the weariness of sitting still, have singing in the middle of the sermon, and one pastor follows his sermon with a few moments of silent prayer."[63]

Churches of this period also had evening services, but these, the report noted, were more subject to variety in content than were the morning services. Generally speaking, the evening services were shorter and less formal, although preaching continued to be a mainstay within them. Their emphasis was more evangelistic, with added time given to music, particularly congregational singing. In some cases, the report added, churches adapted their evening services especially to the young.

In its analysis of the nature and purpose of worship, the committee urged a balance between worship's "didactic" and "liturgic" elements. The effort to improve worship should not be at the cost of losing the teaching aspect that it had long contained. Eternal truths are communicated through the preaching of the Word, and the service with its prayers and hymns can "prepare the mind and heart" for their consideration and reception. Yet, the report noted, it is cause for rejoicing that recent improvements in worship have made the church "more emphatically a house of prayer and a house of praise," instead of "a mere lecture hall . . . as it has sometimes been."[64]

Nevertheless, the committee concluded, additional improvements must be sought, and several were proposed. For example, public prayer can be enriched. Too often it is wearisome with "vain repetitions," when it should be inspiring. Each prayer in the service should have its own special purpose and not impinge upon any other. Even extempore prayer should always be premeditated and planned. Also, prayers should be shorter than was generally the custom. "Tedious prolixity here," the report declared, "is an evil to be radically reformed." Moreover, use of historic prayers of the church was commended, for, said the committee, "we are quite at liberty to borrow what we please from the treasured wealth of the world's liturgies."[65] Some of those prayers, it added, might even be repeated in unison by the congregations, such as the General Confession or the General Thanksgiving from the Anglican Book of Common Prayer. A considerable liturgical distance had been traveled since early Puritan days!

Further improvement, the report urged, could come by enriching the quality of music in the service. Gospel hymns, it said, have served an important purpose and can continue to do so, but they should be restricted to "evangelistic work" and only "sparingly used in the ordinary service of the church." Standards should be set high and efforts made "to cultivate the taste" of members so that the noblest music could be employed. The "praise songs of the church universal," such as the Gloria Patri, the Gloria in Excelsis, the Sanctus, and the Te Deum, might be introduced and the congregation encouraged to participate.[66] In fact, congregational participation in the church's music of worship is most important of all, for this act of praise must be an act of all the people. Congregational singing also should be led by a strong choir, and, the report recommended, there might even be rehearsals, as some churches have prior to prayer meetings, for the congregation's preparation of music for the Sabbath.

Some additional suggestions were that each pastor compose a lectionary so that Scripture reading throughout a year might cover major portions of the Bible, that in developing a calendar for the year's worship, certain "special days" be observed, and that common services to be recommended for use in all Congregational churches be created. Movement toward the improvement of worship was begun.

In 1904 there was a second effort at stimulating this improvement through recommendations of the National Council. By this time, however, some resistance had developed. The committee commented that in some quarters the work toward improvement was "viewed with suspicion as an attempt to fasten chains of ritual upon our churches, and to make up by form and ceremony for poverty of spiritual life." At this meeting, therefore, little was added to what had already been proposed for alterations in the service. The only major suggestion in 1904 was that worshipers recite some common creed or covenant just prior to the sermon. Attention was focused, rather, upon the personal qualifications of the pastor, and the committee said that the concern was less to enrich the service than to enrich the person who leads the service. It spoke of the training, the self-discipline, and the quality of spiritual life essential for this sacred task. And, it concluded, those who come with adequate preparation for this "representative priestly service" will "surely find it a joy" to themselves and "a blessing to the household of God."[67]

In 1910 the National Council returned to the matter of the worship service and its enrichment. Convinced that Congregational churches could profit from further specific suggestions, the preceding national gathering had charged a committee to bring to this council an "Order for Common Worship, catholic in spirit, evangelical in doctrine, and truly expressive of our heritage in the reformed faith and our larger communion with ancient saints and the church throughout the world." The result was the Order of Service, presented in both "shorter form" and "fuller form," which offered to the churches much concrete help for planning the Sabbath morning worship. The council then authorized that "it be printed in convenient form for such churches as may adopt it."[68]

Although the "parent stem" of this Order of Service remained essentially what it was in 1889, the content was abundantly enriched by the inclusion of prayers and music from classic Christian sources. For most of the spoken parts of the service several options among scriptural sentences and traditional prayers were printed, providing for variety within the continued use of the same order. Participation by the worshipers was encouraged not only in the hymns and chants, but also in the prayers and in the reading of scripture. The General Confession, General Thanksgiving, and Lord's Prayer were included, along with a responsive reading and options for unison reading of other biblical passages. A further option was the congregation's recital of the Apostles' Creed. Beyond the order itself, the committee offered a further collection of prayers, drawn again from a variety of historical sources, "for occasional use." Strong effort was therefore made in this committee and council action to begin developing a liturgy for what had largely been nonliturgical churches. In explanation of its underlying assumptions, the committee declared that although "the message of the preacher should be regarded as a leading feature of public worship, . . . the sermon should not be so magnified as to overshadow the service of praise and prayer, in which, face to face with God, we pour out our confessions, our thanksgivings, and our supplications."[69]

Other Services

During the course of the next seven years, the National Council, through its Committee on Order of Worship, prepared and then authorized for publication several additional services for other occasions of public worship. The council records of 1913, 1915, and 1917 show the committee continuously at work. It was the increasing hope that these services not only would meet the needs of the more successful churches of the denomination, where pastors could adapt them to their special local situations, but also would serve to keep open the many churches struggling without pastoral leadership. In 1917 it was reported that 1,118 Congregational churches were without ministers. Frequently, it was noted, those churches would close for lengthy periods until new pastors could be obtained. So one part of the council's hope was that these churches, under lay leadership, could be kept active by using the Sabbath morning Order of Service, as well as such other worship services as were applicable to their needs.

These additional services were fitted for a variety of occasions. For general use the committee provided a vesper service and a Sabbath evening service. For more occasional use it developed a service for receiving new members, a missionary service, a home missionary service, a marriage service, and a funeral service. For use in the celebration of special days, it prepared a Children's Day service, a Forefathers' Day service, a Thanksgiving Day service, and a Service of Patriotism. It also prepared services for the celebration of the sacraments.

Sacraments

In keeping with the Congregational tradition of liturgical simplicity in the celebration of the sacraments, the services for baptism and the Lord's Supper remained essentially plain and unadorned. Enrichment from classic sources was limited in each instance to a single option chosen from the Book of Common Prayer. The main reliance was upon the use of Scripture, in addition to newly prepared simple liturgy and prayer. This was in accord with the "low church" manner in which the sacraments continued to be viewed. In an address given to the National Council in 1901 on the function of the sacraments, the speaker identified them as the "simple ordinances"[70] of the church. Although the term *sacrament* continued in use, the different terminology represented a greater emphasis upon human responsibility and obedience than upon divine initiative and gift. *Ordinance* suggests a prescribed rite to be celebrated, whereas *sacrament* suggests a channel of grace. In 1916 William E. Barton, in his volume on Congregational usage, made clear his preference for the term *ordinance* as well.

This manner of viewing the sacraments appeared particularly in the order for infant baptism commended by the council of 1913. The service was also designated an order for the consecration of infants, and the content stressed primarily a parental dedication of the child to the service of God and a corresponding promise to raise the child "in the knowledge of God and the spirit of Jesus Christ."[71] The nearest the service came to the classic Congregational sacramental idea of baptism representing God's covenanting act was in the parental acknowledgment that the child is a gift of God and in the promise that this will be taught in the child's upbringing. The earlier sense of God's covenanting with the church or with the individual in an act of grace was now liturgically replaced by the commitment to parental responsibility for Christian nurture. This was in accord with the understanding of baptism as connected with family life, which had prevailed in Congregationalism throughout much of the nineteenth century. At the beginning of the twentieth century, Washington Gladden broadened this understanding by seeing baptism as a "beautiful symbol" of the universal unity of the whole human family, for it "reiterates the fact that God is the universal divine Father of all children" and of all humanity.[72]

The order for the administration of the Lord's Supper maintained a more traditional stance. It was a service of repentance and the seeking of forgiveness, and its reference to the elements portrayed them as "witnesses and signs" of grace. It was also a service promising personal renewal, the concluding prayer of which asked "that we may so partake of the very life of Christ, that he may live again in us." However, it likewise was a service of memorial in which memory of Christ's life and death can heal. "Impress and quicken our hearts with the memory of our Master, . . ." read one prayer, "till we feel it to be no task to serve him." It also was a service emphasizing the subjective experience of both personal and corporate communion, where the individual came "to seek a Presence" and "all our brethren everywhere" were remembered in prayer.[73] Commentary in the early twentieth century on the meaning of the Lord's Supper, however, stressed more strongly than did this liturgy the idea of corporate fellowship. Particularly with impediments to admission to the Lord's table by this time largely removed, the conviction was shared with the National Council by a speaker in 1901 that the "communion" experienced at the Lord's Supper is "all the richer because of an unrestricted invitation to all who have confessed Christ, in whatever church, and who love him in sincerity."[74] The two-centuries-old ecumenical hope of Cotton Mather was being fulfilled.

MISSION

For Congregationalism the late nineteenth and early twentieth centuries were a time of progress in development of the church's mission. Under the impact of the New Theology and social gospel and through the leadership of the National Council, the denomination increasingly became engaged in matters of social concern and responsibility. Moreover, its foreign missions program shared in the heightened enthusiasm of a period in which American Protestant churches generally were committed to world evangelization. Altogether these were decades of growth for Congregationalism, and its ministry of outreach was part of that expansion.

Foreign Missions

In 1883 the General Association of California, meeting at Santa Cruz, telegraphed the following message to the National Council of Congregational Churches, meeting in Concord, New Hampshire: "We are with you in sympathy and faith, and propose to raise a million yearly to save the country to Christ, and three fourths to convert the world." The telegraphed reply from the National Council said: "We join you in your noble purpose to devise liberal things for the salvation of the country and the world."[75] It was not until 1900 that John R. Mott, leading twentieth-century Methodist missionary advocate, popularized the phrase "the evangelization of the world in this generation," but

Congregationalists on the West Coast, if not also on the East, seem to have had that hope and its enthusiasm some while earlier!

In the 1880s a period of expansion began in Congregational foreign missions under the direction of the American Board of Commissioners for Foreign Missions. Two major legacies, totalling $1.5 million, were received and used over the next two decades as supplement to the contributions regularly provided by the churches. Moreover, new youth movements, Christian Endeavor in the churches and the Student Volunteer Movement on college campuses, challenged young people to enter missionary service and became a productive source for missionary volunteers. In 1880 the American Board established a west central Africa mission in Angola. In 1883 it founded five additional missions: in Shansi and Kwangtung provinces in China, Nagato Province in Japan, the province of Inhambane in east central Africa, and the state of Chihuahua in Mexico. The Shansi mission was an Oberlin project, planned and staffed by Oberlin students. In 1902 a new mission was begun in Mindanao in the Philippines, and in 1903 students from Yale initiated the Yale-in-China mission in Ch'ang-sha. Meanwhile older missions were more fully staffed and supplied, and finally in 1918 students from Grinnell established the Grinnell-in-China project in north Shantung Province. Also in that year the first African-American missionary to represent African-American Congregational churches received his commission for work in the west central Africa mission. Throughout these decades of expansion, moreover, an increasing number of single women were commissioned for missionary service, selected and supported by the regional Woman's Boards of Mission.

The foreign mission program, however, did not simply expand through this period, for in response to modernizing tendencies it changed. The American Board faced the necessity of adapting and shifting course as new practical and theological challenges appeared. A major practical concern questioned the nature of missionary activity itself and the degree to which nonevangelistic humanitarian service could have its own missionary validity. Medical ministry was one activity that, in due time, gained this recognition. Although physicians were on the mission field in the early decades of the ABCFM, some were there as part-time preachers, and others were present for the health care of the mission personnel. In time these physicians began to offer their medical help more broadly to the native communities in which they worked, but it was not until near the end of the nineteenth century that American Board policy changed to acknowledge this as an independent form of Christian mission. A booklet titled *The Medical Arm of Missionary Service*, carrying testimonies concerning their work by fourteen of the physicians, was helpful in the process, and in 1897 the board voted that medical personnel in its service should have the full status of "missionary," similar to persons engaged in evangelistic work. Mission stations now could be established for medical purpose.

A somewhat different course was followed in recognizing secular education, particularly higher education, as an independent and valid form of Christian mission. Elementary schools were often part of a mission program, but were used for their instrumental value in developing a literacy necessary for Bible reading and religious instruction. In time more advanced schools developed on the field, initiated by native pastors and local sponsoring bodies, and some of these attained college rank. Although the ABCFM also accepted a sponsorship role for these colleges, its relationship to them was somewhat tentative until the beginning of the twentieth century. Secular education, many feared, could divert interest and energy from Christian conversion. In 1907, however, following a long and careful study disclosing the value of the native colleges for community and national leadership, the Board voted to set up a higher education fund and to seek $2 million to endow the sixteen collegiate institutions to which it was already related. From this point on, higher education was recognized as an important and legitimate part of the missionary enterprise. Throughout this period similar study was given to agricultural and industrial education, both of which had been gradually introduced in mission stations. At first this practical training was viewed simply as a help to students, making it possible for them to provide some labor in return for their schooling. But here, too, the value of such skills for the welfare of the students' native communities became apparent, and in due course agricultural and industrial missions were incorporated into the American Board's total program.

In the 1880s the ABCFM faced a troubling theological problem. Known as the "Andover controversy," the problem arose out of the theological liberalization occurring on the Andover Theological Seminary faculty and embraced the question of the finality of divine judgment at the time of death. Several Andover theologians, under the leadership of Egbert Smyth, came to feel that although salvation depended upon confessing Christ as savior, a loving God could not condemn to eternal punishment persons who in their lifetime had never had the opportunity to hear of Christ and respond to him. Therefore there must be for such persons a time of "future probation" in which Christ is somehow presented so that the critical decision can be made. Others objected to this idea, out of faithfulness to the prevailing New England theology and out of inability to find any scriptural warrant for the proposed change. The controversy reached the ABCFM in 1886 after its conservative home secretary and Prudential Committee had withdrawn support from one missionary and rejected the candidacies of other nominees who had found the new conviction particularly appropriate in approaching non-Christian lands. Debate was intense, and at one point Lyman Abbott attempted to pacify it by asking, "Must Congregationalism split into three denominations, one of which is sure of a future probation, one of which is sure there is no future probation, and the third of which is simply sure that God is good and love is love, and all things are in His hands?"[76] Conservatism, however, prevailed for the next seven years, until finally in 1893 the American Board modified its policy and the theological dispute on future probation was put to rest.

Soon, however, this particular controversy was seen within a much broader context. In 1885 Egbert Smyth had written, "The question of the salvation of the heathen is simply one aspect of the fundamental religious question of our time: the claim of Christianity to be the perfect and final religion."[77] Progressive missionary thought was then directed to a comparative study of world religions and to the search for what William R. Hutchison has termed "an exportable Christianity."[78] The task was to examine the nature of Christianity's finality in relation to other faiths and thereby provide more adequate shape for the message of the Christian mission. In 1895 George A. Gordon presented an important address to the ABCFM on this matter in which he emphasized disengaging Christianity from its transient forms. Yet his steps in this process were still tentative. While urging that missionaries "preach Christ" rather than doctrines about Christ, he continued to find a supremacy in Christianity's proclamation of "the eternal sacrifice in the heart of God mediated by the personal sacrifice of Christ."[79] Further, said Gordon, Christianity should be presented in a manner separated from its cultural embodiment; yet he also claimed moral superiority for Western and American cultures because of their Christianization. The difficult problem of developing a liberal apologetic for Christian missions had now appeared and would remain a matter for the American Board's continuing reflection.

Industrial Relations

On the domestic front Congregationalism's home missions continued through the church extension program of the American (after 1893, Congregational) Home Missionary Society and the work with racial minorities conducted by the American Missionary Association. In the 1890s the latter organization expanded its activity, heretofore mainly with African Americans, American Indians, and Asian immigrants, to include Inuit in Alaska and Hispanics in Puerto Rico. Similarly, the other "home" boards, concerned with church building, Sunday School growth, higher education, and ministerial relief, maintained their services to the denomination. Within this period, however, a new direction for the churches' mission developed, generated by the impulses of the social gospel. It did not become institutionalized in the same manner as other concerns, but it did call forth denominational commitment in efforts to apply Christian influence to the solution of the nation's growing problems in industrial relations.

In 1891 William J. Tucker, Andover faculty member, wrote in criticism of Andrew Carnegie's view concerning industry and wealth, "I can conceive of no greater mistake more disastrous in the end to religion if not to society, than that of trying to make charity do the work of justice."[80] For the next three decades this became a basic conviction lying at the heart of social gospel thinking when applied to the economic order. The desperate conditions of urban poverty, produced by the underpayment of labor in an economy where all competitive advantages lay with the employer, led to the prolonged cry for such improvement in wages as would provide for workers a fair share of the product of their labors. It was not enough for poverty to be assuaged by the good will giving of the wealthy. Although other matters, such as child labor and working conditions, were important, economic justice as measured by adequate wages was a primary demand.

For Congregationalists, as for all supporters of the social gospel, Washington Gladden's was a leading voice. Gladden's theology, when applied to perfecting social relations, focused on the importance of the "Christian law of love." The ideal for society was not competition, but cooperation, and in that idealized state there could be cooperative arrangements of profit sharing developed for the benefit of owners and workers alike. But in the present state of affairs, Gladden acknowledged, a different approach was needed. In an important address, titled "Is It Peace or War?" and delivered in 1886, Gladden affirmed that there were three possible relations between capital and labor: subjugation of labor to capital through slavery, a warfare between the two in the wage system, and a uniting of the two in cooperation. Society had not reached the last stage, but it had passed the first, and now struggled in the wage system. The struggle, Gladden believed, must involve a "war" for justice until the final ideal is attained. Moreover, he said, "If war is the order of the day, we must grant labor belligerent rights."[81] For Gladden this meant the recognition of labor's right to unionize and to use its power of organization for the purpose of collective bargaining. It also meant the sanction of strikes if in the process of bargaining they became a necessity for labor's cause. At the same time Gladden cautioned restraint in the use of such confrontation. He deplored all violence in strikes, whoever might be the perpetrator. Although he continued throughout to uphold a union's right to strike, he urged that the right be employed sparingly, lest in overuse it lessen its own effectiveness as an instrument for justice.

Gladden also advocated other reform measures for the improvement of industrial relations. Several of these involved action by the government, such as factory inspections, the regulation of work hours, the abolition of child labor, and the control of monopolies. In his social philosophy, however, Gladden advocated a middle way between individualism and the socialism being promoted by more radical secular reformers. State socialism, he felt, had false economic values, required an undesirable political bureaucracy, and endangered the development of individual character. It was more desirable to "socialize the individual," for, Gladden wrote, "the remedy needed is not the destruction but the Christianization of the present order."[82] The ultimate task of the church in industrial relations was to encourage that Christianization on the part of both capital and labor. The two must be brought together into a worker-management partnership, where the keynote would be cooperation rather than competition, and the impelling motivation would come from the "Christian law of love."

In advancing these ideas in the 1880s and 1890s Gladden was ahead of his time, but, in company with other pioneers, he provided impetus for growing Protestant sensitivity concerning industrial issues. At times his efforts to apply that sensitivity encountered difficulties even in his own denomination, and his conflict in 1905 with the American Board of Commissioners for Foreign Missions was a case in point. The ABCFM had received a gift of $100,000 from John D. Rockefeller, and Gladden objected to this acceptance of "tainted money" gained through monopolistic business practices. Although Gladden's criticism was heard at the American Board's next annual meeting, the money was retained. Nevertheless, Gladden's influence upon Congregationalism's economic views was immense, and his moderatorship of the National Council, 1904–7, was particularly significant.

Throughout the first two decades of the twentieth century the National Council consistently gave time and energy to industrial matters, hearing and responding to reports of its Industrial Committee, and encouraging its conferences, associations, and local churches to become engaged in bringing Christian perspectives to bear upon these troubling issues. In 1910 the council affirmed the Declaration of Principles concerning industrial relations adopted by the Federal Council of Churches upon its founding in 1908, and in this act identified itself more precisely with the growing movement for economic justice and industrial reform. Five years later, after these principles had been amplified into the Social Creed for the Federal Council, the National Council urged each local Congregational church to adopt the statement as its own social commitment. In 1913 the National Council institutionalized further efforts toward Christianization of industrial relations by placing denominational responsibility for its progress in the hands of the Congregational Men's Brotherhood (to use "the masculine forces of the denomination") and under the general overview of a Committee on Social Service. In 1915 the National Council accepted the view that nearly all the problems of society relate to the problems of industry and that the ultimate goal must be a "social salvation" in which all human affairs can "be changed and made a part of the Kingdom of God." Dealing constructively with industrial problems had become an important mission of the church.

Other Social Reforms

Earlier social causes, taken up in the mid-nineteenth century through the voluntary societies, continued to be matters of Congregational concern as the twentieth century arrived. The protecting and honoring of the Sabbath was one such consideration, although as time went on the passion put into this cause and the hope for its success gradually declined. Throughout the 1880s and 1890s the National Council maintained strong interest in this issue, but after 1895 reports by the Committee on Sabbath Observance were replaced by only occasional resolutions. The final report of 1895, however, continued to urge the long-standing conviction that "when the Sabbath is left behind, we do not need to go very far to find atheism and godlessness." The report did deplore a "rigid Sabbatarianism," which it felt "the flexible spirit" of New Testament Christianity did not require, and yet the conduct of business, the pursuit of amusements, and the increased neglecting of things sacred were deemed desecrations of a holy day.[83] The intermittent resolutions enacted by the National Council in the following two decades kept the issue alive. In 1913 all Congregational churches were encouraged "to counteract in every way possible the customs and influences tending to secularize" the Sabbath, and in 1919 approval was specifically expressed for several states' "enactment of proper Sunday laws" and cooperation was urged upon all for protection of a six-day work week.[84] But times were changing, and preservation of Sabbath sanctity became increasingly a losing cause.

The story was different during this period for the cause of temperance, a second area of concern inherited from the early and mid-nineteenth century. Again the struggle was a lengthy one, as the National Council consistently repeated its condemnation of the liquor industry and deplored the habits of those who supported it through their patronage. Various means of moral influence toward abstinence were encouraged, including a vote in 1892 recommending the use of unfermented wine in all Congregational celebrations of the Lord's Supper. As early as 1889, moreover, a committee of the National Council sent a memorial to the United States Congress proposing exploration of the possibility of a national prohibition amendment. Yet this was only a tentative approach to the idea of such national action, and in the ensuing years support was given to state legislation and local option laws. In 1913, however, as desire for national prohibition mounted, the council voted overwhelmingly, 517 to 14, to join in a campaign for a constitutional amendment for that purpose. With the passage of the Eighteenth Amendment by the United States Congress in 1918 and subsequent ratification by forty-five states, the National Council of 1919 was ready to rejoice. After detailing the legislative process bringing this about, the Commission on Temperance reported: "Thus National Prohibition became an accomplished fact. . . . Praise God from whom all blessings flow!"[85] But the work was not yet finished, the committee affirmed, for ahead lay the task of persuading a nation to accept abstinence and, more than that, the task of campaigning again, this time for world prohibition!

Race relations comprised a third area of social concern for late nineteenth- and early twentieth-century Congregationalism, although it has been noted by historians that this in some measure constituted a blind spot in the social gospel. It is true that no special organized efforts were generated by leaders of the churches in this period to deal systematically with broad problems of discrimination and denial of equality. Yet an impressive program of ministry to racial minorities was carried on by the American Missionary Association, and from time to time the National Council turned with sensitivity to the racial issue to set policy and encourage remedy. In fact, the council made a strong declaration on this matter at its first meeting in 1871 at Oberlin. There it declared that "it is the duty, and should be the privilege" of the churches "to throw open the doors" of "churches, schools and colleges, to the full participation of these our fellow-citizens, without any discrimination on account of color." This was a plea for desegregation at the very outset, and later councils continued to speak to racial concerns as situations directed. In 1892 the National Council called for "the right to cast a full ballot and have that ballot counted as cast, without distinction of race."[86] In 1913 it appealed to President Wilson to prevent racial discrimination in government employment. And in 1919, in the face of widespread lawlessness and racial hatred, it called for "negro equal rights before the law and the complete citizenship guaranteed by the constitution." The sensitivity of the National Council was also illustrated by an incident occurring in 1886. One of its African-American members had been refused service in a Chicago restaurant, and it responded by voting, "*Resolved*, That, as a Council, we put on record our sense of indignation at this act of discourtesy and barbarity, and express the hope that the proprietor of the restaurant will not be permitted to escape the penalty for such action imposed by the laws of Illinois."[87]

Other social concerns, such as prison reform and the struggle against war, received attention from time to time in national Congregational thought. But these were matters pursued with lesser intensity and in these decades did not figure large in the denomination's priorities. Apart from the growing commitment to the cause of improved industrial relations, the social mission of Congregationalism of the early twentieth century largely replicated the areas of concern pursued throughout the nineteenth.

SUMMARY

The half-century from 1870 to 1920 was a time of significant growth and important change for American Congregationalism. It was, in fact, Congregationalism's most expansive period throughout the course of its three hundred years of American history. It was also a time anticipatory in several ways of future denominational characteristics.

First, within this period Congregationalism essentially brought into final form its denominational structure. The early nineteenth-century movement onto the expanding national scene carried with it the necessity for development of regional and national agencies by means of which the churches could coordinate their labors. Under the Plan of Union in the first half-century, this did not occur as Congregationalism organizationally floundered. However, in the late 1800s associations, conferences, and the National Council were brought into being, creating the denomination's institutional structure for the twentieth century.

Second, during these years Congregationalism adapted itself to scientific discoveries that were to affect significantly the content of Christian faith. Openness to views of biological evolution and biblical criticism became the basis for a theological liberalism that, although later altered in detail, continued to characterize Congregational thought. Third, this period brought increased diversity into Congregationalism and its ways. New racial groups were incorporated into what had been predominantly a white establishment, and a larger role for women began to appear in a church structure heretofore under male domination.

Fourth, Congregational worship in these years recognized its need for improvement through enrichment of its content. To that end it drew for the first time upon the historic Christian treasury of prayers and other forms of devotion, a practice continued more fully later in the twentieth century. And fifth, Congregationalism in these turn-of-the-century years introduced a more broadly applied social gospel focused boldly on Christian response to economic ills. This became prelude to a steadily growing and more explicit sense of social responsibility as Congregationalism continued in succeeding decades to enlarge its understanding of its God-given mission.

CHAPTER SEVEN

TENSIONS AND TRANSITIONS
1920–1957

Times of tension in the questioning of old ways and periods of transition in the developing of new ways were ever present in the three-centuries-long history of American Congregationalism leading to 1920. While retaining continuity with their past, the Congregational churches of those years lived in a changing world and adapted to the challenges of new ideas and circumstances. Their life was both "rooted" and "in process," an evolving witness to a historic faith.

Yet more than any earlier period in Congregational history, the thirty-seven years between 1920 and 1957 can be characterized as a time of "tension and transition." Living in the midst of the mid-twentieth century's ever-quickening pace of life and exposed to its broadened opportunities as well as to its tragedies, Congregationalism was required as never before to rethink and respond. Both the surrounding changes in society and an internal concern for more fully authentic Christian witness brought occasions for struggle and new direction.

Theologically Congregationalism shared in the period's increasingly diverse efforts to mold a form of inherited Christian faith that would be true to new intellectual discoveries and yet not misled by the false optimism they too easily encouraged. In its foreign missions it sought to find a more contemporary style for worldwide Christian witnessing while contending with decline in local interest and support. Its commitment to the church's social responsibility generated controversy between liberal and conservative viewpoints, but also produced increased levels of moral concern and involvement. And above all, its long-standing ecumenical interest led in the closing years of this period to a denominational merger that precipitated Congregationalism's most divisive controversy and at the same time pointed toward its potentially most significant contribution to Christian unity. So by the year of the merger, 1957, when the major portion of American Congregationalism became part of a newly founded United Church of Christ, much had been put to test and much was in the process of transition. A new life was in preparation, but its fuller embodiment was still ahead.

HISTORY

The Twenties and Thirties

The Jazz Age, the Flapper Age, and the Roaring Twenties are among the names applied to the decade in America following the First World War. Although these designations capture some of the exuberant, and even uninhibited, self-expression of a period recoiling from the anxieties and sacrifices of the war years, they fail to identify the more complex character of this still-troubled time.

On the one hand, this was indeed a boisterous period, even in the conduct of its business life. The 1920s provided a time of prosperity for the American economy, which ended only with the stock market crash of 1929. Big business reigned as new technologies and mass production made automobiles, radios, refrigerators, and other consumer goods available to increasing numbers of American households. More developed sales techniques and advertising methods added to the intensity of business operations, and speculative investing, searching for windfall profits, reached new heights. For some, living in the lap of increased luxury, the times were good and to be enjoyed.

On the other hand, the 1920s were a time of disillusionment. Shocked by the immense tragedy of the war and wearied by the struggle to make the world safe for democracy, especially after the defeat in the Senate of President Wilson's peace policies in 1919, many gave up on the moral idealism present in earlier decades. A new skepticism found its way into national life, led by prominent intellectuals of the day. The sharp pens of H. L. Mencken and Sinclair Lewis, for example, along with the critical writings of Joseph Wood Krutch, ridiculed the church and its piety in an attack on what they termed the outmoded "puritanism" of American religion. But beyond this attack from lofty levels, there was the more profound shaking of the foundations among the populace at large. Life for many did not contain the moral challenges that might capture their loyalties, and altogether there was loss of disciplined commitment, whether in private or public behavior. So the period of Warren G. Harding's presidency, beginning in 1921, has been identified as a "return to normalcy," that is, a journey back into a general mood of moral complacency, and it was followed by more of the same during the Calvin Coolidge succession. The apathy of the time to moral concern was expressed in Mencken's observation that "doing good" was "in bad taste."

This general cultural malaise also affected the churches. The economic depression began in 1929, but historian Robert Handy has shown that the spiritual depression within the American Protestant churches began as early as 1925. Although church membership continued slowly to increase throughout the decade, that affiliation had decreasing significance for many, as convention replaced commitment. Churches struggled with the problem of declining attendance, and many congregations discontinued their traditional Sunday evening services due to lack of interest. Although money was still plentifully available for church use, it was often contributed more for elaborate building programs than for ongoing support of the church's activities. By mid-decade a serious decline in missionary giving developed, reflecting a growing apathy toward both foreign and domestic missions on the part of local churches. The problem was magnified by a growing shortage of college youth willing to commit themselves to a missionary vocation. In these and other statistical evidences of a loss of vitality in the churches Congregationalism fully shared. A report to the National Council of Congregational Churches indicates that from 1921 through 1929 the number of its churches declined from 5,873 to 5,419; net annual additions to membership from 19,046 to 1,672; annual per capita giving for local church expenses from $25.67 to $22.87; and for missionary benevolences from $6.54 to $4.36. The report, moreover, added the explicit judgment that the Congregational churches were "in an ebb-tide" of numerical growth and "of popular adherence to religious practices."[1]

Still further, the "spiritual depression" in the churches was evidenced by their increasing accommodation to the values and conventions of secular society. Particularly infectious were the manners of big business, its methods of achievement and its standards of success. Entrapped by a numbers psychology in which larger is better, many churches concentrated on new and improved ways to "merchandise" their religion. Techniques of commercial salesmanship were employed, and congregations looked for results in terms of business criteria. One of the most popular religious books of the decade, *The Man Nobody Knows*, was written by an advertising executive, Bruce Barton, and portrayed Jesus of Nazareth as a leader of executive ability and an early founder of successful advertising and management ways. A further aspect of this emphasis was a continuation of the late nineteenth-century tendency to see wealth as God's gift to the deserving. Before his death in 1925 Russell H. Conwell preached his famous "Acres of Diamonds" sermon six thousand times, bringing to millions of hearers his depiction of religion as the way to prosperity.

Then in October 1929 the stock market crashed, shattering the American economy. During the next three years the national income dropped by more than 50 percent and unemployment skyrocketed to a level previously unknown. Former workers sold apples on the streets, stood with their families in bread lines, and joined the homeless to sleep in parks, subways, and improvised shelters. All levels of society were affected, and the churches suffered severely. Their decline, begun in the 1920s, continued into the 1930s. Memberships fell, budgets were even more severely curtailed, missionary giving almost disappeared, ministers were dismissed and churches were closed for lack of financial support. Again Congregationalism fully shared in this depression of the churches. The General Council of Congregational and Christian Churches (successor after 1931 to the National Council of Congregational Churches) postponed for a year its scheduled meeting for 1933, announced a series of economies at its gathering in 1934, and prefaced its meeting of 1936 with a special crisis announcement sent to all delegates warning of the dangers of the continued decline. The statistical report at that meeting indicated that though the number of churches had increased due to a 1931 merger with the Christian Convention, the net annual change of membership for 1934 was a loss of 7,569, and per capita annual giving had declined for local church expenses to $14.91 and for missionary benevolences to $1.98. In the crisis announcement the delegates were told that "something more is needed to revive churchgoing than Loyalty Campaigns and Church Advertising." "The foundation of our Congregational structure," it added, "is crumbling"—so "more attention must be given to our FOUNDATIONS."[2]

By the mid-1930s, however, both the economic and the ecclesiastical situations were changing. With the presidential election of Franklin Delano Roosevelt, the program of the New Deal was initiated in 1933, and although this failed to accomplish immediately all that was desired, the American economy began to pull out of its depression. Equally the churches by late in the decade were experiencing their own stirring of rejuvenation that, apart from renewed growth, took two significant forms.

One was the resurgence of theological concern and particularly the effort to find a theological corrective for the extreme evolutionary optimism, with its doctrine of inevitable progress, inherited from the early 1900s. The tragedies of world war and national depression had shattered that dream, and now something more realistic was needed. Contending for consideration initially was a newly born European "theology of crisis," which looked to Karl Barth in Germany as its founder and was introduced by the 1930s to the American scene. For many, however, this represented an extreme near the other end of the theological spectrum, offering a strong Calvinist emphasis upon human sin and divine sovereignty. Thus the theological effort of the 1930s and early 1940s for much of Congregationalism sought a more middle way, a liberalism chastened but not denied. In 1940 the General Council appointed the Theological Commission to work on this task, "with a view to restating the Congregational faith in the light of present issues and interpretations."[3]

The second expression of new vitality in the churches of the mid-1930s was in a resurgence of interest in the social gospel. In actual fact, as Robert Moats Miller has pointed out, the social gospel was never entirely abandoned, for "even in the Roaring Twenties the churches continued to interest themselves in social matters."[4] But in the time of the churches' "spiritual depression" the social gospel's message had been muted, and now it emerged again in fuller voice. Symbolizing as well as energizing this new boldness was a volume published in 1935 by H. Richard Niebuhr, Wilhelm Pauck, and Francis P. Miller, titled *The Church Against the World*. Its pungent criticism, stated by Niebuhr, deplored the trend of recent years by holding that "the church has adjusted itself too much rather than too little to the world in which it lives. It has identified itself too intimately with capitalism, with the philosophy of individualism, and with the imperialism of the West." But, Niebuhr added, it must now turn away from this secular worldliness, moving "toward its eternal relations and so become fit again for its work in time."[5]

Actually, by 1934 the General Council of Congregational and Christian Churches had moved in the direction of implementing that renewed prophetic concern by establishing its Council for Social Action. Then, in the years immediately following, further steps were taken to deal with matters related to labor, race, militarism, and other social issues. Such new activity, however, was not unopposed. Among many Congregationalists, both clergy and laity, a social conservatism prevailed. A 1936 poll showed 70 percent of Congregational clergy opposed to the New Deal and 78 percent of Congregational voters having cast presidential ballots for Roosevelt's Republican opponent, Alf Landon. So as early as 1935 James W. Fifield, a Congregational pastor, organized Spiritual Mobilization, a movement critical of many of the denomination's social action efforts, and the tensions, destined to be long lasting concerning matters of social witness, began more fully to appear. Soon, however, all came under the larger domination of the threat of new global conflict, and the churches, viewing Hitler's conquests in Europe, were faced once again with the question of whether to go to war.

Church Union in the Twenties

Despite the "spiritual depression" of these years of disillusionment Congregationalism continued in the 1920s to pursue its ecumenical interests and to strive for larger unity within Protestantism. In 1919 the National Council joined wholeheartedly in an ambitious exploratory effort bringing twenty-three (later reduced to eighteen) Protestant denominations together under the broad designation American Council on Organic Union of the Churches of Christ. Representatives of the participating groups drew up the Plan of Union for the cooperative bonding of their churches, and this proposal was referred to the separate national bodies. In actuality, the plan did not envisage complete organic union, despite the name under which it was created, but it did foresee a structure more integrated than the simple federation that already existed in the Federal Council of Churches. When presented to the National Council of Congregational Churches in 1921, the plan was approved in substance and recommended to the local churches for their action through district and state meetings. By 1923 it was reported to the National Council that forty-four out of fifty-one state conferences approved and that, although many district associations had not yet voted, 138 had registered their approval against seven that had disapproved. The National Council then voted to send its endorsement to the other participating denominations. Subsequently, however, the whole cause was lost, as most of the other national organizations either declined or deferred, and at the National Council's meeting of 1925 the matter was simply dropped from its agenda.

The National Council meeting of 1925 did produce a church union, however, and though not of the magnitude the multidenominational effort had projected, it brought a warmly welcomed group of German Evangelical Protestants into American Congregationalism. The German Evangelical Protestant Church of the mid-1920s was composed of twenty-seven congregations of the descendants of German immigrants, located chiefly in Pennsylvania and Ohio. Their American history went back to 1782 when their first congregation, the Smithfield Church, was gathered in Pittsburgh. The larger immigration leading to other like-minded congregations did not occur, however, until the nineteenth century, and the denomination itself was formed as a distinctive American body in 1885.

Coming out of the German Lutheran and the German Reformed traditions, and out of their combined migrations to the American Midwest, these immigrants could not find a satisfactory church home with either of their parent bodies. Curtis Beach, recent pastor of the Smithfield Church, has pointed to three characteristics of these immigrant churches separating them from their heritage. First and foremost was their emphasis on freedom of thought. Although they deemed the teachings of Scripture to be normative, these churches had no creed and, wrote Beach, "they allowed members to fashion faith for themselves, based on their own thinking and experience."[6] Second, these churches insisted upon the autonomy of each local congregation, even delaying lengthily their own denominational development. And third, although respecting the special responsibilities of the clergy, these congregations stressed the role of the laity in the governance and decision making of the local church. In all of these areas, it became clear, there was much similarity with the corresponding emphases of Congregationalism.

Thus in 1922, under the leadership of Carl August Voss, then pastor of the Smithfield Church, the German Evangelical Protestants initiated merger negotiations with the National Council. By 1925 preparations were completed, and at the council meeting of that year the union was voted, designating the German Evangelical Protestant Church a separate conference in the Congregational structure, "on a parity with Congregational State Conferences [and] with representation in the Council accordingly."[7] For several years this arrangement as a separate conference prevailed, with its churches divided into two associations, one clustered around Pittsburgh and the other around Cincinnati. In 1935, however, the former became part of the Congregational Conference of Pennsylvania, and in 1947 the latter entered the Congregational Christian Conference of Ohio. These actions fully absorbed the German Evangelical Protestant Church into the now-enlarged life of the Congregational Christian churches.

The Congregational and Christian Merger (1931)

The Congregational union with the General Convention of the Christian Church was consummated on the national level in 1931, the result of a second effort after the unsuccessful attempt in 1895 had long passed into memory. Three late eighteenth- and early nineteenth-century movements lay behind the origin of this Christian church. Its earliest component came from Virginia in the 1790s where a group of dissident Methodists left their church under the leadership of James O'Kelly. An ardent patriot in the American Revolution and a Methodist lay preacher (though later ordained), O'Kelly was committed to democracy in the church and for two decades struggled against Methodism's American leader, Francis Asbury, who not only took for himself the title "bishop" but exercised the church's functions in an autocratic way. Finally in 1792 O'Kelly and thirty others withdrew and two years later founded their own communion. The basic motivation was an issue of polity, the question of bishops and their power, but there was also more involved. In their resistance to oppressive authority the dissidents rejected the use of creeds and turned exclusively to the Bible as the sufficient rule of faith and practice. Moreover, as the Bible revealed early followers of Jesus to have been known as Christians, the dissidents determined that to be their name as well. Further, each church was to be a simple community of disciples, unburdened by human restrictions in a freely expressed loyalty to Christ. Thousands responded to the plain-speaking evangelism and democratic spirit of O'Kelly and of the other clergy who joined him in this ministry, and the movement spread southward through Virginia into North Carolina and westward to Kentucky and Ohio. O'Kelly was also an able writer, but upon his death his widow burned many of his manuscripts, fearing that they, as human writings, would have undue effect upon these churches seeking only the biblical way.

A second strand entering this Christian church came from New England Baptists, whose early clergy leaders were Abner Jones in Vermont and Elias Smith in New Hampshire. Like O'Kelly these men desired biblical simplicity for the church, including the abandonment of creeds and the adoption of the name Christian. In Calvinist New England, however, they also felt more explicitly compelled to deny what they considered oppressive doctrines from their theological heritage, such as the Trinity, substitutionary atonement, predestination, and everlasting punishment. For some years Smith sympathized with Universalism, although he rejected that name along with all other sectarian designations. Both men insisted, moreover, that Christian character should be the sole criterion for church membership. In 1801 Jones, moved by his biblical study, left a fledgling medical career and gathered a dozen residents of Lyndon, Vermont, into a church in which each was to have freedom to interpret the Scripture in his or her own way. The following year Jones was ordained by three Free Will Baptist pastors, though with the prior understanding that he was not to be called a Baptist but simply a Christian, the name by which he likewise identified his congregation. In 1803 Smith, up to that time a Baptist preacher, founded a similar church in Portsmouth, New Hampshire, and shortly thereafter joined Jones in evangelistic work that spread the new movement throughout New England, where it became known as "the Christian Connexion." Pursuing the goal of unity, Smith traveled to Virginia, establishing contact with the Christian movement there. Altogether, however, the New England group experienced hostility in the early years, for their emphasis upon "gospel-liberty" erased much of the classic distinction between clergy and laity and gave heavy precedence to individual conscience over established ecclesiastical authority. Ironically, Congregationalism's merger partner in later years suffered in its New England beginnings at the hands of Congregationalism's Standing Order.

The third stream flowing into the development of this Christian church came from Presbyterians in Kentucky, particularly through the leadership of Barton W. Stone. These persons had been deeply affected in their personal religious experience by a mighty interdenominational revival at Cane Ridge, Kentucky, in 1801, but they also became convinced that sectarian quarreling over the harvest of converts was an utter violation of the Christian unity that should prevail. Moreover, when Presbyterian authorities began to press heresy charges against some of their clergy for having engaged in preaching not fully in accord with strict Calvinism during the revival, the dissidents decided to find a way of greater liberty. Led by Stone, who had given up much of the Calvinist theology, they first attempted to reorganize as a new Presbyterian body, the Springfield Presbytery. But fearing by 1804 that it, too, could be sectarian, they wrote its Last Will and Testament, declaring it dissolved to "sink into union with the Body of Christ at large."[8] Further influenced by one of James O'Kelly's earlier associates, they took the name Christian and committed themselves to living by the Bible alone as their rule of faith and practice. As a champion of the movement, Stone promoted it extensively in frontier settlements in Tennessee, Ohio, Indiana, Illinois, and Missouri, and ultimately this growing group of churches in the Midwest contributed the greatest numerical strength to the national uniting of the three branches into a single Christian church.

A unifying national consciousness developed for these like-minded groups in the early decades of the nineteenth century, initiated through the travels of their evangelists from one area to another. Contributing even more fully to this ripening, however, was Elias Smith's publication of a religious newspaper, the *Herald of Gospel Liberty*. Conveying consistently Smith's advocacy for religious liberty as a major characteristic of New Testament Christianity, this paper went into almost every state of the union and became a means for uniting and defining the Christian movement. By the 1820s national conferences were held, and gradually a more complete unification took place, largely accomplished by mid-century. It was not until 1922, however, that the final denominational name was adopted, the General Convention of the Christian Church.

Somewhat tangential to the General Convention was another group of Christian churches in the South, the African-American churches of the Afro-Christian Convention. Their history went back to the time of the Civil War, for upon emancipation many African Americans formed churches patterned after the white Christian churches organized by their former masters. Although their style of worship was different, drawing upon the musical gifts and emotive characteristics of their own distinctive life, these Afro-Christian churches paralleled closely in theology and structure the white Christian movement. Particularly indicative of this relationship was their acceptance of the Five Cardinal Principles of the Christian Church: Jesus Christ as the church's only head, *Christian* as a sufficient name for the church, the Bible as a sufficient rule for faith and practice, Christian character as a sufficient test for church membership, and the right of private judgment in matters of Christian belief. Subsequently the Colored Christian Conferences were formed in Virginia and North Carolina, and in 1892 these were joined into an Afro-Christian Convention. In the 1880s the Afro-Christian churches established their own school, Franklinton Literary and Theological Institute (later Franklinton Christian College), which served them until closed by the depression in 1930. By the time of the merger with Congregationalism the Afro-Christian Convention had membership in the General Convention of the Christian Church, but in actuality the relationship was distant, and the African-American churches carried on their life quite independently.

The union of the Congregational National Council and the Christian General Convention occurred in 1931. There were differences between the two denominations, the Christians representing a more rural and less affluent constituency and being accustomed to a more informal and evangelistic style of worship than generally found among Congregationalists. But there was much similarity in church polity, with emphasis on the local church's autonomy and also upon openness to freedom of conscience and rejection of binding creedal authority. Both groups, moreover, were strongly committed to church union. Conversations began in the mid-1920s, and two actions of the National Council in 1927 underscored the high degree of Congregational interest. One action was to drop reference to the Kansas City Statement in the negotiations, lest it appear as a creedal authority. The other was to indicate willingness to give up the name *Congregational*, returning to the historic designation *Churches of Christ*, if that would further church union. The change in name, however, was not made, and by 1931 the National Council and the General Convention had accepted, in both cases unanimously, a new constitution creating the General Council of the Con gregational and Christian Churches (later the "and" was dropped from the name). In succeeding years, where there was geographical duplication, the two denominations' state and district bodies, and in some cases local churches, united.

It remained, however, for the African-American congregations, both Congregational and Christian, to become more thoroughly integrated into the new denomination's life. Segregation, both racial and denominational, continued to take its toll, with African-American Christians clustered in their Afro-Christian Convention and southern African-American Congregationalists isolated in churches founded by the American Missionary Association. A significant step forward was taken in 1950 under the leadership of J. Taylor Stanley, when the denominational impasse was broken through the bringing of African-American Christian and African-American Congregational churches together into the Convention of the South. Now the two denominational backgrounds were merged and African-American Congregational Christians shared a common identity. Not until the founding of the United Church of Christ in 1957, however, was the racial impasse institutionally overcome. Racial inclusiveness was one of the requirements of the new denomination's constitution, adopted in 1961, and shortly thereafter the African-American Congregational Christian churches of the Convention of the South were merged into the appropriate state conferences of the United Church of Christ.

The Council for Social Action (1934)

At its meeting in 1925 the National Council of Congregational Churches adopted the Statement of Social Ideals proposed by its Commission on Social Service. The statement spoke about the necessity of "making the social and spiritual ideals of Jesus our test for . . . the development of a new and better world social order."[9] And then it specified in considerable detail what this could mean when translated into the field of education, into industrial and economic practices, into the occupation of agriculture, into racial relationships, and into international affairs. By such means the social gospel remained alive in Congregationalism throughout the 1920s, leading in the next decade to the establishment of the denomination's Council for Social Action (CSA). When the General Council of Congregational and Christian Churches in

1934 created this special church funded agency for encouraging the church's social witness, it took a bold step in further identifying the denomination's priorities. Frederick L. Fagley, assistant secretary of the General Council, wrote later of the event, "All realized that the Council was making history. Not since 1810, when the Massachusetts Association of Ministers voted to approve the organization . . . which was to become the American Board of Commissioners for Foreign Missions, had the churches been asked to give official sanction to . . . a denominational agency of such importance."[10] Like other mission commitments, Gladden's "applied Christianity" was now given major emphasis within Congregationalism.

The prescribed task of the Council for Social Action was threefold. First, it was to conduct research into the social problems of the day, gathering material relevant to making specific moral judgments. Second, its work was to be educational, directed particularly at informing local churches concerning the matters it had studied, though envisaging likewise, said its mandate, "the cultivation of public opinion." And third, the authorization declared that "the Council may on occasion intercede directly in specific situations."[11] Primary emphasis in the council's practice was placed upon the first two of these directives. It developed a monthly magazine, *Social Action*, which won high praise for the quality of its presentation of social issues from the perspective of sensitive Christian understanding. It sponsored conferences and institutes helpful to individual Christians and local churches in finding their way through conflicting social views. From the outset it selected four general areas in which it would primarily focus its work: (1) international relations, with "the moral imperative of doing what we can to create a peaceful world"; (2) industrial relations, including "the issues of unionism, civil liberties, standards of living, and the protection of the unemployed"; (3) country life, with its "issues of the farmer's economic and social status"; and (4) race relations, "with its economic and social implications."[12] As it carried out its research and made its recommendations, noted Robert Moats Miller, the Council for Social Action held to a general political position that was "New Deal liberal," but not "radical." Moreover, said Miller, at least in its early years the council was "the sanest, least biased, and certainly least doctrinaire of almost all the church [that is, the several denominations'] social agencies."[13]

Despite this moderation and despite the fact that its establishment in 1934 was by an almost unanimous vote of the General Council, the CSA soon encountered vigorous criticism and even hostile opposition. Some of this resulted from the generally more conservative outlook of Congregational churches, but an added and major cause lay in another action of the 1934 General Council, when a more extreme group within the council managed to pass an "anti-profit-motive" resolution. The resolution was adopted at a late-night session after three-quarters of the delegates had left the council meeting, and it soon became the storm center of much controversy. Prepared by persons critical of capitalism and sympathetic to the development of a democratically planned social-ist economy, the statement described profit-seeking as exploitative and creative of industrial strife. It pledged working for the abolition of profit incentives and urged striving for a cooperative economy in which private ownership of the means of production would be modified for the sake of social good. Although the resolution had no connection with the establishment or constitution of the Council for Social Action, reaction in the churches tended to associate the two, and quickly the CSA itself came under fire for presumably being allied with this more extreme point of view. During the following biennium, therefore, the Executive Committee of the General Council found it necessary to affirm its faith that "the Council for Social Action will proceed with wisdom, vision and courage to perform the important function for which it was cre-ated."[14] And the next session of the General Council, meeting in 1936, voted its further endorsement of the Council for Social Action as an agency valuable for the denomination at large in studying matters pertaining to economic life.

Although controversy over the anti-profit-motive resolution then subsided, it broke out again in the late 1940s and early 1950s—and with it, once more, controversy over the Council for Social Action. The conservative opposition, which had arisen in the 1935 founding of Spiritual Mobilization, became increasingly active following the Second World War, and by early 1952, through its Committee Opposing Congregational Political Action, had laid several charges against the CSA in a booklet titled *They're Using Our Church*. In this publication the establishment of the social action agency was again linked with the 1934 criticism of capitalism, and the organization itself was portrayed as continuing radical economic tendencies through support of compulsory health insurance, a full-employment bill, and peacetime price controls and rationing, all of which were viewed in the booklet as forms of socialization of the national economy. Moreover, in this time of developing McCarthyism, the CSA was charged with being sympathetic to international communism as developed in the Soviet Union and China, and some of its staff were alleged to be involved in American "communist fronts." Still further, the CSA was criticized for misuse of political lobbying methods through its Washington office. Rather than simply speak for itself in the effort to influence legislators, so the charge ran, the CSA often gave the impression that it spoke representatively for all Congregationalists and their churches. Pressing these criticisms, the booklet then urged delegates to the 1952 General Council to be prepared to stop this "using our church . . . to play politics."[15]

The 1952 General Council responded with several actions. For one thing, it dealt with the 1934 resolution and its socialist inclination by noting that it "was passed in a time of unusual economic stress," and did not represent the view of the present body. Rather, the council said, its own conviction was that "no economic system embodies the perfect will of God," and each "must be evaluated . . . in the light of the Christian Gospel," as the teachings of Christ are "brought to bear upon the corporate problems of our society."[16] Further, a strong endorsement was voted for the Council for Social Action's work, although a program of associates was established, giving 250 elected persons an advisory voice on social action matters. Finally it was agreed that a board of review should examine the CSA mandate and performance in greater detail. The examination was completed by the General Council meeting of 1954. Although the CSA was then urged to be more self-consciously representative of the entire denomination's views in public statements, the overall result was a reaffirmation of the Council for Social Action's important role in the life of the Congregational churches.

War and the Forties

The early decades of the twentieth century provided occasion for anguished struggle within American Protestantism concerning war and its endorsement. The 1920s began with a growing sense of guilt on the part of many church leaders for the uncritical support they had given to the First World War. They had made it into a glorious crusade, and subsequently some of its misguided justification as well as horrible cost became plain. Thus there was a sizable about-face, and many stepped forward in the 1920s, and on into the 1930s, to lead in a newly born peace movement. Although aspects of the social gospel suffered decline in the moral hesitancy of the 1920s, a condemnation of militarism and war was sustained. The Federal Council of Churches led the way in 1921 with a conference in Washington that lobbied for disarmament. Then, influenced by prominent preachers such as Harry Emerson Fosdick, Ernest Fremont Tittle, and Ralph W. Sockman, an increasing number of clergy declared themselves to be Christian pacifists. In a 1931 poll responded to by 19,372 Protestant ministers, 12,076, or 62 percent, expressed themselves as unwilling to support any future war. The Fellowship of Reconciliation, committed to a pacifist program, flourished throughout those years, finding support particularly in seminaries and among younger clergy. But antiwar feeling, whether pacifist or nonpacifist, was expressed most widely in resolutions of the national bodies of many Protestant denominations, as the churches of the land mustered their strength and influence for the cause of permanent peace.

The National Council of Congregational Churches took its first step in that direction in 1921, passing a resolution requesting the United States government to call an international conference for the purpose of moving toward world disarmament. Thereafter, at each biennial meeting preceding the Second World War some action was taken, first by the National Council and then by the General Council, allying the denomination with the broadly ecumenical voice for the promotion of peace. Throughout the 1920s and into the mid-1930s the council voted persistently to urge governmental authorization for the United States to join the League of Nations and the World Court. In 1927 the Council opposed compulsory military training in tax-supported public schools and colleges. In 1929 it urged U.S. ratification of an international convention regulating the sale and exporting of arms. In 1931, in light of the signing of the Pact of Paris, it asked local churches and ministers to support this international agreement in order that the U.S. government might "lead the way by drastic reduction in every kind of armament on land, and sea and in the air." In 1934 these peace efforts attained their strongest expression when the General Council adopted the categorical declaration, "The Church is through with war!" and called upon "the people of our churches to renounce war and all its works and ways and to refuse to support, sanction or bless it."[17] The council in 1934 also requested the CSA to provide guidance in policies and programs for ministers and churches willing to take this stand. A peace plebiscite conducted among Congregationalists by the CSA in the following biennium showed that only 6 percent of the respondents would fight in any war declared by the United States. On the other hand, 15 percent were pacifist, and 33 percent would fight only in a war in which U.S. territory had been invaded.

By the late 1930s, however, events led many to a modification of their antiwar convictions. The rise of Hitler and Mussolini in Europe, their support of the Fascists in the Civil War in Spain, the expansionist design of Germany in acquiring Austria and the Sudentenland of Czechoslovakia, the violent anti-Semitism of Hitler's policy, and finally the 1939 German invasion of Poland leading to all-out European war posed anew the question that had been faced in 1917: should the forces presumably destroying civilization and its freedoms, even though far across the sea, be resisted by American military means? As early as 1937 President Franklin Delano Roosevelt called for economic support of the European Allies and asserted that the United States could not keep out of war if it were to come, for the attack would ultimately reach even the Western Hemisphere. In succeeding years, as the tensions mounted and the hostilities in Europe began, he managed the supplying of military aid. As a consequence, the nation was drawn into an extended debate between those committed to a policy of "collective security" increasingly openly supported by the government and an "isolationism" resistant to all international commitments that might lead the nation into the war.

Meanwhile a change was taking place within much of Protestant thinking concerning the ethical issues related to war and peace. Reinhold Niebuhr, an Evangelical and Reformed pastor in Detroit and later a professor at New York's Union Theological Seminary, was the catalyst. Initially in his *Moral Man and Immoral Society*, published in 1932, and then in a torrent of subsequent writings, Niebuhr found the principles of pacifism inapplicable to the struggles between societies. He had been a pacifist in earlier years as a member of the Fellowship of Reconciliation, but now concluded that although Christ's mandates against violence apply to interpersonal relations, no such absolute good is possible within the social order where all values are relative. Within societal relations there is no place for perfectionism, and moral choices must be made between relative evils. On the basis of this "realism" Niebuhr went on to examine the various elements in the international struggle and concluded that the immense evil of Hitler's nazism must be resisted, even by America, through the evil of war.

The political pressure for support of the European Allies against fascism and the growing influence of Niebuhr's assessment of the ethical issues pertinent to the struggle gave long pause to many earlier antiwar protagonists in American Protestant churches. Moreover, Japan was now an addition to the group of active international aggressors, and for Americans the threat to their ideals, and even to their homeland, was transpacific as well as transatlantic. As a consequence, many again struggled with the militarism issue. The pacifist viewpoint was most prominently expressed by Charles Clayton Morrison, editor of the widely read *Christian Century*. In response Reinhold Niebuhr and others founded *Christianity and Crisis*, a journal on ethical issues dedicated to a Niebuhrian view. And altogether Protestant clergy and laity were increasingly compelled to make their personal decisions in one direction or another on this matter. Disagreement within Congregationalism is seen in the fact that leadership in the Council for Social Action divided on the issue, with one portion resigning. Moreover, the General Council in 1940 passed a resolution on "Christian Attitudes in a Warring World," which recognized two contrasting attitudes affirmed by Christian persons. For some, it said, the fact that Christians are "citizens of a Kingdom not of this world" and are committed to test their methods "by the mind of Christ" means the elimination of all justification of the use of military force. For others, it added, there is the tragic dilemma of living in a sinful society and of recognizing the need for "constant compromise between coercive power and moral principles," leading to use of force on some occasions, even in the midst of detesting war. Clearly there was no unanimity identifying "a Christian position." At that same meeting, however, the General Council questioned aspects of the government's war preparation and urged that if there were to be conscription for military service, careful provision must be made "for just and considerate treatment of all conscientious objectors."[18]

On 7 December 1941 the Japanese attacked Pearl Harbor, and the decision for many between war resistance and war support was sealed. It was now time, so the vast majority felt, to rally to the government's call to fight the free world's aggressors. When war was declared not only against Japan but also against the other Axis powers, Protestant churches across America supported the national effort. Throughout the next four years they provided chaplains for military service, supplied Bibles and devotional literature for troops in the field, and extended moral support to the war cause in a variety of ways. Yet the mood of this church support was different from the unrestrained adoption of the war spirit that had characterized the churches' crusading during the First World War. There was now a sense of agony, and even penitence, in pursuing what the *Christian Century* came to call an "unnecessary necessity." Six months after the war's declaration the General Council of Congregational Christian Churches, in its 1942 meeting, described the catastrophe as "due to human blindness, apathy, and selfishness not only in other nations but also in our own." Then, after detailing some of the failures in international behavior leading to the war, it added, "These things are wrong. They are sins, calling for humility, confession, and repentance."[19]

During the war the General Council continued to recognize the two options Christians faced in making their individual decisions concerning war support. Both were presented as valid choices in 1942 and 1944. Moreover, throughout these years the council continued to express its concern about conscientious objectors and their fair treatment by the government. The Selective Service law allowed for conscientious objection on religious grounds, and those approved were assigned for alternative service to Civilian Public Service camps operated by the three "peace churches" (Mennonites, Quakers, and Church of the Brethren), but under government control. Among the internees throughout the war 210 were Congregationalists. Under the auspices of the General Council a Congregational Christian Committee for Conscientious Objectors was organized, chaired by Albert W. Palmer, president of Chicago Theological Seminary. Although the internees suffered considerable neglect from the churches as a whole, the committee's pastoral, as well as financial, efforts were of valuable aid. Since many of the objectors were not released until several months after the war ended, the General Council, as late as June 1946, was still pressing the U.S. government for more respectful treatment in such matters as significance of work assignments for the internees, adequacy of remuneration and dependency allotments for wives and children, and a "fair rate" of demobilization now that peace had come.

During these years Congregationalists also took up other causes concerned with relieving the war's suffering. In 1940 the General Council created the Committee for Assistance to War Victims, commissioned to cooperate with a similar agency of the Federal Council of Churches in response to foreign relief appeals from war-torn areas. Later renamed the Committee for War Victims and Reconstruction, it was composed of several representatives from each of thirty-eight state conferences, and throughout its several years of existence raised and distributed significant funds for refugee relief and the reconstruction of churches and church life in Europe and Asia. Subsequently the Congregational Christian Service Committee was created to coordinate the work of the ABCFM, the BHM (newly created for home missions), and the CSA in carrying further the work of relief and reconciliation. Out of this came a program for relocating wartime-displaced persons into American communities under church sponsorship. Much was accomplished, including one massive relocation of three thousand Russians whose migrations had taken them through China and the Philippines and finally as a group to California's San Francisco! One special regional concern emerged in the West, the plight of Japanese Americans who had been interned at the war's beginning. In 1942 the General Council deplored the manner by which this had been done, without inquiry into individuals' national loyalty, and condemned attempts at general disenfranchisement. In 1944 the council added its concern for restoration of constitutional rights and liberties to Japanese American citizens and urged Congregational churches and their members to create sentiment favorable to the ultimate reintegration of the evacuees.

Religious Revival and the Fifties

The first half of the twentieth century in America brought substantial differences in receptiveness toward religion. Skepticism and apathy followed closely upon the First World War, but the Second World War led to religious revival. For a decade and a half following the war's end in 1945 American religion was given public support and esteem to a degree hardly before known in the nation's history. The *Yearbook of American Churches* report for 1957 indicated that 61 percent of the American people were formally identified with some church. Even more revealing, the U.S. Census Bureau reported in the same year that when asked "What is your religion?" 96 percent of the respondents offered the name of a religious body. Not all were formal members, but almost all thought of themselves as possessing a specific religious identity. Two years earlier Will Herberg's *Protestant, Catholic, Jew* had appeared, advancing the view that the widely accepted "American way of life" was in reality the universal American religion, though under the rubrics of the "triple melting pot" found in the three historic religious traditions. In this sense a religious identification was part of being an American.

The religious revival of the late 1940s through the 1950s was more, however, than simply a matter of name identification. The churches prospered, as their memberships, attendance, financing, benevolences, and building programs all attained new heights. Nor was this renewal of religious interest limited to the so-called mainstream Protestant churches that had been the dominant force in American religious history up to the early twentieth century. Roman Catholicism and Judaism, as Herberg noted, had taken positions of prominence in American life by the 1950s. And within Protestantism itself new diversity developed. Pentecostal, spirit-filled groups came into being, while within the historic denominations theological divisions became more widespread.

For Protestant conservatives this fresh religious concern often took the form of a renewed revivalism in which appeal was also made to the mainstream. Outstanding among the revivalists of this period was Billy Graham, who was ordained by Southern Baptists in the late 1930s and whose tent meetings in Los Angeles in the late 1940s brought him into national prominence. In 1950 he developed the Billy Graham Evangelistic Association and throughout succeeding years was the major voice of fundamentalist Protestant evangelism. His popular revivalistic campaigns in major American cities attracted thousands to make their "commitments to Christ" and to promise to follow those commitments with participation in the programs of local churches. Many Congregationalists, however, questioned the theology and the results of these crusades. It was often noted that the major motive for conversion was an escaping from eternal punishment and that the effect of conversion was more a temporary emotional experience than a lasting transformation in life-style and behavior. For liberal Congregationalists these characteristics rendered the new revivalism suspect, and they were generally reluctant to take part. In the decades since the latter part of the nineteenth century Congregationalism, on the whole, had distanced itself considerably from its earlier revivalist ways.

Meanwhile, at the other end of the theological spectrum there was also renewed religious interest. Beginning in the tensions of the war years and continuing by virtue of its popular appeal, a movement developed portraying religious faith chiefly as a means of psychological healing for the anxieties and insecurities of modern life. In 1946 Joshua Liebman, a Jewish rabbi, published his *Peace of Mind*, which became a forerunner for similar volumes by other clergy of the major faiths. Liebman's book also provided a commonly accepted name for the cult of reassurance that followed. For Roman Catholics Monsignor Fulton J. Sheen contributed his *Peace of Soul* in 1949, and Protestant Norman Vincent Peale published his *Guide to Confident Living* in 1948 and his immensely popular *The Power of Positive Thinking* in 1952. Avoiding the "hard" elements of Jewish and Christian theology, such as sin, repentance, conversion, sacrifice, and commitment to social justice, the "peace of mind" movement looked to the utilitarian value of religious faith in comforting the troubled mind and providing confidence for the anxious soul. In Peale particularly a Pollyanna-like conviction prevailed that through firm faith and positive thought success in reaching one's goals could be achieved. In the 1950s millions of readers were attracted to this assurance, and it in fact represented a kind of a broad religiosity common to American culture during those years. Significantly, the generalized spirituality of President Eisenhower contributed to this, stressing the importance of "faith in faith" for personal and national well-being. Congregationalism therefore faced this type of "religious renewal" as well, and without question absorbed it to some degree in its expanding ministry. Although many within the Congregational churches resisted the reduction of the Christian gospel to a peace-of-mind psychology, Congregationalism's growth in the 1950s, especially in the fast developing communities of suburbia, undoubtedly was helped by this larger national phenomenon.

Congregationalism's prosperity in the upsurge of religious interest in the midcentury is reflected in its yearbook reports of the denominational statistics. Steady growth marked this progress over those years. From 1945 through 1957 total membership in Congregational Christian churches increased from 1,130,824 to 1,392,632, with new members added at a rate of more than 100,000 a year in the latter portion of that period. Similarly, church school membership increased in those years from 494,129 to 800,683. The latter figure represents the steady addition of young families to church life during the baby boom following the war. Church membership statistics, however, also show an increase in removals over the years, particularly by transfer of letter and revision of the rolls, indicative of the new mobility of population that the postwar era brought. Although changes in dollar figures must be interpreted in the light of inflation, the increase there was notable. Again in the twelve-year period leading to 1957 total benevolence giving grew from $3,951,495 to $9,600,849, and giving for local church expenses increased from $19,301,121 to $52,708,714. In addition $27,934,406 was given in 1957 for building construction, reflecting the new church-building boom then under way. Although these figures do not represent a spectacular expansion, they do show a constant denominational strengthening leading to the moment of entrance into the United Church of Christ. Yet that progress must be kept in perspective. In 1956 Howard E. Spragg, an executive of the Board of Home Missions, noted this "curious paradox," that "the strengthening of religious forces is paralleled by an increasing secularization of our common life"—to which he added the judgment that "the current revival of religion [therefore] represents something less than the fullness of our tradition, for we inherit the Puritan dreams of a Holy Commonwealth and the frontier dreams of a New Jerusalem, the conviction that all of life and culture is under the claim of the Gospel."[20]

Congregationalism and World Ecumenism

The broad vision of the American Congregational tradition also reached out in the twentieth century to ecumenical relations across the seas. Particularly in two developing international organizations American Congregationalists found fruitful contact and a responsible place. The first was the International Congregational Council (ICC), an organization drawing together the Congregational unions and associations from many countries and mission fields around the world. Contacts between British and American Congregationalists in the latter half of the nineteenth century, when delegates and observers were exchanged for their national meetings, led to the founding of the ICC in London in

1891. Subsequent gatherings of worldwide representatives of Congregationalism were held in Boston (1899), Edinburgh (1908), Boston (1920), Bournemouth, England (1930), Wellesley, Massachusetts (1949), and St. Andrews, Scotland (1953). At the Wellesley meeting delegates representing Congregationalism in twenty-four countries were present, and a new constitution was adopted, giving more permanent structure to the organization. Douglas Horton, minister and secretary of the General Council of Congregational Christian Churches in the United States, was elected moderator of the International Congregational Council, and other Americans were chosen for membership on the Executive Committee. The ICC sought particularly to encourage acquaintance and goodwill among Congregationalists from all parts of the world as it considered their common concerns and experiences. However, a larger ecumenical context was provided by the fact that the council also included the United Churches into which Congregationalists had merged, such as those of Canada, South India, North India, and the Philippines.

The second international organization in which American Congregationalism assumed an important role was the World Council of Churches, founded in Amsterdam in 1948. The direct antecedents to the World Council were two movements of the 1920s and 1930s concerned with the need for greater cooperation among the world's Christian churches in different aspects of the ecumenical task. One was the Life and Work movement, committed to bringing churches together in practical ways to minister to human needs, despite vast differences on theological, sacramental, and polity matters. Its theory was that doctrine divides but service unites. Two international conferences were held to pursue this goal, one at Stockholm in 1925 and the other at Oxford in 1937. The latter conference was of particular significance in its stress upon the Church as a God-given community transcending divisions of nation, race, and class, and providing visible evidence of what God means society as a whole to be. As a consequence, it declared its confidence in growing Christian unity. Meanwhile, a second movement, Faith and Order, was under way, committed to facing up to the divisive matters set aside by Life and Work. Again two conferences were held, one at Lausanne in 1927 and the other at Edinburgh in 1937. At the Lausanne conference a comprehensive theological statement was unanimously adopted by the 127 national and denominational churches represented—a remarkable achievement! But the story was different when it came to polity matters concerning the ministry and sacraments, for here serious disagreements surfaced and could not be overcome. Ten years later at Edinburgh the impasse remained. That conference ended by saying, "We humbly acknowledge that our divisions are contrary to the will of Christ, and we pray God in His mercy to shorten the days of our separation and to guide us by His Spirit to the fullness of unity."[21]

Thus it was that with continued desire for greater unity despite division, Faith and Order joined with Life and Work to bring about the World Council of Churches. The original plan looked for this international union to occur in 1941. The war, however, intervened, postponing the event for seven years. But the war experience added to the bonding then to come, for it led to the development of common ministries to war victims and to preparations for the World Council's postwar work of reconstruction of church life in devastated countries. Present at the Amsterdam meeting in 1948 were 351 delegates representing 147 denominational and national churches from 44 countries. As they formed themselves into the World Council of Churches, they affirmed their underlying unity by saying, "We are divided from one another, but Christ has made us His own and He is not divided." Despite diversity, they would be together and, they added, "We intend to stay together."[22] The World Council was not, however, to be a "super-church" with authority over its participating churches, for its members retained full independence. Yet its cooperative activity was significant.

The Commission on Faith and Order was established in the World Council to continue exploring the differences, largely concerning polity and sacraments, that kept the churches divided. A world conference was held in Lund, Sweden in 1952 to deal with those matters, but there was no significant breakthrough. Beyond this continuing inquiry, however, additional steps in cooperative action were taken throughout the 1950s. The Department of Interchurch Aid and Service to Refugees was established to coordinate the work of the member churches in this area. The Commission of the Churches on International Affairs was developed to seek a common mind on world issues and to bring Christian influence to bear on international problems. The Commission on the Life and Work of Women in the Church was organized to conduct studies and to promote action concerning the advance of women in church life. The Ecumenical Institute was created to help Christian laypersons face the problems of a Christian life in a secular environment, and the Secretariat for Evangelism was organized to promote exchange of experiences and to discover new methods of evangelism for the modern day. These and other activities gave to the World Council a position of strength and influence within many of the Protestant and Eastern Orthodox communities of Christendom.

American Congregationalism heartily supported and participated in this international ecumenical venture. When the two preliminary conferences were held in 1937 at Oxford and Edinburgh, American representatives of the General Council of Congregational Christian Churches participated in their joys, their sorrows, and their ultimate hopes. In a sermon at the General Council meeting of 1938 the council preacher, Oscar E. Maurer, referred to the experiences the Congregational Christian delegates had recounted. They had been, he said, on a Mount of Transfiguration where they had seen a mystic vision. It was a vision of the holy catholic church, the one and universal communion of the saints: "The Holy Ghost opened their minds and they saw." However, they also saw "the jagged mountain peaks of difference, some doctrinal, some temperamental, some governmental." Yet the vision predominated and, coming down from the mount, he concluded, these delegates became ecumenism's evangelists, returned from world conferences filled with "flaming zeal."[23] That zeal continued into the formation of the World Council and the development of its program. Representatives of the Congregational Christian Churches of the United States took part at all levels and accepted posts of responsibility. The General Council heard biennial reports from executives of the World Council to keep abreast of its activities and provided continued financial support. In practical matters the Congregational Christian Service Committee worked with the World Council in programs promoting international friendship and postwar relief. In theological study Congregational Christians contributed scholarly help as Oberlin College in 1957 hosted the Faith and Order Conference, where some three hundred delegates wrestled with the conference theme, "The Nature of the Unity We Seek." Also included in this conference were two unofficial Roman Catholic observers and consultants from three major conservative Protestant denominations normally not participants in ecumenical discussions. Congregationalism now shared fully in the frustrations, as well as in the hopes and successes, of a worldwide Christian ecumenism.

Merger with the Evangelical and Reformed Church (1957)

During these same years the General Council of Congregational Christian Churches proceeded through steps leading to the most consequential of its ecumenical accomplishments, merger in 1957 with the Evangelical and Reformed Church to form the United Church of Christ. The Evangelical and Reformed Church, itself the product of a church union in 1934, brought together two former German immigrant denominations of the eighteenth and nineteenth centuries.

The first to arrive in America were the German Reformed, who came in the early 1700s. They came from the upper Rhineland area known as the Palatinate, where under the sixteenth-century rule of a devout prince, Frederick the Pious, a distinctive Germanic form of the Calvinist tradition was developed. Its major document, the Heidelberg Catechism, was the work in 1563 of Zacharius Ursinus and Caspar Olevianus, whom Frederick in a time of bitter church conflict had charged with the task of quieting the "madness of theologians." The catechism was a statement of the church's teaching presenting Christianity not as a system of doctrine to be believed, but as a transforming awareness of God's love to be confessed. The personal and experiential emphasis in the writing was reflected in its first question, "What is your only comfort, in life and death?"—and then in the answer, "That I belong . . . not to myself, but to my faithful Savior, Jesus Christ, . . . [who] makes me wholeheartedly willing and ready from now on to live for him."[24] Used for the instruction of youth, for devotions in the family, and for worship in the church, the Heidelberg Catechism served as an instrument for religious education and the development of committed discipleship In addition the writers of the catechism produced two other documents defining the nature of this church. The Palatinate Liturgy prescribed a simplified form of worship in which altars were replaced by tables, baptismal fonts by zinc vessels, chalices by ordinary cups, and communion wafers by common bread. The Consistorial Order prescribed a presbyterial form of government for the church, functioning through a system of synods composed of lay and clergy members. For a century and a half the German Reformed practiced this faith throughout the Rhineland.

Invasion by the Roman Catholic French under Louis XIV in the early 1700s, however, brought this to an end. Persecution culminated in 1719 with an act forbidding the use of the Heidelberg Catechism, and out of this crisis came the migration of many German Reformed, first to England and then to America. Located mainly in Pennsylvania following 1720, the churches as independent and sometimes pastorless congregations relied initially upon the Dutch Reformed church for counsel and ordained ministry. Beginning in the 1740s, however, under the leadership of Michael Schlatter, a synodical structure for these churches gradually emerged, becoming in 1793 the fully independent German Reformed Church in the United States of America.

While the major concern of the German Reformed movement in the colonial years was its institutional form and growth, the following century brought a significant theological and liturgical development. This was the Mercersburg movement, led in the 1840s and 1850s by two faculty members of the denomination's theological seminary at Mercersburg, Pennsylvania (later moved to Lancaster). John Williamson Nevin, a theologian, and Philip Schaff, a historian, combined their teaching and writing to emphasize more strongly than before the catholic, as contrasted with the evangelical, elements in the Calvinist tradition. Strongly opposed to the individualism of the revivalist movement then dominant in America, they urged a central role for the historic church and its tradition for genuine revival and growth of the religious life. Through the church, in their judgment, the life of Christ was communicated to its members by means of the catechetical system and an altar-centered liturgy, both of which drew upon treasures of the past as channels of enrichment. The Lord's Supper was particularly significant in this regard, for it brought to the communicant the spiritual presence of Christ as food for the soul. As the German Reformed church grew in the nineteenth century, the Mercersburg movement developed a strong following, but it also met with strong opposition from the "Old Reformed." As a consequence, "high church" and "low church" tensions continued on into the twentieth century. Yet throughout, the German Reformed church was dominated by the confessionalism of the Heidelberg Catechism, which continued as the uniting bond.

The second strand in the Evangelical and Reformed church of the mid-twentieth century also came from Germany, but not until the early 1800s. Its people were the Evangelicals, who initially fled from Prussia in resistance to the government's creation in 1817 of the Church of the Prussian Union, an imposed merger between Lutherans and Reformed.

Their resistance, however, was not to the idea of union, but to the autocratic enforcement of it by the Prussian prince. These Evangelicals were strongly committed to church union, but on the basis of a pietism that stressed the common bonds of saving religious experience. In this they resisted not only governmental control but also the rationalism that had edged its way into a Lutheran scholasticism. That emphasis had led many Lutherans into excessively valuing "right doctrine" as necessary for the Christian life. But the pietist Evangelicals were intolerant of the niceties of such dogmatism and were satisfied with viewing the authoritative confessions of both the Lutheran and Reformed traditions as testimonies, rather than tests, of faith. Missionary enthusiasm was likewise a product of their pietism. In the 1820s the Evangelicals developed missionary societies in Germany and Switzerland that encouraged and facilitated their migrations to America.

Settling in the Midwest, these immigrants initially developed congregations independent of one another. Neither the Lutheran nor Reformed denomination appealed them, and basically they were skeptical of any church organization that might compromise congregational autonomy. Much emphasis was placed on the pastoral leadership within each local congregation, for "where the pastor is, there is the church." Assistance for the fledgling churches came, however, from the German and Swiss missionary societies, and also from such nondenominational frontier organizations as the American Bible Society, the American Tract Society, and the American Home Missionary Society. In 1841 the Evangelical churches in Missouri and Illinois organized a *Kirchenverein* (church union) for "fellowship and fraternal cooperation," although at first this was simply for lay and clergy individuals from the churches and not an organization of the churches themselves. Later the churches created a loosely uniting structure that ultimately became the Evangelical Synod of North America. As these churches developed their own ministry, they founded Elmhurst College in Illinois and Eden Theological Seminary in Missouri. Among the graduates of these institutions were Reinhold Niebuhr and H. Richard Niebuhr, the brothers whose theological contributions came to be of immense importance in twentieth-century American religious thought.

When the two Germanic traditions were joined in 1934 to constitute the Evangelical and Reformed church, members shared much in common and were willing to accommodate what differences remained.

So when the resulting denomination began conversations a few years later with the Congregational Christians, it brought a distinctive blend of characteristics into the deliberations. For one thing, the Evangelical and Reformed church spoke for a creedal and catechetical tradition. The creeds and confessions of its combined Calvinist and Lutheran heritage were highly valued, although not dogmatically prescribed. Further, it perpetuated a sacramental tradition, stressing the objectivity of the sacraments and their significance as genuine channels of divine grace. Again, it spoke for a constitutional tradition, in which lines of authority and orderly procedures in church government were clearly prescribed. Its own form of government was presbyterial, employing the principle of representative authority at all levels, from the local to the national. However, in many of its practices it encouraged large freedom for the local church. Still further, the Evangelical and Reformed church perpetuated a "high" sense of the role of the ministry in the local church. It carried on the German tradition of the "Herr Pastor" who was the voice of authority and guardian of discipline but also the caring shepherd of the flock and intermediary for sacramental grace. Yet again, it held true to its pietism and concern for dedicated discipleship, a matter evidenced particularly in its immense program of health and welfare agencies, orphanages, hospitals, and homes for the aged. But as much as all else, it perpetuated for the mid-twentieth century its long-standing commitment to church union. So when representative Congregational Christians began formal conversations with Evangelical and Reformed delegates in 1940 concerning possible merger, two denominations with strong ecumenical histories and aspirations entered into what was to be a long, but ultimately fruitful, journey. However, it was also a divisive time.

The length of the journey from 1940 to 1957, as well as its divisiveness, was due to the complexity of uniting two different polities, congregational and presbyterial, and more specifically to the intense opposition encountered from some Congregational Christian leaders who felt that crucial Congregational principles were being jeopardized in the process. As an early consequence, the instrument created in 1943 to define the merger, called Basis of Union, was subjected over a five-year period to ten rewritings, including the addition of a series of eight Interpretations, prior to its initial approval by the General Council of Congregational Christian Churches for submission to the churches in

1948 and its initial endorsement by the Evangelical and Reformed General Synod in 1949.

Throughout that period Congregational critics expressed several reservations concerning the contemplated union. Most pervasive was the fear that the merger would result in a "authoritarian church" in that local autonomy would be lost to higher judicatories exercising control over a congregation's property rights, choice of minister, and even declaration of faith. Related to this was the further question as to whether the General Council had the legal right to participate in the creation of a union which presumably would define a new arrangement for autonomous local Congregational churches and their cooperative bodies. Still further, this questioning focused on the proposal of a constitution for the new denomination, seeing added danger there of a constricting of historic freedoms. Likewise the questioning turned to the proposed union of the several Congregational Christian mission boards and agencies with their corresponding partners in the Evangelical and Reformed church, charging that such merging would lead to violation of historic fiduciary obligations through placing Congregationally committed funds under "alien" control. By 1947 this opposition had grown to the point of its calling a convention in Evanston, Illinois, and its organizing the Committee for the Continuation of Congregational Churches.

Proponents of the merger answered opponents' fears of loss of local church autonomy by pointing to statements in the Basis of Union affirming autonomy's guarantee. Further, in the added Interpretations they made clear their conviction that the General Council acts only for itself, and not for all the churches, in entering into merger, and that although a constitution will "define and regulate" the role of the new General Synod, it will only "describe" the "free and voluntary relationships" into which the local churches, as well as associations and conferences, enter.[25] Proponents also denied the charges made against the mergers of the boards by affirming the latter's independence in administering their funds. Believing, in its efforts, therefore, the General Council submitted the question of merger to the local Congregational churches for their endorsement. Although it publicly hoped for a 75 percent positive return from the voting churches, the result by the next year showed 72.8 percent support. Accepting this as sufficient approval, the council voted in 1949, by a count of 757 to 172, to move toward union. Shortly thereafter, supported by thirty-three out of its thirty-four regional synods, the General Synod of the Evangelical and Reformed Church, by a count of 249 to 41, voted likewise to move ahead. Presumably the merger would soon be consummated.

On 18 April 1949, however, the Cadman Memorial Church, Brooklyn, New York, filed suit against Helen Kenyon, moderator of the General Council of Congregational Christian Churches, to prevent the union. To the familiar charges of violations of Congregational polity the suit added the allegation that the General Council had acted with insufficient support from the local Congregational churches. Four years of legal contest now began. In 1950 a lower court in New York rendered judgment favoring the Cadman Church and also enjoined the General Council from any actions further pursuing the union. However, at the urging of a moderate contingent among dissenters the General Council did bring together opponents and proponents of the union in the joint Committee on Free Church Polity and Unity. Its task was to study Congregational polity in its historic documents and as currently practiced in order to seek a way of resolution. But a reconciling conclusion never materialized, although the committee submitted a lengthy report in 1954. Meanwhile, the General Council appealed the Cadman decision, leading to a reversal in 1952. The Cadman Church then appealed the reversal, and finally on 3 December 1953, in the third court decision on this matter, the New York Court of Appeals upheld the position favoring the General Council and dismissed the Cadman case. The way was now legally open to complete the union.

The long delay, however, had created new difficulties. The patience of many in the Evangelical and Reformed church had been put to test. Moreover, it seemed to some among them that over the years the General Council's efforts to accommodate its internal opposition had led it to a more explicit emphasis on key Congregational principles for the union than was originally intended. Yet the Evangelical and Reformed commitments to union were strong, and by mid-1954 negotiations were renewed. But with the restoration of discussions, resistance to the union was itself renewed by dissenters among the Congregational Christians. Some opponents favored ultimate union, but sought further changes in the plans. Others, more extreme in opposition, took added steps in 1955 to maintain the continuity of their conception of the Congregational way. Calling together delegates from dissenting churches for a founding meeting in Detroit, they brought into preliminary form the National Association of Congregational Christian Churches (NACCC), composed of those congregations that would choose it in preference to the United Church of Christ. In 1961, after the final break with the UCC had been made, the NACCC completed its organization into a full-fledged denomination, although it interpreted that status as being simply a continuation of the long stream of historic American Congregationalism. Approximately 5 percent of the Congregational Christian churches in the United States then joined the NACCC. Headquarters were located in Milwaukee and later moved to Oak Creek, Wisconsin.

Final actions authorizing the merger creating the United Church of Christ were taken by each of the two participants in 1956. Despite the vigorous renewal of opposition and the intensity of debate (which continued to the very end), the General Council of Congregational Christian Churches voted, 1,310 to 179, to proceed to union and gave its authorization for the Uniting General Synod to be held in 1957. Shortly thereafter the General Synod of the Evangelical and Reformed Church cast its vote for acceptance of the total plan. There were important issues yet to be decided. A constitution needed to be written and approved. A statement of faith needed to be prepared and accepted. The merging of the national boards of the two churches needed to be achieved. Consolidation needed to be attained on the local, district, and state levels. But trusting that all these things could be done, and done well, the two denominations chose to go ahead. And on 25 June 1957, in Cleveland, Ohio, under the leadership of Fred Hoskins for the Congregational Christians and James Wagner for the Evangelical and Reformed, the delegates of the Uniting General Synod spoke this word: "We do now . . . declare ourselves to be one body and our union consummated in this act establishing the United Church of Christ, in the name of the Father, and of the Son, and of the Holy Spirit. Amen."[26]

THEOLOGY

Theological developments within Congregationalism during the decades following 1920 were shaped by ecumenical influences far more pervasive than those of any earlier period in Congregational history. This was due in part to the declining of Congregationalism's dominance in American religious life, but also to Congregationalism's increased role in cooperative endeavors. Throughout the seventeenth and eighteenth centuries, Congregationalism had been a leader among American denominations and the major force in the formation of American religious thought. The nineteenth century, however, brought a reduced role for Congregationalism as a denomination in the midst of America's growing religious diversity and, similarly, a more shared role for its leaders in the theological development of American Protestantism. With the acceleration of the ecumenical movement in the twentieth century, that sharing was further expanded to worldwide proportion. As wholehearted participants in the national and international consultations of Christian leaders, Congregational theologians increasingly carried on their labors within the framework of the larger Christian community.

The Decline of Liberalism

Writing in the *Christian Century* in 1933, John Bennett said, "The most important fact about contemporary American theology is the disintegration of Liberalism."[27] In due time that liberalism was to be reconstructed, with Bennett as one of Congregationalism's leading participants in the process of its rebuilding, but for the moment the most striking fact about it was its demise. The liberalism of the late nineteenth and early twentieth centuries had encountered two major difficulties in the 1920s and 1930s. For one thing, it became apparent in that time of growing skepticism that one consequence of the current liberal approach to theology was further abandonment of the historic character of Christian faith. Committed to the modernization of religious thought through employment of advancing scientific knowledge, some Protestants on the outer edge of the movement were being led to a humanist religion-without-God as the ultimate outcome of their efforts. Those who allowed themselves to be cut adrift from anchorage in either supernatural revelation or churchly tradition by this dedication to scientism were therefore endangering the most basic theological foundations on which their thought was originally based.

More significant, however, was the devastating effect of the times upon efforts to advance a liberal Christian theology of the style of the early twentieth century. There was little or no way that its evolutionary optimism could withstand the onslaught of the First World War and the Great Depression. The assumption that human nature was fundamentally good and that through the working of divine immanence all was moving progressively toward an ultimate societal perfection was soon laid to rest by the monumental calamities of the times. The Christian faith had traditionally spoken harder words in coming to grips with human evil—and similarly in understanding divine redemption. Now those words seemed necessary again. H. Richard Niebuhr voiced the critical appraisal of many when he characterized current liberal faith as maintaining that "a God without wrath brought men without sin into a kingdom without judgment through the ministrations of a Christ without a cross."[28] That liberalism needed to be replaced if Christian thought were again to be faithful to its roots as well as relevant to its times.

Fundamentalism

From the middle of the nineteenth century advocates of a biblical literalism resisted the new science of biblical criticism. The strongest academic source of this opposition was in the conservative Presbyterianism of Princeton Theological Seminary, but unwillingness to accept the methods and conclusions of the new critical approach to the Bible was widespread among many denominations. By the early twentieth century this broad defensiveness congealed into the fundamentalist movement, which considered acceptance of certain conservative "fundamentals" of doctrine to be crucial for Christian faith. In one widely accepted version these essentials of belief were the inerrancy of Scripture, the virgin birth of Jesus, the substitutionary atonement, Jesus' physical resurrection, and his imminent bodily second coming. As a consequence, the 1920s brought prominent heresy trials in several instances where the fundamentalist-modernist conflict was particularly intense.

Congregationalism was spared the agony of heresy hunting because fundamentalism was never prominent in its life. However, a theologically conservative attitude sufficiently prevailed among some local Congregational churches to lead them in the mid-1930s to seek each other for mutual support. In 1945 these churches withdrew from mainstream Congregationalism to form a separate denomination, the Conservative

Congregational Christian Conference (CCCC). Subsequent additions to this movement came from formerly independent Community churches or Bible churches, evangelical in outlook and congregational in polity. The denomination grew to more than 180 churches and, like the National Association of Congregational Christian Churches, viewed itself as the heir of historic Congregationalism. Its basic theological foundation was a scriptural literalism in which the Bible was described as "the only, inspired, inerrant, infallible, authoritative Word of God written,"[29] and its denominational statement of faith included the main beliefs of fundamentalism. Yet the group's congregational polity prevented a legalistic denominational intrusion upon the life of the local church, and further doctrinal interpretation of biblical content was left in the hands of each congregation. The CCCC headquarters were located in St. Paul, Minnesota.

Neoorthodoxy

In the 1930s, however, the major theological criticism and corrective of liberalism came through the "theology of crisis" or, as it is more commonly designated, *neoorthodoxy*. Although this movement brought a return to several of the theological emphases of an earlier Calvinist "orthodoxy" in American Protestant thought, its broad tone was vastly different from that of Protestant fundamentalism. The theologians of neoorthodoxy had come out of the liberal heritage and accepted fully the principles of modern biblical criticism. Yet their theology was a biblical theology, for they took the Bible seriously, though not literally, and found in it the controlling source of their faith.

In its approach to religious truth neoorthodoxy drew upon an existentialist perspective represented in the writings a century earlier of a Danish philosopher-theologian, Søren Kierkegaard. For Kierkegaard sound religious thought begins not in abstract reflection, but with a concrete person in a concrete situation, where commitment is called for in an all-important life decision. Rather than engage in detached philosophical explorations concerning the nature of existence, one must face the reality of one's own existence, its sinfulness, and the commitment necessary to receive God's proffered redemption. This constitutes a leap of faith in response to the offerings of the gospel, and in this one receives God's grace. Christian theology, therefore, emerges not out of a spectator's reflections on metaphysical matters, but out of one's awareness of being personally addressed by God and one's willingness, as a participant by faith, to hear and obey.

Drawing upon Kierkegaard's existentialism and his own strong biblicism, Karl Barth inaugurated a new theological era for European, and ultimately American, Protestantism with his commentary in 1918 on Paul's Letter to the Romans. Interpreters have noted that he took a first-century epistle written in ancient Greek and made it into a special delivery letter to the twentieth century. The address of God to human rebellion and sin was laid heavily upon every soul. All pretensions to human goodness and the powers of self-reliance were here boldly condemned. The call was to repentance and faith, for only in God's forgiveness is there restoration and new life. Not until 1928 was Barth made available to America through an English translation of some of his writings, but soon thereafter serious attention was paid to him by America's leading theologians. In the early 1930s he fled Germany for Switzerland because of his refusal to take the loyalty oath to Hitler's regime. There he wrote extensively, his multivolume *Church Dogmatics* becoming a major source for developing neoorthodox theology.

Barth's own theological beginnings had been within liberal circles, but his neoorthodoxy faulted liberal theology in major ways. For example, liberalism's reliance on human reason and experience for discovering God, Barth believed, had started the theological process wrong end to. God is "Wholly Other," beyond all access through human inquiry and probing, and knowledge of God can come only by God's self-revelation, given in Jesus Christ to those who in faith will receive it. Moreover, Barth's focus on the transcendence of God contrasted sharply with liberalism's almost exclusive emphasis upon God's immanence, for the sovereign God of eternity was not to be confined to limits posed by the realm of time. Still further, Barth maintained, the gulf between God and humanity was deepened by the fact of sin. Barth's appraisal of the human condition magnified the reality of human pride and its rebellion against God's will and correspondingly found the only resolution to this tragedy of life in God's initiative and grace. Rejecting vigorously the optimism of liberalism concerning human potential for goodness, Barth saw all life to be in crisis, and even the preacher was "a dying man speaking to dying men." But the preacher can proclaim the Word of God, and through this God speaks and acts to save.

A second European leader of neoorthodoxy was Emil Brunner, a native Swiss theologian who, in the 1930s and 1940s, added several important volumes to the growing literature of this movement. Brunner's emphasis, however, was a little less harsh than Barth's in describing humanity's condition in its relation to God. Whereas Barth spoke of the "infinite distance" between God and humanity, Brunner affirmed a "point of contact" residual in fallen human nature. This meant for Brunner the possibility of some natural knowledge of God, though it is always distorted by sin and must be tested by the criterion of biblical truth. Moreover, when Brunner spoke about knowledge of God, it was in the distinctive form of knowledge through personal encounter. Barth had affirmed this, but Brunner made it more crucial. Knowledge of God for Brunner was more than simply ideas about God, even ideas drawn from reading the Bible. In the Bible, he said, God "does not deliver to us a course of lectures in dogmatic theology."[30] Rather, God's address, mediated by the Bible, is heard in the meeting of an "I" with a "Thou" in personal relationship. This makes for a difference in both knowledge and behavior. Propositional knowledge of God does not affect behavior, for it is not life changing and can even be used unlovingly. But in personal encounter, where faith responds to God's address, the knowledge of God is transforming. Then knowledge of God is not a commodity to be possessed, but a condition of being possessed and renewed by the gift of love freely given. So in the final analysis, said Brunner, knowledge of love and existence in love are the same. It was out of this that Brunner developed a special concern for the importance of Christian life in society. To some extent, despite his resistance to Hitler, Barth gave up on the social order. Brunner developed more specifically a social ethic based on Christian conviction and expectation.

Neoorthodox thought was mediated to America initially by two Congregationalists, Douglas Horton and Wilhelm Pauck. There was no single system of neoorthodox doctrines, for variations were as many as the individuals involved, but the basic tone and thrust of neoorthodoxy became in the 1930s and 1940s a creative force in American Protestant theology. It would be impossible to ascertain the precise effect on Congregational teaching and preaching, but Congregational students read neoorthodox theologians in their seminary studies for ministry, and a sobering of the thought of Congregational writers is evident when seen in relation to the extreme liberalism of the preceding era. Of the Europeans Brunner was more appreciatively received than Barth, although perhaps in part because he lectured in America in the 1950s. As to Barth, Wilhelm Pauck's early comment is indicative of a later general view. In 1931 Pauck published his *Karl Barth: Prophet of a New Christianity?* He answered the question in the title with a yes and a no. Barth's criticism of liberal theology, said Pauck, "can hardly be refuted." Further, Pauck found lasting significance in Barth's "rediscovery of the transcendence of God," his emphasis on "the infinite, qualitative difference between time and eternity," and his understanding of the nature of the religious "crisis." But Barth was found wanting in his mode of defense of these ideas. He is returning, said Pauck, to the arbitrariness of outmoded theological methods and is ignoring new insights of the sciences, even "the science of religion," that have come in recent decades. No longer can one defend the absoluteness of the Christian religion by asserting an exclusiveness for God's revelation in Bible and Christ. The old authorities must give way to more modern and broader understanding. So Barth, maintained Pauck, is not "*the* prophet of a new Christianity," but he is the "preacher in the wilderness" and is preparing the way.[31]

Neoliberalism

By the mid-1940s "the way" for theology within Congregationalism came, however, to be generally more liberal than neoorthodox. For the most part Congregational theologians did not abandon the long-developed direction of liberal thought, its openness to the sciences and new knowledge, its concern for this life and human progress, its conviction of God's immanent presence, and its confidence in human capacity to respond to redeeming power. Yet the liberalism developing in mid-century was a chastened liberalism, made more "realistic" by its exposure to the magnitude of human suffering and returned by the influence of neoorthodoxy to a more traditional understanding of Christian faith. Some have termed this a *neoliberalism*, developed interdenominationally in postwar American Protestantism and in which Congregationalism broadly shared.

In 1946 the Theological Commission, appointed six years earlier to draw up a theological statement for use in Congregational Christian churches, made its final report to the General Council. A draft of the document had been printed earlier by Walter Marshall Horton in a denominational study volume titled *Our Christian Faith*, and also it had been circulated among clergy and churches for response. The revised form presented to the council thus represented a broad spectrum of Congregational thought and may be seen as an expression of the re-shaped theological liberalism of the time.

One striking emphasis present at the very outset was on the transcendence of God. Time and space, we are told, do not wholly contain God, and were the whole universe to collapse into nothing, its Creator would remain. But transcendence also means sovereignty within the universe and its history, for should all earth's tyrants combine in their oppression, they would still be powerless against God. Such transcendence and power are really beyond our comprehension, and we read that God cannot be captured by the nets of human thinking. Yet God does not remain aloof and away, but in divine sovereignty takes the initiative to establish communion with the children of divine creation. And in that meeting there is the joyous discovery that before our love for God was born we were loved by God.

As we come to know ourselves in relation to God, continued the statement, we find that we are made in the divine image and are co-creators, even co-rulers, within God's universe. This is a limited potential, but its proper exercise through fulfillment of God's will can be the occasion of great happiness. However, life witnesses to a persistent and tragic tendency toward our human rebellion against God's way, in which we seek our own good and yield to self-centered desires. This is sin, and in that rebellion God appears to us as Judge and God's law is seen as one of retributive justice. Even the saint whose love and obedience for God are great, we are told, knows this moral failure and that God's sovereignty cannot be mocked.

But the good news of God is that the Judge, who is above history, is also the Redeemer, who has entered into history and has acted in Jesus Christ to offer forgiving love even before we are willing to receive it. Indeed, God pursues prodigals who flee divine judgment until they realize that their flight is not from an enemy, but from their best Friend. The love of God is revealed in Christ as sacrificial, displayed through Christ's life and death. However, such love, the statement affirms, must always have been the nature of God's way with humanity, even before and outside of Christ. But through Christ this love was most persuasively revealed, sufficient to change persons' entire point of view and bring them to a higher level of existence. It was by virtue of God's coming in Christ that persons learned to love others sacrificially, even as they themselves had been so loved by God.

Moreover, we are told, our response to God's invitation to love is itself encouraged by God's guidance. This is the work of the Holy Spirit witnessing within the human heart. Within us there is that which we sense to be the urging of God, interpreted throughout our lives by parents and church, and constantly encouraging us to decide for Christ. There has always been the help of a still, small voice. Elijah experienced it, as did Socrates. But particularly since Pentecost have Christian hearts been kindled by this awareness of God's inward presence and power. And this completes, in the statement's understanding, the threefold work of God. As Father, God is transcendent Creator; as Son, God enters into our history through Christ; and as Holy Spirit, God touches our hearts with guidance and encouragement to choose the Christian way.

The loving summons of God, however, calls communities, as well as individuals, into new life. The statement of faith speaks of a turning point in history at the time of God's coming in Christ, for then a new and redeemed humanity began and the foundations of God's Kingdom were freshly laid. There had always been a Kingdom, inclusive of all early individual responses to God's love, but from the time of Christ there has been the church, a human community consciously committed to God's purposes. And it is a community that prays daily for the final coming of God's Kingdom.

The totality of our human responses to God are then, in summary, represented by the statement as the responses of "faith," "fellowship," and "freedom." Our faith in God cannot be supported by proof, but it is assisted by a continuous line of witnesses as a ministry of the living Word is transmitted in the church though the ages. Nor can the words of our faith adequately describe God, for divine transcendence exceeds all human conception. Our fellowship is in the church, modeled and energized by the sacrificially shared fellowship of Christ. This is especially important for Congregational Christian churches, the statement notes, as they find their distinctive character not in external forms, but in God-centered mutuality of affection and interdependence. Our freedom is exercised under the guidance of the Holy Spirit, by whom we are led to creative and liberating endeavors. These may be the work of the artist, the scientist, the reformer, breaking shackles that impede or making things beautiful, true, or good. And again this is important in Congregational Christian churches, where freedoms of worship and conscience have been a bulwark against oppressive authorities and traditions.

It is also through the terms *faith*, *fellowship*, and *freedom* that the church's mission in the world can be described. The church's primary function to the outside world is to extend the faith. It preaches the Word, woos humanity, and is committed to a missionary enterprise. But the church also must carry on Christ's work by creating bonds of fellowship throughout the world, calling both individuals and institutions to devotion to the common good of all humanity. This responsibility must be seen as applicable to institutions at all levels in society, even expressed in concern for an ordering of international life, where fragmentation needs to be overcome if peace and progress are to be attained. The church likewise is charged with promoting freedom. It must encourage and protect the free exercise of conscience, but equally it must be a liberating force in the struggles of the social order. The statement makes clear the conviction that the church's mission includes a social responsibility to labor for the eradication of evils, political and economic, which enslave whole peoples and lead to their degradation. In facing such evils the church is summoned to act, but always with methods in harmony with its own nature and calling.

Finally the statement turns to the far future and asks if the evils of life will ever be completely overcome. This is the question of an earthly Kingdom, an eschatological completion of history by the coming of God's reign on earth. The answer given is that such earthly consummation is improbable, for all things temporal are incomplete. But faith moves beyond time and history and knows that God is the final Destination, in whom there is deliverance from every ill. However, a division of humanity beyond history is also implied as possible, for the statement's concluding affirmation is that to be united with God in time and eternity means life and joy, but to separated from God means torment and disaster.

Congregational thought, as represented in the 1940s by this Statement of Faith, is a chastened liberalism. However, it also might be called an evangelical liberalism, for its chastening has brought it back into closer relation to the traditional form of Protestant faith. Throughout the statement both the impact of neoorthodoxy and the continuance of a liberal perspective are seen. God is transcendent and sovereign, but experience of God's familiar and fatherly love is the Christian's source of joy. God takes the initiative in revelation, but nowhere is this limited to the Bible as its means. Sin is real and brings judgment, but the human potential for goodness is great and, strangely, sin never seems to have infected the church. Christ's death is a sacrifice, but its function appears to be that of attracting loyalty rather than redeeming from sin. God's love is supremely conveyed in Christ, but it also exists and is known outside of Christ. The Kingdom of God is beyond all earthly realization, and yet the focus of the Christian's life and effort must be for its consummation. Congregationalists had relearned some of the traditional theology of the past, but they had not given up their liberal ways.

POLITY

In the three hundred years from 1620 to 1920 American Congregationalism had grown from simple localism in organization to the more complex forms necessary for a national structure. In the process the autonomy of the local church had been preserved, but much else had been added. District associations, state conferences, and a national council were now in place, along with mission boards for extending the church's witness. In the main the polity structure to be carried into the 1957 merger to form the United Church of Christ was now settled. Beginning in the 1920s additional developments appeared with respect to women's work in the denomination, and at that time there were also adjustments in the mission structure and in certain practical matters related to ministry. But the major polity issues of the mid-twentieth century had to do with the merger itself.

Women's Organizations

The four Woman's Boards of Mission, established in the early 1870s, provided throughout half a century remarkable agencies for women to work at all levels in assisting the foreign missionary program of the Congregational churches. Based in the local churches, but rising through district and state organizations to national support of the American Board of Commissioners for Foreign Missions, the women's groups raised and administered their own funds and selected and financed their own women missionaries who were then commissioned by the ABCFM for the foreign field. It was a large and successful program, and it became the major way women were able to contribute their skills and efforts to organized church work. The barriers to their participation were otherwise still high. In 1923, although women delegates made up 10 percent of the National Council, there were no women members of the Executive Committee and only four women among the sixty-one persons constituting the Commission on Missions. In 1934 the General Council felt the necessity of voting encouragement for local churches to include women on their planning committees "in such numbers that the women will feel that the plans of the church are their own."[32]

In the early 1920s, however, pressures developed to incorporate the autonomous program of the Woman's Boards of Missions into the structure of the ABCFM. Although some missionaries had asked for this to simplify their relation to their authorizing and supporting agencies, the main cause was male desire for institutional consolidation, which presumably could lead under centralized administration to greater business efficiency. In 1925 the National Council approved a report from its Committee of Twelve proposing the placing of the Woman's Boards' activities under the ABCFM, in exchange for which the women would receive one-third of the elected positions on the ABCFM's Prudential Committee and the assurance that women could be named as departmental executives to supervise the American Board's work. Although the Woman's Boards felt that the one third female representation was inadequate, especially because parity was earlier implied in the negotiations, they consented to the plan, and consolidation occurred in 1927. But when the hoped for financial and organizational benefits did not result, many women considered the sacrifice of their unique independent missionary program to have been high cost for still insufficient gains.

Meanwhile, women's groups continued in Congregational churches and also in association and state conference organizations, carrying on a variety of activities. Some of this work was through the Women's Home Missionary Federation, supportive of the program of the Congregational Home Missionary Society, some of it continued to focus on the work of the ABCFM, and some was more independently directed. By 1940, however, these groups were brought together into a loose structure to coordinate and encourage women's work in the churches, and responsibility for its nurture was given to the Commission on Missions. One early and significant result of this cooperation was the initiation of the "Woman's Gift," developed as a "plus gift" from individual women throughout the churches over and beyond their regular contributions to their churches' benevolence budgets. The first gift was presented at the General Council meeting in 1942, and its presentation was continued biennially, becoming an increasingly important occasion at General Council sessions. The gift was always designated for the mission work of the church, and by 1956 it was divided among the American Board of Commissioners for Foreign Missions, the Board of Home Missions (Department of Christian Education), the Council for Social Action, and the Congregational Christian Service Committee. In 1955 a formal structure was adopted by this growingly unified women's movement through the acceptance of a constitution at a meeting of its state conference presidents, and the newly adopted name was the National Fellowship of Congregational Christian Women. Continuing under the administration of the Missions Council (successor to the Commission on Missions), on which women now had considerably larger representation, the National Fellowship's program focused strongly on the precise mission areas to which its gift was being given. By 1956 women had gained larger representation in other areas as well. Five of the eighteen members of that year's Executive Committee were female, and selection of equal numbers of lay women and lay men was now mandated for delegations to the General Council of Congregational Christian Churches.

Further Mission Consolidation

In the early twentieth century three actions by the National Council of Congregational Churches helped to initiate closer relationship with the local churches and with each other on the part of the earlier autonomous benevolent societies that became Congregationalism's mission agencies. In 1913 the churches' delegates to the National Council were made voting members of the boards of the societies, and the coordinating Commission on Missions was created. In 1923 the first step in merging home mission agencies was taken through an agreement among the Home Missionary Society, the Church Building Society, and the Sunday School Extension Society for cooperative planning and administration under broader identification as the church extension boards. And in 1925 the council action, completed in 1927, was to integrate the work of the Woman's Boards of Mission into the structure and program of the American Board. In the understanding of the denomination's leaders, however, two tasks remained to bring fuller coherence into the total mission program.

The first was the task of further unification of the home mission agencies. An elaborate plan for this was presented to the National Council in 1925 as part of the report also recommending the merging of the Woman's Boards and the ABCFM. Although there was much support for the home agencies union, the complexities of this consolidation necessitated deferment and dependence on the processes of more gradual unification. By 1931, however, the term *Home Board* was employed to designate the totality of home mission agencies, as their separate reports to the General Council were gathered under this rubric, and finally in 1936 the formal consolidation was achieved. The consolidation set up a single corporation, chartered by the legislatures of Connecticut, Massachusetts, and New York, which became recipient of all the legal authorizations possessed by the seven agencies in their respective charters, and under which these agencies would subsequently operate as a single unit. Separate divisions were established for different program functions, but all was legally organized under a single board of directors and administrative leadership. This bound together for united planning and action the three Church Extension Boards, the American Missionary Association, the Congregational Education Society, the Congregational Publishing Society, and the Congregational Board of Ministerial Relief. The name under which all were to be known was the Board of Home Missions of the Congregational and Christian Churches.

Administrative consolidation, however, left a second important task, the unification of the promotion to the churches of the various aspects of the denomination's mission work and particularly the centralizing of appeal for churches' and individuals' support. This problem had been complicated in the early twentieth century not only by the presence of several agencies all separately asking for funds but also by the fact that appeals from state missionary societies were often not coordinated with those of the national organizations. Again, success was achieved only by gradual development. An attempt at unification was made in 1925 through the establishment of the Promotional Council, composed of the promotion secretaries of all the agencies. The understanding was that each would promote the entire program and not simply that of the particular agency represented, but this became a wholly unrealistic expectation!

By 1931 wiser cooperative promotional methods were established, including the publication of a joint missions magazine. The work of the Commission on Missions had likewise been helpful, but its assistance was hampered by the fact that its inclusion of many persons not representing mission boards kept it from truly being an instrument of those agencies. That, however, was rectified in 1936 in connection with the unification of the home boards. Through the General Council's action in that year membership on the Commission on Missions (later, Missions Council) was limited to representatives of the mission agencies, including the Council for Social Action, and at the same time cooperative arrangement was established between state organizations and the national bodies. After 1936, therefore, promotion to the churches of the mission program, both foreign and domestic, was fully coordinated, and the churches were presented annually with one joint appeal for their support. Subsequently another means of planning became an additional help. That was the "midwinter meeting," developed by the early 1940s, in which the Missions Council and representatives of the mission groups (ABCFM, BHM, and CSA) met annually with many others in the denomination's executive positions (the Executive Committee of the General Council, state conference superintendents, women's state presidents, and presidents of laymen's state fellowships, to name a few). The meetings were organized by the Missions Council, and the planning accomplished generally became the program of the national and state agencies for the subsequent year.

Ministry

In the twentieth century Congregationalism encountered two major polity problems related to the nature and employment of its professional ministry. The first concerned the matter of standards and the manner by which they could best be achieved. The struggle known in nineteenth-century Congregationalism for an adequate numbers of ministers continued into the twentieth. In 1938 there were 3,108 Congregational Christian ministers in full standing available for 5,378 active Congregational Christian churches. Some of the churches were yoked churches, where a pastor served more than one parish. But 658 of the churches had vacant pulpits, 527 were served by ordained clergy of other denominations, 207 by Congregational Christian licentiates, 40 by licentiates from other denominations, and 92 by lay men or women. Clearly the need for more successful recruitment continued to be great, and consistently throughout these decades the National Council, and then the General Council, sought means for its advancement.

The polity problem, however, had to do with standards. The shortage of clergy led too easily to acceptance of less-than-qualified persons for ministerial leadership. In 1938 the Committee of Eleven on the Problems of the Ministry reported to the General Council on this issue. The study was continued during the following biennium by the national Commission on Ministry, and its report was adopted by the General Council in 1940. One important aspect concerned transfers by clergy from other denominations. The report recognized that the Congregational Christian ministry had been enriched in the past and should continue to be enriched by such transfers, but it also called for their more careful handling and approval. Mainly the report urged that no minister of another denomination be recommended to a Congregational Christian church by any interested party until approval for transfer had previously been granted by an association or conference committee on ministerial standing. Moreover, those committees should apply the same standards to transferring clergy as they would to new candidates for ministry. Although this maintenance of standards could be accomplished only by voluntary compliance, the council's action expressed grave concern for more careful admission of non-Congregational Christian clergy into the denomination.

Similarly, the General Council in 1940 defined more carefully its recommended criteria and procedures for first entrance into Christian ministry. A new step was added to begin the process, the status of being *in care of association*. This would serve the purpose of early acquaintanceship between the candidate and the denomination—a way of recruitment through more deliberate exposure to the calling of ministry, as well as a means of evaluation of the individual's qualifications for continuation toward ordination. Then came *licensure*, defined as a one-year intermediary status (though twice renewable) for candidates on the way to ordination. Normally licensure would indicate association or conference approval for the candidate's engaging in acts of ministry, with the exception of administering the sacraments or performing the ceremony of marriage. Special approval for either or both of the latter would be further necessary. Only in exceptional instances, the council urged, should licensure be granted to a lay preacher unable to complete the ordination requirements, for it was basically a probationary and learning status for those intending to be ordained. *Ordination* followed and was the responsibility of the association or of the conference if associations had given it into the latter's hands. Upon receiving ordination the candidate also received ministerial standing, which was held in either the association or the conference. Ordination by vicinage council, called by a local church, continued to be recognized, but ministerial standing for clergy ordained in this manner must further be granted after examination by the association or conference.

Beyond this clarification of procedures leading to ordination the 1940 General Council identified certain general qualifications it deemed essential for entrance into ministry: (1) "a vital and growing Christian faith," (2) "high moral character," (3) "appropriate reasons" for seeking ministerial ordination, (4) "satisfactory experience" as a licentiate, (5) "membership in a Congregational Christian church," and (6) "adequate education" for work in ministry. With regard to the latter, the council indicated its pleasure that in these years the American Association of Theological Schools was beginning evaluation and accrediting of seminaries, thereby giving clearer standards for academic acceptability. The candidate's total approval, however, was subject to "references from persons competent to judge" and to satisfactory examination by the ordaining council. The latter could be wide ranging, including questions on the subject matter of the candidate's seminary education and "insight into practical issues of a pastor's work," as well as others dealing with matters of personal experience, faith, and theological understanding. The council additionally urged that the ordination service, with its celebratory dinner, be scheduled no less than two weeks subsequent to the date of the council examining the candidate—

an important guard against forced approvals because the meal is ready to be served! Altogether, therefore, efforts were made in these times both to guard against aberration and to improve the general quality of ministry accompanying the credential of ordination.

The second polity problem affecting the ministry concerned the placement of pastors in new positions when vacancies occurred. The problem was one of discovering ways of assisting the healthy matching of pastors and churches without violating the freedom possessed by local congregations to be unobstructed in their choices or the freedom of pastors to be uninhibited in their searches. Many felt that it was a particularly sensitive and difficult matter. Said the 1940 General Council, "Not only do we feel ourselves to be a long way from knowing all the answers, but we have yet to find anyone else who thinks he knows them."[33] Yet at least tentative steps could be taken, and these were spelled out in the 1940 report. One was to recognize that the denominational official most centrally involved in the relocation of ministers was the state superintendent. It was the superintendent more than any other who could be a source of information and counsel to both pastor and church. But the superintendent could not handle all this alone and therefore should have counsellors, clergy and lay, for support in these delicate tasks. Further, printed material should be used to guide wisely the actions of all concerned.

Beyond these steps, the report urged, thought should be given to establishing a national registry, under the supervision of the Commission on Ministry, in which pastors and churches can record information concerning themselves that would then be available, upon inquiry, for general use. One special advantage of this registry, it was noted, was the likelihood of its facilitating ministerial changes across conference borders. Actually, no such registry was immediately developed, but the seed for greater cooperation on the national level in ministerial placement had been sown. In 1944 the General Council voted to establish the national Department of Ministry for the Congregational Christian churches. In 1946 authorization was given for the creation of a national registry of Congregational Christian clergy. Finally, in 1948 the council provided a full-time executive for the Department of Ministry and announced that the compiling of the registry was well under way. At least some steps had been taken toward dealing with placement difficulties.

Polity and the Merger

The most critical polity issue in the merger controversy of the 1940s and 1950s, namely, the autonomy of the local church, was not a matter of polity disagreement among Congregationalists in the long internal dispute. Persons on both sides of Congregationalism's debate strongly supported this principle. Throughout the entire decade and a half of controversy, Congregational declarations, whether favoring or opposing the merger, continued to assert, as a centerpiece of church government, the freedom of the gathered community of believers under the headship of Christ. However, the issue was a matter of legal dispute, for a basic question of law was whether or not the documents on which the merger was to be based fully guaranteed that local autonomy. Opponents of the merger claimed they did not, maintaining that the Basis of Union was ambiguous on the matter and could be read as potentially sanctioning structures or procedures compromising local freedom. In response proponents added to the Basis of Union the supplementary Interpretations, which presumably made clearer the guarantee of autonomy, but that document, too, was looked upon by the opponents with skepticism. In the eyes of the court, however, the documents were seen as sufficient for this declared purpose. The final judgment, rendered by the Court of Appeals, affirmed that the Basis of Union gave adequate assurance that local Congregational churches entering the merger would continue to possess the same freedoms which they had earlier enjoyed.

Several serious disagreements concerning polity principles did arise, however, within Congregationalism during the course of the controversy. An early challenge by opponents questioned the authority of the General Council to enact a union affecting the status of local churches, for the uniting document identified the merger as the "Union of The Congregational Christian Churches and the Evangelical and Reformed Church." More than one issue was involved here. Proponents of the merger clarified one aspect of this matter through adding in the Interpretations an identification of the uniting parties as the General Council of the Congregational Christian Churches and the General Synod of the Evangelical and Reformed Church, whose union would bring about the General Synod of the United Church of Christ. Although this limitation was not the earlier expectation of the Evangelical and Reformed leaders, they accepted the clarification. Moreover, behind this clarification, from the merger proponents' point of view, was the affirmation that the General Council, as an autonomous church body, had the authority to act for itself in such matters. This involved additional dispute as to whether the council was not rather an agent of the churches and dependent upon their authorization for entrance into union. Although there was no explicit final court judgment on this matter, the General Council acted freely and independently (though with counsel from the churches) through its majority vote for union with the Evangelical and Reformed General Synod.

Yet the union ultimately came to include the local churches as well, for the intention remained that although the first act simply created the new General Synod of the United Church of Christ, the final goal was the uniting of all parts of the two communions to constitute a single denomination. So the question arose as to the manner of a local church's becoming a member church in the United Church of Christ. Opponents of the merger held that a church becomes a member only by its affirmative vote. Proponents held that a church is a member unless it votes dissent. Actually, churches were in due time provided with two opportunities for voting. The first was early in the process, when the Basis of Union and the Interpretations were initially submitted to the congregations, and the second was late in the process, when the constitution for the United Church of Christ was finally written and submitted to the local churches for approval. In the final outcome full membership in the United Church for former Congregational Christian churches depended on a church's vote of approval. However, the UCC Year Book carries two additional categories. Both are made up of former Congregational Christian churches that continue to relate to their former conferences by submitting annual reports and yet have not given their approval to the union. One category is of churches that have never voted or have voted to abstain from voting. The other is of churches that have voted not to be a part of the United Church but by their reporting continue a tenuous relationship. No such problems arose for the state conferences, all of which voted for their consolidation with the Evangelical and Reformed synods.

The Basis of Union's plan for the writing of a constitution for the United Church of Christ precipitated further polity disagreements within Congregationalism. Again more than one issue was involved. From the outset there was strong conviction among the Congregational critics of the merger plans that no general constitution should be written for the entire United Church of Christ if the union were to come to pass. Although the Evangelical and Reformed Church had a denominational constitution, there was no corresponding document for the Congregational Christian churches. The General Council had a constitution governing its own activities, but the conferences, associations, and local churches were not controlled by it, for that would be infringement on their autonomy. In response to this concern, therefore, the Interpretations stated that the constitution "will define and regulate as regards the General Synod but describe the free and voluntary relationships which the churches, associations, and conferences shall sustain with the General Synod and with each other."[34] Yet this was also protested, for opponents believed that nothing even describing the churches should be in a constitution. A constitution could in all likelihood be subject to amendment, and rights therefore could not be permanently guaranteed. This view, however, did not prevail.

One additional matter concerned the timing of the writing of a constitution, for opponents continued to feel that its preparation and adoption should precede the act of union in order that full assurance concerning the desired local church freedom could be obtained. At this point, however, the General Council insisted that uniting be based on trust and that constitution-making profit from some experience of living together by the uniting denominations. Moreover, the Basis of Union and its Interpretations were the agreed-upon foundation for the new constitution and could guarantee the freedoms desired.

Finally, polity disagreement was encountered among Congregationalists in contemplation of the merging of the mission Boards of the two denominations. Opponents of the merger viewed past contributions to the endowments of the ABCFM and the BHM to have been committed under the restriction of continued use for Congregational purposes. A merging with the Evangelical and Reformed could therefore alienate their usage from the original intent. Proponents of the merger rejected this interpretation, seeing the funds as unrestricted with regard to use and the boards therefore free to merge and to employ the endowments for joint mission projects. Although the former view was affirmed in the first court judgment, the second and third judgments explicitly upheld the latter. This dispute was then dropped from consideration during the final stages of the controversy.

WORSHIP

The "improvement of worship" initiated by the National Council of Congregational Churches from the late nineteenth through the early twentieth century remained an important concern in the continuing decades of the twentieth. The new name for it, however, was *liturgical renewal*. The simple worship forms of Congregationalism had long excluded more elaborate liturgy, but the passing of the generations, as well as new appreciations of earlier worship practices within historic Christianity, led to a fresh openness. In the early twentieth century Congregational worship appropriated selected prayers from what was increasingly viewed as the treasury of the past, and a new era of liturgical examination and appreciation began. Yet within Congregationalism not all were similarly inclined. The freedom of the local church to determine its own manner of worship left results to local desire. But the denominational movement as a whole was toward a liturgically enriched worship.

The Christian Year

One aspect of the reappropriation of earlier liturgical tradition was the introduction of an ecclesiastical calendar into Congregational awareness. Seventeenth-century Congregationalists had firmly rejected as "papist" all honoring of special religious days, except for the Sabbath, as well as all observing of special religious seasons. Even Christmas and Easter initially suffered this repudiation through Puritan conviction and determination. In time New England Congregationalists developed their own special days of penitence and thanksgiving, but long continued to ignore the traditional calendar of the church's holy days.

Change first came in 1918 through recommendations of the newly established Commission on Evangelism and Devotional Life. In that year the commission offered to the churches a suggested program for the Lenten period that would reach a climax on Easter Sunday. Its executive, Frederick L. Fagley, later recalled how gradually, and even strategically, this had to be introduced. During the first year, he said, the word *Lent* was not used, and only in the second year was the period termed the *Lenten season*. Further, the devotional booklet, *The Fellowship of Prayer*, recommended in 1919 for use in this program, was designed in its first year to begin daily devotions with the first Sunday in Lent, and not until the following year did it properly open the Lenten season with devotional material for Ash Wednesday. In Fagley's recollection the acknowledgment of Ash Wednesday was looked on by the Commission as "a rather bold step" in its effort to restore for Congregationalism elements of the classic church year.[35] However, by 1923 it was reported to the National Council that approximately 50 percent of the churches were observing a Lenten program of renewal that would conclude with the reception of new members into the congregation on Easter Sunday. In 1935 the commission expanded this denominational appropriation of a church year by adding materials to be used during the Advent season.

Further observance in Congregationalism of the Christian calendar appeared in the services of worship prepared and published during the next decade under the sponsorship of the General Council. The council had earlier authorized a *Book of Church Services* printed by its Commission on Worship in 1923. This worship guide paid scant attention to the church year, simply containing a "Christmas Service" and an "Easter Service," while largely continuing the early twentieth-century pattern of worship commended for the churches. However, significant changes appeared with the publication of *A Book of Worship for Free Churches* in 1948. This volume, also authorized by the General Council, was prepared by a seminar on worship made up of several Congregational pastors who met for a decade under the direction of the Commission on Evangelism and Devotional Life. Along with other forms for worship, their book contained a seventy-five-page section on "Orders of Worship for the Christian Year," following the year from the Sundays of Advent in December through All Souls' Day the following November. Lenten season services were provided for the Sundays in Lent and particularly for the special times in Holy Week, where services for Palm Sunday, Maundy Thursday, Good Friday, and Easter Sunday were proposed. Worship suggestions for Epiphany, Whitsunday, and Trinity Sunday were likewise included, along with a supplementary section of "Prayers for the Christian Year."

Word and Sacrament

The movement of liturgical renewal sought, among other things, to restore a more equitable balance between the preaching of the Word and the administration of the sacrament of the Lord's Supper. At the beginning of the Protestant Reformation sermon and sacrament shared responsibility for the communication of God's Word. The sermon was the Word spoken, the sacrament was the Word enacted. Both were channels of grace, conveying the promises of God and their fulfillment to those who respond in faith. In this they were the "marks" of the church, both Luther and Calvin maintaining that the church could be known as present wherever the Word was faithfully preached and the sacraments were properly administered. Calvin added the conviction that because faith is often frail and easily shaken, God has used earthly elements in the sacraments as visible instruments for conveying the life of the spirit. Particularly through the bread and the wine of the Lord's Supper the communicant receives the gift of the spiritual presence of Christ. With this sacramental understanding Calvin desired to have the Lord's Supper celebrated weekly in conjunction with the preaching. Church authorities in Geneva, however, settled for a monthly celebration, a practice continued by Calvinist Congregationalists when they came to America.

Throughout the eighteenth and nineteenth centuries the meaning and role of the Lord's Supper changed considerably in American Congregationalism. For communication of the gospel, primary emphasis was accorded to preaching, and both preaching and the sacrament were valued increasingly in terms of their effects in subjective experience. Revivalist preaching aimed at individual heart warming and the Lord's Supper at an enriched communal experience. Moreover, the sacrament had come to be celebrated with less frequency, quarterly communion being most common. But with the advance of the twentieth century, more changes occurred. The influence of neoorthodoxy brought a fresh awareness of the objectivity of the divine Word to be proclaimed in the sermon, and the movement of liturgical renewal restored value to the sacrament as an instrument of grace. In the latter instance the ecumenical movement of the twentieth century also contributed significantly to changing Congregational awareness. Interdenominational gatherings through the World Council of Churches confronted Congregationalists more directly with the sacramental traditions of other church bodies. Study conferences sponsored by the Faith and Order Commission, such as the conference at Oberlin in 1957, encouraged new theological understanding of the sacraments, and participation in ecumenical intercommunion often gave restored liturgical importance to the Lord's Supper as a meal central to Christian practice. In 1938 Congregationalism, as a denomination, began participation in the celebration of "World Wide Communion," joining other churches in this annual sacramental testifying to Christian wholeness despite continuing divisions.

Congregational leaders shared broadly in the developing liturgical movement of the 1940s and 1950s. Theological seminaries were open to these new impulses, and especially many among younger clergy became committed to sacramental renewal. Yet the changes remained within the context of Congregationalism's historic resistance to liturgy, as well as its suspicion of any sacramentalism threatening to devalue the preached Word. So midcentury provided a mixed picture within Congregational churches. One assessment of the relative strength of the liturgical movement appeared in a survey conducted in 1960 by Michael J. Taylor, S.J., and published under the title *The Protestant Liturgical Renewal*. Questioning fifteen hundred "mainstream" Protestant pastors, 215 of whom were Congregational, Taylor found evidence of considerable liturgical interest in all five denominations explored. His primary question was, "Are you personally interested in the liturgical renewal, i.e., in giving greater stress to the Sacrament and liturgy of the Lord's Supper in Sunday worship?"[36] Among the Congregationalists who responded, 55 percent were unreservedly in favor of the renewal, 15 percent mildly interested, and 30 percent indifferent or opposed. And in response to a related question, 70 percent favored achieving a better balance between Word and sacrament in worship. Moreover, 88 percent viewed the Lord's Supper as essential for Christian worship, whereas 10 percent saw it as important but not absolutely so, and the remaining 2 percent dismissed it as accidental. As to the nature of the Lord's Supper, 17 percent regarded it as a memorial, and the remaining 83 percent extended its meaning to include some form, generally spiritual, of the presence of Christ. Among "indifferent" pastors, 90 percent were satisfied with their quarterly celebration, whereas among "interested" pastors, 35 percent celebrated monthly or more often and others felt restrained from greater than quarterly frequency by their congregations' resistance. Although limited in its scope, this sampling is suggestive of the impact of the sacramental renewal on the thought of many of the clergy serving Congregational churches.

Symbolism

The liturgical renewal in the decades of the mid-twentieth century likewise was expressed through enrichment of the symbolism employed in worship. If there was a stark symbolism in the austere simplicity and beauty of the colonial meetinghouse, it was lost in the nineteenth century with its platforms to accommodate the idiosyncrasies of revivalist preachers and the large balconied auditoria to house the audiences who came either to respond or perhaps simply to be entertained. But the twentieth century saw new developments in church architecture. Most significant was the return to the divided chancel, where the center pulpit of the past was replaced by an altar surmounted by a cross. Whether encased in a classic Gothic-style cathedral or in a sanctuary of innovative contemporary design, this architecture reflected the new direction of worship, with greater focus on the sacramental and larger attention given to the ceremony of worship as the praise of God.

The 1948 *Book of Worship for Free Churches* included an introductory essay on "Symbolism," which took note of this new development. However, its main point on this matter of architectural change was that the acceptance of an altar with its implications, as replacement for a communion table, was by no means universal in Congregationalism. Some prefer an altar to provide a greater sense of the presence of God and of Christ's sacrifice, whereas others prefer the sense of a gathered communion that the table can connote. But, the authors added, both perspectives are important and, in either instance, should be present. Christ's Last Supper with his disciples was a time of communion amongst them, yet also a preparation for his sacrificial death. The two themes do go together, and both can well be suggested by the symbolism of either altar or table. Nevertheless the divided chancel with its altar was being newly employed in Congregational worship, and the essay on symbolism went on to offer numerous suggestions concerning the manner of dressing the altar and its use. Linens, candles, flowers, and vessels were all seen to have their meaningful place.

The essay also spoke of other forms of symbolism in the newly developed settings for Congregational worship. The church itself was often built in the shape of a cross. Moreover, because the narthex and the nave historically have represented the world and the chancel has symbolized heaven, the long aisle from narthex on into chancel can image the pilgrimage of life from birth to eternity. In this connection the essay suggested that as the altar is located at the far conclusion of the journey, the baptismal font should be at the entrance to signify the beginning of the Christian's life. The use of liturgical colors was recommended for the different seasons of worship, predominantly purple (denoting penitence) for Advent and Lent, white (purity) for Christmas through Epiphany and Easter through Whitsunday, red (Holy Spirit) for Whitsunday and the brief period following, black (mourning) for Good Friday and funerals, and green (growth and hope) for the remainder of the church year. Clergy vestments were portrayed as having symbolic significance in worship, particularly the black Geneva gown descended from earlier academic use and the stole that from its fourth-century origin represented a yoke of obedience in monastic orders and now is a sign of ordination.

Other symbols, the essay added, are found in the decorative arts. The IHS (first three letters in the Greek spelling of Jesus) or the Chi Rho (first two letters in the word for Christ) might be used in monograms or even embedded upon the altar cross. A triangle in various forms can symbolize the Trinity. The symbols of a fish, a lamb, a rock, or a door can be used to represent Jesus. The four evangelists may be pictured through their historic images, a winged man (Matthew), a winged lion (Mark), a winged ox (Luke), an eagle (John). And much more was proposed as useful for Congregational worship. The essay concluded with the warning that "there is grave and constant danger of losing our sense of values in the minutiae of forms."[37] But Congregational worship in the 1940s and 1950s was beginning to seek enrichment through both the beautification and the restored traditionalism mediated by the liturgy.

MISSION

Throughout four centuries of Congregational history, reaching from the first stirrings of English Separatism in the mid-1500s to the entrance of the main body of American Congregationalism in 1957 into the United Church of Christ, the most decisive transformation in characteristics of the evolving denomination occurred in the interpretation of the church's mission. Whatever the reasons for such change, ranging from altered theological and ethical views to variations in the social and political contexts of the life of the churches, the fact of history is that a once self-isolated Congregationalism increasingly took on a role of responsibility for influencing life in the larger society. The church that once viewed itself as a "walled garden" separated from the world became a church committed to working within the world for the purposes of evangelism, social justice, and Christian compassion.

Foreign Missions

The foreign mission program of American Congregationalists originated in the early 1800s, reached a peak of enthusiasm in the late 1800s, suffered a serious decline following the First World War, and gradually regained some of its lost stature during the course of the mid-twentieth century. In that modern period the returning prosperity of the churches, along with an improved international awareness, contributed to the restoration of support for foreign missionary activities. American Board of Commissioners for Foreign Mission financial records reveal the changes that occurred. From 1924 to 1939 the American Board suffered a series of deficits, leading to continuous cuts in appropriations to mission churches, hospitals, schools, and social centers. Indicative of the deepening crisis was the announcement to the General Council in 1934 that the foreign mission budget for 1935–36 would be no more than one-half of what it had been seven years earlier. However, this was in accord with the general financial hardship experienced by the churches during those years, a condition brought on by both the spiritual and the economic depression. Total benevolence giving for Congregational (and later, Congregational Christian) churches declined from $5,366,181 in 1923 to $1,907,439 in 1939. Recovery in church contributions began in 1940, and total benevolences for Congregational Christian churches rose in 1957 to $9,600,849 and in 1958 to $10,155,582. The 1940s and 1950s provided more prosperous times for the churches than did the two decades preceding.

However, the ABCFM continued to face serious difficulties throughout these later years. Some were posed by the conflict of the

Second World War. In Japan the work of American missionaries was given over to Japanese Christians, the Americans having been urged by their Japanese colleagues to leave in 1941, shortly before the war with the United States began. In the Philippines, however, many of the American mission personnel were trapped by the hostilities, and several were captured and interned. Not all mission work was terminated in China, for twenty missionaries were able to continue at their posts, but a much larger number were forced to leave the areas occupied by the Japanese. The disruptive effects of the war were likewise felt by American missionaries in Bulgaria and Greece in southern Europe and in Turkey and Syria in the Near East. And altogether the war's total tragedy left immense wounds to which the American Board responded with postwar work of reconciliation and rehabilitation. In the years following the war, the American Board also confronted new political situations reflecting growing anti-colonialism and emerging nationalism. Restrictions were encountered in India, Angola, Turkey, and South Africa. Missionary work was cut off completely in China by its communist government.

During this period the ABCFM was additionally called upon to rethink the purpose and function of its mission program. Although this rethinking had begun in the late nineteenth century, a new focus was provided in 1932 by the Laymen's Foreign Mission Inquiry. Financed by John D. Rockefeller, Jr., the inquiry was conducted by a New York social research organization in evaluation of the foreign mission programs of several Protestant denominations. Researchers consulted with missionaries in India, Burma, China, and Japan, and brought data to a committee for appraisal. The committee's final report, titled _Rethinking Missions_, was prepared under the editorship of the chairman of the appraisers, William Ernest Hocking, professor of philosophy at Harvard University. For those committed to traditional views of missionary activity the report was deeply troubling, and it was in fact rejected by conservative groups. It not only criticized the denominational fragmentation in missionary work, recommending a unified nondenominational administration for greater efficiency, but it also proposed a radical rethinking of the very nature of the missionary task. Although commending the "educational and other philanthropic aspects of mission work," it urged that they should be free from responsibility for "direct and conscious evangelization." Additionally it pled for a mission program in which responsibility for direction was shared with indigenous leadership. In a key statement the report said, "We must be willing to give largely without preaching; to cooperate with non-Christian agencies for social improvement; and to foster the initiative of the Orient in defining the ways in which we shall be invited to help."[38]

In 1933, under the leadership of its executive vice-president, Fred Field Goodsell, the American Board responded to the "Rethinking Missions" document by expressing appreciation for its careful work of evaluation and by indicating acceptance of its main recommendations. The board said, "We are at one with the Commission in their emphasis on the necessity of adjusting the missionary enterprise to the present-day world." The one place of slight disagreement related to theological presuppositions, the American Board affirming that it preferred to "state with greater emphasis its conviction of the uniqueness of the revelation of God in Christ." Thus claim for the finality of Christianity in relation to other world religions, questioned half a century earlier, was still a matter of concern in the board's interpretation of the purpose of Christian mission. Yet this claim, the board said, should be reflected in missionary efforts to manifest Christ's spirit in all dealings with other cultures, not in efforts to assert dominance for a particular theological doctrine concerning the preeminence of Christ. And altogether, the board added, it was necessary to draw upon the wisdom and experience of the mission fields' non-Christian cultures that the religion of Jesus might "express itself everywhere in truly indigenous ways."[39]

Holding to this understanding, the American Board continued in the mid-twentieth century to shape its program in newer ways. For one thing, it increasingly stressed the importance of self-determination for mission churches and an ultimate participation with them as colleagues in the world mission of the church. This cooperation would erase the somewhat invidious earlier distinction between "older and younger" churches and provide greater parity in interchurch relations. Further, that parity should lead to recognition that world mission is a two-way project and that as mission churches come of age they must send missionaries as well as receive them. Indeed, some of those who are sent might well be profitably received by American churches for a learning from non-American Christian experience. And finally, the board committed itself to greater church unity on the mission field, by encouraging Congregational Christian participation in national church unions, such as those in South India, North India, China, Japan, and the Philippines. Even when the polity of the unions strayed from Congregationalism, the feeling prevailed that, by uniting, the churches were advancing the spirit of Christ.

Domestic Mission

With the consolidation of the various home mission organizations in 1936 to form the Board of Home Missions, a large portion of the domestic mission program of the Congregational Christian churches was united under a single agency for direction and administration. The board then organized itself into five divisions, through which different specialized aspects of its work were channeled. These were essentially a continuation of the special functions of the agencies that had been brought together in the consolidation, and they remained as such within the Board of Home Missions throughout the succeeding years leading to its merger with the Evangelical and Reformed Board of National Missions in the forming of the United Church of Christ.

A major concern for the home missions program was founding new churches in unchurched areas and strengthening existing churches at points where national assistance could help. This was basically the work of the Division of Church Extension and Evangelism, and it largely continued the earlier commitments of the American (later, Congregational) Home Missionary Society of the nineteenth century and the Commission on Evangelism of the twentieth. But the situation in the mid-twentieth century was different, for time had brought its changes. No longer were churches being founded on a rough and advancing western frontier, for the settling of the nation was essentially complete. Now, however, there were new frontiers, suburbs developed out of expanding cities, and there, too, the church needed to be present. So the church-founding energies of the 1940s and 1950s were directed in large measure toward the "high potential" areas where young families were clustering in their escape from metropolitan life.

This required new approaches to evangelism, along with the development of Sunday schools and, ultimately, the assistance of church-building projects that could provide for the needs of these growing congregations. Here, too, the Division of Church Extension and Evangelism served, continuing the work of the earlier Sunday School Extension and Church Building societies. Moreover, beyond this expansion program the division gave assistance to rural churches through its Department of Town and Country. Despite the flight to the cities and the suburbs, Congregationalism in the 1950s continued to have some four thousand churches in small towns and rural areas. Financial and program help for their well-being remained, therefore, a part of the domestic mission.

Four other divisions within the Board of Home Missions served the denomination in a variety of ways. The Division of Christian Education inherited the traditional responsibility of assisting, through guidance and financial help, the programs of Congregational colleges and seminaries, along with the responsibility of preparing educational materials for use in the Sunday schools of Congregational Christian churches. By the mid-twentieth century, as religious concerns were felt increasingly in public as well as church institutions, the work in higher education included development of campus ministries for Congregational Christian students in college and university settings. For many years this became a particularly vigorous program in which Congregationsal Christian chaplains carried on the ministries either in connection with local churches or in ecumenical cooperation.

Likewise the task of creating Sunday school curriculum materials increased tremendously as a consequence of church growth, and for the year 1956 the Division of Christian Education reported that its editors had prepared two hundred separate pieces of instructional material, of which a total of four million copies had been distributed to the churches! Also under the care of the Division of Christian Education was the Pilgrim Fellowship, a rapidly expanding program for Congregational Christian youth. Founded in 1936 and led by talented youth directors, Pilgrim Fellowship not only attracted large groups of young people to its societies in local churches but also developed a strong national organization with ecumenical connections to the National Council of Churches through the United Christian Youth Movement and to the World Council of Churches through its Youth Department. By 1956 more than 148,000 Congregational Christian youth were enrolled in this movement.

The Pilgrim Press Division was the publishing arm for the denomination, a descendant of the Congregational Publishing Society, which had been founded in 1841. In addition to curriculum materials, it provided a large range of publications, including devotional materials, successive editions of the Pilgrim Hymnal (1931, 1935, 1958), and a variety of books on religious subjects. The Division of Ministerial Relief provided regular and emergency assistance to retired clergy and clergy widows in financial need. In addition to regular grants, special gifts were made available through the Christmas Fund. Finally, the American Missionary Association Division continued the long-standing work of its parent namesake organization in serving the special needs of racial minority groups for whom several of its programs were initiated in the nineteenth century. Particularly under its care were the African-American schools, colleges, and churches in the South that had been developed by the AMA after the abolition of slavery.

The domestic mission of the Congregational Christian churches involved more, however, than simply the extension and preservation of the denomination's institutions. For one thing, the Board of Home Missions knew that both through the churches and beyond the churches its mission was sharing the Gospel's good news in Christian action in society. In 1946 Truman B. Douglass, executive vice-president of the board, described its responsibilities as including engaging "the ministries of uncalculating Christian love to those who are carrying some burden of disadvantage—especially the disadvantages imposed by prejudice and injustice."[40] But more, this aspect of the church's domestic mission was also shaped and furthered, from 1934 onward, by the Council for Social Action and, throughout all these twentieth-century years, by the Congregational National Council and its successor, the General Council of the Congregational Christian Churches. One of the distinctive aspects of the denomination in its premerger development was the fact that at all institutional levels the social responsibility of the churches was more seriously recognized and more forthrightly assumed.

The National Council continued into the 1920s its earlier concern over temperance. Now, however, the slogan became "Obey the law." In 1923, 1925, and 1927 the National Council urged support for its Commissions on Temperance and on Law Enforcement and encouraged financial help for the Anti-Saloon League of America for its efforts to enforce the prohibition laws of the states and of the nation. In 1934, after the repeal of the national prohibition amendment, the council voted to inaugurate educational programs throughout the churches that would encourage total abstinence, cooperate with other groups in seeking legal restrictions over the liquor industry, and work toward the ultimate abolition of all "traffic in intoxicants."

Immediately following the First World War the National Council renewed its earlier efforts for the Christianization of industrial relations. One approach was through resolutions urging specific reforms. In 1921 the council expressed the hope that labor could be more adequately represented, by its unions or shop councils, in the shaping of its relations with management. The effort of one group to dictate conditions of life for another is, the council said, contrary to the spirit of Christ. Thus, it added, "an industrial order pervaded by the sense of brotherhood must be achieved."[41] In 1923 the council deplored the American Iron and Steel Institute's continued favoring of a twelve-hour workday for the steel industry, saying that "the whole church should protest against it with no uncertain voice."[42] In 1925, in its elaboration of its Statement of Social Ideals, the council called for the abolition of child labor, introduction of an eight-hour workday and a six-day workweek, provision of sanitary and safe working conditions, and development of a "minimum comfort wage" in return for which "all labor should give an honest day's work for an honest day's pay."[43] By 1931 it was urging "a five-day work week without a decrease in the wage levels" and a program of unemployment benefits that would provide "self respecting aid to the unavoidable labor surplus at any time."[44]

Beyond these specific concerns the National Council urged a more profound reconstruction of the economic order in which the profit motive would be modified by the service motive. For a decade and a half following the end of the First World War, much liberal Protestant economic thought was attracted to socialist ideas as promising a better system than laissez-faire capitalism for the nation's economic life. In 1919 the council held that there was no divine right to private property and maintained that only the use of property for service justified private possession. In its concern for equalizing social benefits, it further advocated efforts "to abolish all special economic privileges which enable some to live at the expense of others." In 1923 it repeated these themes, criticizing further those who "consider legitimate the acquisition of financial success without regard to questions of whether Society has been served or exploited." In 1925 it urged that "all ownership is a social trust" and that "the unlimited exercise of the right of private ownership is socially undesirable."[45] And in 1931 it advocated inauguration of a planned national economy to bring about social control in the productive and distributive processes.

All this lay behind the "anti-profit-motive" resolution of 1934 that created such a storm of protest and also tarnished, improperly, the Council for Social Action. Opinions changed, however, by the 1950s, the 1952 General Council stating that the 1934 declaration did not represent its current view. Yet the commitment to social responsibility, including political advocacy, remained. In 1954 the council voted to commend a public housing bill in Congress that would finance the clearance of slum areas for new multi-unit housing projects. Moreover, throughout these years, the Council for Social Action steered a steady course in leading local churches into increasing awareness of their own social responsibility in relation to economic matters. In 1939 the CSA conducted an economic plebiscite among Congregationalists that showed strong favor for federal relief for the unemployed and for the organization of consumer cooperatives, along with majority support for unionization of labor, federal underwriting of agricultural prices, and public ownership of electric utilities. The domestic mission of the church clearly continued to include responsibilities in the economic order.

Despite the early social gospel's "blindness" with respect to issues of racial discrimination, the importance of contesting this social evil grew steadily in Congregationalism's consciousness until it became by the 1940s and 1950s a major cause in the church's social mission. The tardiness is indicated by the fact that no denominational commission was charged with responsibility for handling racial concerns until 1923, and then they were included in the portfolio of the catchall Commission on International and Inter-racial Relations and the Near East. The National Council in 1925, however, separated the responsibility for interracial considerations and assigned them to a special commission. In 1934 the Council for Social Action assumed this concern as one of the four social areas in which it was to work.

Similarly, the National Council gave only sporadic attention to racial matters in its resolutions of the 1920s and early 1930s. In 1923 it expressed support of the Dyer Anti-Lynching Bill being considered by the United States Congress. In 1931 it voted to hold its future meetings only in cities where hotel accommodations were integrated. And in 1934 it criticized the idea of Nordic superiority as "a rationalization growing out of a desire to keep other races in subjection," and further urged the newly founded Council for Social Action to lead local churches into an overcoming of prejudice and its consequences "through education, social, and political persuasion and pressure." Beginning in 1942, however, and in each succeeding biennial session, the General Council dealt more vigorously and thoroughly with the evils of racial discrimination. In 1942 it termed this denial of human dignity to be "a chief national sin."[46] In 1944 it urged abolition of the poll tax as a prerequisite for voting. In 1946 it spoke out against "restrictive housing covenants, differential employment practices, . . . and segregated use of community facilities." In 1948 it reaffirmed an earlier call for a "non-segregated church in a non-segregated society."[47] In 1954 it called for a "tolerant implementation" of the Supreme Court decision integrating public education.[48] And in 1956 it summarized much that had gone before with a lengthy statement on racial integration as applied to education, housing, employment, business practices, judicial processes, and church life.

Beyond these major issues the General Council of the Congregational Christian Churches interpreted its responsibilities within the nation to include the expression of moral judgments on other sensitive matters relevant to both its own membership and the surrounding society. Thus, as situations gave warrant, it reflected and spoke over the years on matters such as birth control, adequate housing, American Indian rights, civil liberties, atomic energy, free speech in the light of anti-Communist hysteria, and innumerable aspects of the way to disarmament and world peace. Throughout their pilgrimage the Congregational churches in America came to know themselves as responsible institutions in a needy world. Theirs was the mission to be a channel of God's grace, not only for the soul's redemption but also for the healing of the social order.

SUMMARY

The nearly four decades in the twentieth century leading to entrance into the United Church of Christ were years of much struggle for American Congregationalism. Embedded in part within the struggles of American society itself, these trials put the Congregational churches to test, facing them with large challenges to maintain their viability and fidelity.

Problems of morale and financial distress were encountered primarily in the 1920s and the 1930s, when all American churches suffered through the spiritual and economic depressions. Battling postwar skepticism and moral lethargy, as well as severe economic hardship, Congregationalism managed more than simple survival in those years. Merger with the Christian Convention, establishment of the Council for Social Action, and consolidation of the home boards were testimonies to its resiliency in trying times. Equally, the 1920s and 1930s put Congregational theologizing to test. Nineteenth-century liberalism's failure to speak to twentieth-century crises left wide the temptations to abandon its valuing of reason for a more authoritarian faith. Fundamentalism never appealed, but neoorthodoxy did. Yet in the end, though much fluidity in theology remained, Congregationalism inclined toward a chastened liberalism, more rooted in the classic Protestant tradition but still open to new intellectual developments in the formulating of faith.

Although the 1940s and 1950s brought renewed growth and financial well-being to the churches, Congregationalism felt new pressures against the social liberalism it had developed over the decades. The Council for Social Action was accused of irresponsible radicalism, particularly in economic areas, and organized opposition took shape against the general advocacy of the social gospel within the denomination. Ultimately the CSA was exonerated, and social responsibility remained important in Congregationalism's understanding of its mission, but the tensions created were never fully resolved. And finally, there was the struggle connected with the merger creating the United Church of Christ. Lasting more than a decade and a half, this conflict's severity was immense. It did lead to a division within the denomination. But the commitment of the large majority was to an ecumenical goal it felt this church union could help fulfill. Thus, even at great cost, it remained faithful to that commitment.

NOTES

1. OLD WORLD ANTECEDENTS, 1558–1660

1. Champlin Burrage, *The True Story of Robert Browne (1550?–1633), Father of Congregationalism* (London: H. Frowde, 1906), 12.

2. R. W. Dale, *History of English Congregationalism* (New York: A. C. Armstrong and Son, 1907), 93.

3. B. R. White, *The English Separatist Tradition From the Marian Martyrs to the Pilgrim Fathers* (Oxford: Oxford University Press, 1971), 47.

4. Timothy George, *John Robinson and the English Separatist Tradition* (Macon, Ga.: Mercer University Press, 1982), 37.

5. Ibid., 43–44.

6. Ibid., 54.

7. Dale, *History of English Congregationalism*, 158.

8. Ibid., 183.

9. George, *John Robinson*, 85.

10. John Robinson, "An Answer to a Censorious Epistle" (1608), in *Works*, by John Robinson, ed. Robert Ashton (Boston: Doctrinal Tract and Book Society, 1851), 3:407.

11. John Robinson, "A Justification of Separation from the Church of England" (1610), in *Works*, 2:88, 132.

12. Henry Jacob, *Reasons . . . Proving A Necessity of Reforming our Churches in England* (1604), 5.

13. Champlin Burrage, *The Early English Dissenters in the Light of Recent Research (1550–1641)* (New York: Russell & Russell, 1912), 2:294.

14. John Cotton, *The Way of Congregational Churches Cleared* (London, 1648), 8.

15. *An Apologeticall Narration* (London, 1643), 11, 31.

16. John Calvin, *Institutes of the Christian Religion* (Philadelphia: Westminster Press, 1970), 1:7, 1.

17. Perry Miller, *The New England Mind: The Seventeenth Century* (Cambridge: Harvard University Press, 1954), 206.

18. William Strong, *A Discourse of the Two Covenants* (London, 1678), 153.

19. William Ames, *The Marrow of Sacred Divinity* (London, 1642), 1.

20. William Perkins, "A Reformed Catholic," in *Works*, by William Perkins (London: I. Legatt, 1631), 1:576.

21. Thomas Sutton, *Lectures on the 11th Chapter of Romans* (London, 1632), 403.

22. Richard Sibbes, "The Bride's Longing for her Bridegroom's Second Coming," in *Works*, by Richard Sibbes (Edinburgh: James Nichol, 1863), 6:542.

23. Ames, *The Marrow of Sacred Divinity*, 127.

24. Paul Baynes, *A Help to True Happiness* (London, 1635), 92.

25. William Haller, *The Rise of Puritanism* (New York: Harper & Bros., 1938), 142.

26. Robert Jenison, *Concerning God's Certain Performance* (London, 1642), 120.

27. Thomas Blake, *Vindiciae Foederis, Or A Treatise of the Covenant of God Entered into with Mankind* (London, 1658), 111.

28. Jenison, *Concerning God's Certain Performance*, 120.

29. Ames, *The Marrow of Sacred Divinity*, 176–77.

30. Williston Walker, *The Creeds and Platforms of Congregationalism* (Boston: The Pilgrim Press, 1960), 19.

31. Ibid., 25.

32. Ibid., 22.

33. Ibid., 26.

34. Henry Jacob, *An Attestation of many Learned, Godly, and famous Divines* (1613), 122.

35. Horton Davies, *The Worship of the English Puritans* (London: Dacre Press, 1948), 50.

36. Richard Greenham, *Works*, 3d ed. (London: F. Kyngston 1601).

37. Haller, *The Rise of Puritanism*, 131.

38. George, *John Robinson*, 149.

39. Ibid., 151.

40. Stephen Mayor, *The Lord's Supper in Early English Dissent* (London: The Epworth Press, 1972), 32.

41. Ibid., 31.

42. Walker, *Creeds and Platforms of Congregationalism*, 408.

2. NEW WORLD BEGINNINGS, 1620–1660

1. Herbert Schneider, *The Puritan Mind* (New York: H. Holt & Co., 1930), 8.

2. Walker, *Creeds and Platforms of Congregationalism*, 90.

3. Gaius Glenn Atkins and Frederick L. Fagley, *History of American Congregationalism* (Boston: The Pilgrim Press, 1942), 60.

4. Walker, *Creeds and Platforms of Congregationalism*, 92.

5. Atkins and Fagley, *History of American Congregationalism*, 74.

6. Walker, *Creeds and Platforms of Congregationalism*, 116.

7. Ibid., 103–4.

8. Michael McGiffert, ed., *God's Plot* (Amhert: University of Massachusetts Press, 1972), 55.

9. Conrad Cherry, ed., *God's New Israel: Religious Interpretation of American Destiny* (New York: Prentice-Hall, 1971), 42–43.

10. Ibid., 39.

11. Sidney James, ed., *The New England Puritans* (New York: Harper & Row, 1968), 84.

12. Richard Mather, *Church Government and Church Covenant Discussed* (London, 1643), 83.

13. Thomas Hooker, *A Survey of the Summe of Church Discipline* (London, 1648), 1:13.

14. Schneider, *The Puritan Mind*, 54.

15. Edmund S. Morgan, *The Puritan Dilemma* (Boston: Little, Brown, 1958), 117.

16. Ibid., 118

17. Ibid., 120.

18. David D. Hall, ed., *The Antinomian Controversy, 1636–1638* (Middletown, Conn.: Wesleyan University Press, 1968), 7.

19. Williston Walker, *A History of the Congregational Churches in the United States* (New York: Christian Literature Company, 1897), 141.

20. Hall, *Antinomian Controversy*, 337.

21. Schneider, *The Puritan Mind*, 68.

22. Perry Miller, *Roger Williams* (Indianapolis: Bobbs-Merrill, 1953), 103.

23. Charles W. Sorenson, "John Davenport's Errand into the Wilderness," *Bulletin of the Congregational Library* 29, no. 3 (1978): 9.

24. Larzer Ziff, ed., *John Cotton on the Churches of New England* (Cambridge: Belknap Press, Harvard University Press, 1968). 27.

25. Walker, *Creeds and Platforms of Congregationalism*, 138.

26. William Perkins, "A Treatise Tending unto a Declaration, Whether a Man be in the Estate of Damnation or in the Estate of Grace," in *Works*, 1:410.

27. McGiffert, *God's Plot*, 43–45.

28. David D. Hall, *The Faithful Shepherd: A History of the New England Ministry in the Seventeenth Century* (Chapel Hill: University of North Carolina Press, 1972), 164.

29. Charles E. Hambrick-Stowe, *The Conversion Process in the Work of Thomas Hooker* (Master's thesis, Pacific School of Religion, Berkeley, Calif., 1972), 75, 93, 89.

30. Norman Pettit, *The Heart Prepared: Grace and Conversion in Puritan Spiritual Life* (New Haven: Yale University Press, 1966), 129.

31. Hambrick-Stowe, *Conversion Process*, 86–87.

32. William K. B. Stoever, "Nature, Grace, and John Cotton," *Church History* 44 (1975): 26.

33. William Perkins, "Christ's Sermon in the Mount," in *Works*, 3:149.

34. John Cotton, *Several Questions of Serious and Necessary Consequence* (London, 1647), 4.

35. Stoever, "Nature, Grace, and John Cotton," 30.

36. Ibid., 29.

37. Hall, *The Antinomian Controversy*, 231.

38. Philip Schaff, *The Creeds of Christendom* (New York: Harper & Brothers, 1877), 3:637.

39. Hooker, *Summe of Church Discipline*, 1:51.

40. Walker, *Creeds and Platforms of Congregationalism*, 208.

41. Ibid., 131.

42. Champlin Burrage, *The Church Covenant Idea* (Philadelphia: American Baptist Publication Society, 1904), 93.

43. Walker, *Creeds and Platforms of Congregationalism*, 117.

44. Wil[liam] Bartlet, *A Model of the Primitive Congregational Way* (London, 1647), 109.

45. Edmund S. Morgan, *Visible Saints* (New York: New York University Press, 1963), 100.

46. Ibid.

47. John Cotton, *The Way of the Churches of Christ in New England* (London, 1645), 58.

48. Walker, *Creeds and Platforms of Congregationalism*, 205

49. Ibid., 222.

50. Ibid., 219.

51. John Norton, *The Answer*, (Cambridge: Belknap Press, Harvard University Press, 1958), 98.

52. Hall, *Faithful Shepherd*, 111.

53. Ibid., 117.

54. Walker, *Creeds and Platforms of Congregationalism*, 220.

55. Walker, *History of the Congregational Churches*, 46.

56. Walker. *Creeds and Platforms of Congregationalism*, 229–30.

57. Ibid., 232–33.

58. Ibid., 234.

59. Doug Adams, *Meeting House to Camp Meeting* (Austin: Sharing Company, 1981), 20.

60. Winton U. Solberg, *Redeem the Time: The Puritan Sabbath in Early America* (Cambridge: Harvard University Press, 1977), 154.

61. E. Brooks Holifield, *The Covenant Sealed: The Development of Puritan Sacramental Theology in Old and New England, 1570–1720* (New Haven: Yale University Press, 1974), 140.

62. Walker, *Creeds and Platforms of Congregationalism*, 224.

63. Holifield, *The Covenant Sealed*, 164.

64. Charles E. Hambrick-Stowe, *The Practice of Piety: Puritan Devotional Disciplines in Seventeenth-Century New England* (Chapel Hill: University of North Carolina Press, 1982), 167.

65. Charles E. Hambrick-Stowe, ed., *Early New England Meditative Poetry* (New York: Paulist Press, 1988), 96.

66. Robert Pierce Beaver, *Church, State, and the American Indians* (St. Louis: Concordia Publishing House, 1966), 27.

67. Alden T. Vaughan, *New England Frontier: Puritans and Indians, 1620–1675* (Boston: Little, Brown, 1969), 260.

68. Ibid., 281.

69. Miller, *The Seventeenth Century*, 470.

3. CONTINUITY AND CHANGE, 1660–1730

1. Elizabeth C. Nordbeck, *The New England Diaspora: A Study of the Religious Culture of Maine and New Hampshire, 1613–1763* (Ph.D. diss., Harvard University, 1978), vi, 105.

2. Ibid., 1.

3. Robert Middlekauff, *The Mathers: Three Generations of Puritan Intellectuals, 1596–1728* (New York: Oxford University Press, 1971), 114, 169.

4. Walker, *Creeds and Platforms of Congregationalism*, 253.

5. Ibid., 328.

6. H. Keith Watkins, *The Ecclesiastical Contributions of Increase Mather to Late Seventeenth and Early Eighteenth Century Puritan Thought* (Th.D. diss., Pacific School of Religion, Berkeley, 1964), 158.

7. Walker, *Creeds and Platforms of Congregationalism*, 311–12.

8. Watkins, *Ecclesiastical Contributions*, 192–93.

9. Ibid., 193.

10. Emory Elliott, *Power and the Pulpit in Puritan New England* (Princeton: Princeton University Press, 1975), 114.

11. Watkins, *Ecclesiastical Contributions*, 200.

12. Walker, *Creeds and Platforms of Congregationalism*, 426, 433.

13. Ibid., 436.

14. Watkins, *Ecclesiastical Contributions*, 245; Schneider, *The Puritan Mind*, 90.

15. Watkins, *Ecclesiastical Contributions*, 246, 247.

16. Walker, *Creeds and Platforms of Congregationalism*, 479.

17. Ibid., 492.

18. Watkins, *Ecclesiastical Contributions*, 366.

19. Ibid., 366, 369, 368.

20. Perry Miller, *The New England Mind: From Colony to Province* (Cambridge: Harvard University Press, 1953), 128.

21. Watkins, *Ecclesiastical Contributions*, 368, 365, 383.

22. Ibid., 374.

23. Miller, *From Colony to Province*, 374.

24. Watkins, *Ecclesiastical Contributions*, 384.

25. Miller, *From Colony to Province*, 411.

26. Watkins, *Ecclesiastical Contributions*, 385.

27. Middlekauff, *The Mathers*, 169, 165.

28. James W. Jones, *The Shattered Synthesis: New England Puritanism Before the Great Awakening* (New Haven: Yale University Press, 1973), 80.

29. Ibid., 77.

30. Thomas Goodwin, "Christ the Mediator," in *Works* (London, 1692), 3:26.

31. Elliott, *Power and the Pulpit*, 160, 177.

32. Middlekauff, *The Mathers*, 253–55.

33. Ernest Benson Lowrie, *The Shape of the Puritan Mind: The Theology of Samuel Willard* (New Haven: Yale University Press, 1974), 27, 30.

34. Jones, *Shattered Synthesis*, 95–97.

35. Lowrie, *Puritan Mind*, 226.

36. Holifield, *The Covenant Sealed*, 175.

37. Walker, *Creeds and Platforms of Congregationalism*, 324, 334.

38. Middlekauff, *The Mathers*, 126.

39. Henry M. Dexter, *The Congregationalism of the Last Three Hundred Years as Seen in its Literature* (New York: Harper & Bros., 1880), 488.

40. Ibid., 483.

41. Watkins, *Ecclesiastical Contributions*, 276.

42. Ibid., 185, 277.

43. Ibid., 277.

44. Roland H. Bainton, *Christian Unity and Religion in New England* (Boston: Beacon Press, 1964), 224.

45. Walker, *History of the Congregational Churches*, 232.

46. Miller, *From Colony to Province*, 258.

47. Walker, *Creeds and Platforms of Congregationalism*, 219.

48. Dexter, *Congregationalism*, 484.

49. Hall, *Faithful Shepherd*, 208.

50. Harry S. Stout, *The New England Soul: Preaching and Religious Culture in Colonial New England* (New York: Oxford University Press, 1986), 162.

51. Walker, *Creeds and Platforms of Congregationalism*, 503.

52. Ibid., 505.

53. Walker, *History of the Congregational Churches*, 210–11.

54. Stout, *The New England Soul*, 30.

55. Walker, *History of the Congregational Churches*, 246.

56. Watkins, *Ecclesiastical Contributions*, 214.

57. Dexter, *Congregationalism*, 486.

58. Ibid., 487.

59. Williston Walker, "The Congregational idea of worship," *Hartford Seminary Record*, December 1894: 17.

60. George Punchard, Unpublished MS for *History of Congregationalism*, vol. 6 (Boston: Congregational Publishing Society, 1880–81), Congregational Library, Boston.

61. Alf E. Jacobson, "The Evolution of Worship in Congregational New England," Part 1, *Bulletin of the Congregational Library* 14, no. 3 (May 1963): 7.

62. Ibid.

63. Punchard, Unpublished MS, n.p.

64. Holifield, *The Covenant Sealed*, 186; Hall, *Faithful Shepherd*, 251.

65. Walker, *Creeds and Platforms of Congregationalism*, 222.

66. Holifield, *The Covenant Sealed*, 191, 190.

67. Hambrick-Stowe, *Early New England Meditative Poetry*, 162.

68. Holifield, *The Covenant Sealed*, 202.

69. George H. Ide, *The Congregational Churches and Christian Education* (Boston: Alfred Mudge and Son, 1887), 15–16.

70. Alden T. Vaughan, ed., *The Puritan Tradition in America, 1620–1730* (New York: Harper & Row, 1972), 236–37.

71. Winthrop S. Hudson, *Religion in America* (New York: Charles Scribner's Sons, 1981), 38.

72. Vaughan, *Puritan Tradition in America*, 245.

73. Stout, *The New England Soul*, 57.

74. Miller, *From Colony to Province*, 38.

75. Roland H. Bainton, *Yale and the Ministry* (New York: Harper & Brothers, 1957), 8.

76. Ortho T. Beall, Jr., and Richard H. Shryock, *Cotton Mather: First Significant Figure in American Medicine* (Baltimore: Johns Hopkins Press, 1954), 51.

77. Stephen Foster, *Their Solitary Way: The Puritan Social Ethic in the First Century of Settlement in New England* (New Haven: Yale University Press, 1971), 151.

4. REVIVAL AND REVOLUTION, 1730–1800

1. Sydney Ahlstrom, *A Religious History of the American People* (New Haven: Yale University Press, 1972), 281.

2. Hudson, *Religion in America*, 65.

3. Edwin S. Gaustad, *The Great Awakening in New England* (New York: Harper & Brothers, 1957), 28.

4. Hudson, *Religion in America*, 65.

5. Stout, *The New England Soul*, 190.

6. Ibid., 194.

7. Gaustad, *Great Awakening*, 34.

8. Jonathan Edwards, *Works*, 4 vols. (New York: Jonathan Leavitt and John Trow, 1843), 4:317–18.

9. Bainton, *Yale and the Ministry*, 24.

10. Ibid., 17.

11. Gaustad, *Great Awakening*, 100.

12. C. C. Goen, *Revivalism and Separatism in New England, 1740–1800* (New Haven: Yale University Press, 1962), 21.

13. Gaustad, *Great Awakening*, 39.

14. Walker, *History of the Congregational Churches*, 264.

15. Stout, *The New England Soul*, 203.

16. David Harlan, *The Clergy and the Great Awakening in New England* (Ann Arbor, Mich.: UMI Research Press, 1980), 56.

17. Stout, *The New England Soul*, 203

18. Harlan, *Clergy and the Great Awakening*, 57.

19. Gaustad, *Great Awakening*, 98.

20. Jonathan Edwards, *A Treatise Concerning Religious Affections* (New Haven: Yale University Press, 1959), 383.

21. Walker, *History of the Congregational Churches*, 265.

22. Harlan, *Clergy and the Great Awakening*, 1.

23. Goen, *Revivalism and Separatism*, 58.

24. Stout, *The New England Soul*, 243.

25. Ibid., 250, 253, 251.

26. Bainton, *Yale and the Ministry*, 13.

27. Gaustad, *Great Awakening*, 119.

28. Richard L. Bushman, *From Puritan to Yankee* (Cambridge: Harvard University Press, 1967), 222.

29. Hudson, *Religion in America*, 91.

30. Goen, *Revivalism and Separatism*, xv.

31. Stout, *The New England Soul*, 305.

32. J. Walter Sillen, "Manasseh Cutler: A Congregational Minister's Influence Upon the Northwest Ordinance of 1787," *Bulletin of the Congregational Library* 38, no. 3 (Spring-Summer 1987): 6.

33. Ibid., 4.

34. Daniel T. Fiske, "New England Theology," *Bibliotheca Sacra* 22, no. 87 (1865): 507.

35. Frank Hugh Foster, *A Genetic History of the New England Theology* (Chicago: University of Chicago Press, 1907), 175.

36. Robert L. Ferm, *Jonathan Edwards the Younger, 1745–1801* (Grand Rapids, Mich.: Eerdmanns, 1976), 123.

37. Foster, *Genetic History*, 111.

38. Fiske, "New England Theology," 507.

39. Foster, *Genetic History*, 123.

40. Jones, *Shattered Synthesis*, 137, 177.

41. Ibid., 135.

42. Ibid., 190.

43. Ibid., 195.

44. Harlan, *Clergy and the Great Awakening*, 89.

45. Ibid., 90.

46. Ibid., 93.

47. Goen, *Revivalism and Separatism*, 31, 58.

48. Stout, *The New England Soul*, 217.

49. Mary Beth Norton, *Liberty's Daughters: The Revolutionary Experience of American Women, 1750–1800* (Boston: Little, Brown, 1980), 130–32.

50. Walker, "The Congregational idea of worship," 23.

51. Alf E. Jacobson, "The Evolution of Worship in Congregational New England," Part 2, *Bulletin of the Congregational Library* 15, no. 1 (October 1963): 8.

52. Ibid.

53. Ibid., 9.

54. Stout, *The New England Soul*, 221.

55. Ibid.

56. Robert J. Dinkin, "Seating the Meeting House in Early Massachusetts," *New England Quarterly* 43, no. 3 (September 1970): 455.

57. Bernard Rosenthal, "Puritan Conscience and New England Slavery" *New England Quarterly* 46, no. 1 (March 1973): 70.

58. Daniel K. Richter, "'It is God Who Has Caused Them To Be Servants': Cotton Mather and Afro-American Slavery in New England," *Bulletin of the Congregational Library* 30, no. 3 (Spring-Summer 1979): 6.

59. Rosenthal, "Puritan Conscience," 75.

60. Beaver, *Church, State*, 39.

61. Harlan, *Clergy and the Great Awakening*, 119.

62. Hudson, *Religion in America*, 112.

5. EXPANDING HORIZONS, 1800–1870

1. Charles C. Cole, Jr., *The Social Ideas of the Northern Evangelists, 1826–1860* (New York: Columbia University Press, 1954), 11.

2. Sherwood Eddy, *The Kingdom of God and the American Dream* (New York: Harper & Brothers, 1941), 134.

3. Sanford H. Cobb, *The Rise of Religious Liberty in America* (New York, 1902), 513.

4. Sidney E. Mead, *Nathaniel William Taylor, 1786–1858: A Connecticut Liberal* (Chicago: University of Chicago Press, 1942), 50–51.

5. Samuel H. Willey, *American Congregationalism in the Nineteenth Century* (San Francisco: George Spalding, 1902), 8.

6. Albert E. Dunning, *Congregationalists in America* (New York: J. A. Hill, 1894), 302.

7. Mead, *Nathaniel William Taylor*, 137.

8. Ibid., 28.

9. H. Shelton Smith, Robert T. Handy, and Lefferts A. Loetscher, eds., *American Christianity: An Historical Interpretation with Representative Documents* (New York: Charles Scribner's Sons, 1960), 1:521.

10. Edwin S. Gaustad, *A Religious History of America* (New York: Harper & Row, 1966), 151.

11. Hudson, *Religion in America*, 199.

12. G. M. Stephenson, *The Puritan Heritage* (New York: Macmillan, 1952), 157.

13. Walker, *Creeds and Platforms of Congregationalism*, 533.

14. Ibid.

15. *Proceedings of the General Convention of Congregational Ministers and Delegates in the United States, Held at Albany, N.Y., 5th-8th of October, 1852* (New York: S. W. Benedict, 1852), 70.

16. Ibid., 72.

17. Walker, *Creeds and Platforms of Congregationalism*, 540.

18. John R. Bodo, *The Protestant Clergy and Public Issues, 1812–1848* (Princeton: Princeton University Press, 1954), 162.

19. Colin B. Goodykoontz, *Home Missions on the American Frontier, with Particular Reference to the American Home Missionary Society* (Caldwell, Idaho: Caxton, 1939), 20.

20. Andrew L. Drummond, *Story of American Protestantism* (Edinburgh: Oliver and Boyd, 1949), 257.

21. Gaustad, *A Religious History of America*, 151.

22. Stephenson, *The Puritan Heritage*, 99–100.

23. Lois Kimball Mathews, "Some Activities of the Congregational Church West of the Mississippi," in *Essays in American History Dedicated to Frederick Jackson Turner* (New York: Henry Holt and Company, 1910), 11.

24. William Warren Sweet, *Religion on the American Frontier: The Congregationalists, 1783–1850* (Chicago: University of Chicago Press, 1939), 32.

25. Gordon A. Riegler, *Socialization of the New England Clergy, 1800–1860* (Greenfield, Ohio: Greenfield Publishing, 1945), 14.

26. *Proceedings of the General Convention*, 27.

27. Mrs. John T. Beach, *The Albany Convention of 1852 or aid to our feeble churches of the west, adapted from the minutes of the convention*, MS, Congregational Library, Boston.

28. *Proceedings of the General Convention*, 25.

29. Atkins and Fagley, *History of American Congregationalism*, 205.

30. Walker, *Creeds and Platforms of Congregationalism*, 560.

31. Ibid., 563.

32. Commission on Congregationalism and Missions, *The Missionary History of Congregationalism* (New York: National Council of Congregational Churches, 1920), 19.

33. Ahlstrom, *A Religious History*, 657.

34. Hudson, *Religion in America*, 224.

35. Ibid.

36. William Ellery Channing, "Unitarian Christianity," in *The Works of William E. Channing, D.D.* (Boston: American Unitarian Association, 1890), 371.

37. Ibid., 373.

38. Ibid., 378–80.

39. George Nye Boardman, *A History of New England Theology* (New York: A. D. F. Randolph, 1899), 109.

40. Ibid., 107.

41. Mead, *Nathaniel William Taylor*, 190.

42. Bainton, *Yale and the Ministry*, 101.

43. Charles G. Finney, *Memoirs of Rev. Charles G. Finney* (New York: A. B. Barnes, 1876), 189.

44. William G. McLoughlin, *Revivals, Awakenings, and Reform* (Chicago: University of Chicago Press, 1978), 125.

45. Ibid., 125–26.

46. Theodore T. Munger, *Horace Bushnell, Preacher and Theologian* (Boston: Houghton Mifflin, 1899), 76.

47. H. Shelton Smith, *Changing Conceptions of Original Sin, A Study in American Theology Since 1750* (New York: Charles Scribner's Sons, 1955), 161–63.

48. John Wright Buckham, *Progressive Religious Thought in America* (Boston: Houghton Mifflin, 1919), 27.

49. Bainton, *Yale and the Ministry*, 116.

50. H. Shelton Smith, ed., *Horace Bushnell* (New York: Oxford University Press, 1965), 26.

51. Bainton, *Yale and the Ministry*, 120.

52. *Official Record of the National Congregational Council Held at Boston, June 14–24, 1865* (Boston: Proprietors of the Congregational Quarterly, 1865), 165.

53. Dexter, *Congregationalism*, 513–54.

54. Joseph E. Roy, *A Manual of the Principles, Doctrines and Usages of Congregational Churches* (Chicago: Church, Goodman, and Donnelly, 1864), 36–37.

55. Ibid., 22–23.

56. Henry M. Dexter, *Congregationalism: What it is; Whence it is; How it works; Why it is better than any other form of Church Government; and its Consequent demands* (Boston, 1865), 2–3, 334.

57. *Official Record*, 166.

58. Thomas Cogswell Upham, *Ratio Disciplinae: or The Constitution of the Congregational Churches* (Portland, Maine: Shirley and Hyde, 1829), 240.

59. A. Hastings Ross, *The Church Kingdom: Lectures on Congregationalism* (Boston: Congregational Sunday School and Publication Society, 1887), 296.

60. *Official Record*, 166.

61. Nathaneal Emmons, *The Platform of Ecclesiastical Government, established by the Lord Jesus Christ* (Providence, R.I., 1826), 10.

62. *A Manual of Congregationalism, Prepared for the General Conference of the Congregational Churches of Maine* (Portland, Maine: Hyde & Lord, 1848), 42.

63. Ahlstrom, *A Religious History*, 405–6.

64. *Official Record*, 103, 168.

65. Ibid., 103–4.

66. Cole, *Social Ideas*, 21, 57.

67. *Official Record*, 104.

68. Norman S. McKendrick, *How Congregationalists Have Worshipped*, Mimeographed MS, n.d., Congregational Library, Boston.

69. Stephenson, *The Puritan Heritage*, 149.

70. *Official Record*, 37.

71. Donald M. Scott, *From Office to Professtion: the New England Ministry, 1750–1850* (Philadelphia: University of Pennsylvania Press, 1978), 144.

72. Ibid.

73. *Official Record*, 106.

74. Fred Field Goodsell, *You Are My Witnesses* (Boston: American Board of Commisioners for Foreign Missions, 1959), 13–18.

75. Ibid., 35.

76. Cole, *Social Ideas*, 125.

77. Mervin M Deems, *Maine—First of Conferences: A History of the Maine Conference, United Church of Christ* (Bangor, Maine: Furbush-Roberts Printing, 1974), 30.

78. *Proceedings of the General Convention*, 19.

79. Stephenson, *The Puritan Heritage*, 181–82.

80. Cole, *Social Ideas*, 108.

81. Stephenson, *The Puritan Heritage*, 183.

82. Deems, *Maine*, 28.

83. Cole, *Social Ideas*, 199.

84. *Official Record*, 127.

6. AN ERA OF PROGRESS, 1870–1920

1. Martin Marty, *Righteous Empire: The Protestant Experience in America* (New York: Dial Press, 1970), 133–76.

2. National Council of Congregational Churches, *Minutes* (Boston, 1871), 29–30.

3. Ibid., 30.

4. National Council, *Minutes* (Boston, 1877), 37.

5. National Council, *Minutes* (Boston, 1880), 187–89.

6. National Council, *Minutes* (Boston, 1913), 342, 345, 352.

7. Winthrop S. Hudson, *The Great Tradition of the American Churches* (New York: Harper & Brothers, 1953), 174; Clifton E. Olmstead, *A History of Religion in the United States* (Englewood Cliffs, N.J.: Prentice-Hall, 1960), 466.

8. Paul A. Carter, *The Spiritual Crisis of the Gilded Age* (De Kalb: Northern Illinois University Press, 1972), 27, 28.

9. William R. Hutchison, *The Modernist Impulse in American Protestantism* (Cambridge: Harvard University Press, 1976), 76.

10. Jon H. Roberts, *Darwinism and the Divine in America: Protestant Intellectuals and Organic Evolution, 1859–1900* (Madison: University of Wisconsin Press, 1988), 150.

11. Lloyd J. Averill, *American Theology in the Liberal Tradition* (Philadelphia: Westminster Press, 1967), 86, 88.

12. Marty, *Righteous Empire*, 157.

13. Ahlstrom, *A Religious History*, 789.

14. Henry F. May, *Protestant Churches and Industrial America* (New York: Harper & Brothers, 1949), 91.

15. Charles Howard Hopkins, *The Rise of the Social Gospel in American Protestantism* (New Haven: Yale University Press, 1940), 84–85.

16. National Council, *Minutes* (New York, 1920), 232.

17. National Council, *Minutes* (Boston, 1889), 244.

18. National Council, *Minutes* (Boston, 1892), 251.

19. National Council, *Minutes* (Boston, 1895), 20

20. May, *Protestant Churches and Industrial America*, 116.

21. Josiah Strong, *Our Country* (Cambridge: Harvard University Press, Belknap Press, 1963), 53.

22. National Council, *Minutes* (Boston, 1889), 45.

23. Robert D. Cross, ed., *The Church and the City, 1865–1910* (Indianapolis: Bobbs-Merrill, 1967), 46.

24. Strong, *Our Country*, 61–62.

25. Ibid., 174.

26. A. Knighton Stanley, *The Children Is Crying: Congregationalism Among Black People* (New York: The Pilgrim Press, 1979), 77, 56, 48.

27. William G. Chrystal, "German Congregationalism," *Hidden Histories in the United Church of Christ*, ed. in Barbara Brown Zikmund (New York: United Church Press, 1984), 69.

28. National Council, *Minutes* (New York, 1921), 40–41.

29. Walker, *Creeds and Platforms of Congregationalism*, 563–64.

30. Ibid., 575.

31. National Council, *Minutes* (Boston, 1874), 62–64.

32. National Council, *Minutes* (Boston, 1898), 316.

33. National Council, *Minutes* (Boston, 1892), 40.

34. National Council, *Minutes* (Boston, 1895), 36.

35. Smith, Handy, and Loescher, *American Christianity*, 2:220.

36. Ira V. Brown, *Lyman Abbott, Christian Evolutionist: A Study in Religious Liberalism* (Cambridge: Harvard University Press, 1953), 170, 171, 177.

37. Robert T. Handy, *A History of the Churches in the United States and Canada* (New York: Oxford University Press, 1977), 306–7.

38. Brown, *Lyman Abbott*, 220–21; Olmstead, *History of Religion*, 511.

39. Averill, *American Theology*, 92.

40. George A. Gordon, "The Collapse of the New England Theology," *Harvard Theological Review* 1, no. 2 (1908): 127–68. All quotations from Gordon in discussion of the New England theology are drawn from this article.

41. Brown, *Lyman Abbott*, 144, 142.

42. Averill, *American Theology*, 71

43. Buckham, *Progressive Religious Thought in America*, 68.

44. Richard D. Knudten, *The Systematic Thought of Washington Gladden* (New York: Humanities Press, 1968), 59.

45. Drummond, *Story of American Protestantism*, 341.

46. Smith, *Changing Conceptions of Original Sin*, 180.

47. Ibid., 170, 180.

48. Knudten, *Systematic Thought*, 86.

49. Ibid., 110.

50. Brown, *Lyman Abbott*, 144–45.

51. National Council, *Minutes* (Boston, 1880), 25.

52. National Council, *Minutes* (Boston, 1913), 340–41.

53. Gabriel Fackre, "The Kansas City Statement As A Confession of Faith," *Bulletin of the Congregational Library* 39, no. 3 (Spring-Summer 1988): 6.

54. National Council, *Minutes* (Boston, 1877), 244; National Council, *Minutes* (Boston, 1880), 72.

55. National Council, *Minutes* (Boston, 1886), 286–87.

56. William E. Barton, *The Law of Congregational Usage* (Boston: The Pilgrim Press, 1923), 156, 150.

57. National Council, *Minutes* (Boston, 1907), 345.

58. Barton, *The Law of Congregational Usage*, 292.

59. National Council, *Minutes* (Boston, 1907), 346.

60. National Council, *Minutes* (Boston, 1886), 319.

61. A. Hastings Ross, "Voluntary societies and Congregational churches," *Bibliotheca Sacra*, October 1890, 537.

62. National Council, *Minutes* (Boston, 1886), 361.

63. National Council, *Minutes* (Boston, 1889), 299–300.

64. Ibid., 303.

65. Ibid., 303–4.

66. Ibid., 305.

67. National Council, *Minutes* (Boston, 1904), 492, 497.

68. National Council, *Minutes* (Boston, 1910), 303, 373.

69. Ibid., 304.

70. National Council, *Minutes* (Boston, 1901), 175.

71. National Council, *Minutes* (Boston, 1913), 324.

72. Knudten, *Systematic Thought*, 94–96.

73. National Council, *Minutes* (Boston, 1913), 327–28.

74. National Council, *Minutes* (Boston, 1901), 181.

75. National Council, *Minutes* (Boston, 1883), 11–12.

76. Brown, *Lyman Abbott*, 134.

77. Hutchison, *The Modernist Impulse*, 111.

78. Ibid., 132.

79. Ibid., 141.

80. Buckham, *Progressive Religious Thought in America*, 170.

81. May, *Protestant Churches and Industrial America*, 173.

82. A. I. Abell, *The Urban Impact on American Protestantism, 1865–1900* (Cambridge: Harvard University Press, 1943), 72.

83. National Council, *Minutes* (Boston, 1895), 142, 144.

84. National Council, *Minutes* (Boston, 1913), 405; National Council, *Minutes* (New York, 1919), 41.

85. National Council, *Minutes* (Boston, 1919), 260.

86. National Council, *Minutes* (Boston, 1871), 59; National Council, *Minutes* (Boston, 1892), 39.

87. National Council, *Minutes* (New York, 1919), 40; National Council, *Minutes* (Boston, 1886), 36.

7. TENSIONS AND TRANSITIONS, 1920–1957

1. General Council of Congregational Christian Churches, *Minutes* (New York, 1931), 19.

2. General Council, *Minutes* (New York, 1936), supplement.

3. General Council, *Minutes* (New York, 1940), 41.

4. Robert Moats Miller, *American Protestantism and Social Issues, 1919–1939* (Chapel Hill: University of North Carolina Press, 1961), 31.

5. H. Richard Niebuhr, Wilhelm Pauck, and Francis P. Miller, *The Church Against the World* (Chicago: Willett, Clark, 1935), 12–13.

6. Curtis Beach, "The German Evangelical Protestants," in *Hidden Histories in the United Church of Christ*, ed. Barbara Brown Zikmund (New York: United Church Press, 1987), 2:39.

7. National Council, *Minutes* (New York, 1925), 21.

8. Smith, Handy, and Loescher, *American Christianity*, 1:576.

9. National Council, *Minutes* (New York, 1925), 51–53.

10. Atkins and Fagley, *History of American Congregationalism*, 261–62.

11. General Council, *Minutes* (New York, 1934), 89.

12. General Council, *Minutes* (New York, 1936), 51.

13. Miller, *American Protestantism*, 81.

14. Executive Committee, General Council of Congregational Christian Churches, 7 January 1935.

15. Committee Opposing Congregational Political Action, *They're Using Our Churches* (n.p.).

16. General Council, *Minutes* (New York, 1952), 39.

17. General Council, *Minutes* (New York, 1931), 211; General Council, *Minutes* (New York, 1934), 105.

18. General Council, *Minutes* (New York, 1940), 45, 47.

19. General Council, *Minutes* (New York, 1942), 35.

20. General Council of Congregational Christian Churches, *Advance Reports* (New York, 1956), 88.

21. Leonard Hodson, ed., *The Second World Conference of Faith and Order* (New York: Macmillan, 1938), 275.

22. Message of The First Assembly of the World Council of Churches, 1948, *Man's Disorder and God's Design* (New York: Harper and Brothers), appendix.

23. General Council, *Minutes* (New York, 1938), 161–62.

24. *The Heidelberg Catechism with Commentary* (Boston: United Church Press, 1963), 17.

25. Louis H. Gunnemann, *The Shaping of the United Church of Christ* (New York: United Church Press, 1977), 224.

26. Ibid., 19.

27. *The Christian Century*, 8 November 1933, 1403.

28. H. Richard Niebuhr, *The Kingdom of God in America* (Chicago: Willett, Clark, 1937), 193.

29. Conservative Congregational Christian Conference, *1991 Year Book* (n.p.), 80.

30. Emil Brunner, *The Divine-Human Encounter* (Philadelphia: Westminster Press, 1943), 110.

31. Wilhelm Pauck, *Karl Barth: Prophet of a New Christianity?* (New York: Harper & Brothers, 1931), 219–20.

32. General Council, *Minutes* (New York, 1934), 15.

33. General Council, *Advance Reports* (New York, 1940), 61.

34. Gunnemann, *United Church of Christ*, 224.

35. Atkins and Fagley, *History of American Congregationalism*, 274.

36. Michael J. Taylor, *The Protestant Liturgical Renewal: A Catholic Viewpoint* (Westminster, Md.: Newman Press, 1963), 281.

37. General Council of Congregational Christian Churches, *A Book of Worship for Free Churches* (New York: Oxford University Press, 1948), xxiv.

38. Schneider, *Religion in Twentieth-Century America*, 96.

39. Goodsell, *You Are My Witnesses*, 118–19.

40. General Council, *Advance Reports* (New York, 1946), 89.

41. National Council, *Minutes* (New York, 1921), 394.

42. National Council, *Minutes* (New York, 1923), 75.

43. National Council, *Minutes* (New York, 1925), 52.

44. General Council, *Minutes* (New York, 1931), 218.

45. National Council, *Minutes* (New York, 1919), 35; National Council, *Minutes* (New York, 1923), 76; National Council, *Minutes* (New York, 1925), 51.

46. General Council, *Minutes* (New York, 1934), 110–11; General Council, *Minutes* (New York, 1942), 39.

47. General Council, *Minutes* (New York, 1946), 47; General Council, *Minutes* (New York, 1948), 74; General Council, *Minutes* (New York, 1954, 42.

SUGGESTED READINGS

GENERAL HISTORIES: AMERICAN RELIGION

Ahlstrom, Sydney E. *A Religious History of the American People*. New Haven: Yale University Press, 1972.

Brauer, Jerald C. *Protestantism in America*. Philadelphia: Westminster Press, 1953.

Drummond, Andrew L. *Story of American Protestantism*. Edinburgh: Oliver and Boyd, 1949.

Gaustad, Edwin S. *Historical Atlas of Religion in America*. New York: Harper & Row, 1962.

————. *A Religious History of America*. New York: Harper & Row, 1966.

Handy, Robert T. *A History of the Churches in the United States and Canada*. New York: Oxford University Press, 1977.

Hardesty, Nancy A. *Great Women of Faith*. Grand Rapids, Mich.: Baker Book House, 1980.

Hatch, Nathan O. *Democratization of American Christianity*. New Haven: Yale University Press, 1989.

Hudson, Winthrop S. *Religion in America*. 3d ed. New York: Charles Scribner's Sons, 1981.

McLoughlin, William G. *Revivals, Awakenings, and Reform*. Chicago: University of Chicago Press, 1978.

Marty, Martin E. *Righteous Empire: The Protestant Experience in America*. New York: The Dial Press, 1970.

Olmstead, Clifton E. *A History of Religion in the United States*. Englewood Cliffs, N.J.: Prentice-Hall, 1960.

Smith, H. Shelton. *Changing Conceptions of Original Sin, A Study in American Theology Since 1750*. New York: Charles Scribner's Sons, 1955.

Sweet, William Warren. *Religion in the Development of American Culture*. New York: Charles Scribner's Sons, 1952.

GENERAL HISTORIES: CONGREGATIONALISM

Atkins, Gaius Glenn, and Fagley, Frederick L. *History of American Congregationalism*. Boston: The Pilgrim Press, 1942.

471

Barton, William E. *Congregational Creeds and Covenants*. Chicago: Advance Publishing, 1917.

Dexter, Henry Martyn. *The Congregationalism of the Last Three Hundred Years as Seen in its Literature*. New York: Harper & Brothers, 1880.

Foster, Frank Hugh. *A Genetic History of the New England Theology*. Chicago: University of Chicago Press, 1907.

Goodsell, Fred Field. *You Shall Be My Witnesses*. Boston: American Board of Commissioners for Foreign Missions, 1959.

Holifield, E. Brooks. *The Covenant Sealed: The Development of Puritan Sacramental Theology in Old and New England, 1570–1720*. New Haven: Yale University Press, 1974.

Stephenson, George M. *The Puritan Heritage*. New York: Macmillan, 1952.

Starkey, Marion L. *The Congregational Way: The Role of Pilgrims and Their Heirs in Shaping America*. Garden City, N.Y.: Doubleday, 1966

Stout, Harry S. *The New England Soul: Preaching and Religious Culture in Colonial New England*. New York: Oxford University Press, 1986.

Youngs, J. William T. *The Congregationalists*. New York: Greenwood Press, 1990.

Walker, Williston. *The Creeds and Platforms of Congregationalism*. New York: The Pilgrim Press, 1991. (Originally published in 1893.)

Walker, Williston. *A History of the Congregational Churches in the United States*. New York: Christian Literature Company, 1897.

Winslow, Ola. *Meetinghouse Hill, 1630–1783*. New York: Macmillan, 1952.

Zikmund, Barbara Brown, ed. *Hidden Histories in the United Church of Christ*. Vols. 1 and 2. New York: United Church Press, 1984, 1987.

CHAPTER 1: OLD WORLD ANTECEDENTS, 1558–1660

Burrage, Champlin. *The Early English Dissenters in the Light of Recent Research*. Vols. 1 and 2. New York: Russell & Russell, 1967. (Originally published in 1912.)

Collinson, Patrick. *The Elizabethan Puritan Movement*. London: Jonathan Cape, 1967.

Coolidge, John S. *The Pauline Renaissance in England*. Oxford: Clarendon Press, 1970.

Dale, R. W. *History of English Congregationalism*. New York: A. C. Armstrong and Son, 1907.

Davies, Horton. *The English Free Churches*. London: Oxford University Press, 1952.

———. *The Worship of the English Puritans*. London: Dacre Press, 1948.

George, Timothy. *John Robinson and the English Separatist Tradition*. Macon, Ga.: Mercer University Press, 1982.

Haller, William. *The Rise of Puritanism*. New York: Harper & Brothers, 1938.

Knappen, M. M. *Tudor Puritanism*. Chicago: University of Chicago Press, 1939.

New, John F. H. *Anglican and Puritan: The Basis of Their Opposition, 1558–1640*. London: Adam & Charles Black, 1964.

Nuttall, Geoffrey. *Visible Saints, The Congregational Way, 1640–1660*. London: Oxford University Press, 1957.

Sprunger, Keith L. *The Learned Doctor William Ames*. Urbana: University of Illinois Press, 1972.

von Rohr, John. *The Covenant of Grace in Puritan Thought*. Atlanta: Scholars Press, 1986.

Wallace, Dewey D., Jr. *Puritans and Predestination: Grace in English Protestant Theology, 1525–1695*. Chapel Hill: University of North Carolina Press, 1982.

White, B. R. *The English Separatist Tradition from the Marian Martyrs to the Pilgrim Fathers*. Oxford: Oxford University Press, 1971.

CHAPTER 2: NEW WORLD BEGINNINGS, 1620–1660

Bartlett, Robert M. *The Faith of the Pilgrims: An American Heritage*. New York: United Church Press, 1978.

Levy, Babette May. *Preaching in the First Half Century of New England History*. Hartford: American Society of Church History, 1945.

Miller, Perry. *Errand into the Wilderness*. Cambridge: Harvard University Press, 1956.

————. *The New England Mind: The Seventeenth Century*. Cambridge: Harvard University Press, 1939.

————. *Orthodoxy in Massachusetts*. Cambridge: Harvard University Press, 1933.

Morgan, Edmund S. *The Puritan Dilemma: The Story of John Winthrop*. Boston: Little, Brown, 1958.

————. *Visible Saints: The History of a Puritan Idea*. New York: New York University Press, 1963.

Morison, Samuel Eliot. *Builders of the Bay Colony*. Boston: Houghton Mifflin, 1930.

Pettit, Norman. *The Heart Prepared: Grace and Conversion in Puritan Spiritual Life*. New Haven: Yale University Press, 1966.

Scholes, Percy. *The Puritans and Music*. London: Oxford University Press, 1934.

Solberg, Winton U. *Redeem the Time: The Puritan Sabbath in Early America.* Cambridge: Harvard University Press, 1977.

Stoever, William K. B. *'A Faire and Easie Way to Heaven': Covenant Theology and Antinomianism in Early Massachusetts.* Middletown, Conn.: Wesleyan University Press, 1978.

Vaughan, Alden T. *New England Frontier: Puritans and Indians, 1620–1675.* Boston: Little, Brown, 1969.

Ziff, Larzer. *The Career of John Cotton: Puritanism and the American Experience.* Princeton: Princeton University Press, 1962.

CHAPTER 3: CONTINUITY AND CHANGE, 1660–1730

Bushman, Richard L. *From Puritan to Yankee.* Cambridge: Harvard University Press, 1967.

Butler, Jon. *Awash in a Sea of Faith.* Cambridge: Harvard University Press, 1990.

Donnelly, Marian Card. *The New England Meeting Houses of the Seventeenth Century.* Middletown, Conn.: Wesleyan University Press, 1968.

Foster, Stephen. *Their Solitary Way: The Puritan Social Ethic in the First Century of Settlement in New England.* New Haven: Yale University Press, 1971.

Hall, David D. *The Faithful Shepherd: A History of the New England Ministry in the Seventeenth Century.* Chapel Hill: University of North Carolina Press, 1972.

———. *Worlds of Wonder, Days of Judgment.* New York: Knopf, 1989.

Hambrick-Stowe, Charles E. *The Practice of Piety: Puritan Devotional Disciplines in Seventeenth-Century New England.* Chapel Hill: University of North Carolina Press, 1982.

Jones, James W. *The Shattered Synthesis: New England Puritanism Before the Great Awakening.* New Haven: Yale University Press, 1973.

Lovelace, Richard F. *The American Pietism of Cotton Mather: Origins of American Evangelicalism.* Grand Rapids, Mich.: Eerdmanns, 1979.

Lowrie, Ernest Benson. *The Shape of the Puritan Mind: The Theology of Samuel Willard.* New Haven: Yale University Press, 1974.

Middlekauf, Robert. *The Mathers: Three Generations of Puritan Intellectuals, 1596–1728.* New York: Oxford University Press, 1971.

Miller, Perry. *The New England Mind: From Colony to Province.* Cambridge: Harvard University Press, 1953.

Pope, Robert G. *The Half-Way Covenant: Church Membership in Puritan New England.* Princeton: Princeton University Press, 1969.

CHAPTER 4: REVIVAL AND REVOLUTION, 1730–1800

Baldwin, Alice M. *The New England Clergy and the American Revolution.* Durham, N.C.: Duke University Press, 1928.

Cherry, Conrad. *The Theology of Jonathan Edwards: A Reappraisal.* Garden City, N.Y.: Doubleday, 1966.

Gambrell, Mary L. *Ministerial Training in Eighteenth-Century New England.* New York: Columbia University Press, 1937.

Gaustad, Edwin S. *The Great Awakening in New England.* New York: Harper & Brothers, 1957.

Gerstner, John H. *Steps to Salvation: The Evangelistic Message of Jonathan Edwards.* Philadelphia: Westminster Press, 1960.

Goen, C. C. *Revivalism and Separatism in New England, 1740–1800: Strict Congregationalists and Separate Baptists in the Great Awakening.* New Haven: Yale University Press, 1962.

Greene, Lorenzo. *The Negro in Colonial New England, 1620–1776.* New York: Columbia University Press, 1942.

Griffin, Edward M. *Old Brick: Charles Chauncy of Boston, 1705–1787.* Minneapolis: University of Minnesota Press, 1980.

Harlan, David. *The Clergy and the Great Awakening in New England.* Ann Arbor: UMI Research Press, 1980.

Hatch, Nathan O. *The Sacred Cause of Liberty: Republican Thought and the Millennium in Revolutionary New England.* New Haven: Yale University Press, 1977.

Heimart, Alan. *Religion and the American Mind: From the Great Awakening to the Revolution.* Cambridge: Harvard University Press, 1966.

Morgan, Edmund S. *The Gentle Puritan: A Life of Ezra Stiles, 1727–1795.* New Haven: Yale University Press, 1962.

Wilson, Robert John. *The benevolent deity: Ebenezer Gay and the rise of rational religion in New England, 1696–1787.* Philadelphia: University of Pennsylvania Press, 1984.

CHAPTER 5: EXPANDING HORIZONS, 1800–1870

Bodo, John R. *The Protestant Clergy and Public Issues, 1812–1848.* Princeton: Princeton University Press, 1954.

Brownlee, Frederick Leslie. *New Day Ascending.* Boston: The Pilgrim Press, 1946.

Clark, Joseph B. *Leavening the Nation: The Story of American Home Missions.* New York: Baker and Taylor, 1903.

Cole, Charles C., Jr. *The Social Ideas of the Northern Evangelists, 1826–1860.* New York: Columbia University Press, 1954.

Goodykoontz, Colin B. *Home Missions on the American Frontier, with Particular Reference to the American Home Missionary Society*. Caldwell, Idaho: Caxton, 1939.

Henry, Stuart C. *Unvanquished Puritan: A Portrait of Lyman Beecher*. Grand Rapids, Mich.: Eerdmanns, 1973.

Mead, Sidney E. *Nathaniel William Taylor, 1786–1858: A Connecticut Liberal*. Chicago: University of Chicago Press, 1942.

Munger, Theodore T. *Horace Bushnell, Preacher and Theologian*. Boston: Houghton Mifflin, 1899.

Phillips, Clifton Jackson. *Protestant Americans and the Pagan World: The First Half Century of the American Board of Commissioners for Foreign Missions, 1810–1860*. Cambridge: Harvard University Press, 1969.

Scott, Donald M. *From Office to Profession: The New England Ministry, 1750–1850*. Philadelphia: University of Pennsylvania Press, 1978.

Smith, Timothy L. *Revivalism and Social Reform: In Mid-Nineteenth Century America*. Nashville: Abingdon, 1957.

Wright, Conrad. *The Beginnings of Unitarianism in America*. Boston: Beacon Press, 1955.

CHAPTER 6: AN ERA OF PROGRESS, 1870–1920

Abell, A. I. *The Urban Impact on American Protestantism, 1865–1900*. Cambridge: Harvard University Press, 1943.

Abrahms, Ray H. *Preachers Present Arms*. New York: Round Table Press, 1933.

Averill, Lloyd J. *American Theology in the Liberal Tradition*. Philadelphia: Westminster Press, 1967.

Barton, William E. *The Law of Congregational Usage*. Boston: The Pilgrim Pres, 1923. (Originally published in 1916.)

Brown, Ira V. *Lyman Abbott, Christian Evolutionist: A Study in Religious Liberalism*. Cambridge: Harvard University Press, 1953.

Buckham, John Wright. *Progressive Religious Thought in America*. Boston: Houghton Mifflin, 1919.

Hopkins, Charles Howard. *The Rise of the Social Gospel in American Protestantism, 1865–1915*. New Haven: Yale University Press, 1940.

Hutchison, William F. *The Modernist Impulse in American Protestantism*. Cambridge: Harvard University Press, 1976.

Knudten, Richard D. *The Systematic Thought of Washington Gladden*. New York: Humanities Press, 1968.

May, Henry F. *Protestant Churches and Industrial America*. New York: Harper & Brothers, 1949.

Roberts, Jon H. *Darwinism and the Divine in America: Protestant Intellectuals and Organic Evolution, 1859–1900*. Madison: University of Wisconsin Press, 1988.

Szasz, Ferenc Morton. *The Divided Mind of Protestant America, 1880–1930*. Tuscaloosa, Ala.: University of Alabama Press, 1982.

CHAPTER 7: TENSIONS AND TRANSITIONS, 1920–1957

Bennett, John C. *Social Salvation*. New York: Charles Scribner's Sons, 1935.

Burton, Malcolm K. *Destiny for Congregationalism*. Oklahoma City: Modern Publishers, 1953.

————. *How Church Union Came: A Critical Evaluation of the Methods and Representations Used by Churchmen to Establish the United Church of Christ*. Marshalltown, Iowa: Committee for the Continuation of Congregational Christian Churches of the United States, 1966.

Carter, Paul A. *The Decline and Revival of the Social Gospel: Social and Political Liberalism in American Protestant Churches, 1920–1940*. Ithaca, N.Y.: Cornell University Press, 1954.

Cavert, Samuel McCrea. *The American Churches in the Ecumenical Movement, 1900–1968*. New York: Association Press, 1968.

Dunn, David, ed. *A History of the Evangelical and Reformed Church*. Philadelphia: The Christian Education Press, 1961.

Gray, Henry David. *The Mediators*. Ventura, Calif.: American Congregational Center, 1984.

Gunnemann, Louis H. *The Shaping of the United Church of Christ*. New York: United Church Press, 1977.

————. *United and Uniting: The Meaning of an Ecclesial Journey*. New York: United Church Press, 1987.

Horton, Douglas. *Congregationalism: A Study in Church Polity*. London: Independent Press, 1952.

Horton, Walter Marshall. *Our Christian Faith*. Boston: The Pilgrim Press, 1945.

Maurer, Oscar E., ed. *Manual of the Congregational Christian Churches*. Boston: The Pilgrim Press, 1954.

Miller, Robert Moats. *American Protestantism and Social Issues, 1919–1939*. Chapel Hill: University of North Carolina Press, 1958.

Morrill, M. T. *A History of the Christian Denomination in America*. Dayton, Ohio: Christian Publishing Association, 1912.

Schneider, Herbert W. *Religion in Twentieth-Century America*. Cambridge: Harvard University Press, 1952.

Stanley, A. Knighton. *The Children Is Crying: Congregationalism Among Black People*. New York: The Pilgrim Press, 1979.

Stanley, J. Taylor. *A History of Black Congregational Christian Churches of the South*. New York: United Church Press, 1978.

Williams, Daniel D. *What Present Day Theologians Are Thinking*. New York: Harper & Brothers, 1952.

INDEX